A MACMILLAN
ILLUSTRATED ENCYCLOPEDIA

ANIMALS

VOLUME 2
BIRDS

First published as three volumes in 1999 by Macmillan Library Reference USA

Macmillan Library Reference USA
1633 Broadway, 7th Floor
New York, New York 10019

Consultant Editor: **Dr. Philip Whitfield**
Biology Department, King's College, University of London
This edition updated by **Richard Walker**
Consultants:
Mammals: **Professor D. M. Stoddart,**
Zoology Department, University of Tasmania, Hobart, Australia
Birds: **I. C. J. Galbraith,**
Ornithology Department, British Museum (Natural History), Tring, Hertfordshire
Reptiles and Amphibians: **Professor Barry Cox,**
Biology Department, King's College, University of London
Fishes: **Alwyne Wheeler,**
British Museum (Natural History), London

Artists:
Mammals: **Graham Allen**
Dick Twinney
Birds: **Michael Woods**
Malcolm Ellis
Keith Brewer
Reptiles and Amphibians: **Alan Male**
Fishes: **Colin Newman**

1 2 3 4 5 6 7 8 9 10

ISBN
0-02-865417-X (Volume 1)
0-02-865418-8 (Volume 2)
0-02-865419-6 (Volume 3)
0-02-865420-X (3 Volumes)

Manufactured by Imago, Singapore

Cataloging-in-Publication Data available

This paper meets the requirements of ANSI/NISO Z39.48-1992 (Permanence of Paper).

CONTENTS

BIRDS

Feathered conquerors of the air.

DISTRIBUTED OVER THE SURFACE OF THE EARTH AND INHABITING ALMOST EVERY POSSIBLE AREA OTHER THAN THE DEEP OCEAN ARE OVER 9,000 SPECIES OF BIRD. RANGING IN SIZE FROM TINY HUMMINGBIRDS, WEIGHING ONLY A FEW GRAMS, TO THE OSTRICHES THAT STAND TALLER THAN THE AVERAGE HUMAN BEING, BIRDS HAVE A SPECIAL PLACE IN HUMAN CONSCIOUSNESS. BIRDS ARE OFTEN BOLDLY MARKED OR COLORED, HAVE COMPLEX FAMILY AND GROUP BEHAVIOR, ARE EASILY OBSERVED AND, ABOVE ALL, HAVE THE POWER OF FLIGHT. CONSEQUENTLY THEY HAVE ALWAYS STIMULATED MUCH INTEREST, PLEASURE, WONDERMENT, EVEN ENVY, IN HUMAN BEINGS.

Reed Cormorant

Birds are warm-blooded, air-breathing vertebrates with four limbs, the front pair of which are modified to provide muscle -powered wings that, in the vast majority of living birds, give the potential for active flight. Birds can be unambiguously identified as such by their feathers – a feature which all birds, without exception, possess, and which no other member of the animal kingdom shares.

Much of the unique nature of a bird's body structure is linked to its need for a low take-off weight and a good power-to-weight ratio. Like mammals, birds are descended from reptilian ancestors. They have taken, evolutionarily speaking, the heavy-boned, scaly, elongate body of a reptile and turned it into a light, compact flying machine with a feather-covered outer surface. The bones have become slim, thin-walled and filled with air sacs, deriving from the walls of the lungs. All skeletal structures are pared down to produce maximum strength with minimum weight, and the heavy reptilian skull has changed to a light, almost spherical cranium, terminating in a toothless beak covered with horny plates.

Like reptilian scales and mammalian hairs, feathers are constructed largely from the tough protein keratin. They exist in a vast range of shapes, sizes and colors and have a variety of functions: first, they provide a light, flexible, thermally insulating protective layer over the bird's surface, crucial for maintaining the bird's high constant body temperature, which can reach (42°C) 107.6°F. Second, the colors and patterns of feathers are the prime means of visual communication between birds; third, and perhaps most importantly, the large aero-foiled shaped feathers of the wings and those of the tail provide the bird's flight surfaces. The wing feathers are attached to the highly modified bones of the forelimbs and provide the main lift and thrust for flight, while the tail feathers help the bird steer during flight. The tail feathers are attached to a stumpy remnant of a tail, quite unlike that of the birds' reptilian ancestors.

The earliest fossil bird, *Archaeopteryx*, dating from the upper Jurassic period 160 million years ago, demonstrates an intriguing intermediate stage in the progressive loss of reptilian characteristics as birds evolved. *Archaeopteryx* had feathers and wings, but it also had teeth in its jaws and a typically reptilian set of tail vertebrae – it was, effectively, a feathered, winged reptile.

Although air offers relatively little resistance to motion, take off and active flight require a massive output of power from the bird. The relatively huge breast muscles of a bird,

Northern Goshawk

Black Capped Lory

attached to a deep keel on the breastbone, deliver this power to the basal bone of the wing, the humerus. For these muscles to operate at the necessary high power output, good blood circulation is required and an exceptionally efficient respiratory system, to supply oxygen at the required rate. Birds have four-chambered hearts, similar to those of mammals, but independently evolved, which can operate extremely rapidly: a sparrow's heart beats 500 times a minute, a hummingbird's up to 1,000 times a minute in flight.

Equally a bird's respiratory system seems to take the air-breathing lung to the limits of its capability. Paired lungs, with throughflow, are only one part of the bird's extensive and efficient respiratory system, which also includes many air sacs.

The ability to extract oxygen from the air much more rapidly and efficiently than a mammal is able to do helps to explain the astoundingly fast wing-beats of a hummingbird, the lightning flight of some swifts and the capacity of some birds to fly at altitudes where the atmosphere contains little oxygen.

In some bird families it is usual for males and females to have similar plumage; in others the sexes differ in appearance. Although there are some interesting exceptions (for example, the females of many species of birds of prey are larger than the males), when the sexes differ, the male bird is the larger and more colorfully feathered, and the female has duller plumage, which may help to conceal her on the nest. For most, but not all birds, there is a single breeding season in any year. Typically in this period, cock birds find and protect nesting territories and may sing or display to intimidate rival males and attract mates. Fertilization is internal, but apart from a few species, the male bird does not possess a penis but only a small erectile protuberance at the base of his cloaca (the reproductive opening) through which sperm passes into the female's cloaca.

Birds lay eggs containing large yolks, the food reserves for the developing embryo, surrounded by a tough, mineralized shell. The egg is formed as the ovum passes from the ovary down the oviduct to the outside world, successive layers of white, inner and outer shell membranes, being added on the way. Most birds lay their eggs in some form of nest, where they are incubated, or kept warm, by one or both parents while the embryo develops. The young of some birds, such as ducks and pheasants, hatch covered with downy feathers and are able to walk immediately, while the young of others, such as blackbirds and most other songbirds are born naked and helpless and need a period of feeding and care from the parents.

Among the 23 orders of living birds, a remarkable variety of modifications has taken place to the basic avian body, with the most crucial adaptations being to feet, legs, beaks and wings. There are large long-legged walking birds, such as ostriches, rheas, emus and cassowaries, that have completely lost the power of flight. There are other flightless birds, such as the penguins, that have wings adapted as underwater paddles. At the opposite extreme are the insectivorous swifts, birds so aerial that it is possible that their only contact with the ground throughout life may be at the nest. There are highly specialized predators of the night (owls, nightjars) and of the daylight hours (eagles, hawks, falcons), with strong beaks and killing talons. Almost any type of small animal or vegetable food is the diet of some bird species – a shrike pouncing on a grasshopper, a hummingbird extracting nectar and a parrot feeding on a jungle fruit, all testify to the breathtaking diversity of the bird kingdom.

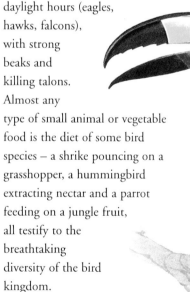

Laminated Toucan

Cladogram showing possible phylogenetic relationships of birds. Traditionally, birds have been placed in 27 or 28 orders. This classification has been in place since the 1930s and was based originally on evidence from fossil birds with more recent modifications. As with any classification it can be difficult to tell the difference between true phylogenetic relationships and the similarities found between completely unrelated species that are the result of convergence, the independent evolution of similar characteristics and life-styles. Unrelated species have in the past been "lumped" together in groups such as the "flycatchers" simply because of similarities that have arisen independently. Attempts to take a more objective view of bird classification have included the use of

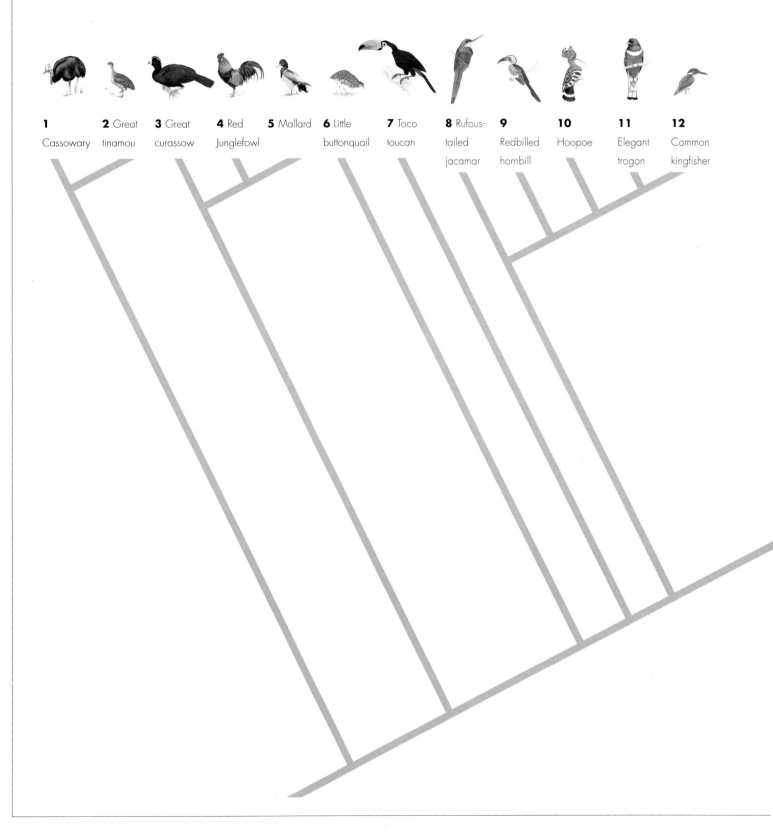

1 Cassowary

2 Great tinamou

3 Great curassow

4 Red Junglefowl

5 Mallard

6 Little buttonquail

7 Toco toucan

8 Rufous-tailed jacamar

9 Redbilled hornbill

10 Hoopoe

11 Elegant trogon

12 Common kingfisher

DNA analysis to determine affinities between birds. DNA (deoxyribonucleic acid) is the genetic material found in all body cells that determines an organism's characteristics. The more closely related two species are, the more similar the chemical composition of their respective DNA molecules. A new classification based on DNA analysis recognizes 23 orders, and is the one shown on this cladogram and the one used throughout this book. Although this provides a new framework for bird classification, it is still very much under review and will undoubtedly change in the future as new evidence appears and new criteria are employed to determine relationships between birds.

13 Speckled mousebird

14 Common cuckoo

15 Yellow-crowned amazon

16 White-throated swift

17 Ruby-throated hummingbird

18 Red-crested turaco

19 Northern hawk owl

20 Victoria crowned pigeon

21 Sunbittern

22 Greater flamingo

23 Red-eyed vireo

KEY TO BIRD CLADOGRAM

1 Struthioniformes (ratites)

2 Tinamiformes (tinamous)

3 Craciformes (curassows, guans, megapodes)

4 Galliformes (gamebirds)

5 Anseriformes (waterfowl)

6 Turniciformes (buttonquail)

7 Piciformes (barbets and woodpeckers)

8 Galbuliformes (jacamars and puffbirds)

9 Bucerotiformes (hornbills)

10 Upupiformes (hoopoes)

11 Trogoniformes (trogons)

12 Coraciiformes (kingfishers, rollers, bee-eaters)

13 Coliiformes (colies)

14 Cuculiformes (cuckoos)

15 Psittaciformes (parrots)

16 Apodiformes (swifts)

17 Trochiliformes (hummingbirds)

18 Musophagiformes (turacos)

19 Strigiformes (owls and nightjars)

20 Columbiformes (pigeons)

21 Gruiformes (cranes and rails)

22 Ciconiiformes (waterbirds and birds of prey)

23 Passeriformes (songbirds)

RATITES

ORDER STRUTHIONIFORMES

Ratites is the informal name given to a mixed group of running birds with some dramatic morphological differences from all other birds that belong to the order Struthioniformes. Apart from the fowl-sized kiwis of New Zealand, ratites are all extremely large ground-living birds, with massive, muscular legs for powerful running. Their wings are much reduced in size and are not functional. The ratite breastbone is flat and small and has no central keel – in other birds this keel serves for the attachment of the flight muscles. The word "ratite" means "raft-like" as opposed to carinate, applicable to all other birds and meaning "keeled".

There are four living ratite families – ostrich, emu and cassowaries, rheas, and kiwi.

STRUTHIONIDAE: OSTRICH FAMILY

Ostriches are the largest living birds. There is now only a single species, living in Africa, but formerly the family's range extended from southern Europe to Mongolia as well as throughout Africa.

Ostrich *Struthio camelus*

RANGE	Africa
HABITAT	Grasslands, arid land
SIZE	6–9 ft (1.75–2.75 m) tall

The ostrich is too big to fly but has become so perfectly adapted to high-speed running that it is the fastest creature on two legs. At speeds of up to 44 mph (70 km/h), it can easily outstrip

most enemies. Powerful legs, flexible knees and supple two-toed feet are its adaptations for speed. The ostrich has lost its strong wing feathers, but the male has soft, curling plumes which were once much in demand for fashionable hats and boas. Female birds are slightly smaller than males and have brownish plumage and off-white wings and tails. Juveniles are grayish-brown.

Ostriches eat mostly plant food, but occasionally feed on small reptiles. They are nomadic, wandering in small groups in search of food. At breeding time, the male collects a harem of 2 to 5 females. One female scrapes a shallow pit in the ground in which to lay her eggs and the rest of the harem probably use the same nest. The eggs are the largest laid by any bird – the equivalent in volume of about 40 hen's eggs. The male bird takes over the incubation of the eggs at night and shares in the task of nurturing the young.

RHEIDAE: RHEA FAMILY

Rheas are the South American equivalents of the ostrich and are the heaviest of the New World birds. Although they have larger wings than other ratites, they are still unable to fly, but they are good swimmers and fast runners. There are two species.

Greater Rhea *Rhea americana* **LR:nt**

RANGE	South America, east of the Andes
HABITAT	Open country
SIZE	5 ft (1.5 m) tall

Greater rheas live in flocks of between 20 and 30 birds. Male and female birds look much alike. They feed on plants, seeds, insects and some small animals. At breeding time, the male bird displays, and gathers together a harem of females. He then leads his mated females to a shallow nest which he has prepared, and they all lay their eggs in this one nest making a clutch of up to 18 eggs in total which the male rhea then incubates.

CASUARIIDAE: CASSOWARY FAMILY

This family contains the one surviving species of emu – the second largest living bird – and three species of cassowaries. Emus live in the open country of Australia and can run fast. Cassowaries are found in the tropical forests of Australasia, including some islands. They are large, powerful birds, well adapted for forest life. Because of the isolating effects of island habitats, many races have evolved with minor differences.

Emu *Dromaius novaehollandiae*

RANGE Australia

HABITAT Arid plains, woodland, desert

SIZE 6½ ft (2 m) tall

Emus have remained common in Australia despite having been destroyed as serious pests on farmland. They can run at speeds of up to 30 mph (48 km/h) and also swim well. Fruit, berries and insects make up the bulk of their diet. The female lays between 7 and 10 dark-green eggs, with a characteristic pimply texture, in a hollow in the ground. The male incubates the eggs for about 60 days.

Southern Cassowary *Casuarius casuarius* **VU**

RANGE N. Australia, New Guinea

HABITAT Rain forest

SIZE 5 ft (1.5 m) tall

The southern cassowary is an impressive bird with long, hairlike quills which protect it from the forest undergrowth. Its wings are vestigial, but its legs are extremely powerful and armed with sharp-toed feet, capable of inflicting severe wounds. The bald but brightly colored head and neck bear brilliant wattles

and a horny casque. As the cassowary moves through the dense forest in search of seeds, fruits and berries, it holds this prominent casque well forward to help break a path. Male and female look alike, but the female is larger. The female lays 3 to 6 green eggs in a shallow, leaf-lined nest on the ground.

APTERYGIDAE: KIWI FAMILY

Kiwis are flightless forest birds. There are 3 species, all of which are found in New Zealand only.

Brown Kiwi *Apteryx australis* **VU**

RANGE New Zealand

HABITAT Forest

SIZE 27½ in (70 cm)

The brown kiwi, which is the national emblem of New Zealand, is a rarely seen, nocturnal creature. It has rudimentary wings concealed under coarse, hairlike body feathers. Its legs are short and stout with powerful claws, which it uses for scratching around the forest floor in search of the insects, worms and berries which make up its diet. The nostrils are at the tip of the bird's pointed bill and it seems to have a good sense of smell – rare among birds.

Females are larger than males, but the sexes otherwise look similar. The female lays 1 or 2 eggs in a burrow where they are incubated by the male. Each egg weighs about 1 lb (450 g) and is exceptionally large in proportion to the adult bird's body.

TINAMOUS, MEGAPODES AND CURASSOWS

ORDER TINAMIFORMES

TINAMIDAE: TINAMOU FAMILY

Tinamous are fowllike ground birds, found in a variety of habitats from Mexico to Argentina. They can fly, but are weak and clumsy and, although built for running, their best defence is to remain still, relying on their protective coloring. They feed on seeds, berries and insects. There are 47 species of tinamou.

Great Tinamou *Tinamus major*

RANGE S. Mexico to Bolivia and Brazil

HABITAT Rain forest, cloud forest

SIZE 18 in (46 cm)

The great tinamou, like all members of its family, is polygamous and females lay up to 12 eggs, often in different nests. With their vivid, clear colors – blue, green and pink – and highly glazed surface, these eggs are among the most beautiful of all birds' eggs.

ORDER CRACIFORMES

This order of moderate to large gamebirds includes two families – megapodes are ground-dwellers with a unique nesting technique; curassows, guans and chachalacas live in forests and are predominantly arboreal although curassows spend some time on the ground.

MEGAPODIIDAE: MEGAPODE FAMILY

The 19 species in this family all occur from the Philippines to Australia and central Polynesia. Males and females look more or less alike, and all have large, strong legs and feet. They feed on insects, small vertebrate animals, seeds and fruit.

Megapodes do not brood their eggs in the normal way, but lay them in mounds of decaying vegetation or sand, and allow them to be incubated by natural heat.

Malleefowl *Leipoa ocellata* **VU**

RANGE S. Australia

HABITAT Mallee (arid eucalyptus woodland)

SIZE 21½–24 in (55–61 cm)

Despite its arid habitat, the male malleefowl manages to create an efficient incubator mound, which he is engaged in tending for much of the year. In winter, he digs a pit and fills it with plant material. Once this has been moistened by the winter rains, he covers it with sand, and the sealed-off vegetation starts to rot and to build up heat. The malleefowl keeps a constant check on the temperature by probing the mound with his beak and keeps it to about 91°F (33°C). He controls any temperature fluctuations by opening the mound in order to cool it, or by piling on more sand.

The laying season lasts some time, since the female lays her 15 to 35 eggs one at a time, at intervals of several days in holes made in the mound by the male. The chicks hatch about 7 weeks after laying and struggle out unaided. They are wholly independent and can fly within a day.

Common Scrubfowl *Megapodius freycinet*

RANGE E. Indonesia to Melanesia; N. and N.E. Australia

HABITAT Rain forest and drier areas

SIZE 17¾ in (45 cm)

An active, noisy bird, the scrubfowl seldom flies, but seeks refuge in trees if disturbed. In some areas these birds make simple incubation mounds in sand, which are then warmed by the sun or, on some islands, by volcanic activity. In rain forest, they make huge mounds, up to 16 ft (5 m) high, containing decomposing plant material. The eggs are laid in tunnels dug into the mound.

CRACIDAE: CURASSOW FAMILY

There are about 50 species in this family, found in the neotropical zone from south Texas to northern Argentina. All are nonmigratory forest birds, often adapted for a tree-dwelling life. Many species have crests or casques on their heads.

Great Curassow *Crax rubra*

RANGE Mexico to Ecuador

HABITAT Tropical rain forest

SIZE 37 in (94 cm)

Great curassows roost and nest in trees, but also spend a good deal of time on the ground. They feed on fruit, leaves and berries. The males have a loud, booming ventriloquial call that seems to be amplified by the elongated trachea. This call is used in courtship display and to threaten other males.

Curassows make an untidy nest of twigs and leaves in a bush or tree and lay 2 eggs. Both parents feed and care for the chicks.

Nocturnal Curassow *Nothocrax urumutum*

RANGE South America: upper Amazon basin

HABITAT Tropical rain forest

SIZE 26 in (66 cm)

The nocturnal curassow is, in fact, active during the day, searching for its plant food. It sings only at night, however, making a booming call. In males, the voice is amplified by means of an extended trachea. The sexes look alike, with bare, brightly colored faces, ample crests and brown and rufous plumage.

Crested Guan *Penelope purpurascens*

RANGE Mexico, south to Venezuela, Ecuador

HABITAT Lowland rain forest and drier areas

SIZE 35 in (89 cm)

Primarily tree-living birds, crested guans forage in small groups up in the treetops, walking slowly along the branches and leaping across gaps. They will, however, come down to the ground to collect fallen fruit and seeds and to find drinking water. Male and female birds look alike.

In the breeding season, guans perform a wing-drumming display. While in flight, the bird begins to beat its wings at twice the normal speed, producing a whirring sound that is maintained for several seconds. A bulky nest, sited in a tree, is made from twigs and lined with leaves. The usual clutch is 2 or 3 eggs, and the female guan does most of the incubation.

Plain Chachalaca *Ortalis vetula*

RANGE USA: extreme S. Texas; Mexico, Central America

HABITAT Brush, thickets in rain forest; drier areas

SIZE 20–24 in (51–61 cm)

The plain chachalaca's common name is derived from its three syllable call, "cha-cha-lak", and like the curassow's, its voice is amplified by its elongated trachea. Groups of birds set up a deafening chorus, morning and evening. Primarily a tree-dwelling bird, the plain chachalaca feeds on berries, fruit, leaves and shoots and some insects. It also comes down to the ground to search for some of its food. A small frail nest is made of twigs, up in a tree or bush, and the female incubates the clutch of 3 or 4 eggs. Male and female chachalacas look alike.

PHEASANTS, GROUSE AND TURKEYS

ORDER GALLIFORMES

Galliformes are typical gamebirds. There are three families in the order – pheasants and their relatives; guineafowl; and New World quails.

PHASIANIDAE: PHEASANT, GROUSE, AND TURKEY FAMILY

This large and complex family of small to large gamebirds includes quails, partridges, pheasants, Old World quails, grouse, and turkeys. The 177 species in the family are found in open to forest habitats from arctic tundra to tropical forests in all continents apart from South America and Antarctica. Most are plump, rounded birds which usually feed and nest on the ground, but often roost for the night in the trees. Their wings are short and powerful and capable of strong, but not sustained, low-level flight. Most are seed-eating birds which scratch around for food with their stout, unfeathered legs and strong claws, but many also eat insects and other small invertebrates as well as fruits and berries.

Males and females have different plumage coloration in many species, particularly the larger pheasants. Some of the smaller, plainer birds are monogamous, while in the more ornate species, the males tend to be polygamous. The nest is usually simple, often a scrape on the ground; chicks are born fully covered with down and can leave the nest soon after hatching.

Many members of this family have been successfully introduced outside their native range. Some are well known as gamebirds, hunted for sport and eaten by humans.

Common Quail *Coturnix coturnix*

RANGE Europe, Asia, east to Lake Baikal; N. India, Africa; winters Mediterranean coast, Africa, Asia to S. India, Thailand

HABITAT Grassland, farmland

SIZE 7 in (18 cm)

One of the smallest birds in the pheasant family, the quail is a neat, rounded bird with a weak bill and legs. The female resembles the male in build, but has an unmarked buff throat and a closely spotted breast. A rarely seen bird, the quail forages in the undergrowth and although it can fly it tends to run through vegetation in order to escape danger, rather than flying. It flies considerable distances when migrating. It feeds mainly on seeds, but eats some small invertebrates, particularly in the summer.

Breeding takes place in early summer, and the female lays one clutch of 9 to 15 eggs in a plant-lined scrape on the ground. She incubates her eggs for 16 to 21 days.

Painted Quail *Coturnix chinensis*

RANGE India to S.E. China, Malaysia, Indonesia, Australia

HABITAT Swamp, grassland

SIZE 6 in (15 cm)

This tiny bird is typical of the eastern quails, which tend to be more boldly patterned than the European birds. The female painted quail has duller plumage than the male, being mainly buff-colored with a barred breast. Painted quails forage in vegetation and feed on seeds and insects.

The female lays 4 to 8 eggs in a shallow scrape on the ground. She incubates the clutch for about 16 days.

Himalayan Snowcock *Tetraogallus himalayensis*

RANGE W. Himalayas

HABITAT Mountain slopes

SIZE 22 in (56 cm)

The Himalayan snowcock is one of 7 species of snowcock, all of which are found at high altitudes in Asia. Typical of its group, it is a large bird with coloration which blends well with its environment. In the early morning, pairs or groups of up to 5 snowcocks fly down the hillsides from their roosts to find water to drink. The rest of the day is spent slowly coming back up, feeding on the way on roots, tubers, green plants, berries and seeds.

Breeding takes place between April and June. Courting males are especially noisy at this time, making loud five-note whistles. The female lays 5 to 7 eggs in a hollow scrape in the ground among stones. She incubates the clutch for 27 or 28 days.

Red-legged Partridge *Alectoris rufa*

RANGE S.W. Europe to S.E. France, N. Italy, Corsica; introduced in Britain, Azores, Madeira and Canary Islands

HABITAT Scrub, moorland, farmland

SIZE 12½–13¼ in (32–34 cm)

A typical partridge, with a larger bill, stronger legs and longer tail than the quails, the red-legged partridge is distinguished by the white stripe above each eye, the black-bordered white throat and the red bill and legs. Males and females look alike, but juveniles are less vividly colored. These birds roost in trees and bushes but feed on the ground, mainly on plants, although they occasionally eat insects and frogs. They are reluctant to fly, and prefer to escape danger by running. Breeding begins in April or May. Red-legged partridges are monogamous and make long-lasting pair bonds. The female lays 10 to 16 eggs in a shallow scrape which the male makes on the ground and lines with leaves. The clutch is incubated by both parents for about 23 or 24 days.

Red-necked Francolin *Francolinus afer*

RANGE Africa, south of the Equator, except S.W.

HABITAT Bush, cultivated land, savanna

SIZE 16 in (41 cm)

The francolins are large gamebirds, with strong bills and characteristic patches of bare skin on the head or neck. Over 30 species occur in Africa, but a few francolins live in Asia. The red-necked francolin has red skin around its eyes and on its neck. It is typical of the group. Its breast is covered with broad dark streaks which help to camouflage it. Males and females look alike.

In small family groups, francolins forage for plant food and insects. They fly well and take refuge in trees if disturbed. They nest on the ground and females lay 5 to 9 eggs.

Red Spurfowl *Galloperdix spadicea*

RANGE India

HABITAT Brush, scrub, bamboo, jungle, woodland

SIZE 14¼ in (36 cm)

A type of partridge, the male red spurfowl has distinctive scalloped plumage and naked red skin around each eye. The female's grayish plumage is barred and spotted with black.

Pairs or groups of up to 5 spurfowl forage together, scratching in the undergrowth for seeds, tubers and berries, as well as slugs, snails and termites.

The timing of the breeding season varies from area to area, according to conditions; although this is usually between January and June, it can be at any time of year. The nest is a shallow scrape on the ground dug among bamboo or scrub, and scantily lined with a few leaves or blades of grass. The female lays 3 to 5 eggs which she incubates alone. The male helps to care for the young.

Crested Partridge/Roulroul *Rollulus rouloul*

RANGE Myanmar to Sumatra and Borneo

HABITAT Floor of dense forest on lowland or hills

SIZE 10 in (25.5 cm)

The crested partridge is the most attractive and unusual of the wood partridges. The male is instantly recognizable by his red brushlike crest; he also has red skin around the eyes and a red patch on his bill.

The female bird has a few long feathers on her head but lacks the crest.

These partridges move in mixed groups of up to 12, occasionally more, feeding on seeds, fruit, insects and snails. They lay 5 or 6 eggs in a domed nest, which is atypical for the family. The young return to the nest at night.

PHEASANTS CONTINUED

Temminck's Tragopan *Tragopan temminckii* **LR:nt**

RANGE Mountains of W. China, N. Myanmar and S.E. Tibet

HABITAT Forest

SIZE 25¼ in (64 cm)

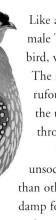

Like all the 5 species of tragopan, the male Temminck's tragopan is a striking bird, with beautiful, elaborate plumage. The female is much plainer, with rufous to grayish-brown plumage on the upperparts and a buff or white throat and light-brown underparts.

This tragopan is even more unsocial and more arboreal in its habits than other tragopans and prefers cool, damp forest. It feeds on seeds, buds, leaves, berries and insects.

At the start of the breeding season, the male courts his mate by displaying his brilliant plumage. The nest is made in a tree, and the female lays 3 to 6 eggs.

Red Junglefowl *Gallus gallus*

RANGE Himalayas to S. China, S.E. Asia, Sumatra, Java; introduced in Sulawesi, Lesser Sunda Islands

HABITAT Forest, scrub, cultivated land

SIZE 17–30 in (43–76 cm) including tail: 11 in (28 cm) in male

The ancestor of the domestic fowl, the red junglefowl is a colorful bird. The female is much smaller and duller than the male. She has mainly brown plumage and some chestnut on the head and neck. Several races of red junglefowl occur which vary slightly in appearance.

They are gregarious birds, gathering in flocks of up to 50 or so to feed on grain, grass shoots and crops, fruit, berries, insects and their larvae.

The breeding season is usually March to May. The female scrapes a hollow in the ground near a bush or bamboo clump and lines it with leaves. She incubates the clutch of 5 or 6 eggs for 19 to 21 days.

Gray Peacock-pheasant *Polyplectron bicalcaratum*

RANGE Himalayas to Hainan; S.E. Asia: Burma, Thailand, Indo-China

HABITAT Forest

SIZE 22–30 in (56–76 cm)

The gray peacock-pheasant is one of 6 species in the genus *Polyplectron*, all of which occur in India, Southeast Asia or Sumatra. The female is smaller than the decorative male and has fewer, smaller eye-spots, which are black with white borders. They are secretive, yet noisy, birds and feed on grain, fruit, berries and insects.

The male displays to his mate, calling as he spreads his tail and wing coverts. The female lays 2 to 6 eggs in a nest on the ground and incubates the clutch for about 21 days.

Golden Pheasant *Chrysolophus pictus* **LR:nt**

RANGE W. China; introduced in Britain

HABITAT Scrub on rocky hillsides; introduced in woodland

SIZE Male: 38½–42½ in (98–108 cm)

Female: 24–25½ in (63–65 cm)

The spectacularly beautiful male golden pheasant has brilliant plumage and a crest of golden feathers. The female bird is much plainer, with various shades of brown plumage, streaked with black. Wild golden pheasants move in pairs or alone and are shy birds, alert to any danger. They have short wings and are reluctant to fly, preferring to run from danger. Seeds, leaves, shoots and insects are their main foods.

Little is known of the breeding habits of this pheasant in its natural habitat, but in Britain, it makes a shallow scrape on the ground and lines it with plant material. The female lays 5 to 12 eggs, which she incubates for 22 days, apparently hardly ever, if at all, leaving the nest during this period.

Common Pheasant

Phasianus colchicus

RANGE Caspian area, east across C. Asia to China, Korea, Japan and Myanmar; introduced in Europe, N. America, New Zealand

HABITAT Woodland, forest edge, marshes, agricultural land

SIZE Male: 30–35 in (76–89 cm) Female: 20¼–25¼ in (53–64 cm)

Extremely successful as an introduced species, the pheasant is probably the best known of all gamebirds. So many subspecies have now been introduced and crossed that the plumage of the male is highly variable, but a typical bird has a dark-green head and coppery upperparts, with fine, dark markings; many have a white collar. The female is less variable and has brown plumage.

In the wild, pheasants feed on plant material, such as seeds, shoots and berries, and on insects and small invertebrates. They are ground-dwelling birds and spend much of their time scratching for food in undergrowth. They run fast, and their flight is strong over short distances, although low.

Male pheasants are polygamous and have harems of several females. The female scrapes a shallow hollow in the ground, usually in thick cover, which she lines with plant material. She lays 7 to 15 eggs on consecutive days and begins the 22 to 27-day incubation only when the clutch is complete. The young are tended and led to food by the female, rarely with any help from the male. Pheasants produce only one brood a season.

Indian/Blue Peafowl

Pavo cristatus

RANGE India, Sri Lanka

HABITAT Forest, woodland, cultivated land

SIZE Male: 3–4 ft (92 cm–1.2 m) without train; 6½–7¼ ft (2–2.25 m) in full plumage; Female: 33¾ in (86 cm)

The magnificent Indian peafowl is so widely kept in captivity and in parks and gardens outside its native range that it is a familiar bird in much of the world. The cock is unmistakable, with his iridescent plumage, wiry crest and glittering train, adorned with eyespots. The smaller female, or peahen, has brown and some metallic green plumage and a small crest.

Outside the breeding season, peafowls live in small flocks of 1 male and 3 to 5 hens, but after breeding, they may split into groups made up of adult males or females and young. They feed in the open, early in the morning and at dusk, and spend much of the rest of the day in thick undergrowth. Seeds, grain, groundnuts, shoots, flowers, berries, insects and small invertebrates are all eaten by these omnivorous birds, and they may destroy crops where they occur near cultivated land.

In the breeding season, the male bird displays – fully spreading his erect train to spectacular effect by raising and spreading the tail beneath it. With his wings trailing, he prances and struts in front of the female, periodically shivering the spread train and presenting his back view. The female may respond by a faint imitation of his posture. In the wild, the nest scrape is made in thick undergrowth, and the female incubates her 4 to 6 eggs for about 28 days.

Congo Peafowl *Afropavo congensis* **VU**

RANGE Africa: Congo basin

HABITAT Dense rain forest

SIZE 23½–27½ in (60–70 cm)

First described in 1936, the Congo peafowl is the only gamebird larger than a francolin native to Africa. The male bird has dark, glossy plumage and a crest of black feathers on the head, behind a tuft of white bristles. The female has a crest, but no bristles, and is largely rufous brown and black, with some metallic green plumage on her upperparts. The habits of Congo peafowls in the wild have seldom been documented, but they are believed to live in pairs and to take refuge and roost in trees. They feed on grain and fruit.

Congo peafowls are monogamous in captivity and build a nest of sticks in a tree. The female incubates the 3 or 4 eggs for about 26 days.

GROUSE, TURKEYS, GUINEA FOWL AND NEW WORLD QUAIL

Black Grouse *Tetrao tetrix*

RANGE N. Europe, N. Asia

HABITAT Moor, forest

SIZE 16–20 in (41–51 cm)

Social display is a particularly well-developed activity in the black grouse. In spring males, or blackcocks, gather at a traditional display ground, known as a lek which is used year after year. Each day at about sunrise, males call, dance and posture – each in his own patch of the lek – in order to attract the females. The male black grouse has a distinctive lyre-shaped tail which he spreads and displays in courtship. Females, or grayhens, are smaller than males and have mottled brown plumage and forked tails.

Black grouse are polygamous birds and a successful dominant male may mate with many females. Each female lays a clutch of 6 to 11 eggs in a shallow leaf-lined hollow on the ground. She incubates the eggs for 24 to 29 days.

Prairie Chicken *Tympanuchus cupido*

RANGE C. North America

HABITAT Prairie

SIZE 16½–18 in (42–46 cm)

This increasingly rare bird was once common over a large area of North America. Male and female birds look similar, but females have barred tail feathers and smaller neck sacs. Prairie chickens feed on plant matter, such as leaves, fruit and grain. In the summer, they catch insects, particularly grasshoppers. Male birds perform spectacular courtship displays,

inflating their orange neck sacs and raising crests of neck feathers. They give booming calls and stamp their feet as they posture, to make the display even more impressive. Female birds lay 10 to 12 eggs and incubate them for 21 to 28 days.

Ptarmigan *Lagopus mutus*

RANGE Holarctic

HABITAT Forest, tundra

SIZE 13–15½ in (33–39 cm)

The ground-dwelling rock ptarmigans depend on camouflage for defence. In order to achieve this in the changing background of their northerly range, they adopt different plumages according to the season. The summer plumage is mottled to blend with the forest while, during the winter snows, ptarmigans have white plumage, only the tail feathers remaining dark. Rock ptarmigans feed on leaves, buds, fruits and seeds, and also eat some insects in the summer.

They are monogamous birds; the male defends a small territory at the breeding grounds. The female lays 6 to 9 eggs in a leaf-lined hollow on the ground and incubates them for 24 to 26 days.

Common Turkey

Meleagris gallopavo

RANGE USA, Mexico

HABITAT Wooded country

SIZE 36–48 in (91–122 cm)

The common turkey is one of two turkey species. Both are large birds with bare skin on head and neck. Males and females look similar, but females have duller plumage and smaller leg spurs. The wild turkey has a lighter, slimmer body and longer legs than the domesticated version. Turkeys are strong fliers over short distances. They roost in trees, but find most of their food on the ground and eat plant food, such as seeds, nuts and berries, as well as some insects and small reptiles.

A breeding male has a harem of several females. Each female lays her eggs in a shallow leaf-lined nest on the ground; sometimes two or more females use the same nest. The female incubates the clutch of 8 to 15 eggs for about 28 days and cares for the young. The sexes segregate after breeding.

NUMIDIDAE: GUINEAFOWL FAMILY

The 6 species of guineafowl are heavybodied, rounded gamebirds with short wings and bare heads. Males and females look virtually the same. All species occur in Africa and Madagascar. The helmeted guineafowl is the ancestor of the domestic guineafowl.

Helmeted Guineafowl *Numida meleagris*

RANGE E. Africa

HABITAT Forest, dry brush

SIZE 25 in (63 cm)

The helmeted guineafowl, which is named for the bony protuberance on its crown, has the distinctive spotted plumage of most species of guineafowl. It feeds on insects and on plant material, such as seeds, leaves and bulbs.

The female lays a clutch of 10 to 20 eggs in a hollow scraped in the ground. She incubates the eggs and her mate helps her to care for the young.

ODONTOPHORIDAE: NEW WORLD QUAIL FAMILY

There are about 31 species of New World quail, distributed from Canada to northeast Argentina. Many are hunted for sport and food. They are larger, more diverse and more strikingly colored than the Old World quails and differ from them in certain anatomical features, the most important of which is the stronger, serrated bill, typical of the American birds.

Northern Bobwhite *Colinus virginianus*

RANGE E. USA to Guatemala; introduced in West Indies

HABITAT Brush, open woodland, farmland

SIZE 9–10½ in (23–27 cm)

The common name of this species is an imitation of its call. Bobwhites are gregarious birds for much of the year, moving in coveys of 30 or so. In spring the coveys break up, and the birds pair for mating.

Male and female birds look alike, but the male has striking face markings, while the female's face is buff-brown. The nest is a hollow in the ground. The average clutch is 14 to 16 eggs and both parents incubate the eggs.

California Quail *Callipepla californica*

RANGE W. USA

HABITAT Rangeland and agricultural land

SIZE 9½–11 in (24–28 cm)

The State bird of California, this quail is an attractive bird with a characteristic head plume. Females look similar to males and have head plumes, but they lack the black and white facial markings; they have buff-brown heads and chests.

California quails move in flocks, mostly on foot. They do not fly unless forced to do so. They feed on leaves, seeds and berries, and some insects.

The female lays her clutch of 12 to 16 eggs in a leaf-lined hollow on the ground and generally she incubates them for 18 days.

SCREAMERS, MAGPIE GOOSE, WHISTLING DUCKS AND DUCKS

ORDER ANSERIFORMES

A highly successful and diverse group of birds, this order contains 2 families – the Anatidae (ducks, geese and swans), and the Anhimidae (screamers).

ANHIMIDAE: SCREAMER FAMILY

The 3 species of screamer are similar to geese in body size but have longer legs and large feet with only partial webbing. The toes are long, enabling the birds to walk on floating vegetation. All species live in South America.

Northern Screamer *Chauna chavaria* **LR:nt**

RANGE N. Colombia, Venezuela

HABITAT Marshes, wet grassland

SIZE 28–36 in (71–91 cm)

The northern screamer has a typically noisy, trumpeting call (the origin of its common name) which it uses as an alarm signal. It feeds mostly on water plants. The female lays 4 to 6 eggs in a nest of aquatic vegetation and both parents incubate the eggs.

ANSERANATIDAE: MAGPIE GOOSE FAMILY

The single species in this family is a long-legged, long-necked goose that leads a semi-aquatic existence in swamps.

Magpie Goose *Anseranas semipalmata*

RANGE N. Australia, S. New Guinea

HABITAT Swamps, flood plains

SIZE 30–34 in (76–86 cm)

An interesting, apparently primitive species, the magpie goose is the only true waterfowl to have only partially webbed feet. Its bill is long and straight, and the head is featherless back to the eyes. Females resemble males but are smaller. Plant material is its major food source, and this goose forages by grazing and digging and by bending down tall grasses with its feet in order to reach the seeds. Magpie geese are gregarious and move in flocks of several thousands. Mates are usually kept for life, but a male may mate with two females. The female lays about 8 eggs in a nest of trampled vegetation; both partners incubate the clutch for 35 days and feed the chicks.

DENDROCYGNIDAE: WHISTLING DUCK FAMILY

The nine species of medium-sized ducks in this family are found from Asia to Australia, and from the Americas to tropical Africa. They have long legs, a long neck, and an upright stance. Whistling ducks are sociable and live and feed in large flocks.

White-faced Whistling Duck *Dendrocygna viduata*

RANGE Tropical South America, Africa, Madagascar

HABITAT Lakes, swamps, marshes

SIZE 17–19 in (43–48 cm)

The white-faced whistling duck eats aquatic insects, mollusks, crustaceans and plant matter such as seeds and rice. It will often dive for food. Much foraging activity takes place at night; during the day the birds roost near the water, often in flocks of several hundred. Mutual preening plays an important part in the formation of pairs and maintenance of bonds. Between 6 and 12 eggs are laid in a nest in a hole in a tree. Both partners incubate the eggs for 28 to 30 days.

ANATIDAE: TYPICAL WATERFOWL FAMILY

This family contains an assemblage of water birds, found in all areas of the world except continental Antarctica and a few islands. The 148 species include ducks, geese and swans.

All members of the family are aquatic to some degree and obtain plant and animal food from the surface of the water or beneath it by up-ending or diving. The majority are broad-bodied with shortish legs, and feet with front toes connected by webs. Beaks vary according to feeding methods, but are usually broad, flattened and blunt-tipped, with small terminal hooks. In many species males have brightly colored plumage and females plain, brownish feathers. Generally in such sexually dimorphic species, the female performs all parental duties.

Most ducks molt all the flight feathers simultaneously after the breeding season and undergo a flightless period of 3 or 4 weeks. During this period males of some species adopt "eclipse" plumage, similar to the female's muted plumage. After breeding, many species migrate to winter feeding grounds.

Tundra Swan *Cygnus columbianus*

RANGE Holarctic

HABITAT Tundra, swamps and marshes

SIZE 45–55 in (114–140 cm)

The whistling swan (above) and Bewick's swan (below) are sometimes treated as two separate species despite the fact that they interbreed freely. Both breed in the far north of their range and migrate to winter in Europe, China, Japan and the USA. Males and females look alike – the female is sometimes slightly smaller – and juveniles have mottled grayish plumage. The swans feed in shallow water on aquatic vegetation. Mating bonds are strong and permanent. They are formed and maintained by mutual displays. The female lays 3 to 5 eggs in a nest of sedge and moss lined with down, usually near water. She incubates the eggs for 35 to 40 days.

Graylag Goose *Anser anser*

RANGE Europe, Asia

HABITAT Hood plains, estuaries

SIZE 30–35 in (76–89 cm)

The graylag is the most numerous and widespread goose in Eurasia. Males of this sturdy, large-headed species are bigger than females, but otherwise the sexes look alike. The geese feed

on plant materials, such as roots, leaves, flowers and fruit. A nest of vegetation and twigs is made on the ground near a tree or bush or in reed beds, and the female incubates the 4 to 6 eggs for 28 days. The male helps to defend the goslings.

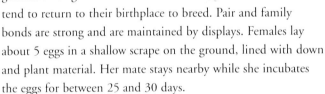

Canada Goose *Branta canadensis*

RANGE N. America; introduced into Europe and New Zealand

HABITAT Varied

SIZE 22–43 in (56–110 cm)

Habitats of the 12 geographically distinct races of Canada goose vary from semidesert to temperate rainforest and arctic tundra. Races also vary greatly in size. Canada geese feed by day on grassland vegetation and aquatic plants. This migratory species uses the same routes from generation to generation and birds tend to return to their birthplace to breed. Pair and family bonds are strong and are maintained by displays. Females lay about 5 eggs in a shallow scrape on the ground, lined with down and plant material. Her mate stays nearby while she incubates the eggs for between 25 and 30 days.

Common Shelduck *Tadorna tadorna*

RANGE Europe, C. Asia

HABITAT Coasts and estuaries

SIZE 24 in (61 cm)

Shelducks are large gooselike ducks. They feed on mollusks, particularly on the estuarine snail *Hydrobia*, as well as on fish, fish eggs, insects and their larvae, and algae. Females are smaller than males and have white feathers between eyes and bill. Pair bonds are strong and thought to be permanent. At breeding grounds the pairs take up territories. The female lays about 9 eggs in a burrow or cavity nest or in the open. While she incubates the clutch for 28 to 30 days, the male defends her.

DUCKS CONTINUED

Falklands Steamer Duck *Tachyeres brachypterus*

RANGE Falkland Islands

HABITAT Coasts

SIZE 24–29 in (61–74 cm)

Steamer ducks are heavily built marine diving ducks and 2 of the 3 species are flightless. The female is smaller than the male and has a yellow-green bill and dark-brown head with white rings around the eyes.

These coastline foragers feed primarily on mollusks, bivalves, crabs and shrimps – there is a record of one bird found to have 450 mussel shells in its stomach and crop. The Falklands duck makes a nest on grass or dry seaweed, or even in an abandoned penguin burrow, and lines it with down. The female lays 5 to 8 eggs and the male guards her attentively while she incubates them.

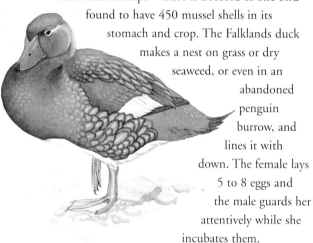

Mallard *Anas platyrhynchos*

RANGE Throughout northern hemisphere

HABITAT Almost anywhere near water

SIZE 16–26 in (41–66 cm)

The mallard is a typical dabbling duck often feeding tail-up in shallow water. Female mallards have plain brownish plumage, with distinctive blue feathers on the wings. Pair bonds are renewed each year with a prolonged period of intricate social displays, including the ritualized preening of the bright wing patches.

The female lays her 8 to 10 eggs in a nest on the ground. Her mate deserts her early in the incubation period and flies off to undergo his annual molt with the other males.

The mallard duck is the ancestor of all domestic ducks except for muscovies.

Northern Shoveler *Anas clypeata*

RANGE Europe, Asia, N. America

HABITAT Inland marshes, coastal waters

SIZE 17–22 in (43–56 cm)

The shoveler's distinctive spatulate bill is an adaptation for feeding on plankton. As the bird swims, it sucks water into the bill; the water is strained out through hairlike lamellae lining the bill which retain the tiny planktonic creatures.

Female birds have much duller plumage than males; they are mostly brown, but have blue and green feathers on the wings. Northern shovelers usually move in small groups or pairs for most of the year.

The female makes a nest in a reed bed and lays 7 to 14 eggs which she incubates for 23 to 25 days. The ducklings are born with normal bills; the spatulate shape develops as they mature.

Common Eider *Somateria mollissima*

RANGE Circumpolar (north)

HABITAT Coasts, inland rivers and lakes

SIZE 22–28 in (56–71 cm)

Like most ducks, the female eider lines her nest with down plucked from her breast. The down of the eider is particularly soft and warm and has long been collected and used by man. The female duck has barred, brownish plumage, and both male and female have Y-shaped bill extensions of membrane reaching almost up to the eyes. During the breeding season, eiders frequent coasts and feed on mollusks, crustaceans and other small creatures. They nest in colonies but fight over nest sites, and each pair holds its own territory. The female incubates the clutch of about 5 eggs alone for 27 to 28 days while her mate goes off with the other males to undergo his annual molt.

Greater Scaup *Aythya marila*

RANGE Circumpolar (north)

HABITAT Coastal and inland waters

SIZE 16–20 in (41–51 cm)

One of the group of ducks known as pochards, the scaup breeds in tundra regions and winters to the south. It feeds on small invertebrates, such as mollusks and crustaceans. Like other pochards, such as the canvasback, *A. valisineria*, and the tufted duck, *A. fuligula*, it is an excellent diver and frequently dives as deep as 26 ft (8 m) in search of food. Scaups gather in huge flocks, and at breeding grounds pairs overlap their ranges. The female lays 8 to 10 eggs which she incubates for 23 to 27 days.

Mandarin Duck *Aix galericulata* **LR:nt**

RANGE E. Asia, Korea, China, Japan; introduced in Britain and N. Europe

HABITAT Inland swamps, lakes and pools

SIZE 17–20 in (43–51 cm)

The mandarin has been celebrated in Japanese and Chinese art for centuries. Mandarins are most active at dawn and dusk; they feed on plant food, such as seeds, acorns and rice, and on insects, snails and small fish. They are social ducks, and the pair bond continues from year to year when possible. Courtship displays are particularly elaborate, including ritualized preening of the enlarged saillike feathers on the flanks and display drinking. The female lays 9 to 12 eggs, often in a tree-hole nest, and incubates them. The closely related wood/Carolina duck, *Aixsponsa* of North America is also brilliantly marked.

Red-breasted Merganser *Mergus serrator*

RANGE Holarctic

HABITAT Coastal and inland waters

SIZE 19–26 in (48–66 cm)

Mergansers are fish-eating, diving ducks with long, thin, serrated bills, well-adapted for catching fish under water. They also feed on crustaceans. Courtship rituals are complex. The male stretches his neck and sprints over the water; before copulating he performs a series of drinking, preening and wingflapping movements. The female lays her 9 or 10 eggs in a hole or cavity. The male deserts his mate early in the incubation period. Once the young have hatched, several females collect their young together into one brood which they tend together.

Muscovy Duck *Cairina moschata*

RANGE Central America, tropical South America

HABITAT Rivers and marshes in forest

SIZE 26–33 in (66–84 cm)

These birds, familiar in their domestic form, are rare in their pure form outside the native range. The male has warty skin around the eyes and an enlarged bill base; the female's head is entirely feathered and there is no bill enlargement. The wild form is attractive, but some of the domestic strains have grotesque warts and huge bill carbuncles. Muscovies eat plants, seeds, small fish and insects and termites, which are plentiful in their habitat. Muscovies have no real migratory pattern, but may move to coasts in dry seasons. They do not form large flocks, and pair and family bonds are weak. Courtship displays are simple and brief. The female lays 8 to 15 eggs in a hollow or among rushes. She incubates them alone. The male plays no part in the care of the young.

Ruddy Duck *Oxyura jamaicensis*

RANGE USA, Central America, Andes; introduced in Britain

HABITAT Inland lakes and rivers; estuaries

SIZE 14–19 in (35–48 cm)

The ruddy duck is one of a group of ducks known as stifftails. All are small, stocky, freshwater diving ducks with the habit of holding the tail up at an angle while swimming. Ruddy ducks are usually active at night and feed on aquatic plants, insects and small invertebrates. They are not highly developed socially and do not hold nesting territories. Females lay about 8 eggs in a ground nest, but may lay more eggs in other nests.

BUTTONQUAIL, HONEYGUIDE AND WOODPECKERS

ORDER TURNICIFORMES

TURNICIDAE: BUTTONQUAIL FAMILY

There is a single family in this order. The 17 species of buttonquail are dumpy, ground-living birds, which closely resemble quails, but have only three toes on each foot. Their wings are short and rounded and they seldom fly. Females are larger and more brightly plumaged than males. All species occur in tropical and subtropical regions of the Old World.

Little Buttonquail *Turnix sylvatica*
RANGE S. Spain, Africa; S. Asia to Indonesia, Philippines
HABITAT Grassland, scrub
SIZE 6 in (15 cm)

A shy, secretive bird, the little or small buttonquail spends much of its time in the undergrowth, although it is able to fly. It feeds on plants, seeds and insects. The female bird takes the dominant sexual role, displaying to the male and competing with other females. Both birds make the nest, which is usually a hollow in the ground, lined with grass.

From 3 to 8 oval eggs, usually 4, are laid, and the male incubates the clutch for an average of 13 days – one of the shortest incubation periods for any bird.

ORDER PICIFORMES

This order includes 5 families of mostly tree-dwelling, cavity-nesting birds – Indicatoridae (honeyguides), Picidae (woodpeckers), Megalaimidae (Asian barbets), Lybiidae (African barbets), and Ramphastidae (New World barbets and toucans). The 355 species in the order have in common a zygodactyl foot – a foot with two toes pointing forward and two pointing backward – which aids climbing up vertical tree trunks.

INDICATORIDAE: HONEYGUIDE FAMILY

There are 17 species of honeyguide. Most are found in Africa with one species in Southeast Asia and one in the Himalayas. Honeyguides feed on wax and larval bees, and some species have developed the habit, for which the family is named, of leading humans and other mammals to bees' nests in the hope that they will break the nests open. The birds are unique in being able to feed on wax, which they can digest by means of symbiotic bacteria in their intestines. They also feed on other insects, some of which they catch in the air.

As far as is known, all species are brood parasites and lay their eggs in the nests of barbets and woodpeckers. Male and female look slightly different in most species.

Greater/Black-throated Honeyguide *Indicator indicator*
RANGE Africa, south of the Sahara
HABITAT Varied, forest edge, arid bush, acacia woodland, cultivated land
SIZE 73 in (20 cm)

The greater honeyguide is one of the 2 species in the family that actively lead other creatures to bees' nests. Chattering loudly, the bird approaches a human being or another honey-eating mammal, such as the ratel, and having attracted the attention, leads the way to the nest, flying a short distance at a time. The honeyguide needs the help of another creature to break open the nest and, once this has been done, will feed on the remains of the honey, the wax and larval bees. The skin of this bird is particularly thick and must guard it against stings. Like all honeyguides, this bird also feeds on other insects.

The honeyguide lays its eggs in the nests of other birds and its young are reared by their foster parents.

PICIDAE: WOODPECKER FAMILY

Woodpeckers and their relatives the wrynecks and piculets must be among the best-known of all specialized tree-living birds. There are about 215 species, found almost worldwide except in Madagascar, Australia, the Papuan region and most oceanic islands. Males and females have slight plumage differences.

Woodpeckers are highly adapted for climbing in trees, extracting insect food items from bark and wood and making holes in tree trunks. The woodpecker clings tightly to the bark of the trunk with its sharply clawed feet, on which two toes face forward and two backward, giving it maximum grip. The stiff tail acts as an angled strut and gives the bird additional support as it bores into the wood with hammerlike movements of its strong, straight beak. A few woodpeckers are ground-living.

Ivory-billed Woodpecker

Campephilus principalis **EX**

RANGE Formerly S.E. USA, Cuba

HABITAT Swamps, forest

SIZE 20 in (51 cm)

The largest North American woodpecker, this species is characterized by its pointed crest and long, ivory-colored bill. The destruction of this woodpecker's habitat – mature forest – has led to a dramatic decline in its numbers. Although there may be a few birds left in remote parts of Cuba, it is listed as extinct by the IUCN.

It feeds on the larvae of insects, especially of the wood-boring beetles that live between the bark and wood of dying or newly dead trees, and also eats some fruit and nuts. Both members of a breeding pair help to excavate a nest cavity, and the female lays 1 to 3 eggs. The clutch is incubated for about 20 days, the male taking a turn at night, and both parents feed the young.

Northern/Eurasian Wryneck *Jynx torquilla*

RANGE Europe, N. Africa, N. Asia; winters in Africa and S. Asia

HABITAT Open deciduous forest, cultivated land

SIZE 6¼–8 in (16–20.5 cm)

A skulking, solitary bird, the wryneck is an unusual member of the woodpecker family, with a shorter, weaker bill than the true woodpeckers. Although it can cling to tree trunks, it does not have the stiff, supporting tail of the typical woodpecker and more often perches. It does not bore into trees for its food, but picks ants and other insects off leaves or from the ground, using its long, fast-moving tongue. The common name comes from its habit of twisting its head into strange positions while feeding and during the courtship display.

The wryneck breeds in summer in Europe, north Africa and central Asia. It does not excavate its own nest, but uses an existing cavity in a tree trunk, an abandoned woodpecker hole or a crevice in a wall or bank. The female lays 7 to 10 eggs, and both parents, but mainly the female, incubate the eggs for 13 days. Both parents feed insects and larvae to the young, which leave the nest about 3 weeks after hatching. After breeding, some populations of wrynecks migrate south to tropical Asia and Africa for the winter.

Great Spotted Woodpecker *Dendrocopos major*

RANGE Europe, N. Africa, Asia

HABITAT Mixed forest, woodland

SIZE 9 in (23 cm)

The most common European woodpecker, the great spotted woodpecker is an adaptable species, living in all types of woodland, including parks and gardens. As it bores into tree trunks to extract its food – wood-boring insects and their larvae – it makes a characteristic drumming noise, which it also makes in spring in place of a courtship song. It supplements its diet with nuts, seeds and berries and has a habit of wedging a pine cone into a crevice and chipping out the kernels with its bill. The male bird has a red band at the back of his head, which the female lacks, and the juvenile has a red crown.

In Europe, the breeding season begins in mid-May, and both partners help to excavate a hole in a tree, 10 ft (3 m) or more above ground. The female lays 3 to 8 eggs in this unlined nest and, with some assistance from the male, incubates them for 16 days. Both parents care for the young, bringing them insects in their bills. Most great spotted woodpeckers are resident birds, but some northern populations may migrate south in winter to find food.

WOODPECKERS CONTINUED

Eurasian Green Woodpecker *Picus viridis*

RANGE Europe, N. Africa, Turkey to Iran, W. Russia

HABITAT Open deciduous woodland, gardens, parks

SIZE 12½ in (32 cm)

A large, vividly plumaged woodpecker, this species has a short tail and a long, pointed bill. The male has a characteristic red mustachial stripe with a black border; in the female the stripe is all black. Like other woodpeckers, the green woodpecker feeds in trees on the larvae of wood-boring insects, but it also feeds on the ground, where it hops along ponderously, searching for ants. It will also eat fruit and seeds. The flight of this species is typical of the woodpecker family, being deeply undulating, with long wing closures between each upward sweep.

The breeding season starts in April in the south of the range and May in the north. Both partners of a breeding pair help to excavate a nest cavity, often in a rotten tree trunk and usually at least 3¼ ft (1 m) above ground. The female lays 4 to 7 eggs, sometimes as many as 11, which both parents incubate for 18 or 19 days. The chicks hatch naked and helpless and must be fed by their parents on regurgitated food for about 3 weeks, when they are able to fend for themselves.

In a hard winter, green woodpeckers, a non-migratory species, can suffer severe food shortages, which cause large drops in population.

Golden-tailed Woodpecker

Campethera abingoni

RANGE Africa, south of the Sahara

HABITAT Woodland, brush, mountain forest

SIZE 8 in (20.5 cm)

The golden-tailed woodpecker can be identified by the broad black streaks on the white plumage from its chin to its belly and by the yellow-tipped tail feathers. There are some dark-red and black markings on the nape and head and the rest of the plumage is largely green with white flecks. Usually seen in pairs,

these woodpeckers are noisy birds and utter calls like derisive laughter; they also give a screeching alarm signal. They are restless birds, continuously on the move, with swift deeply undulating flight, in search of the arboreal ants and the larvae of other insects, such as beetles, that form their main foods.

The nest hole is usually excavated in the soft wood of a dead tree, and the female lays 2 or 3 eggs.

Great Slaty Woodpecker *Mulleripicus pulverulentus*

RANGE Asia: N. India to S.W. China, Sumatra, Java, Borneo, Palawan

HABITAT Forest, swamp forest

SIZE 20 in (51 cm)

The great slaty woodpecker is a large species that associates in groups of about 6 birds, which follow one another from one tree-top to the next, calling noisily with loud cackles as they fly. Their flight is leisurely, without the normal woodpecker bounds and undulations. The larvae of wood-boring beetles and other insects are the main foods of this woodpecker, and it drills into trees with its powerful bill to find them. Both males and females of this species have some buffy-brown plumage on the chin and neck, but males also have mustachial streaks, which the females lack. Juvenile birds resemble the females but they are a darker and duller color, with more pale spots on the underparts.

In the breeding season, the groups break up into pairs, which then excavate their nests high up in tree trunks, often in dead or decaying wood. Both parents incubate the 3 or 4 eggs, which are laid in the unlined nest cavity, and share in the care and feeding of the nestlings.

Ground Woodpecker *Geocolaptes olivaceus* **LR:nt**

RANGE South Africa

HABITAT Dry, open hill country

SIZE 11 in (28 cm)

This woodpecker lives almost entirely on the ground and hops everywhere. On the rare occasions when it does take to the air, it flies heavily and only for short distances, its red rump feathers showing conspicuously. Male and female look alike, with gray plumage on the head, olive-brown upperparts flecked with white, and rose-pink chest and belly. Juvenile birds are duller, with mottled olive and off-white plumage on the belly.

Ground woodpeckers live in small groups of up to 6 or so and are usually found on high ground above 2,000 ft (600 m), where they perch on rocks or boulders or, very occasionally, on the low branches of trees and bushes. They feed on ants and other ground-living insects and their larvae, which they find by probing under rocks and stones. Their call is sharp and metallic, and they may also utter highpitched whistles.

This species nests on the ground in a long tunnel with a small chamber at the end, which both partners dig in a bank of clay or sand. The female lays 4 or 5 eggs.

Greater Flame-backed/Golden-backed Woodpecker

Chrysocolaptes lucidus

RANGE India, S.E. Asia to the Philippines

HABITAT Woodland, forest fringe, mangroves

SIZE 13 in (33 cm)

This medium-sized woodpecker is widespread in the wooded areas of India and Southeast Asia, where many races of the species inhabit a variety of forest types. Often found near flocks of other woodpeckers, drongos, bulbuls and babblers, these birds usually associate in pairs. After flying noisily from tree to tree, with characteristic bounds and undulations, they alight on a trunk and, working their way up in jerky spirals, bore into the wood with their beaks in order to feed on insect larvae. Flamebacked woodpeckers have also been observed catching winged termites in the air. They seldom feed on the ground. However they are known to occasionally drink the nectar of some flowers.

Although this is an extremely variable species, greater flamebacks can generally be identified by the two black mustachial streaks, separated by a patch of white plumage, on each side of the bill. The female bird lacks the male's distinctive red crest and has a flat black crown, spotted with white.

In the breeding season, the male flamebacked woodpecker drums particularly energetically as a courtship signal. The birds nest in a hole in a tree trunk, and the hole may be used many times, with a fresh entrance, which always leads to the same breeding chamber, being cut each season. It is not known whether the same birds return to the same hole every year.

The female lays a clutch of 4 or 5 eggs, which are incubated for 14 or 15 days, and the young woodpeckers remain in the nest being fed and cared for by the parents until they are able to fly at between 24 and 26 days old.

Blond-crested Woodpecker

Celeus flavescens

RANGE South America: Amazonian Brazil, Paraguay, N.E. Argentina

HABITAT Forest

SIZE 11 in (28 cm)

With its long, shaggy crest, the blond-crested woodpecker may appear to be rather larger than it actually is. The yellow feathers of the crest are narrow and soft so that when they are held erect they blow freely in the breeze.

This species is particularly widespread in southeastern Brazil, however, the blond-crested woodpecker is not confined to the lowlands, but has been observed at altitudes of up to 3,000 ft (900 m).

WOODPECKERS, ASIAN BARBETS AND AFRICAN BARBETS

Rufous/White-browed Piculet *Sasia ochracea*

RANGE N.E. India through S.E. Asia and S.E. China

HABITAT Woodland, especially bamboo

SIZE 9 cm (3½ in)

This tiny, dumpy, stub-tailed woodpecker is an active, restless bird. It is usually seen singly or in pairs. With jerky movements, it creeps over thin twigs of low trees and bushes or hops around the litter of the woodland floor, searching for its food – mainly ants and their larvae. The female bird looks similar to the male but lacks his golden forehead.

The piculet's nest is a tiny hole about 1 in (2.5 cm) across, drilled in a decaying, hollow bamboo or an old tree. The female lays a clutch of 3 or 4 eggs.

Yellow-bellied Sapsucker

Sphyrapicus varius

RANGE Canada, N. and E. USA; winters in Central America, West Indies

HABITAT Forest, woodland

SIZE 8 in (20.5 cm)

The sapsucker migrates northward in the spring from its wintering grounds in Central America and the West Indies. On reaching its breeding range, it drills rows of holes in the bark of trees and returns from time to time to drink the oozing sap and to eat the insects that are attracted to it. The bird also collects other insects in and around the trees using its brushlike tongue.

A breeding pair bores a nest hole, usually in the trunk of a dead tree, with the male doing most of the excavation work. The cavity takes 2 to 4 weeks to complete.

The female lays 5 to 7 eggs, which both birds then incubate for about 12 days.

Northern/Common Flicker *Colaptes auratus*

RANGE Alaska to Mexico, Cuba, Grand Cayman Island

HABITAT Woodland, open country

SIZE 10–14 in (25.5–35.5 cm)

The flicker is a ground-feeding bird, which lives on ants and other insects. It also eats fruit and berries. There are 2 forms, now considered to be subspecies of the same species – the eastern birds have yellow wing linings, and the western birds, red wing linings. The two subspecies are often called yellow-shafted and red-shafted flicker respectively. In the Midwest, the forms meet and interbreed.

During courtship, or to communicate possession of its territory, the flicker drums with its bill on a tree or the metal roofing of buildings.

The male flicker selects a site for the nest hole, usually a hole in a tree trunk, stump or telegraph pole, and does most of the excavation work. Both parents incubate the eggs for about 12 days, the male taking the night shift.

White-barred Piculet *Picumnus cirratus*

RANGE South America: Guyana to N. Argentina

HABITAT Forest, woodland, parks

SIZE 3½ in (9 cm)

A small, busy woodpecker, the white-barred piculet scrambles over trees, hanging upside down, moving over, under and around the branches in search of larvae to feed on.

Predators are deterred from attacking this piculet because of its curious and particularly offensive odor.

The nest is made in a bamboo stem, and to excavate it, the piculet clings to the bamboo in true woodpecker fashion, speedily chipping it away with its beak.

MEGALAIMIDAE: ASIAN BARBET FAMILY

Barbets are small to medium-sized chunky birds that are often brightly-colored and are found in tropical areas of Asia, Africa, and the Americas. They have large heads, and a stout, sometimes notched, beak often fringed with tufts of bristles. Males and females look alike in most species.

Most barbets are solitary, tree-dwelling birds that feed on insects and fruit. Once grouped together in a single family, barbets are now placed in three separate families – Megalaimidae (Asian barbets), Lybiidae (African barbets) and Ramphastidae – this family includes both the American barbets and the toucans. Asian barbets are generally larger than other barbet species. The 26 species are found in forest and woodland from south Tibet and south China to Indonesia and the Philippines. They nest in a hole bored into a tree.

Coppersmith/Crimson-breasted Barbet

Megalaima haemacephala

RANGE Pakistan east to China and Philippines, south to Sri Lanka, S.E. Asia, Sumatra, Java and Bali

HABITAT Woodland, gardens, urban areas

SIZE 6 in (15 cm)

A stocky bird, the coppersmith barbet is identified by the patches of bright red and yellow plumage on the throat and head, and the streaked belly. Alone, or sometimes in pairs or small groups, the coppersmith hunts in the trees for fruit particularly figs, or may make clumsy aerial dashes after insects.

The breeding season lasts from January to June, and the barbets excavate a hole in a dead or rotting branch, which their beaks can penetrate easily. Both parents incubate the clutch of 2 to 4 eggs and tend the young birds.

LYBIIDAE: AFRICAN BARBET FAMILY

The 42 species of African barbets form the most diverse barbet family. They resemble the Asian barbets, but also include the tiny tinkerbirds, which are just 3 in (8 cm) long, and other species that live in open savanna or scrub.

While most species nest in tree holes, three more sociable species make nesting burrows in banks or termite mounds and feed mainly on insects.

Double-toothed Barbet *Lybius bidentatus*

RANGE Africa: S. Sudan, Ethiopia, south to Uganda, W. Kenya, Tanzania

HABITAT Light forest, wooded savanna, cultivated land

SIZE 9 in (23 cm)

Identified by its deep-red throat and breast, the double-toothed barbet feeds on fruit, particularly figs and bananas, and will often invade plantations.

The nest is excavated in a dead branch of a tree, and the female is thought to lay 3 or 4 eggs. Like all barbets, both partners of a pair share the nesting duties.

TOUCANS

RAMPHASTIDAE: NEW WORLD BARBET AND TOUCAN FAMILY

This family includes two subfamilies: the 14 species of American barbets which resemble the African and Asian barbets and live in similar habitats; and the 41 species of toucans. The toucans are among the most extraordinary birds in the world. All toucan species are found living in the canopy layers of the dense rain forests of the Amazon basin and in neighboring forested areas of South America. They are medium-sized birds, ranging in size from 12 to 24 in (30 to 61 cm), and have enormous, boldly colored beaks that account for almost half the total body length. These bills are constructed of a honeycomb of bony material and are consequently light but very strong. The gaudy coloration varies greatly, not only between species but within a species. The plumage is usually dark, often black, with patches of boldly contrasting color on head and neck, which accentuates the bill colors. Toucans' wings are short and rounded and their flight weak. The legs are strong, and the claws well adapted for grasping branches, with two toes pointing forward and two backward. Male and female look alike in most species.

The specific functions of the toucan's remarkable beak are poorly understood. It may act as an important visual signal in territorial or courtship behavior or, it has been suggested, it may help the bird to obtain food otherwise out of its reach. Many other birds, however, manage without such bills. The bill may even help to intimidate other birds when the toucan raids their nests for young. Toucans feed on fruit of many types and on large, tree-living insects; occasionally they take larger prey such as nestling birds, eggs and lizards. The toucan seizes food with the tip of its bill and then throws its head back to toss the morsel into its mouth. An extremely long, narrow tongue, with a bristlelike appendage at the tip, aids manipulation of the food.

Toucans nest in tree cavities, either in natural holes or abandoned woodpecker holes. A few species line their nests with leaves, but in others regurgitated seeds from food-fruit form a layer on the nest floor. The 2 to 4 eggs are incubated by both parents, who are able to flex their long tails forward over their backs so as to accommodate to the confines of the nesting cavity. Young toucans hatch naked and blind and develop slowly. At 3 weeks their eyes are only just opening, and they are not fully fledged for more than 6 weeks. They have specialized pads on their heels, on which they sit, which may be a form of protection against the rough floor of the nest. Both male and female feed and care for the young during this period.

Emerald Toucanet *Aulacorhynchus prasinus*

RANGE S. Mexico to Nicaragua, Venezuela, Colombia, Ecuador and Peru

HABITAT Humid mountain forest, open country with trees

SIZE 14 in (35.5 cm)

The shy emerald toucanet lives at altitudes of between 6,000 and 10,000 ft (1,800 and 3,000 m). The birds sit inconspicuously among the foliage or fly for short distances in pairs or small groups to forage for food, calling to one another as they do so with a variety of noisy sounds. Their diet is wide ranging and includes insects, small reptiles and amphibians, and the eggs and young of other bird species, as well as the more usual fruit and berries. Striking birds, emerald toucanets are unmistakable with their bright green plumage and bold yellow and black bills.

The nest is made in a hole in a tree, often an old woodpecker hole. Emerald toucanets have even been known to harass woodpeckers until they give up their nests. Both parents incubate the 3 or 4 eggs and bring food, mostly fruit, to the nestlings. The young of the emerald toucanet, like all toucans, hatch naked and develop their first feathers at about 2 weeks. Their beaks, however, grow faster than their bodies, and the young toucanet has a full-sized, 3 in (7.5 cm) bill before its body is even half the size of that of the adult.

Saffron Toucanet
Baillonius bailloni **LR:nt**

RANGE S.E. Brazil

HABITAT Forest

SIZE 14 in (35.5 cm)

The saffron toucanet has fine, gold-colored plumage, which is especially lustrous on the cheeks and breast. Shy, graceful birds, they live in small groups and feed mainly on berries, preferring to forage high in the tree-tops rather than in the lower levels of the forest.

Plate-billed Mountain Toucan *Andigena laminirostris* **LR:nt**

RANGE Andes in Colombia, W. Ecuador

HABITAT Forest

SIZE 20 in (50 cm)

Also known as the laminated toucan, this species lives at altitudes of between 1,000 and 10,000 ft (300 and 3,000 m). The bill is about 4 in (10 cm) long and extremely unusual in shape. On each side of the upper bill there is a horny yellow plate, which grows out from the base of the bill. The function of these plates is not clearly understood, since little is known of the habits of these toucans.

Spot-billed Toucanet *Selenidera maculirostris*

RANGE Tropical Brazil, south of the Amazon to N.E. Argentina

HABITAT Lowland rain forest

SIZE 13 in (33 cm)

An uncommon toucanet, this species has a patch of feathers, usually orange or yellow, behind each eye – a feature which is peculiar to the *Selenidera* genus and is thought to be important in the male's courtship display. The bill of the male is distinctive, with a yellowish tip and black markings on the upper mandible; the female's bill is less clearly marked.

The spot-billed toucanet feeds on berries and large fruit – swallowing them whole and then disgorging the skins, stones and seeds. All toucans aid the seed dispersal of a number of fruit-bearing plants in this way.

Once their eggs are hatched, spot-billed toucanets often visit citrus plantations in groups, in order to feed and find termites and other small insects to take to their young.

Toco Toucan *Ramphastos toco*

RANGE E. South America: the Guianas to N. Argentina

HABITAT Woodland, forest, plantations, palm groves

SIZE 24 in (61 cm)

A common toucan and one of the largest of its family, the toco toucan lives in small groups and frequents coconut and sugar plantations, as well as the normal toucan habitats. Its golden-yellow bill is about 7½ in (19 cm) long, and it feeds on a wide range of fruit but has a particular preference for capsicums. Toco toucans are not at all shy and will enter houses, steal food and tease domestic pets.

Curl-crested Aracari

Pteroglossus beauharnaesii

RANGE Amazonian Peru, W. Brazil, N. Bolivia

HABITAT Forest

SIZE 14 in (35.5 cm)

This toucan is normally shy and nervous, but can be aggressive and active. It has curious plumage quite unlike that of any other toucan. The feathers on its crown are like shiny, curly scales, and those on the cheeks and throat have black scaly tips. It has pronounced jagged notches in its beak.

Groups of 5 or 6 adult aracaris roost together in an abandoned woodpecker hole or in a hollow in a tree, folding their tails over their backs so as to fit into the confined space.

JACAMARS, PUFFBIRDS AND HORNBILLS

ORDER GALBULIFORMES

Jacamars and puffbirds are the two families that make up this order. Both are tree-dwelling insect eaters that are found in Central and South America. Jacamars and puffbirds have zygodactyl feet, with two toes in front and two behind.

GALBULIDAE: JACAMAR FAMILY

The 18 species of jacamar are graceful, long-billed birds. They look similar to bee-eaters and catch insects on the wing in a similar way, but they are unrelated. Males are often brightly colored, but females are a little duller. Jacamars dig tunnels in the ground to nest in. Jacamars occur from Mexico to Brazil.

Rufous-tailed Jacamar
Galbula ruficauda

RANGE Mexico, Central America, through tropical South America to N. Brazil; Trinidad and Tobago and from E. Brazil to N.E. Argentina

HABITAT Forest clearings, second growth forest, scrub

SIZE 9–11 in (23–28 cm)

The rufous-tailed jacamar is brightly plumaged, with glossy iridescent upperparts. The female has a buff throat. Young birds are duller. The jacamar sits on a branch, watching for insects. It darts after them with swooping flight, snapping them out of the air, then returns to its perch to eat its catch, and may beat large specimens against the branch to kill them.

The female jacamar digs a breeding tunnel in the ground. Both birds incubate the eggs for 19 to 23 days. The young are fed until they can fly, at about 3 weeks old.

BUCCONIDAE: PUFFBIRD FAMILY

The 33 species of puffbird and nunbird are insect-eating birds, found from Mexico south through Central and tropical South America. Puffbirds are stouter, more lethargic birds than the agile jacamars, although they do make aerial sallies after prey. Male and female look more or less alike, both with large heads for their size and sober plumage.

White-necked Puffbird
Notharchus macrorhynchos

RANGE Central and South America to N.E. Argentina

HABITAT Open forest, forest edge, savanna with trees

SIZE 10 in (25.5 cm)

This species has the typical puffbird habit of fluffing out its plumage as it perches watching for prey, thus creating a bulky appearance, which is the origin of the common name. Once an insect is sighted, the puffbird flies out to catch it in the air with its broad, hook-tipped bill.

Breeding white-necked puffbirds excavate a tunnel in the ground and then camouflage the entrance with leaves and twigs. The female lays 2 or 3 eggs in a leaf-lined chamber at the end of the tunnel, and both birds incubate the clutch.

Black-fronted Nunbird
Monasa nigrifrons

RANGE East of the Andes: Colombia to Peru, N.E. Bolivia, Brazil

HABITAT Forest

SIZE 11½ in (29 cm)

Puffbirds of the genus Monasa have black or black and white plumage, hence the common name – nunbirds. They are more gregarious than other puffbirds and often gather in flocks. Otherwise they are similar in their habits. They perch on branches to watch for insects and then fly out to seize the prey in the air.

Breeding pairs excavate tunnels in which to nest, and the female is thought to lay 2 or 3 eggs.

ORDER BUCEROTIFORMES

There are two families in this order of long-beaked birds – Bucerotidae (typical hornbills), the group to which most species belong; and Bucorvidae (ground-hornbills).

BUCEROTIDAE: HORNBILL FAMILY

The 54 species of hornbill occur in Africa, south of the Sahara, and in tropical Asia, south to Indonesia. Most have brown or black and white plumage, but are instantly recognizable by their huge bills, topped with horny projections, or casques. Despite its heavy appearance, the hornbill's beak is actually a light honeycomb of bony cellular tissue, encased in a shell of horn. Many hornbills live and feed in trees in forest and savanna. Most are omnivorous, eating fruit, insects, lizards and even small mammals. Male and female look similar in some species but differ in others.

Hornbills are probably best known for their extraordinary nesting habits. Once the female has laid her eggs in a suitable nest hole, the entrance is walled up with mud, leaving a small slitlike opening. The male may do this or the female may barricade herself in, using material that the male supplies. She remains there throughout the incubation and part of the fledgling period, totally dependent on her mate for food supplies, but perfectly protected from predators. The male brings food, which he passes to her through the slit.

While she is a captive, the female molts, but by the time the appetites of the young are too much for the male to cope with, her feathers have regrown. Using her beak, she hacks her way out of the nest, and the young repair the barricade. Both parents then bring food until the young hornbills can fly. Details vary slightly between species, but all hornbills keep their nests clean, throwing out food debris and excreting through the slit.

Red-billed Hornbill

*Tockus
erythrorhynchus*

RANGE W., E. and S.E. Africa

HABITAT Dry savanna,
open woodland

SIZE 18 in (46 cm)

Although brightly colored, the beak of the red-billed hornbill has little, if any casque. Male and female look similar with gray and brownish-black plumage and light markings on the wings. The female does not always have a black base to the lower bill. Usually in pairs or small family parties, red-billed hornbills feed on the ground and in trees on insects, such as grasshoppers, locusts and beetles, and on fruit.

The female lays her 3 to 6 eggs in a hole in a tree, which is barricaded with mud in the usual manner of hornbills.

Helmeted Hornbill

Buceros vigil **LR:nt**

RANGE Malaysian Peninsula, Sumatra, Borneo

HABITAT Forest

SIZE 4 ft (1.2 m)

The greatly elongated central tail feathers of this huge hornbill may add as much as 20 in (50 cm) to its length. The female is slightly smaller than the male.

This bird is unusual in that while all other hornbills have bills that are deceptively light, its casque is formed of solid ivory making its skull the heaviest of any bird's. This heavy head could cause problems for the bird when in flight, but the elongated central tail feathers help to counterbalance the skull. Unfortunately the attributes of the helmeted hornbill have created much demand for it, and it has long been hunted both for its ivory casque and its tail feathers.

Helmeted hornbills feed on fruit, lizards, birds and their eggs. The breeding procedure is believed to be similar to that of other hornbills.

Great Indian Hornbill

Buceros bicornis

RANGE India, S.E. Asia, Sumatra

HABITAT Forest

SIZE 5 ft (1.5 m)

Although a large bird, the great Indian hornbill has a top-heavy appearance, with its huge bill and casque. The female bird is much smaller, particularly her bill and casque, and has white instead of red eyes, but she is otherwise similar to the male.

These hornbills spend much of their time in trees, feeding on fruit, especially figs, as well as on insects, reptiles and other small animals.

The female bird lays 1 to 3 eggs in an unlined nest hole in a tree and walls up the entrance from within, using her own feces and material brought to her by the male. She incubates the eggs for about 31 days.

GROUND-HORNBILLS, HOOPOES, WOOD-HOOPOES AND TROGONS

BUCORVIDAE: GROUND-HORNBILL FAMILY

The two species of ground-hornbills are large birds that inhabit savanna, arid grasslands, and open woodlands in tropical Africa.

Southern Ground-Hornbill *Bucorvus cafer*

RANGE	Parts of Africa south of the equator
HABITAT	Open country
SIZE	42 in (107 cm)

The southern ground-hornbill and the closely related Abyssinian ground-hornbill, *B. abyssinicus*, are the largest African hornbills. These mainly ground-living, turkey-sized birds walk in pairs or small family groups, eating insects, reptiles and other animals.

Females lay 1 to 3 eggs in a hole in a tree or stump, lined with leaves. She is not walled up in the nest, but comes and goes freely, covering the eggs with leaves when she is not sitting.

ORDER UPUPIFORMES

The members of this order all have long, slightly downcurved beaks used for probing the ground and crevices for insects and other small animals. There are 3 families – Upupidae (the hoopoe), Phoeniculidae (woodhoopoes), and Rhinopomastidae (scimitar-bills). The hoopoe is found in Eurasia, Asia and Africa, while the woodhoopoes and 3 species of scimitar-bills are found in Africa south of the Sahara desert.

UPUPIDAE: HOOPOE FAMILY

The single hoopoe species is ground-living. The sexes look similar, but females may be smaller and duller.

Hoopoe *Upupa epops*

RANGE	Europe (not Scandinavia or Britain), N. Africa, C. and S. Asia; tropical Africa, S. Asia
HABITAT	Open country with trees, forest edge, parks, gardens, orchards
SIZE	11 in (28 cm)

The hoopoe has pinkish to cinnamon body plumage, boldly barred wings and tail and a huge crest, which is usually held flat. It walks and runs swiftly, probing the ground with its bill for worms, insects and invertebrates. The hoopoe perches and roosts in trees and flies efficiently, if slowly. It may occasionally hunt insects in the air.

The female lays 5 to 8 eggs (but up to 12) in a hole in a tree, wall or building. The male feeds his mate while she incubates the clutch for 16 to 19 days.

PHOENICULIDAE: WOODHOOPOE FAMILY

The 5 species of woodhoopoe live in wooded grassland, forest and forest edge in central and southern Africa. The sexes look similar, but the female is often smaller and sometimes browner.

Green Woodhoopoe *Phoeniculus purpureus*

RANGE	Africa, south of the Sahara
HABITAT	Woodland, often near rivers
SIZE	15 in (8 cm)

This woodhoopoe has glossy dark-green and purple plumage and a long, deep-purple tail. Its distinctive red bill is long and curves downwards. Male and female look alike, but young birds have brownish neck and breast plumage and black bills. These noisy, gregarious birds fly from tree to tree in small parties, searching for insects to eat and calling harshly.

Females lay 3 to 5 eggs in a hole in a tree. She incubates the clutch. Her mate helps to tend and feed the young.

ORDER TROGONIFORMES

TROGONIDAE: TROGON FAMILY

Trogons are a family placed in its own order. The 39 species are among the most colorful birds in the world. Males are more brilliantly marked than females. Trogons inhabit forests in the southern regions of Africa; India and Southeast Asia; and Central and South America.

Trogons are between 9 and 14 in (23 and 35.5 cm) long with short, rounded wings and long tails. Their feet are zygodactyl, (two toes point forward and two point back).The first and second digits point forward. (In other birds with such feet, the first and fourth digits do so.) Trogons are mainly arboreal. They eat insects, small invertebrates, berries and fruit.

Resplendent Quetzal *Pharomachrus mocinno* **LR:nt**

RANGE Mexico, Central America

HABITAT High-altitude rain forest

SIZE Body: 11¼ in (30 cm)
Tail feathers: 24 in (61 cm)

The quetzal has greatly extended feathers overlying the tail (coverts), which form a magnificent train but are shed and regrown after each breeding season. These feathers were highly prized for ceremonial use by the ancient Mayans and Aztecs. Females are plainer than males. Their upper tail coverts do not form a train.

Quetzals are quite solitary birds, which inhabit the lower layers of the tropical forest. They eat fruit, insects, frogs, lizards and snails. The nest is a hole in a tree and 2 or 3 eggs are laid. The male helps to incubate them, bending his tail forward over his head, so that it hangs out of the nest hole. His feathers become damaged from moving in and out of the nest.

Coppery-tailed/Elegant Trogon *Trogon elegans*

RANGE Extreme S.W. USA to Costa Rica

HABITAT Forest, woodland

SIZE 11–12 in (28–30.5 cm)

This trogon has a stout yellow bill and a broad, blunt tail which is coppery-red seen from above, but gray and white from below, with a black band at the base. The female is duller, with a brownish head. This is the only species of trogon in the USA.

These birds are solitary and generally quiet, but they do make monotonous, froglike calls. They perch in the trees for long periods then take to the air, to dart about the branches in search of insects, small animals and fruit. Most feeding is done in flight, and the birds sometimes hover in front of leaves to glean food from their surfaces. The trogon's legs and feet are weak and used almost entirely for perching.

Both partners of a breeding pair help to excavate a hole in a tree for use as a nest, or they take over an existing hollow or abandoned woodpecker hole. The 3 or 4 eggs are incubated by both the male and female, probably for 17 to 19 days. The young hatch naked and helpless and are cared for and fed by both parents and leave the nest at 15 to 17 days old.

Red-headed Trogon *Harpactes erythrocephalus*

RANGE Nepal: Himalayas, S. China; S.E. Asia, Sumatra

HABITAT Forest

SIZE 13¼ in (34 cm)

There are 11 species of trogon in Asia, all in the genus *Harpactes*. All are beautifully colored, with broad, squared-off tails. The male has distinctive dark-red plumage on its head, while the female has a brownish head, throat and breast. They are mainly solitary and perch on trees, darting out to catch insects. They also eat leaves, berries, frogs, and lizards. Both parents incubate the 3 or 4 eggs in an unlined hole for about 19 days.

Narina Trogon *Apaloderma narina*

RANGE S. Africa, S. and E. coastal regions

HABITAT Forest, scrub

SIZE 11½ in (29 cm)

This is one of 3 African trogon species. It lives in the lower levels of dense forest and perches for long periods on a branch or creeper in a hunched posture. It eats mainly insects, which it catches among the branches, and occasionally fruit. The 2 or 3 eggs (laid in a hollow tree trunk) are incubated for about 20 days.

ROLLERS, GROUND-ROLLERS, CUCKOO-ROLLERS, MOTMOTS AND BEE-EATERS

ORDER CORACIIFORMES

There are 9 families in this order – rollers, ground-rollers, cuckoo-roller, motmots, todies, bee-eaters, and three families of kingfisher. The birds generally have large bills in proportion to their body size and bright plumage.

CORACIIDAE: ROLLER FAMILY

Most of the 12 species of roller live in Africa, although they occur in warm temperate and tropical parts of the Old World, from Europe to Australia. They are brightly colored, stocky birds, with large heads, long, downward-curving bills and long wings. Their common name originates from their tumbling, aerobatic courtship displays. Males and females look alike.

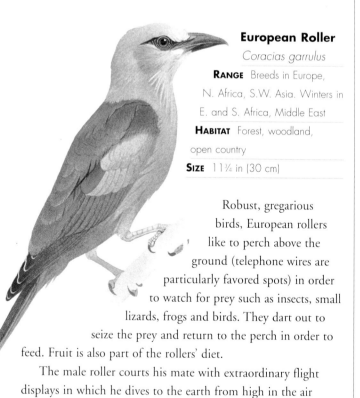

European Roller
Coracias garrulus

RANGE Breeds in Europe, N. Africa, S.W. Asia. Winters in E. and S. Africa, Middle East

HABITAT Forest, woodland, open country

SIZE 11¾ in (30 cm)

Robust, gregarious birds, European rollers like to perch above the ground (telephone wires are particularly favored spots) in order to watch for prey such as insects, small lizards, frogs and birds. They dart out to seize the prey and return to the perch in order to feed. Fruit is also part of the rollers' diet.

The male roller courts his mate with extraordinary flight displays in which he dives to the earth from high in the air tumbling and rolling as he descends.

The nest is made in an existing hole in a tree, wall or bank. Alternatively, the abandoned nest of another bird species is used. Both parents incubate the clutch of between 4 and 7 eggs for a total of 18 or 19 days and also share the care of the young.

BRACHYPTERACIIDAE: GROUND ROLLER FAMILY

The 5 species of ground roller all live in Madagascar. They differ from the rollers in that they are ground-living rather than arboreal.

Short-legged Ground Roller
Brachypteracias leptosomus **VU**

RANGE E. Madagascar

HABITAT Dense forest to 6,000 ft (1,800 m)

SIZE 10–12 in (25.5–30.5 cm)

Typical of its family, the short-legged ground roller is a squat bird, with short wings, strong legs and a stout, downward curving bill. It lives on the forest floor, feeding on insects and reptiles, and flies up into trees only when alarmed.

LEPTOSOMATIDAE: CUCKOO-ROLLER FAMILY

The cuckoo-roller is related to true rollers and ground rollers. However the sexes look unalike.

Cuckoo-roller *Leptosomus discolor*

RANGE Madagascar, Comoro Islands

HABITAT Forest, savanna

SIZE 16–18 in (41–46 cm)

Cuckoo-rollers are noisy birds. They live in trees and feed on insects (especially hairy caterpillars) and lizards. Their short legs are weak, but they are strong, spectacular fliers. The female is plainer than the male, with rufous plumage and black markings.

MOMOTIDAE: MOTMOT FAMILY

Motmots are beautifully plumaged birds, with decorative, elongated tail feathers. There are 9 species of motmot, found from Mexico to northeastern Argentina. All have slightly downward-curving bills with serrated edges, which they use to seize prey from the dense vegetation among which they live. Male and female look alike, or nearly so.

Blue-crowned Motmot *Momotus momota*

RANGE Mexico, Central America, South America to N.W. Argentina; Trinidad and Tobago

HABITAT Rain forest, plantations

SIZE 15–16 in (38–41 cm)

The blue-crowned motmot has two greatly elongated central tail feathers with racket-shaped tips. Although the feathers are initially fully vaned, the vanes just above the ends of the feathers are loosely attached and fall away as the bird preens or brushes against vegetation, leaving the racket tips. The motmot perches to watch for prey, such as insects, spiders or lizards, often swinging its tail from side to side like a pendulum while it waits. It darts out from the perch to seize prey, then returns to consume the item, having briefly beaten it against a branch.

Motmots nest in a burrow, which is dug by both members of a breeding pair, in a bank or opening off the side of a mammal's burrow. The burrow may be up to 13 ft (4 m) long and have several sharp turns. In the enlarged chamber at the end of the tunnel, the female lays her 3 eggs on bare ground. Both parents incubate the eggs for about 21 days.

TODIDAE: TODY FAMILY

The 5 species of tody all live in the West Indies and are extremely similar in size and appearance, with mostly green and red plumage. Males and females look alike. They are insect-eating birds which catch their prey, flycatcher-fashion, in the air.

Jamaican Tody *Todus todus*

RANGE Jamaica

HABITAT Wooded hills and mountains

SIZE 4 in (10 cm)

The Jamaican tody is typical of its family, with its small, compact body, relatively large head and long, sharp bill. It hunts close to the ground, catching flying insects and, occasionally, baby lizards.

Todies live in pairs or singly and are strongly territorial. They nest in burrows, which they dig with their bills, usually in the sides of banks. The nest tunnel is about 11¾ in (30 cm) long, with a tiny entrance just big enough for the birds to squeeze through. It opens out at the end into a breeding chamber. Both parents incubate the 3 or 4 eggs and care for the young.

MEROPIDAE: BEE-EATER FAMILY

The 26 species of bee-eater are brightly plumaged birds, with streamlined bodies, long wings and small, weak legs. They occur in tropical and warm temperate areas of the Old World. As their name suggests, they are adept at the aerial capture of insects, such as bees and wasps, which they seize with their long, downward-curving bills. While they are considered a menace by beekeepers, these birds are much appreciated in the tropics, where they consume large numbers of locusts.

Bee-eaters are gregarious birds, feeding together and nesting in colonies of sometimes hundreds of pairs. Males and females look alike. Many species are migratory.

European Bee-eater *Merops apiaster*

RANGE Breeds in Europe, S. Russia, N. Africa, S.W. Asia; winters in tropical Africa and Middle East

HABITAT Open country, woodland

SIZE 11 in (28 cm)

One of the most tropical-looking European birds, the gaudy bee-eater makes swift darts from a perch to catch prey, mainly bees and wasps. It rubs its prey against a branch or the ground before swallowing it, presumably to destroy the sting.

Bee-eaters nest in colonies. A pair makes a tunnel 3¼ to 9¾ ft (1 to 3 m) long, often in a river bank. The female lays 4 to 7 eggs at the end of the tunnel, and both parents incubate the clutch for about 20 days. Together, they care for and feed their young.

KINGFISHERS

ALCEDINIDAE ALCEDINID: KINGFISHER FAMILY

Kingfishers are found all over the world, but the majority of the 94 or so known species inhabit the hotter regions of the Old World. They range in length from 4 to 18 in (10 to 46 cm) and have stocky bodies, large heads and short necks. The beak is almost always straight with a pointed tip and is large in proportion to the body. Wings are short and rounded, and tail length is variable. Most kingfishers have multicolored plumage, with patches of iridescent blue, green, purple or red. Male and female differ slightly in appearance in some species.

Several species eat fish and aquatic invertebrates which they hunt by diving headlong from a perch just above the water, but they do not actually swim. Most species, however, feed on dry land on insects, lizards, snakes and even birds and rodents, catching prey by swooping down from a high vantage point.

Kingfishers nest in tunnels, often in river banks, or in cavities in trees or termite nests; there is little or no nesting material. Some northern populations migrate south in winter. There are 3 kingfisher families – the Alcedinid, Dacelonid, and Cerylid Kingfishers. The 24 species of Alcedinid Kingfishers live close to water from temperate Eurasia to Australia and in Africa.

Common Kingfisher *Alcedo atthis*

RANGE Europe, N. Africa to Asia, Indonesia, New Guinea and Solomon Islands

HABITAT Inland waterways, marshes, mangroves, sea shores

SIZE 6¼ in (16 cm)

The common kingfisher is the only European kingfisher. It has a wide range and is unmistakable with its brilliant plumage and long, daggerlike bill. A solitary bird, it lives in the vicinity of water. When hunting, it perches on branches overhanging the water, watching for fish and other small aquatic animals. Alternatively it flies low over the water, often hovering for a few seconds before diving.

A breeding pair excavates a slightly upward-sloping tunnel, up to 24 in (61 cm) long, in the bank of a stream, with a nesting chamber about 6 in (15 cm) across at the end of it. They start the tunnel by hurling themselves repeatedly against the riverbank so that their bills always strike the same spot.

The female lays a clutch of 4 to 8 eggs which both parents incubate in shifts for 19 to 21 days. Both the male and female share in the care and feeding of the young.

African Pygmy Kingfisher *Ispidina picta*

RANGE Africa, south of the Sahara to Zambia

HABITAT Bush, woodland

SIZE 5 in (12.5 cm)

One of the smallest kingfishers, this species has the curious habit of diving from its perch into grass, much as other kingfishers dive into water. Grasshoppers, caterpillars, beetles and other insects, as well as some lizards, make up its diet. The insects are caught in the air or on the ground. The pygmy kingfisher's nest is made at the end of a tunnel in a river bank or in a termite mound or anthill, and the female lays a clutch of 3 to 5 eggs.

DACELONIDAE: DACELONID KINGFISHER FAMILY

Dacelonid kingfishers are stocky, with long tails and blunt, thick beaks. The 61 species occur from southern Asia to Australia, the Philippines and Pacific islands, and in Africa. The family includes kookaburras, white-collared kingfishers, and bush kingfishers. Some species live by water, but others live in dry areas of scrub, forest or open country.

Laughing Kookaburra

Dacelo novaeguineae

RANGE Australia; introduced in Tasmania

HABITAT Dry forest fringe, savanna, any open country with trees

SIZE 18 in (46 cm)

The largest of the kingfishers, the kookaburra is renowned for its noisy, laughlike call. If one bird starts calling, others nearby will join in, particularly at dawn or at dusk. Kookaburras eat practically anything, including large insects, crabs, small reptiles, mammals and birds, as well as rodents and other harmful vermin.

Kookaburras nest in holes in trees or sometimes in arboreal termite nests, in cavities in banks or even on buildings. The female lays 3 or 4 eggs.

Shovel-billed Kingfisher *Clytoceyx rex* **DD**

RANGE New Guinea

HABITAT Forest

SIZE 12 in (30.5 cm)

The soberly colored shovel-billed kingfisher is a solitary bird which inhabits forest at altitudes of up to 7,700 ft (2,350 m). It perches for long periods on tree stumps and branches, swooping down suddenly to catch large insects, larvae and small mice. Using its short, heavy bill as a shovel, it also probes in the mud beside streams and rivers, searching for worms, crabs and reptiles. Little is known about its breeding habits, but it is thought to make its nest on the ground.

White-collared/Mangrove Kingfisher

Todirhamphus chloris

RANGE Ethiopia to India, S.E. China, Australia, S.W. Pacific islands

HABITAT Mangroves, estuaries, rivers, forest clearings

SIZE 10 in (25.5 cm)

This widely distributed kingfisher is found in a variety of habitats but most commonly in mangroves. Perching on branches, it watches for prey; then swoops down to the swamp mud or dives into the water in pursuit of crabs and small fish, its main foods. Before swallowing a crab, the kingfisher will dash it against a branch a few times in order to crush the shell.

These kingfishers nest in holes in trees, among the roots of an arboreal fern or in termite or ant nests. The female lays a clutch of 3 or 4 eggs.

Common Paradise Kingfisher *Tanysiptera galatea*

RANGE New Guinea to Molucca Islands

HABITAT Forest

SIZE 11 in (28 cm)

The common paradise kingfisher has greatly elongated tail feathers, thought to be used in courtship display. Deep in the forest understorey, it perches on branches to watch for its prey, mainly millipedes and lizards, but also insects and other invertebrates. It may dig in the forest litter for earthworms.

Paradise kingfishers are normally solitary birds, but in the breeding season both partners of a pair help to dig a hole in an arboreal termite nest in which to lay their eggs. Alternatively, the birds will nest in patches of vegetation at the forest edge. The female lays a clutch of between 3 and 5 eggs which are incubated by both parents.

CERYLIDAE: CERYLID KINGFISHER FAMILY

The 9 species of Cerylid kingfishers are larger with longer tails than the Alcedinid kingfishers. They live by lakes and rivers, or the sea, in the Americas, Africa and south and south-east Asia.

Belted Kingfisher

Megaceryle alcyon

RANGE Alaska, Canada, USA, south to Mexico and Panama; West Indies

HABITAT Fresh water, coasts

SIZE 11–14 in (28–35.5 cm)

The only American kingfisher occurring north of Texas and Arizona, this common bird inhabits any territory near water. The sexes look similar, but the female has a chestnut band across the breast and down her flanks. Solitary birds out of the breeding season, each holds its own territory. They eat small fish, crabs, crayfish, tadpoles, frogs, lizards and some insects, and generally hover above the water before diving for prey.

Both members of a breeding pair dig a nesting tunnel 4 to 8 ft (1.2 to 2.4 m) long in the river bank, at the end of which they make a nesting chamber. The female lays a clutch of 5 to 8 eggs which are incubated for about 23 days.

MOUSEBIRDS AND CUCKOOS

ORDER COLIIFORMES

COLIIDAE: MOUSEBIRD FAMILY

The 6 species of mousebird, or coly, are a distinctive family that modern taxonomists place in an order of its own. All the forms are similar in appearance, and the sexes look alike in all species. The body of the mousebird is about the same size as that of a house sparrow, but it has extremely long tail feathers of graduated lengths. The plumage is soft and loosely attached to the skin. All species have crests, and their bills are short, curved and quite strong. Mousebirds are distributed in the savanna regions of Africa, south of the Sahara. They are sociable, living in small groups and roosting together, huddled up for warmth.

Speckled Mousebird *Colius striatus*

RANGE Africa, south of the Sahara

HABITAT Savanna, dense forest

SIZE Body: 4¾ in (12 cm)
Tail: 7–7¾ in (18–20 cm)

The speckled mousebird's tail is almost twice the length of its body. It lives mainly in trees and climbs expertly among the branches, using its strong, adaptable feet – the hind toes can be turned forward – and long, sharp claws. This species is gregarious and feeds and roosts in small groups. Soft vegetable matter, particularly young shoots and fruit, is its normal diet, but it will eat insects.

The speckled mousebird makes a nest of twigs and rootlets, lined with leaves, in a tree or bush. Usually 3 eggs are laid, and they are incubated by both parents for 12 to 14 days. Chicks can leave the nest at a few days old and fly at 16 to 18 days old.

ORDER CUCULIFORMES

This order contains 143 species of cuckoos in 6 families – Cuculidae (Old World cuckoos), Centropodidae (coucals), Coccyzidae (American cuckoos), Opisthocomidae (hoatzin), Crotophagidae (anis and guira cuckoos), and Neomorphidae (roadrunners and ground-cuckoos). They range between 6 and 28 in (15 and 71 cm) long, and most are slender bodied, with long tails and short legs. Males and females look alike in most species. Fifty or so Old World cuckoos are nest parasites.

CUCULIDAE: OLD WORLD CUCKOO FAMILY

The 79 species in this family are found from Eurasia south to Africa and Australia. This diverse family includes both tree-dwelling and terrestrial species. Some build nests and rear their own young, but the females of many species in the family lay their eggs in the nests of another species which then incubates and rears her young. In some species this habit of nest parasitism is now highly developed, and the cuckoo's eggs resemble those of the host species. Since parasitic cuckoos generally lay their eggs in the nests of much smaller passerine birds, their eggs must be smaller and hatch more quickly than those of nonparasitic cuckoos.

Common Cuckoo *Cuculus canorus*

RANGE Europe, N. Africa, N. and S.E. Asia;
winters south of range in Africa and S. Asia

HABITAT Forest, woodland, moors

SIZE 13 in (33 cm)

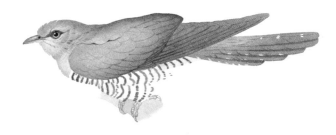

The male cuckoo's song, the origin of its common name, heralds the arrival of spring, when the bird flies north to breed in Europe and Asia. A slim, long-tailed bird, it leads a solitary life outside the breeding season and haunts trees, hedges and thickets, where it eats large insects, particularly hairy caterpillars.

Breeding starts in mid-May, and each female has a well-defined territory in which she searches for nests in which to lay her eggs. She uses the same host species, usually small passerine birds such as dunnocks, wagtails or redstarts, throughout her life. The species she chooses is probably that of her own foster parents. On alternate days, she lays a single egg, each in a different nest, at the same time removing one of the host's eggs, until she has laid a total of 8 to 12 eggs. She must lay her egg stealthily, for if the foster parents are alarmed, they may reject the whole clutch. The young cuckoo hatches in about 12 days. Since it is much the bigger, stronger and faster growing it is able to oust the hosts' own young from the nest. The hosts have to work extremely hard in order to satisfy the demands for food made by the young cuckoo, which is much larger than they are.

African Emerald Cuckoo

Chrysococcyx cupreus

RANGE Africa, south of the Sahara

HABITAT Forest edge and clearings

SIZE 7¼ in (20 cm)

A shy bird which haunts the dense foliage of tall forest trees, the emerald cuckoo is more often heard than seen, for it darts for cover at the slightest hint of danger.

Considered to be one of the most beautiful of African birds, the male has a golden-yellow belly and an emerald-green back. The female has moss green upperparts, a brown crown and a white belly, barred with mossgreen. Emerald cuckoos feed on a variety of insects, including caterpillars, ants and beetles.

The female lays her eggs in the nests of such birds as bulbuls, orioles, puff-back shrikes and black-headed weavers.

The emerald cuckoo is thought to be migratory. A smaller relative, the shining cuckoo, *C. lucidus*, migrates some 2,000 miles (3,200 km) across the southwest Pacific Ocean from New Zealand to the Solomon Islands.

Drongo Cuckoo

Surniculus lugubris

RANGE India, S.E. Asia, S. China, Indonesia

HABITAT Forest, scrub, cultivated land

SIZE 10 in (25.5 cm)

The drongo cuckoo resembles the drongo, *Dicrurus macrocercus*, in its plumage and forked tail, unique among cuckoos, and uses it as a foster-parent in some areas. A solitary, mainly nocturnal bird, it feeds on insects, particularly grasshoppers and caterpillars, and on fruit such as figs. It also catches winged insects by leaping up into the air after them in the manner of the drongo.

The female lays her eggs in the nests of various drongo species and in those of other birds. Juveniles have white flecks in their black plumage, which disappear as the birds mature.

Common/Asian Koel *Eudynamys scolopacea*

RANGE India, Pakistan, Sri Lanka, S. China, S.E. Asia, New Guinea, Australia

HABITAT Forest fringe, scrub, cultivated land, gardens

SIZE 17 in (43 cm)

The koel is a solitary bird, keeping to leafy trees and seldom descending to the ground. It feeds on fruit, particularly

figs, but also eats insects and small invertebrates such as snails. The male and female do not look alike – the male is black and glossy, while the female has brownish plumage, spotted and barred with white and buff.

The female koel lays her eggs in the nest of the house crow, *Corvus splendens*, or of a friarbird or honeyeater. Birds which use the crow as a foster-parent lay several eggs which resemble those of the host species, but are smaller. The young koels are black and look similar to young crows.

Channel-billed Cuckoo

Scythrops novaehollandiae

RANGE Australia to New Guinea, Indonesia

HABITAT Forest, woodland

SIZE 25 in (63.5 cm)

The channel-billed cuckoo is the largest cuckoo of the Australasian region. With its large, deep bill, it is reminiscent of a toucan or hornbill. It will devour almost anything, but insects, fruit and berries are its preferred foods.

Channel-billed cuckoos migrate north in March, returning south in September in order to breed. The female lays 2 or more eggs in the nest of a crow, magpie or currawong. The 2 blind, naked cuckoo chicks attempt to push one another out of the nest at first, but are usually unable to do so, and normally both are reared by the foster parents.

CUCKOOS CONTINUED

Small Green-billed Malkoha *Phaenicophaeus viridirostris*

RANGE S. India, Sri Lanka

HABITAT Forest, scrub, bamboo forest

SIZE 15 in (38 cm)

This distinctive cuckoo is a common Indian species. It has a green bill and sky-blue eye patch, which is the origin of its alternative common name – the blue-faced malkoha.

The small green-billed malkoha flies feebly and reluctantly and spends most of the time under cover of bushes and undergrowth. Large insects, such as grasshoppers, mantids and caterpillars, form the bulk of its diet, and it occasionally catches small lizards.

This nonparasitic species builds a shallow nest, made of sticks and lined with leaves. The female lays 2 eggs.

Running Coua *Coua cursor*

RANGE S.W. Madagascar

HABITAT Arid brush

SIZE 14¼ in (36 cm)

The running coua is a terrestrial bird and usually moves on foot, although it is able to fly reasonably well. Single birds or small groups walk about looking for insects, such as caterpillars; if alarmed, they run quickly away, interspersing their strides with hops. A nonparasitic cuckoo, the coua builds its own nest, but little is known about its breeding habits.

CENTROPODIDAE: COUCAL FAMILY

The 30 species of coucals are terrestrial cuckoos found in forests and grasslands from southern Asia to the Philippines, Australia and sub-Saharan Africa. They have strong legs and either walk or run along the ground, or skulk in dense vegetation.

Buff-headed Coucal

Centropus milo

RANGE Solomon Islands

HABITAT Forest

SIZE 26 in (66 cm)

One of the largest cuckoos, the buff-headed coucal has short wings, a long tail and a big, curved bill. It is a poor flier and spends most of its time on the ground, but even there moves awkwardly. It will sometimes flap up into a tree, moving from branch to branch and then gliding clumsily down. It feeds on large insects, frogs and reptiles.

The coucal's nest is a rounded, domed structure, made of grass and built in the undergrowth just above ground level. The female lays a clutch of 3 to 5 eggs.

COCCYZIDAE: AMERICAN CUCKOO FAMILY

These medium-sized tree dwellers resemble Old World cuckoos, but none of the 18 species is parasitic. They are found from southern Canada to northern Argentina.

Yellow-billed Cuckoo *Coccyzus americanus*

RANGE Breeds from Canada to Mexico and Caribbean islands; winters in Central and South America

HABITAT Woodland, orchards, thickets

SIZE 11–13 in (28–33 cm)

The yellow-billed cuckoo is secretive and shy. It frequents undergrowth and brush, searching for hairy caterpillars, beetles, grasshoppers, tree-crickets, army ants, wasps and flies. It also feeds on summer fruit and small frogs and lizards.

A nonparasitic cuckoo, it builds a nest of sticks in a tree or bush and lines it with dry leaves, grass or even pieces of rag. The female lays 3 or 4 eggs, one every 2 or 3 days, and both parents incubate the eggs, each of which hatches 14 days after laying. The nestlings are almost naked when they hatch, with only a sparse covering of down. Both parents feed and tend the young.

OPISTHOCOMIDAE: HOATZIN FAMILY

The hoatzin is the single species in this family.

Hoatzin *Opisthocomus hoazin*

RANGE South America: Amazon and Orinoco basins

HABITAT Wooded river banks

SIZE 24 in (61 cm)

The hoatzin has large wings and tail, a long neck and a small head, topped with a ragged crest. The sexes look alike. It is a poor flier and uses its wings more for support and balance when moving about in the trees. Hoatzins live in flocks of 10 to 20. They eat fruit and leaves, particularly mangrove and arum leaves.

The hoatzin builds its untidy stick nest in a tree overhanging water so that if threatened, the young birds, which can swim, can drop down into the water to escape. Both parents are believed to incubate the 2 or 3 eggs. The young hoatzin has a pair of hooked claws on each wing, which help it to clamber among the trees. The claws are lost as the bird matures.

CROTOPHAGIDAE: ANI AND GUIRA CUCKOO FAMILY

The 3 anis species and 1 species of guira cuckoo are all gregarious, and roost and breed communally. They occur from southern USA to northern Argentina.

Smooth-billed Ani *Crotophaga ani*

RANGE From C. Florida south to Central and South America, West Indies

HABITAT Forest edge, grassland, pasture

SIZE 13 in (33 cm)

Anis are nonparasitic cuckoos, with long square-ended tails, heavy bills and short wings. They fly weakly and feed mainly on the ground on insects, fruit and berries. Anis often follow grazing cattle which disturb ground insects.

Smooth-billed anis live in flocks of up to 25. They build a bulky communal nest from sticks, weeds and grass in a small tree or bush. Females each lay 3 or 4 eggs, and share the incubation. The whole flock feeds the chicks.

NEOMORPHIDAE: ROADRUNNER AND GROUND-CUCKOO FAMILY

These medium to large cuckoos occur from south-western USA to northern Argentina. They are mainly ground-dwellers that pursue their prey on foot. Of the 11 species, 3 are nest parasites.

Striped Cuckoo

Tapera naevia

RANGE S. Mexico, Central America, South America to N. Argentina

HABITAT Savanna, swamps

SIZE 12 in (30.5 cm)

The striped cuckoo is a shy bird that perches on a tree, calling for hours at a time, often during the hottest part of the day. Its call is a melancholy, carrying whistle, which sounds like "sa-ci". The striped cuckoo has parasitic breeding habits.

Greater Roadrunner *Geococcyx californianus*

RANGE S.W. USA: S. California, Utah, Kansas, south to Mexico

HABITAT Semi-arid open country

SIZE 19¾–23½ in (50–60 cm)

A slender, fowllike bird, with a small, shaggy crest, a long tail and long legs, the roadrunner is a fast-running ground-bird which can attain speeds of 15 mph (24 km/h) or more. Its short, rounded wings are functional and it can fly clumsily. Like its cousin, the lesser roadrunner, *G. velox,* of Mexico and Central America, it lives in dry, open places and eats ground-living insects, such as crickets and grasshoppers, and other small invertebrates, birds' eggs, lizards, snakes (even rattlesnakes) and fruits such as prickly pear. It usually kills with a sudden pounce.

Roadrunners form permanent pair bonds and live in their territory all year round. They build shallow nests of sticks, lined with leaves and feathers, in trees or cactus clumps. The female lays 2 to 6 eggs in April or May which are incubated for about 20 days. The eggs hatch over several days. Both parents care for the young, which hatch naked and helpless. Their eyes open at about 7 days, and they can feed themselves at about 16 days.

PARROTS

ORDER PSITTACIFORMES

PSITTACIDAE: PARROT FAMILY

The 358 species of parrot make up one of the most easily identified groups of birds. Despite a size range of between 4 and 40 in (10 and 101 cm), all types have a general similarity of appearance and structure. Species include lories, cockatoos, lovebirds, budgerigars and lorikeets.

Most parrots are brightly colored tree-living birds. Their beaks are short, powerful and strongly hooked, with a bulging base or cere. The upper part of the parrot's bill is hinged and moved by muscles, and the flexibility that this gives allows the bill to become almost like a third manipulative limb, which is used in climbing and feeding. Although many birds have hinged bills, this feature is more marked in the short-billed parrots. Males and females look alike in most species, but there are plumage differences in a few instances.

Parrots are distributed through the tropical and subtropical zones of both hemispheres. The largest number of species occur in Australasia and the Amazon in South America. In the forests of these regions, parrots feed largely on fruit, nuts, seeds, nectar and fungi. They manipulate food with their feet, beaks and strong, mobile tongues. Many parrots are gregarious and vocal, making screaming and discordant calls. Although they mimic sound in captivity, they are not known to do so in the wild.

Black-capped Lory *Lorius lory*

RANGE New Guinea, Papuan Islands

HABITAT Forest

SIZE 12 in (31 cm)

Several races of this lory, with slight plumage differences, occur on the various islands in its range. Shy birds, black-capped lories frequent the upper levels of the forest, usually moving in pairs or small groups of up to a dozen. They eat pollen, nectar, flowers, fruit, and insects and their larvae. Little is known of the breeding habits of this lory, but it appears that the female lays 2 eggs, which she incubates for about 24 days.

Rainbow Lorikeet *Trichoglossus haematodus*

RANGE E. and N. Australia, Tasmania; Bali, east to New Hebrides

HABITAT Forest, coconut plantations, gardens, parks

SIZE 10¼ in (26 cm)

One of the most attractively plumaged birds in the parrot order, the adaptable rainbow lorikeet inhabits almost any wooded land, even near human habitation. Usually seen in pairs or flocks of anything from 3 or 4 to 100 birds, rainbow lorikeets are active and noisy and continually fly about the trees searching for food and calling loudly. Pollen, nectar, fruit, berries, seeds, leaves, insects and larvae are all included in their diet, and they will feed on grain crops and invade orchards.

Rainbow lorikeets nest in holes in trees, high above the ground. The female lays 2 eggs, rarely 3, which she incubates for about 25 days. Both parents feed the chicks which stay in the nest until they are about 7 or 8 weeks old.

Cockatiel *Nymphicus hollandicus*

RANGE Australia

HABITAT Open country

SIZE 12½ in (32 cm)

The slender cockatiel has long wings and tail and a tapering crest on its head. Males and females differ slightly – males having brighter markings than females. In pairs or small flocks, cockatiels forage on the ground for seeds, and feed in the trees on fruit and berries.

Breeding usually takes place between August and December, but the exact timing depends on the conditions, particularly on rainfall. The 4 to 7 eggs are laid in a hole in a tree and are incubated by both parents for 21 to 23 days.

The young leave the nest at 4 or 5 weeks and males acquire their bright facial markings at about 6 months.

Sulfur-crested Cockatoo *Cacatua galerita*

RANGE New Guinea and offshore islands, Aru Islands, N. and E. Australia, Tasmania; introduced in New Zealand

HABITAT Forest, savanna, farmland

SIZE 19¾ in (50 cm)

Noisy, gregarious birds, sulfur-crested cockatoos move in pairs or family groups in the breeding season, but join in flocks for the rest of the year. In open country, these flocks may number hundreds of birds. Each flock has an habitual roosting site which the birds leave at sunrise, in order to fly to daytime feeding grounds where they forage for seeds, fruit, nuts, flowers leaves, insects and larvae.

After a brief courtship display, culminating in a spell of mutual preening, the sulfur-crested cockatoos nest in a hole in a tree. Both parents incubate the clutch of 2 or 3 eggs for about 30 days, and the young stay in the nest for 6 to 9 weeks.

Kea *Nestor notabilis* **LR:nt**

RANGE New Zealand: South Island

HABITAT Forest, open country

SIZE 18¾ in (48 cm)

The kea is a bold, stocky bird with a long, curving upper bill. The female's bill is shorter and less curved. Keas fly strongly, wheeling in wide arcs, even in stormy, windy weather. They feed in trees and on the ground on fruit, berries, leaves, insects and larvae. They will also scavenge on refuse dumps and eat carrion. The belief has long persisted that keas attack and kill sheep, and many birds have been destroyed by farmers for this reason. Although they may well attack sick, injured or trapped sheep, these activities are thought to have been exaggerated, and keas are now protected by law.

Nesting takes place at almost any time of year, but usually occurs between July and January. Males are polygamous. The nest is made in a crevice, under rocks among the roots of a tree or in a hollow log. The female lays 2 to 4 eggs which she incubates for 21 to 28 days.

Red-breasted Pygmy Parrot

Micropsitta bruijnii

RANGE Buru, Ceram, New Guinea, Bismarck Archipelago, Solomon Islands

HABITAT Mountain forest

SIZE 3½ in (9 cm)

In pairs or small groups, these tiny parrots clamber over branches of trees feeding on the lichens and fungus prevalent in high forest. The short tail has stiff shafts and can be used as a prop in the manner of a woodpecker. Pygmy parrots may also feed on other plant material and insects.

PARROTS CONTINUED

Eclectus Parrot *Eclectus roratus*

RANGE New Guinea, Solomon Islands, Lesser Sunda Islands; Australia: extreme N. Queensland

HABITAT Lowland forest

SIZE 13¾ in (35 cm)

Male and female eclectus parrots differ so radically in plumage that for years they were thought to be separate species. Both are glossy, brilliant birds, males with primarily green plumage and females with red. The body is stocky and the tail short and square. They are noisy, gregarious birds, roosting in groups of as many as 80 and flying off at sunrise in pairs or small groups to feed on fruit, nuts, seeds, berries, leaves, flowers and nectar.

The nest is made high up in a tree at the edge of the forest or in a clearing. The 2 eggs are laid in a hole in the tree trunk and the female incubates them for about 26 days.

Gray Parrot *Psittacus erithacus*

RANGE Central Africa: W. coast to Kenya and N.W. Tanzania

HABITAT Lowland forest, savanna, mangroves

SIZE 13 in (33 cm)

Flocks of gray parrots roost together in tall trees at the forest edge or on small islands in rivers and lakes. At sunrise they fly off swiftly in pairs or small groups to find food, following regular routes to and from the roosting area. Climbing from branch to branch, gray parrots feed in the trees on seeds, nuts, berries and fruit, particularly the fruit of the oil palm.

The timing of the breeding season varies according to area, and there may occasionally be two broods a year. There have been very few observations of nesting in the wild, but the female is believed to lay 3 or 4 eggs in a hole in a tree and to incubate them herself.

Peach-faced/Rosy-faced Lovebird *Agapornis roseicollis*

RANGE S.W. Africa: Angola, Namibia, S. Africa: N. Cape Province

HABITAT Dry open country

SIZE 6 in (15 cm)

Flocks of these noisy, abundant lovebirds maneuver skilfully and swiftly among the trees and bushes. They eat seeds and berries and never move far from some form of water supply. Lovebirds are so called because of their conspicuous mutual preening habits.

Colonies of lovebirds nest in crevices in cliffs or in buildings, or take over large parts of the communal, many-chambered nests of weaver birds. The female is thought to lay 3 to 6 eggs which she incubates for 23 days.

Kakapo/Owl Parrot *Strigops habroptilus* **EW**

RANGE New Zealand: parts of South and Stewart Islands

HABITAT Mountain forest all altitudes to 4,100 ft (1,250 m)

SIZE 25¼ in (64 cm)

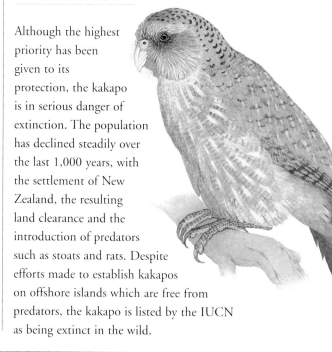

Although the highest priority has been given to its protection, the kakapo is in serious danger of extinction. The population has declined steadily over the last 1,000 years, with the settlement of New Zealand, the resulting land clearance and the introduction of predators such as stoats and rats. Despite efforts made to establish kakapos on offshore islands which are free from predators, the kakapo is listed by the IUCN as being extinct in the wild.

The kakapo is a most unusual parrot. It is a ground-living and flightless, nocturnal bird. During the day it shelters among rocks or bushes or in a burrow and emerges at dusk in order to feed on fruit, berries, nuts, seeds, shoots, leaves, moss and fungi. The kakapo climbs well, using its beak and feet to haul itself up tree trunks and along branches, and can flap its wings to help balance itself as it climbs or jumps from trees.

Courtship habits, too, are different in the kakapo from those of other parrots, for the males display communally in traditional areas, or leks. Each male excavates several shallow, bowl-shaped areas in which he displays: the bowl helps to amplify the booming calls which accompany his show.

The nest is a burrow made among rocks or tree roots and 1 or 2, occasionally 3, eggs are laid. The female is thought to incubate the clutch and to care for the young alone. Kakapos do not appear to breed every year, and breeding may be linked to the availability of food.

Rose-ringed Parakeet

Psittacula krameri

RANGE Central Africa, India to Sri Lanka; introduced in Mauritius, Middle East, Singapore, Hong Kong, Hawaiian Islands

HABITAT Woodland, cultivated land

SIZE 15¾ in (40 cm)

The bold, noisy rose-ringed parakeets are usually seen in small flocks, although they may gather in hundreds at feeding or roosting sites. These parakeets fly well, but tend not to travel far afield. Seeds, berries, fruit, flowers and nectar are the main items of their diet and they are relentless in their search, invading orchards and plantations, decimating sunflower crops and rice paddies and even ripping open bags of stored grain.

Males and females differ slightly in plumage – the female lacks the pink collar and black facial markings and has shorter central tail feathers than the male.

At the onset of the breeding season, the pair perform their courtship ritual, the female rolling her eyes and head until the male approaches her. He then rubs bills with her and feeds her.

They nest in a hole in a tree, which they excavate or take over from woodpeckers or barbets, or under the roof of a building. The female lays a clutch of 3 to 5 eggs which she incubates for 22 days. The young leave the nest about 7 weeks after hatching.

Crimson Rosella *Platycercus elegans*

RANGE E. and S.E. Australia; introduced in New Zealand and Norfolk Island

HABITAT Coastal and mountain forest, gardens, parks

SIZE 14¼ in (36 cm)

Crimson rosellas are bold, colorful birds, abundant in most of their range. Adults live in pairs or groups of up to 5, while juveniles form large groups. Much of the day is spent feeding on the ground or in the trees, mainly on seeds but also fruit, blossoms, insects and larvae.

The breeding season starts in late August or early September. In his courtship display the male lets his wings droop while he fans his tail out, moving it from side to side. The female nests in a hole in a tree and lays 5 to 8 eggs which she incubates for 21 days, leaving the nest only briefly each morning to be fed by her partner. The young leave the nest at about 5 weeks, but remain with their parents for another 5 weeks before joining a flock of other young rosellas.

Budgerigar *Melopsittacus undulatus*

RANGE Australia (interior); introduced in USA: Florida

HABITAT Scrub, open country

SIZE 7 in (18 cm)

So popular as a cage bird, with its many color variations, the budgerigar is a small parrot with mainly green plumage in the wild. Its numbers vary with conditions, but it is generally common and in years of abundant food supplies is one of the most numerous Australian species. Active mainly in the early morning and late afternoon, flocks of budgerigars search on the ground for grass seeds, their main food. They are swift, agile birds in the air and flocks are nomadic, continually moving from one area to another in search of food and water.

Breeding takes place at any time of the year, usually after rains which ensure food supplies. A nest is made in a hollow in a tree stump or log, and 4 to 6, sometimes 8, eggs are laid and incubated by the female for 18 days. The young leave the nest after about 30 days.

PARROTS CONTINUED

Scarlet Macaw *Ara macao*

RANGE Mexico, Central America, N. South America to Brazil and Bolivia

HABITAT Forest, savanna, plantations

SIZE 33½ in (85 cm)

A spectacular, brilliantly plumaged bird, the scarlet macaw is one of the largest and most striking members of its family. A much-photographed and painted species and the most familiar of South American parrots, it is nevertheless declining in numbers because of the widespread destruction of its rain forest habitat and the collection of large numbers of young birds and nestlings for the lucrative cage-bird trade. It is already rare in some parts of its range.

Scarlet macaws maintain strong pair bonds and are generally seen in pairs, family groups or flocks of up to 20. As they make their daily journeys from roosting areas to feeding grounds, pairs will fly together, wings almost touching. They feed up in the trees on seeds, fruit, nuts, berries and other plant matter and, although they eat in silence, they fly off, squawking noisily, at any disturbance.

Surprisingly little is known of the breeding habits of these splendid birds. Nests have been observed in holes in tree trunks well above the ground, but there is little reliable data on clutch size or incubation.

Spectacled Parrotlet *Forpus conspicillatus*

RANGE Central and South America: E. Panama, Colombia (not S.E.), W. Venezuela

HABITAT Open forest, thorn bush

SIZE 4¾ in (12 cm)

About 3 races of this little parrotlet occur within the range, all with slight plumage differences. Generally, however, males have dull, greenish upperparts, with yellow markings on the forehead, cheeks and throat and some blue markings. Females have brighter green upperparts than males and lack the blue markings. Out of the breeding season, spectacled parrotlets move in small flocks of 5 to 20, making constant chattering calls. These busy, active birds, forage in trees and bushes for berries, fruit, buds and blossoms or they search on the ground for the seeds of grasses and herbaceous plants. Their flight is swift and erratic.

During the breeding season, the parrotlets associate in pairs. Little is known of their breeding habits, but it is probable that they make their nests in natural holes in trees or posts. The female is believed to lay a clutch of 2 to 4 eggs. There are several species of parrotlet in the genus *Forpus*, all with similar habits and appearance.

Sun Parakeet *Aratinga solstitialis*

RANGE South America: Guyana, Surinam, French Guiana, N.E. Brazil

HABITAT Open forest, savanna

SIZE 11¾ in (30 cm)

The sun conure is a beautiful bird, with vibrant yellow plumage. It is not a common species, and little is known of its habits. Generally seen in small flocks, conures are noisy birds, which make frequent screeching calls. They feed on seeds, fruit, nuts and berries, usually foraging up in the treetops.

From the few observations of breeding habits, the female lays 3 or 4 eggs which she incubates for 4 weeks. Both parents feed the chicks, which remain in the nest for about 8 weeks.

The golden-capped conure, *A. aurocapilla*, and the jendaya conure, *A. jendawa*, are both similar to the sun conure and may even be races of the same species.

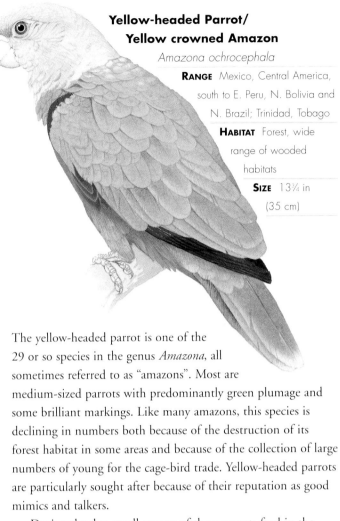

Yellow-headed Parrot/
Yellow crowned Amazon
Amazona ochrocephala

RANGE Mexico, Central America, south to E. Peru, N. Bolivia and N. Brazil; Trinidad, Tobago

HABITAT Forest, wide range of wooded habitats

SIZE 13¾ in (35 cm)

The yellow-headed parrot is one of the 29 or so species in the genus *Amazona*, all sometimes referred to as "amazons". Most are medium-sized parrots with predominantly green plumage and some brilliant markings. Like many amazons, this species is declining in numbers both because of the destruction of its forest habitat in some areas and because of the collection of large numbers of young for the cage-bird trade. Yellow-headed parrots are particularly sought after because of their reputation as good mimics and talkers.

During the day, small groups of these parrots feed in the treetops on fruit, seeds, nuts, berries and blossoms and will also come down to within 6½ ft (2 m) of the ground to find food. Yellow-headed parrots are strong fliers and travel well above the trees except when going only short distances. At dusk they return to regular roosting areas.

A breeding pair finds a hollow in a tree trunk, which both enlarge, and the female lays 3 or 4 eggs. She incubates them for 29 days, during which the male remains nearby. Twice a day, the female leaves the eggs briefly in order to join her mate, who feeds her by regurgitation.

Monk Parakeet *Myiopsitta monachus*

RANGE South America: C.Bolivia, S. Brazil to C. Argentina; introduced in Puerto Rico and N.E. USA

HABITAT Open woodland, palm groves, cultivated land, eucalyptus plantations

SIZE 11½ in (29 cm)

A popular cage bird and abundant in the wild, the monk parakeet is a medium-sized parrot, with long tail feathers and a heavy bill. It is an adaptable species and readily inhabits trees planted by man in orchards or on ranchland, even when near to human habitation. The highly gregarious monk parakeets occur in flocks of 10 to 100 or more and build enormous communal nests, unique in the parrot order. The nest is used for breeding and for roosting and so is inhabited throughout the year and is always the centre of much activity as the birds come and go, shrieking noisily.

Monk parakeets leave the nest in small groups to find food, and if they are feeding in open country or fields, a few birds will sit up in nearby trees to act as sentinels. At the first sign of danger, they call a warning, and the feeding birds quickly disperse. Seeds, fruit, berries, nuts, blossoms, leaves, insects and larvae are all eaten, and monk parakeets can cause much damage by feeding on cereal crops and in orchards.

Although the nest is used all year round, at the start of the breeding season in October, the birds add to it and repair any damage. The nest is usually situated at the top of a tree and is made of twigs, particularly thorny twigs, which hold together well and deter predators. It may start with only a few compartments, but it is gradually added to until it has anything up to 20 compartments, each occupied by a pair of birds. Each compartment has its own entrance at the bottom of the nest, leading into the brood chamber. The whole structure is so strong that other birds may nest on top of it.

The female parakeet lays 5 to 8 eggs, but because of the obvious difficulties of observing behavior in such a structure, little is known of the incubation of the clutch or the care of the chicks. The young birds leave the nest at about 6 weeks old.

SWIFTS AND CRESTED SWIFTS

ORDER APODIFORMES

This order includes 2 families – swifts and crested swifts. All are birds with highly developed flight abilities.

APODIDAE: SWIFT FAMILY

Swifts are the most aerial of birds. The 99 species in this fast-flying family seem to be able to carry out every avian activity on the wing, other than nesting. They catch food, eat, drink, collect material for nest construction and even copulate while flying. Some species may also be able to sleep aloft. Although they can take off with difficulty from flat ground, swifts normally alight only on vertical surfaces, such as cliffs or buildings, and they cannot perch. They are usually active in the daytime and feed on insects.

Swifts range in length between 3½ and 10 in (9 and 25.5 cm), and male and female look alike. Owing to similarity of habits rather than close relationship, swifts have a superficial resemblance to swallows and martins, for they possess the same narrow, pointed, although longer, wings and short, normally forked tails. Their legs and feet are tiny since they seldom, if ever, walk, but they have strong, curved claws for gripping landing and nesting surfaces. In most species, all four toes point forward. The beak is typically short and slightly down-curving and has a wide gape.

All swifts glue their nests together with glutinous saliva from specialized salivary glands.

Brown-backed Needletail

Hirundapus giganteus

RANGE India through S.E. Asia to the Philippines

HABITAT Forest up to 6,000 ft (1,800 m)

SIZE 10 in (25.5 cm)

One of the fastest-flying bird species, the brown-backed needletail can reputedly attain speeds of 155 to 186 mph (250 to 300 km/h). It feeds on insects and will hover motionless, like a hawk, watching for prey. The female lays 3 to 5 eggs in a nest made on the ground.

White-throated Swift *Aeronautes saxatalis*

RANGE W. Canada and USA to Mexico and El Salvador

HABITAT Vicinity of mountain and coastal cliffs, canyons, rugged foothills

SIZE 6–7 in (15–18 cm)

The white-throated swift is able to attain speeds of up to 186 mph (300 km/h) and it is probably the fastest-flying bird in North America. The swift catches insects, such as flies, beetles, bees, wasps, flying ants and leaf-hoppers, on the wing.

The swifts court in flight and copulate either on the wing, with their bodies pressed together as they tumble downward through the air, or in a nesting site. The nest, made in a crack or crevice in a coastal cliff or mountainside, is cup shaped and constructed from feathers and grass, glued together with saliva. The 4 or 5 eggs are laid in May and June and incubation duties are shared by both parents.

African Palm Swift *Cypsiurus parvus*

RANGE Subsaharan Africa

HABITAT Open country

SIZE 7 in (18 cm)

Palm swifts are gregarious birds which move in flocks and are easily distinguished by their unusually long tails. They are especially active at dusk, when many insects swarm.

The palm swift nests on the underside of a palm frond. The breeding pair constructs a pad of feathers, which are glued together and to the leaf with saliva. They then glue their clutch of 1 or 2 eggs to the nest, also with saliva. Assuming a vertical posture and gripping the sides of the nest with their claws, both partners take turns at incubating the eggs. When the chicks hatch, they must cling on to the nest with their claws and maintain their hold until they are fully fledged and ready to fly.

Edible-nest Swiftlet *Collocalia fuciphaga*

RANGE Andaman and Nicobar Islands, S.E. Asia, Philippines

HABITAT Coasts, islands; feeds over forest and scrub

SIZE 5 in (12.5 cm)

This swiftlet is one of 31 similar species in the genus *Collocalia*, all of which are found in Southeast Asia and the islands of the Pacific. The differentiation of the species is extremely difficult but has now been clarified by considering nest construction and sites and the ability to echolocate.

The swiftlets build their nests in caves, often in colonies of many thousands. They find their way in the darkness of the deeper caves by using echolocation, a rare ability among birds. As they fly, they make rapid clicking sounds and use the high-frequency echoes off the cave walls to navigate.

All swiftlets use saliva to make their nests and to glue them to cave walls, but the edible-nest swiftlet's nests are made almost entirely from hardened saliva with only a few feathers included – probably by accident. And it is these nests which give the bird its common name, for they are harvested in huge numbers to make the birds' nest soup which Chinese gourmets consider a delicacy. The female lays 2 or 3 eggs.

Common Swift *Apus apus*

RANGE Breeds in Europe, east to China; N.W. Africa; winters in Africa

HABITAT Over open country, fresh water, urban areas

SIZE 6¼ in (16 cm)

A common, gregarious bird, this swift is almost always seen in the air and only occasionally alights on walls, rocks or buildings. Uttering harsh, screaming cries, it flies in search of aerial insects, alternating rapid wing beats with long spells of gliding flight.

The breeding season starts in mid-May. The swifts select nest sites under the eaves of buildings or in rock crevices and make shallow cup-shaped nests of grass and feathers, glued together with saliva. There are usually 3 eggs in a clutch, laid at intervals of 2 or 3 days, and they are incubated for 14 to 20 days. Both parents feed the young, but may leave them for several days at a time. When this happens, the young burn up their fat stores and development slows down. If the fast is prolonged, the nestlings' body temperature may drop as much as 50°F (27.5°C) and they lapse into torpor, without any ill effects, until food is once again available.

HEMIPROCNIDAE: CRESTED SWIFT FAMILY

The 4 species of crested swift all have crests and long, deeply forked tails. Their plumage is softer and brighter than that of other swifts and they are less aerial in their habits. Unlike true swifts, they are able to perch. Males and females have some slight plumage differences. Crested swifts occur in India and Southeast Asia, south to New Guinea and the Solomon Islands.

Crested/Gray-rumped Tree Swift *Hemiprocne longipennis*

RANGE Malay Peninsula, Indonesia to Sulawesi

HABITAT Forest edge, open woodland

SIZE 8 in (20.5 cm)

The crested swift can perch on branches and telephone wires, from which it swoops down to feed on airborne insects.

Males and females of the species look similar, but the male has a chestnut patch behind the eye, while in the female this plumage is green.

The nest of the crested swift is a tiny cup-shaped structure, made from thin flakes of bark, glued together with saliva and attached with saliva to the branch of a tree. There is just enough room on it for the 1 egg, which both parents take it in turns to incubate by sitting on the branch and puffing up their breast feathers to cover the egg. Both parents care for the chick.

HUMMINGBIRDS

ORDER TROCHILIFORMES

TROCHILIDAE: HUMMINGBIRD FAMILY

This family is the only one in its order. Named for the drone produced by the extremely rapid beating of their wings, the spectacular hummingbirds occur all over the Americas, from Alaska to Tierra del Fuego and high in the Andes, but mainly in the tropics. The 319 or so species include the smallest, and some of the most striking, birds known.

Hummingbirds range in length from 2¼ to 8½ in (5.7 to 21.5 cm), but the tail often makes up as much as half of this length. Their wings are long and narrow relative to body size, and hummingbirds are quite unsurpassed in their aerial agility. They can hover motionless in front of a flower, their wings beating so fast that they are virtually invisible; fly upward, sideways, downward and, uniquely, even backward. The keel of the breastbone in a hummingbird is proportionately bigger than that of any other bird, to support the massive flying muscles needed to power their movements.

The hummingbird's main foods are insects and nectar, which it obtains by plunging its long, slender, often curved bill (which has become adapted for the task) deep inside the flower. It uses its tubular tongue to extract the nectar. The shapes of the bill and tongue are often closely related to the flower shape.

There is a great variety of tail shapes among male hummingbirds, and these decorative feathers are used in courtship display. Females have duller plumage than males and lack the ornamental tail feathers. Except in the breeding season, hummingbirds are solitary and defend their territory aggressively, even against much larger birds. The female builds a cup-shaped nest on a branch, palm frond or a rock, and normally lays 2 eggs. In all but 1 species, she alone incubates the eggs and cares for the young.

Sword-billed Hummingbird *Ensifera ensifera*

RANGE Andes: Venezuela, Colombia, Ecuador, Peru, Bolivia
HABITAT Shrubby slopes at 8,200–10,000 ft (2,500–3,000 m)
SIZE Bird: 3 in (7.5 cm) Bill: 5 in (12.5 cm)

The sword-billed hummingbird has the longest bill, relative to its size, of any bird. The bird probes deep into trumpet shaped flowers with its bill to feed on nectar and insects which feed on the nectar.

White-tipped Sicklebill

Eutoxeres aquila
RANGE Costa Rica, Panama, Colombia, Ecuador, N.E. Peru
HABITAT Forest
SIZE 5 in (12.5 cm)

This little hummingbird's strongly downward curving bill is adapted to obtaining nectar from irregularly shaped flowers, such as *Coryanthes* orchids. The bird will also cling awkwardly to *Heliconia* flowers and probe the blossoms with its bill.

Ruby-throated Hummingbird

Archilochus colubris
RANGE Breeds in S.E. Canada, E. USA; winters in Mexico, Central America and West Indies
HABITAT Woodland, gardens
SIZE 3½ in (9 cm)

This tiny bird migrates 500 miles (800 km) or more across the Gulf of Mexico to its wintering grounds – an extraordinary feat for such a small bird. The male has a distinctive ruby red throat, and the female has white throat plumage and a rounded tail.

Bee Hummingbird

Calypte helenae
RANGE Cuba, Isle of Pines
HABITAT Forest
SIZE 20 in (5.7 cm)

The smallest bird in the world, the bee hummingbird's actual body measures only ½ in (1.25 cm), and its bill is a similar size. The tail makes up the remainder of its length. The bee hummingbird weighs only ¹⁄₁₄ oz (2 g). Its tiny wings beat between 50 and 80 times a second as it hovers in the air in order to feed from flowers.

Giant Hummingbird

Patagona gigas

RANGE Andes from Ecuador to Chile and Argentina

HABITAT Arid land

SIZE 8½ in (21.5 cm)

The largest hummingbird, this species weighs ¾ oz (20 g). It beats its wings only 8 or 10 times a second, and though it feeds at flowers, it also catches insects in flight.

Frilled Coquette

Lophornis magnifica

RANGE E. and C. Brazil

HABITAT Forest, scrub

SIZE 2¾ in (7 cm)

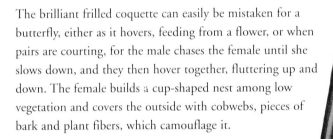

The brilliant frilled coquette can easily be mistaken for a butterfly, either as it hovers, feeding from a flower, or when pairs are courting, for the male chases the female until she slows down, and they then hover together, fluttering up and down. The female builds a cup-shaped nest among low vegetation and covers the outside with cobwebs, pieces of bark and plant fibers, which camouflage it.

Marvelous Spatule-tail

Loddigesia mirabilis **VU**

RANGE Andes in Peru

HABITAT Forest at 7,500–8,500 ft (2,300–2,600 m)

SIZE Body: 5 in (12.5 cm) Tail: 5½ in (14 cm)

The male of this little-known hummingbird species has an extraordinary long tail with only four feathers, two of which are greatly elongated and wirelike and expanded into racket shapes at the ends. During his courtship display, the male bird frames his iridescent throat plumage with his decorative tail feathers and flies back and forth in front of his prospective mate.

Ruby-topaz Hummingbird *Chrysolampis mosquitus*

RANGE Colombia, Venezuela, the Guianas, Brazil, N.E. Bolivia, Trinidad, Tobago

HABITAT Forest, scrub, savanna

SIZE 3½ in (9 cm)

The male of this species has glittering, colorful plumage, while the female's feathers are greenish and gray. It feeds on nectar and insects, both in low vegetation and tall trees.

Long-tailed Sylph Hummingbird *Aglaiocercus kingi*

RANGE Venezuela to Bolivia, Peru and Ecuador

HABITAT Forest, scrub

SIZE Male: 7 in (18 cm)
Female: 3¾ in (9.5 cm)

The outer tail feathers of the male of this species are almost 5 in (12.5 cm) long and are used in courtship display. The female's tail feathers are not elongated, and she has a buff-white throat and cinnamon underparts.

Crimson Topaz *Topaza pella*

RANGE The Guianas, Venezuela, Brazil and east of the Andes in Ecuador

HABITAT Rain forest

SIZE 7¾ in (20 cm)

The glittering, colorful male crimson topaz has two elongated black tail feathers, which are 2¼ in (6 cm) longer than the rest of the tail. The female is less startling, but she also has gleaming green and red plumage and a bronze and violet tail.

Andean Hillstar *Oreotrochilus estella*

RANGE Andes: from Ecuador to Argentina, Chile and N. Peru

HABITAT Rocky slopes

SIZE 4¾ in (12 cm)

The neck and throat plumage of the male Andean hillstar varies, but usually includes glittering green or violet. The female has an olive-green back and head, a white throat and grayish underparts.

TURACOS, BARN OWLS AND OWLS

ORDER MUSOPHAGIFORMES

MUSOPHAGIDAE: TURACO FAMILY

The 23 species of turaco are fowllike, tree-dwelling birds of tropical Africa. Except for the go-away birds, which are gray and white, turacos are glossy and brightly colored, with long, broad tails and short, rounded wings. Many species have hairy crests and bare skin around the eye. The brilliant red of the head and wing feathers of some species is the result of a unique copper complex pigment which is soluble in alkalis. The green pigment is also unique. Turacos have short, stout bills and feed largely on insects and fruit. Males and females look alike.

Red-crested Turaco *Tauraco erythrolophus*

RANGE Africa: Angola, Zaire

HABITAT Woodland, savanna

SIZE 16 in (40.5 cm)

The red-crested turaco is a fruit-eating bird, which lives in trees and seldom descends to the ground. It is a poor flier but is agile and swift in the trees and can run, hop and climb among the branches. In addition to fruit, it eats seeds, insects and snails.

This turaco is almost identical to Bannerman's turaco, *T. bannerrnani*, and the most obvious distinguishing feature is the nostrils: rounded in the red-crested and slit-shaped in Bannerman's turaco. Nothing is known of their breeding habits.

Gray Go-away Bird, *Corythaixoides concolor*

RANGE Africa: Tanzania, Congo River basin to South Africa

HABITAT Open bush, acacia scrub

SIZE 20 in (51 cm)

Although wary, the common go-away bird is not timid. At the hint of danger, it alerts all the animals in the area with its penetrating call which sounds like "g'away, g'away". In pairs or small groups, the go-away birds perch on trees or fly clumsily from one tree to another; they eat berries, fruit and insects. The breeding season is from October to January. The birds display, one partner perches in a treetop and the other hovers above. Both help to build a nest of sticks in dense creepers or an acacia tree. The female lays 2 or 3 large eggs, which both parents incubate for, it is thought, about 18 days.

ORDER STRIGIFORMES

This order contain 9 families and 291 species. Two families – Tytonidae (barn owls) and Strigidae (true owls) contain the owls. With their flattened faces, enormous eyes, taloned feet and predatory, usually nocturnal habits, owls are the nighttime equivalent of hawks, eagles and falcons. Owls kill with their talons – each toe is tipped with a sharp, hooked claw. They swallow prey whole and regurgitate the bones, fur and feathers in pellets. The sexes look alike in most species, although females are sometimes larger.

The remaining 7 families in the order are the Aegothelidae (owlet-nightjars), Podargidae (Australian frogmouths), Batrachostomidae (Asiatic frogmouths), Steatornithidae (oilbird), Nyctibiidae (potoos), Eurostopodidae (eared-nightjars), and Caprimulgidae (nightjars).

TYTONIDAE: BARN OWL FAMILY

The 12 species of barn and bay owl differ from typical owls in many minor details. They have a heart-shaped facial disc, relatively small eyes and long, slender legs. The long, hooked beak is mostly concealed by feathers. The toes are strong with sharp, curved claws. Barn owls are night hunters.

Oriental Bay Owl *Phodilus badius*

RANGE N. India, Sri Lanka, S.E. Asia, Greater Sunda Islands

HABITAT Forest

SIZE 11½ in (29 cm)

The oriental bay owl is similar in appearance to the barn owl. It is strictly nocturnal and is believed to feed mostly on insects, which it hunts in and around the trees. It lays 3 to 5 eggs, usually in a hole in a tree. An African species of bay owl has been discovered recently.

Barn Owl *Tyto alba*

RANGE Worldwide, except temperate Asia and many Pacific islands

HABITAT Open country, woods, inhabited areas

SIZE 13¼ in (34 cm)

The barn owl is a long-legged, usually pale-plumaged bird with a white face. There are over 30 subspecies, found over its wide range, which differ mainly in intensity of plumage coloration. Barn owls generally live alone or in pairs and roost during the day in farm buildings, hollow trees or caves. At night, they emerge to hunt, feeding primarily on small rodents, which they catch and kill on the ground, and also on small birds.

Breeding usually starts in April in the north. The female nests in an old building, a hollow tree trunk or a rock crevice and lays 4 to 7 eggs, which she incubates for about 33 days. The male brings food to her during this period, and both parents care for the young.

STRIGIDAE: OWL FAMILY

The 161 species of typical owl occur the world over, except on some oceanic islands. They are soft-feathered, short-tailed birds, with big heads and enormous eyes set in a circular facial disc. In all species the beak is hooked and is partly hidden by feathers.

Most owls hunt at night and all feed entirely on animals, from insects and invertebrates to birds and medium-sized mammals such as rabbits. They have exceptionally keen eyesight and excellent hearing.

Brown Fish Owl *Ketupa zeylonensis*

RANGE Middle East to S. China, Sri Lanka, S.E. Asia

HABITAT Forested streams and lakes

SIZE 22 in (56 cm)

A specialized, semiaquatic owl, the brown fish owl is always found near water and feeds on fish, as well as on the more typical prey of owls. Its feet and ankles are unfeathered, an adaptation which allows it to wade in the shallows to catch fish without the plumage getting wet.

The breeding season of this species begins in February or March. It makes a nest platform in a tree by joining some branches together, or nests on a ledge or rock. Only 1 or 2 eggs are laid. They are then incubated by both parents for a total of about 35 days.

Elf Owl *Micrathene whitneyi*

RANGE S.E. USA, Mexico

HABITAT Wooded canyons, desert with saguaro cactus

SIZE 5–6 in (12.5–15 cm)

One of the smallest owls in the world the elf owl is distinguished by its short tail from other small owls in its range. During the day, it roosts in a tree or bush and comes out at dusk to hunt. Insects are its main prey, many being caught in the owl's feet while it is in flight. It will also hover over foliage or dart out from a perch after prey like a flycatcher. Beetles, moths, grasshoppers, crickets and scorpions (the sting is removed or crushed) are frequent prey, and it occasionally catches small snakes and lizards.

Elf owls nest in deserted woodpecker holes in cactus plants or tree trunks. The male finds a suitable site and sings to attract a female, who responds and enters the nest. In April or May, she lays 1 to 5 eggs which she incubates for 24 days. The male feeds the female while she incubates and also brings food for her to give to the young when they have hatched.

Eastern Screech Owl

Otus asio

RANGE N. America: S. Canada, E., C., and S. USA, N.E. Mexico

HABITAT Open woodland, cactus desert

SIZE 7–10 in (18–25.5 cm)

A small owl with conspicuous ear tufts, the screech owl roosts during the day in a hollow tree or old building and starts to hunt at dusk. It catches insects and mice, shrews and other small mammals, as well as frogs, lizards and some birds. Breeding starts from February to July, according to area. Screech owls nest in a hole in a tree, such as an abandoned woodpecker hole. Normally 4 or 5 eggs are laid, but there may be as many as 8. The male brings food while the female incubates, but once the eggs hatch, both parents feed the young.

OWLS CONTINUED

Snowy Owl *Nyctea scandiaca*

RANGE Circumpolar: Arctic Canada,
Greenland, N. Eurasia

HABITAT Tundra, marshes, coasts

SIZE 20½–25½ in (52–65 cm)

The snowy owl is a large bird with
distinctive, mainly white plumage.
Females have more dark, barred
markings than males. They usually
hunt during the day. Prey includes
mammals up to the size of arctic
hares, smaller rodents, and birds.
The snowy owl begins nesting in
mid-May in a shallow scrape in the
ground or on a rock, lined with moss and feathers. The female
lays a clutch of between 4 and 15 eggs. The male feeds her while
she incubates the eggs for 32 or 33 days.

Great Horned Owl *Bubo virginianus*

RANGE N., Central and South America

HABITAT Varied, woods, forest, city parks, suburbs

SIZE 18–25¼ in (46–64 cm)

Great horned owls are large, powerful birds.
The ear tufts are feathers and are not
connected with hearing. The owls roost
in trees and hunt mainly at night for
mammals, birds, insects and reptiles.

Breeding time depends on area, but it
can be as early as January or February. The
owl nests in an old nest of another bird, a
cave, a hollow in a tree or on a cliff ledge.
Usually 3 eggs are laid, but there can be as
many as 6. The eggs are incubated for 30 to
35 days by both parents.

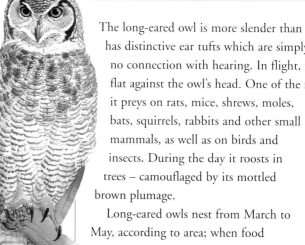

Morepork/Boobook *Ninox novaeseelandiae*

RANGE New Zealand, Australia, Tasmania, S. New Guinea,
Lesser Sunda Islands

HABITAT Forest, scrub, open country with caves for roosting

SIZE 11½ in (29 cm)

The morepork is the most widely distributed owl in New
Zealand and Australia. It is usually seen at dusk when it begins

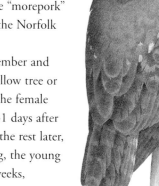

to hunt for its food, which consists largely of insects,
particularly moths, as well as spiders, lizards, small
birds, rats and mice. It occasionally hunts during
the day. The common names are derived from
one of its calls which sounds like "morepork"
or "boobook". One subspecies, the Norfolk
boobook, is now listed as rare.

The morepork nests in November and
lays 3 or 4 eggs in a nest in a hollow tree or
in a patch of thick vegetation. The female
begins her incubation of 30 to 31 days after
laying the first egg, but she lays the rest later,
at 2-day intervals. After hatching, the young
remain in the nest for about 5 weeks,
guarded and fed by their parents.

Long-eared Owl *Asio otus*

RANGE N. America, Europe, N.W. Africa, Asia

HABITAT Coniferous forest, woodland, parks

SIZE 13–16 in (33–40.5 cm)

The long-eared owl is more slender than the tawny owl and
has distinctive ear tufts which are simply feathers and have
no connection with hearing. In flight, the ear tufts are kept
flat against the owl's head. One of the most nocturnal owls,
it preys on rats, mice, shrews, moles,
bats, squirrels, rabbits and other small
mammals, as well as on birds and
insects. During the day it roosts in
trees – camouflaged by its mottled
brown plumage.

Long-eared owls nest from March to
May, according to area; when food
supplies are abundant they may produce
two broods. The female lays 3 to 10
eggs, usually 4 or 5, in an
abandoned nest of another
bird species or even in a
squirrel's nest. Alternatively, she lays her
eggs on the ground under a tree or bush.
She incubates the eggs for 26 to 28 days and
her partner feeds her during this period and for
the 3 to 4 weeks before the chicks leave the nest.

Some northern populations of long-eared owls
migrate south in winter, to Mexico, northern Egypt
and India, and northward again in spring.

Northern Hawk Owl

Surnia ulula

RANGE Canada, extreme N. USA, N. Asia, Scandinavia

HABITAT Open areas in coniferous forest

SIZE 14¼–17 in (36–43 cm)

The hawk owl's tail is longer than usual for an owl. Its has a pale facial disc, bordered with black. Its fairly short, pointed wings give it a hawklike appearance in flight. It hunts by day, swooping from a perch in the trees to catch small mammals, such as mice and voles, as well as birds and insects.

Nesting occurs from April to June, depending on the area. The clutch varies from 5 to 9 depending on food supply. The eggs are laid in the hollow top of a tree stump or an abandoned nest or woodpecker hole and are incubated for 25 to 30 days.

Eurasian Pygmy Owl *Glaucidium passerinum*

RANGE N. Europe, east through Russia and C. Asia to China

HABITAT Open forest

SIZE 6 in (16 cm)

The smallest European owl, the pygmy owl has a small head and a long tail. It hunts mainly at night and feeds on small rodents and birds. Pygmy owls breed from March to May. They often nest in disused woodpecker holes. The male feeds the female while she incubates the 2 to 7 eggs for about 28 days and feeds the young once they are hatched.

Little Owl

Atbene noctua

RANGE Europe, Africa, W. and C. Asia, east to China

HABITAT Forest, open country, urban land

SIZE 8¼ in (21 cm)

The little owl has a frowning expression. It is active in the day. Insects and small rodents are its main foods, but it occasionally eats small birds and carrion. In Europe, it nests from mid-April onward. The female lays 3 to 5 eggs and incubates them for about 29 days. The male feeds the young when they first hatch, but later the parents share the hunting.

Tawny Owl *Strix aluco*

RANGE Britain, Europe, N. Africa, W. and C. Asia to Korea

HABITAT Woods, gardens, parks, urban areas

SIZE 15 in (38 cm)

The tawny owl is a strongly built bird, with mottled plumage, a rounded head and black eyes. One of the most common European owls, it is distinguished from the long-eared and short-eared owls by its lack of ear tufts and its dark eyes. It is strictly nocturnal, roosting in a tree during the day and hunting small rodents, birds and some insects at night.

Breeding starts in late March. The tawny owl nests in a hole in a tree or occasionally on the ground or in an old nest of another species. Usually 2 to 4 eggs are laid, but there can be up to 8. The female incubates the clutch for 28 to 30 days. The male feeds the newly hatched young for the first few weeks, but then both parents hunt. The young leave the nest at about 5 weeks.

Burrowing Owl *Speotyto cunicularia*

RANGE S.W. Canada, W. USA and Florida; Central and South America

HABITAT Semidesert, grassland without trees

SIZE 9–11 in (23–28 cm)

The burrowing owl is a small ground-living owl with a short tail and long legs. It often lives in the abandoned burrows of prairie dogs and other mammals and usually adapts the burrow to its needs by digging with its feet to enlarge the hole and make a nesting chamber. In a complex of burrows, such as those left by prairie dogs, a number of owls may take over and form a colony. The owls do not share burrows with prairie dogs.

Burrowing owls usually hunt in the evening, but are often seen during the day standing at the burrow entrances. They eat small rodents, birds, frogs, reptiles and insects. They often follow animals, such as horses, perhaps to catch prey that they disturb.

Burrowing owls nest from March to July. The female lays 6 to 11 eggs in a chamber at the end of the burrow. Both parents incubate the eggs for about 28 days. Northern populations migrate south in winter.

OWLET-NIGHTJARS, FROGMOUTHS, OILBIRD AND POTOOS

AEGOTHELIDAE: OWLET-NIGHTJAR FAMILY

Owlet-nightjars are small, dumpy birds, which resemble their relatives the nightjars in many respects, but have the flat-faced look of owls. They hunt at dawn and dusk, catching insects in the air or, more often, on the ground, where they move easily. There are 8 species of owlet-nightjar, found in New Guinea, Australia and some nearby islands.

Australian Owlet-nightjar *Aegotheles cristatus*

RANGE Australia, Tasmania, S. New Guinea

HABITAT Forest, woodland, scrub

SIZE 7¾–9½ in (20–24 cm)

A shy, solitary bird, the Australian owlet-nightjar spends the day perched in an upright posture on a branch, disguised by its mottled and barred plumage. It starts to hunt for insects and invertebrates at dusk, taking much of its prey on the ground, but also chasing aerial insects. Its bill is small and flat, but with a large gape, and is almost obscured by erect bristles.

The clutch of 3 or 4 eggs is laid in a hole in a tree or bank, lined with green leaves. The lining is renewed as the leaves wither. There may be more than one brood in a year.

PODARGIDAE: AUSTRALIAN FROGMOUTH FAMILY

The frogmouths are tree-dwelling birds that occur from India through Southeast Asia to New Guinea and Australia. They have a flat, shaggy head and large eyes. Poor fliers, they have short, rounded wings and stumpy tails and a large beak, which is surrounded by tufts of bristles and can open into a wide gape. Poor fliers, they have short, rounded wings and stumpy tails. They are crepuscular and nocturnal feeders that watch for prey on branches or on the ground and then pounce on it. Males and females look more or less alike. There are two families of frogmouths. The 3 species of Australian frogmouths are found in Australia, New Guinea, and the Solomon Islands.

Tawny Frogmouth *Podargus strigoides*

RANGE Australia, Tasmania

HABITAT Forest, open woodland, trees in scrub, gardens, parks

SIZE 13–18¼ in (33–47 cm)

The nocturnal tawny frogmouth spends the day resting in a tree, where its mottled, streaked plumage blends perfectly with the lichen-covered branches. At any hint of danger, the bird stretches out its body, with head and bill pointing upward, and in this posture it is almost indistinguishable from a broken branch or stump. Much of the frogmouth's hunting is done at dusk, when it watches for prey from a tree or post, then descends silently to seize it on the ground. Insects, snails, frogs and even small mammals and birds are all included in its diet. There are at least 7 subspecies of tawny frogmouth, all varying slightly in size and shade of plumage.

The nest is a flimsy platform of sticks and leaves, made on a forked branch, or an old nest of another species may be used. The female incubates the 2 eggs for about 30 days, and both parents feed the young.

BATRACHOSTOMIDAE: ASIATIC FROGMOUTH FAMILY

There are 11 species of Asiatic frogmouths. They are similar to the Australian family. They occur from the Himalayas to the Philippines.

Ceylon Frogmouth *Batrachostomus moniliger*

RANGE Sri Lanka, S.W. India

HABITAT Forest

SIZE 7¼–9 in (19–23 cm)

The Ceylon frogmouth is a tree-dwelling bird, but it takes most of its food on the ground after short flights from a perch;

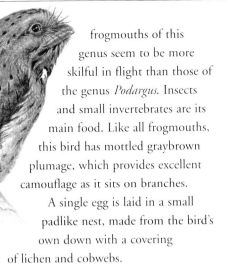

frogmouths of this genus seem to be more skilful in flight than those of the genus *Podargus*. Insects and small invertebrates are its main food. Like all frogmouths, this bird has mottled graybrown plumage, which provides excellent camouflage as it sits on branches.

A single egg is laid in a small padlike nest, made from the bird's own down with a covering of lichen and cobwebs.

STEATORNITHIDAE: OILBIRD FAMILY

The single species of oilbird is sufficiently unusual to merit its own family. A large-eyed nocturnal bird, it has a patchy distribution in northern South America. The male and female birds look alike.

Oilbird *Steatornis caripensis*
RANGE Locally in Peru, through Ecuador, Colombia and Venezuela to French Guiana; Trinidad
HABITAT Seaside and mountain caves
SIZE 17 in (43 cm)

A long-winged, long-tailed bird, the oilbird has small, almost useless legs and feet. It lives in deep, totally dark caves where even its large eyes, specialized for night-time vision, are ineffective. However, it can nest and fly about in these caves with ease by means of a system of echolocation similar to that used by bats. As it flies, the bird makes a series of high-pitched clicking sounds, which bounce off the walls of the cave and enable it to navigate.

After dark, the oilbird emerges to feed on fruit, particularly that of palms. It seizes the fruit in its strong bill, swallows it whole and digests the entire night's intake the following day, back in its roost. The oilbird has a well-developed sense of smell and probably uses this, as well as its good nighttime vision, to find ripe fruit.

Oilbirds live in colonies of up to 50 pairs. The nest is made on a ledge from droppings, mixed with regurgitated fruit, and the female lays 2 to 4 eggs. Both parents incubate the eggs for about 33 days and feed the young on palm fruit.

During their period on the nest, the young oilbirds become enormously fat, weighing at least half as much again as an adult, since they are not able to fly until they are about 4 months old. Local people used to capture these fledglings and render down their fat for use as cooking oil – hence the common name – but this practice is now prohibited by law in most areas.

NYCTIBIIDAE: POTOO FAMILY

The 7 species of potoo occur in the West Indies and adjacent areas of Central and South America. Although related to nightjars and similar to them in appearance, potoos feed like flycatchers, darting out from a perch to catch insects. Males and females look alike, or nearly so.

Common Potoo
Nyctibius griseus
RANGE Jamaica, Hispaniola, Trinidad and Tobago; Mexico, Central America, tropical South America
HABITAT Forest edge, open forest, cultivated land with trees
SIZE 16 in (41 cm)

The common potoo has a long tail, sometimes accounting for as much as half of the bird's total length, and very short legs. Its grayish-brown plumage is heavily mottled and streaked, rendering it almost invisible among the lichen-covered branches of its habitat.

During the day it sits in an extremely upright posture, often on a broken branch or stump, with its head and bill pointing upward so that it looks like part of the tree. At night, the potoo hunts for food, flying out from a perch to catch insects and returning to the same spot to consume them.

The single egg is laid on top of a tree stump and is incubated by both parents. If disturbed, the sitting bird adopts the upright posture and freezes or may retaliate by opening its eyes and bill wide and fluffing out its plumage in threat. Both parents feed the young, which sit in the upright posture in the nest. The young fly about 44 days after hatching.

NIGHTJARS

EUROSTOPODIDAE: EARED NIGHTJAR FAMILY

The 7 species in this family resemble the nightjars although they lack bristles around the bill. They are found in forest and scrub from southern Asia and south China to Australia.

Great Eared Nightjar *Eurostopodus macrotis*

RANGE India: Assam to S.E. Asia, Philippines, Sulawesi

HABITAT Forest, scrub

SIZE 16 in (41 cm)

Mainly solitary birds, these large nightjars occasionally gather in small groups. They feed on insects caught in the air. Flying high around the treetops at dawn or dusk, they perform skilful aerobatics in pursuit of their prey and call constantly, with a clear whistle. The female lays 1 egg on dead leaves, often in the shade at the foot of a tree.

CAPRIMULGIDAE: NIGHTJAR AND NIGHTHAWK FAMILY

The 76 species of this family of nocturnal birds are distributed almost worldwide: they are absent from only New Zealand and some Pacific islands. They do not occur at high latitudes. Many have evocative names, such as nightjar, goatsucker, poorwill and chuck-will's-widow, usually derived from their calls.

Nightjars have long, pointed wings, and large eyes for good night vision. The bill is short and weak, but it opens very wide and is fringed by sensory bristles. Most nightjars call for a period each evening at dusk, before they begin hunting. Flying silently and slowly, they make sudden darts after insects, which the bristles help to funnel into their wide, open mouths. They also

occasionally eat young birds. Nightjars are masterly in flight, but have short, weak legs and avoid walking far on the ground.

During the daytime, nightjars roost in trees or on the ground, hidden from predators by their camouflaging plumage. In trees they perch with their bodies lengthways along the branch. All species have finely mottled gray, black and brown heads and backs, which blend with foliage and vegetation. The sexes do not look alike in most species.

Common Poorwill *Phalaenoptilus nuttallii*

RANGE Breeds S.W. Canada, W. USA; winters S. USA, Mexico

HABITAT Arid bush on hills and mountains, open woodland

SIZE 7–8½ in (18–21.5 cm)

A small, short-tailed nightjar, the common poorwill flits around at night, hunting moths, beetles and grasshoppers on or near the ground. By day, it roosts in shrubbery or tall woods. The poorwill is the only bird known to hibernate. Each October it finds a rock crevice in which to spend the winter. Its temperature falls from about 106°F (40°C) to about 64°F (18°C). Its heartbeat and breathing rates drop to almost undetectable levels in order to conserve energy.

In early summer, poorwills breed. The female lays 2 eggs on bare ground or gravel. The clutch is incubated by both parents.

Lyre-tailed Nightjar *Uropsalis lyra*

RANGE South America: Andes in Venezuela, Colombia, Ecuador, Peru

HABITAT Mountain forest, savanna, open woodland

SIZE Male: 31 in (79 cm); Female: 10 in (25.5 cm)

The male lyre-tailed nightjar has two long lyre-shaped outer tail feathers. They are thought to be used in the male's courtship display. This solitary, nocturnal bird perches on low branches, often near water, and calls at dusk. Little is known of its feeding or breeding habits, but they are probably similar to those of other nightjars.

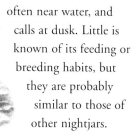

Standard-winged Nightjar *Macrodipteryx longipennis*

RANGE Africa: Chad, Sudan, Ethiopia, N. Uganda, Kenya

HABITAT Wooded savanna, scrub

SIZE 9 in (23 cm)

The standard-winged nightjar feeds on insects, which it catches in the air. A migratory species, it breeds in the southern part of its range from January to March and then moves north to Chad and northern Sudan.

In the breeding season, the male nightjar develops one elongated flight feather on each wing that grows to about 9 in (23 cm) in length. These are used in courtship displays, when the male flies around the female raising his elongated feathers and arching and vibrating his wings. The male is believed to mate with more than one female, each of which lays 2 eggs on the ground. Several birds may lay in the same area. The male bird then migrates, leaving the females to incubate the eggs and to care for the young alone.

Pauraque *Nyctidromus albicollis*

RANGE S.W. USA; Mexico; Central and South America to N.E. Argentina

HABITAT Semiopen scrub, woodland clearings

SIZE 11 in (28 cm)

Perching in a tree at night, the pauraque watches for insects, such as moths, wasps, and beetles, then launches into the air and flies close to the ground to catch them in its wide, gaping bill.

During the day it roosts, hidden among the dead leaves on the woodland floor where it is virtually invisible. Males and females have some plumage differences – the female's outer wing and tail feathers are black, barred with rufous brown, while the male's tail feathers are brown, barred with white, and are conspicuous in flight.

Pauraques live alone or in pairs. The female lays 2 eggs on bare ground, under the cover of bushes, and both parents incubate the clutch. They feed the nestlings by inserting the tip of the bill into a gaping mouth and regurgitating insects from the throat. The young birds begin to hop out of the nest at 2 or 3 days old, although not yet able to fly.

Eurasian Nightjar *Caprimulgus europaeus*

RANGE Breeds in Europe, N. Africa, W. and C. Asia; winters in tropical Africa

HABITAT Open country, forest edge, moors, heaths, semidesert

SIZE 10¼ in (26 cm)

This long-winged, long-tailed bird is the only nightjar that is widespread in Europe, and it tolerates many different habitats.

The male bird has some white spots on the outer wing tips and his tail feathers are tipped with white, but the sexes are otherwise similar in plumage.

After spending an inactive day perching on a branch, or on the ground, the nightjar takes wing at sunset and can be seen wheeling and gliding in the air and making sudden darts after moths and other nocturnal insects. It makes a churring call – the "jar" of its name.

The breeding season starts in mid-May. The male courts the female by clapping his wings together, and both birds sway their tails from side to side before mating.

The female lays 2 eggs in a slight scrape on the ground or on top of vegetation. The parents share the incubation of the eggs – the female takes the day shift and the male the night shift. The eggs hatch after 18 days. Both parents then care for the young, which are able to fly at about 17 or 18 days old. Pairs produce 2 broods of chicks in a season.

PIGEONS

ORDER COLUMBIFORMES

This order includes 2 living families – the sandgrouse and the pigeons – and the now extinct dodo family.

COLUMBIDAE: PIGEON FAMILY

The only family in this order contains 310 species of pigeon and dove, found in most parts of the world except the Antarctic and some oceanic islands. The greatest variety occurs in Asia and Australasia, where there are many extremely beautiful species. The name "pigeon" is generally used to describe larger birds in the family, while "dove" is applied to smaller forms, but there are exceptions to this rule, such as the rock dove.

Pigeons and doves vary in size from birds about the size of a sparrow to a few almost as large as a turkey. Most have dense, soft plumage, rounded, compact bodies and relatively small heads. The sexes look alike in most species, but in a few birds the male has more striking plumage. Both share an unusual reproductive feature – the lining of the crop secretes "pigeon milk", with which they feed their young for the first few days. This nutritious fluid is high in protein and fats and smells like cheese. Pigeons and doves generally lay only 1 or 2 eggs in a flimsy, but effective, nest, made of sticks.

Many pigeons and doves spend much of their lives in and around trees, eating seeds, fruit, buds and other plant material. Others are ground-dwelling, but have much the same diet. Pigeons and doves are strong fliers, with good homing abilities.

Common Ground Dove *Columbina passerina*
RANGE S. USA; Mexico, south to central Ecuador, N. Brazil; West Indies
HABITAT Open scrub, cultivated land
SIZE 6–6¾ in (15–17 cm)

These tiny, ground-living doves walk about briskly in pairs or small groups with heads nodding, picking up seeds, waste grain, insects and small berries and even scraps of human food. The scaly-breasted ground dove is a plump, compact bird with a short, broad tail and rounded wings. The female has much duller plumage than the male.

Mating occurs from February to October over the range. The male courts the female on the ground, puffing up his neck and bobbing his head and neck in time to his monotonous cooing while pursuing her. A flimsy nest is made in a low bush or tree or on the ground, and 2 eggs are laid and incubated by both parents for 13 or 14 days.

Rock Dove/Pigeon *Columba livia*
RANGE Islands and coasts of W. Britain, countries bordering Mediterranean; E. Europe, east to India and Sri Lanka
HABITAT Sea and inland cliffs; fields
SIZE 13–14 in (33–35.5 cm)

This species is the ancestor of all the domestic pigeons, including the homing pigeon, and of the feral pigeons (wild birds descended from birds bred in captivity) found in towns almost worldwide. Rock doves generally move in pairs or small groups, although large flocks are quite frequent. They feed on open ground, mainly on seeds, especially cultivated grains, but also on grasses, snails and other mollusks.

Mating takes place throughout the year, after much bowing, nodding, billing and cooing. The nest is flimsily made of twigs and grass on a sheltered cliff ledge or in a hole in a cliff, in a building or, occasionally, a tree. Two eggs are laid, which are incubated for 17 or 18 days.

Band-tailed Pigeon *Columba fasciata*

RANGE Western N. America, south to Mexico;
Central America, Colombia

HABITAT Coniferous forest, oak woodland in mountainous areas

SIZE 14¼–15¼ in (36–39 cm)

This is a heavily built pigeon. The tail, which is notable in flight and gives the bird its common name, is distinctly banded, with a pale end, a dark band across the middle and a blue-gray base.

The band-tailed pigeon flies strongly and swiftly and spends much time perching in trees, where it also seeks most of its food – nuts, berries, seeds, buds and blooms. It also eats insects and, in autumn, gorges on acorns.

Depending on area, the pigeons mate from March to September, and the female lays 1 egg, occasionally 2, which both parents incubate for 18 to 20 days.

Mourning Dove *Zenaida macroura*

RANGE Temperate areas in Canada; USA: all states;
Mexico, Bahamas, Cuba, Hispaniola

HABITAT Woodland, grain fields with trees,
semi-desert, suburbs

SIZE 11–13 in
(28–33 cm)

The mourning dove has short legs, a rounded body, neat head and a thin delicate-looking bill. The sexes look similar, but the central tail feathers are very long in the male and the wings are long and pointed. In flight the white outer tail feathers are obvious. Juvenile birds are heavily spotted on their wings.

The birds generally move in pairs or small groups, but large numbers may gather at feeding grounds. Ground-living birds, they eat mainly weed seeds or grain spilled in harvesting, but also take snails and other invertebrates.

The common name derives from the sweet, melancholy cooing of the male, which is followed by a courtship flight. Mating begins in January in the south of the range to April in the north. The nest is loosely constructed of twigs in a tree or bush, a roof gutter or chimney corner, or even on the ground. The female lays 2 eggs, which are incubated by both birds for 14 or 15 days. Each season 2 or 3 broods are produced.

Blue-headed Quail Dove *Starnoenas cyanocephala* **EN**

RANGE Cuba, formerly Jamaica

HABITAT Lowland forest and shrubbery; locally highland forest

SIZE 12–13 in (30.5–33 cm)

Numbers of this medium-sized dove are becoming fewer, owing to the destruction of its habitat, and little is known about it. It feeds on the ground in areas where it is able to walk freely, taking mainly seeds, snails and berries. The nest is made low in a tree or shrub or on the ground, and usually 2 eggs are laid.

SUNBITTERN, BUSTARDS, CRANES AND TRUMPETERS

ORDER GRUIFORMES

A diverse group of wading and ground-living birds, this order contains 9 families, 2 of which contain a single species.

EURYPYGIDAE: SUNBITTERN FAMILY

The sunbittern, found in Central and South America, is the sole member of its family. Its exact affinities are uncertain. Males and females of the species look alike.

Sunbittern *Eurypyga helias*

RANGE Central America, South America to Brazil

HABITAT Forest streams and creeks

SIZE 18 in (46 cm)

The sunbittern is an elegant bird, with a long bill, a slender neck and long legs. It frequents the well-wooded banks of streams, where it is perfectly camouflaged in the dappled sunlight by its mottled plumage. Fish, insects and crustaceans are its main foods, which it hunts from the river bank or seizes with swift thrusts of its bill, while wading in the shallows.

In courtship display, the beautifully plumaged wings are fully spread, revealing patches of color. The wing tips are held forward, framing the head and neck. Pairs perform a courtship dance, with tail and wings spread. Both partners help to build a large domed nest in a tree and incubate 2 or 3 eggs for about 28 days.

OTIDIDAE: BUSTARD FAMILY

Bustards are heavily built, ground-dwelling birds, which tend to run or walk rather than fly, although they are capable of strong flight. The majority of the 25 species occur in Africa, but there are bustards in southern Europe, Asia and Australia. Male birds are more boldly plumaged than females.

Great Bustard *Otis tarda* **VU**

RANGE Scattered areas of S. and central Europe, east across Asia to Siberia and E. China

HABITAT Grassland, grain fields

SIZE 29½ in—3¼ ft (75 cm—1 m)

The male great bustard is a large, strong bird, with a thick neck and sturdy legs. The female is smaller and slimmer, lacking the male's bristly "whiskers" and chestnut breast plumage. Insects and seeds are their main foods, but they are omnivorous.

The male performs a courtship display, raising his wings and tail, puffing himself out. The 2 or 3 eggs are laid in an unlined scrape on the ground and incubated by the female for 25 to 28 days.

Black Bustard *Eupodotis afra*

RANGE South Africa

HABITAT Grassland, bush

SIZE 20¼ in (53 cm)

Male black bustards are showy birds, with distinctive markings on the head and neck. Females are quieter, with plumage mottled with black, tawny and rufous spots. Only the underparts are pure black. They live in pairs in a well-defined territory and eat mainly vegetable matter and some insects.

The female usually lays only 1 egg on the ground and incubates it herself.

GRUIDAE: CRANE FAMILY

The 15 species of crane are splendid, long-legged, long-necked birds, which often have brightly colored bare skin on the face and decorative plumes on the head. The larger crane species stand up to 5 ft (1.5 m) tall. They are found over most of the world, except in South America, Madagascar, Malaysia, Polynesia and New Zealand.

Except during the breeding season, when they consort only in pairs, they are gregarious birds and, after breeding, they migrate in large flocks, flying in V-formation or in line, with their necks extended and legs trailing. Males and females have similar plumage.

Whooping Crane

Grus americana **EN**

RANGE N. America

HABITAT Wetlands in prairies and other open habitats

SIZE 4–4½ ft (1.2–1.4 m) tall

Exceedingly rare birds in the wild, whooping cranes have been at the point of extinction, although vigorously protected, since the 1930s when they almost disappeared. They breed in Canada and winter on the Texas Gulf Coast, and their annual migrations are carefully monitored.

An omnivorous bird, the whooping crane feeds on grain, plants, insects, frogs and other small animals.

It lays 2 eggs on a flat nest of sticks on the ground. Both parents incubate the eggs and care for the young.

Black Crowned Crane

Balearica pavonina

RANGE Africa, south of the Sahara

HABITAT Swamps

SIZE 3¼ ft (1 m) tall

The common name of this bird is derived from the crest of yellow feathers on its head. Cranes perform courtship dances in the breeding season and, in a simpler form, through the year. The crowned crane postures with wings outstretched to display its feathers, struts about and jumps into the air. Both parents incubate the 2 or 3 eggs and care for the young.

PSOPHIIDAE: TRUMPETER FAMILY

The 3 species of trumpeter are soft-plumaged, predominantly black birds, with weak, rounded wings. They inhabit the lowland forests of South America. Trumpeters rarely fly, but run swiftly on long legs. The sexes look similar, but males make loud, trumpeting calls.

Gray-winged/Common Trumpeter *Psophia crepitans*

RANGE South America: Amazon basin

HABITAT Forest

SIZE 20¼ in (53 cm)

Common trumpeters are gregarious birds, which move in flocks around the forest floor, feeding on fruit, berries and insects. Trumpeters perform dancelike courtship movements and are believed to nest in holes in trees. The 6 to 10 eggs are incubated by the female.

LIMPKIN, FINFOOT, SUNGEESE, SERIEMAS, KAGU AND MESITES

HELIORNITHIDAE: LIMPKIN AND SUNGREBE FAMILY

This family contains four species. The limpkin is a marsh wading bird, similar to cranes, found from the southern USA to Argentina. It is now protected by law, having been hunted almost to extinction earlier in the 20th century. There are 3 species of sungrebe and finfoot, one in each of the world's major tropical areas: Central and South America, Africa, and Asia (India to Sumatra). They frequent wooded areas near to water and can swim well.

Limpkin *Aramus guarauna*

RANGE USA: S. Georgia, Florida; Mexico, Central and South America; Caribbean

HABITAT Swamps

SIZE 23¼–28 in (59–71 cm)

The limpkin is a long-legged bird, with long toes and sharp claws. It flies slowly and infrequently. The limpkin is most active at dusk and at night, when it uses its sensitive, slightly curved beak to probe the mud for water-snails.

Limpkins breed between January and August, depending on the area, but in the USA the nesting season is usually March or April. A shallow nest is built using sticks, usually on the ground near to water. Both of the parents share the incubation duties for their clutch of 4 to 8 eggs.

African Finfoot *Podica senegalensis*

RANGE Africa: south of the Sahara

HABITAT Wooded streams, pools, mangroves

SIZE 20¼–25 in (53–63.5 cm)

An aquatic bird, the finfoot skulks at the edges of well-wooded streams, among overhanging vegetation. It swims low in the water, sometimes with only its head and neck visible. It is also an accomplished diver.

Once aloft, it flies strongly and also leaves the water to clamber around in vegetation and to climb trees. Insects and small invertebrates, amphibians and fish make up the majority of its diet. Male and female birds of the species look similar, although the male is larger than the female and has buff gray plumage on the front of his neck, while the female's throat and neck are a whitish hue.

The nest is constructed from twigs and rushes on a branch overhanging water or else among flood debris. The female lays a clutch of 2 eggs.

Sungrebe *Heliornis fulica*

RANGE S. Mexico, through Central and South America to N. Argentina

HABITAT Stagnant streams, wooded rivers

SIZE 11 in (28 cm)

Although smaller than the African finfoot, the sungrebe has the same elongate body and lobed toes. Its common name is particularly unsuitable, since the bird frequents shady overgrown margins of streams and rivers and is rarely seen out in the open.

The sungrebe feeds on insects, especially larvae, found on leaves. It also eats small invertebrates, amphibians and fish. It flies strongly, but tends to take cover in undergrowth in order to escape danger, rather than to fly.

The 4 eggs are laid in a bush or tree overhanging water.

CARIAMIDAE: SERIEMA FAMILY

The 2 species of seriema are long-legged, ground-living birds, both of which occur through South America. They are believed to be the only surviving descendants of some long-extinct, carnivorous, ground-dwelling birds, which are known from fossils. Males and females of the species look alike or nearly so.

Red-legged Seriema *Cariama cristata*

RANGE E. Bolivia, Brazil, Paraguay, Uruguay, N. Argentina

HABITAT Grassland

SIZE 28 in (70 cm)

The graceful red-legged seriema runs fast, but rarely flies and tends to rely on its running speed to escape danger. The sharp, broad bill is used to kill reptiles and amphibians, as well as to feed on insects, leaves and seeds. The nest is built from sticks in a tree. Both parents incubate the 2 or 3 eggs for about 26 days.

RHYNOCHETIDAE: KAGU FAMILY

The classification and relationships of the kagu, the sole member of its family, have been the subject of much dispute.

Kagu *Rhynochetos jubatus* **EN**

RANGE New Caledonia

HABITAT Forest

SIZE 22 in (56 cm)

Once abundant, the nocturnal, virtually flightless kagu is now rare, largely due to the onslaught by introduced dogs, cats and rats. The kagu feeds on insects, worms and snails, which it finds on or in the ground by probing with its long pointed bill. The male and female of the species look more or less alike.

In display, the two birds face each other, spreading their wings to show off the black, white and chestnut plumage. They may perform remarkable dances whirling round with the tip of the tail or wing held in the bill. A nest is made on the ground, and both parents incubate the single egg for about 36 days.

MESITORNITHIDAE: MESITE FAMILY

The 3 species of mesite all live in Madagascan forests. They run well but rarely fly, and 1 species, Bensch's mesite, *Monias benschi*, has yet to be seen in flight. Males and females look alike in 2 species, but unalike in Bensch's mesite.

White-breasted Mesite

Mesitornis variegata **VU**

RANGE N.W. Madagascar

HABITAT Dry forest

SIZE 10 in (25.5 cm)

The white breasted mesite is a ground-dwelling bird and spends much of its life searching the forest floor for the insects and seeds that make up its diet.

Mesites generally move about the forest floor in pairs, heads bobbing as they walk.

The nest is built in a bush or a low tree so that the birds can climb up to it. It consists of a platform of twigs, lined with leaves. A clutch of 1 to 3 eggs is laid. There is some doubt as to whether it is the male or female that incubates the eggs.

RAILS

RALLIDAE: RAIL FAMILY

There are 142 species of rail, crake, wood rail, gallinule and coot in this distinctive, cosmopolitan family. They are ground-living birds, often found in or around water and marshy areas, and are well adapted for life in dense vegetation. Typical species are small to medium sized birds – 5½ to 20 in (14 to 51 cm) long – with moderately long legs and toes and short rounded wings. Their bodies are laterally compressed, enabling them to squeeze through clumps of vegetation. Males and females look alike ,or nearly so, in most species, although males are sometimes larger. Most are solitary, secretive birds.

There are two groups within the family: first, the rails, crakes and woodrails, with their camouflaging mottled plumage; and second, the darker gallinules and coots, which are much more aquatic in their habits. Most species fly reasonably well but may ordinarily be reluctant to take to the air, although many make long migrations between winter and summer habitats. Island-dwelling rails have been particularly prone to becoming flightless, which has then led to their extinction.

Diet is varied in the rail family. Species with long, thin bills probe in soft soil and leaf litter for insects, spiders, mollusks, worms and other invertebrates, while species with shorter, thicker bills feed on vegetation. Coots are aquatic feeders and dive or up-end in search of a variety of underwater plant and animal food.

Takahe *Porphyrio mantelli* **EN**

RANGE New Zealand: now confined to Murchison Mountains, South Island

HABITAT High valleys at 2,500–4,000 ft (750–1,200 m)

SIZE 24¾ in (63 cm)

First discovered in 1849, the takahe was sighted only four times in the following 50 years and was assumed to be extinct until it was rediscovered in 1948. Despite careful conservation, however, there were thought to be only 100 pairs alive in 1977. Competition for its plant-food diet from introduced deer and predation by introduced stoats are major reasons for its decline.

A stout bird, the takahe runs well, but it is flightless. It may venture into shallow water, but it does not swim as a rule. It feeds on the coarse fibrous vegetation of its habitat, particularly on snow-grass (*Danthonia*), taking the seed heads and stems. Holding down the clump with one foot, it cuts out stems with its heavy beak and consumes their tender bases.

Pairs remain together for life when possible and usually breed in November. After several trial nests, a nest of grass stalks is made either between or under clumps of grass which provide some shelter. Both parents incubate the clutch of 2 eggs for up to 28 days, but many nests are destroyed by bad weather or predators and only 1 chick from each clutch is ever reared.

Common Moorhen *Gallinula chloropus*

RANGE Worldwide (not Australasia)

HABITAT Swamps, marshes, ponds, slow rivers with cover on banks

SIZE 13 in (33 cm)

A familiar water bird, the moorhen is one of the most adaptable and successful members of its family. It frequents almost any fresh water and adjacent land and readily adapts to man-made environments such as urban parks and farms. It is a lively, active bird, far less secretive than the rail or crake, and swims freely on open water. Plant foods, such as pond weeds, berries and fallen fruit, make up the bulk of the moorhen's diet, but it also eats a small amount of insects.

In the breeding season, the timing of which varies over its vast range, the moorhen pair defends a territory and performs intricate courtship displays on both land and water.

Both sexes help to build a nest of dead reeds and other aquatic plants among reeds or in a bush at the water's edge. The 5 to 11 eggs are laid on consecutive days and are incubated for between 19 and 22 days by both parents. Some pairs may produce a second brood during the season. Northernmost populations migrate south in winter.

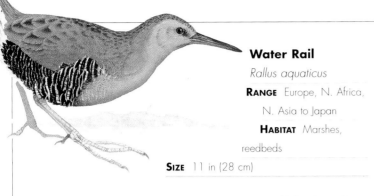

Water Rail
Rallus aquaticus

RANGE Europe, N. Africa, N. Asia to Japan

HABITAT Marshes, reedbeds

SIZE 11 in (28 cm)

The slim-bodied water rail moves easily and skilfully through the tangled aquatic vegetation which it frequents. A shy bird, it runs for cover when alarmed, but is less retiring than the small rails and will come on to open land when the marshes freeze over in winter. It swims short distances near cover. Its varied diet includes plant material, such as roots, seeds and berries, as well as insects, crustaceans, small fish and worms.

April to July is the normal breeding season in most of the rail's range, and it sometimes produces two broods. The nest, which is made of dry reeds and other plants, is situated on the marsh. Both parents share the incubation of the 6 to 11 eggs for 19 to 21 days.

Giant Wood Rail *Aramides ypecaha*

RANGE South America: E. Brazil, Paraguay, Uruguay, E. Argentina

HABITAT Marshes, reedbeds, rivers

SIZE 20¼ in (53 cm)

A large, handsome bird, the giant wood rail is an abundant species in its range. These birds feed alone during the day on plant and animal material, but at night they gather in small groups in the marshes and call in chorus.

The nest is made of grass and plant stems in a low bush just above the marsh surface. About 5 eggs are laid.

American Coot *Fulica americana*

RANGE C. and S. Canada, USA, Central and South America along Andes; Hawaiian Islands, Caribbean, Bahamas

HABITAT Marshes, ponds, lakes, rivers

SIZE 13–15¼ in (33–40 cm)

A dark-plumaged, ducklike species with a white bill, the American coot is a conspicuous, noisy water bird. Its flight is strong and swift, although it seldom flies far unless migrating. It has lobed toes and is a strong swimmer and a good walker.

Water plants are its main food, but it also eats aquatic insects, mollusks and some land plants. Coots often feed in flocks, hundreds of birds swimming together.

In North America, the birds breed from April to May. After prolonged courtship rituals, a cup-shaped nest is made of dried marsh plants in a reedbed or on floating vegetation. The 8 to 12 eggs are incubated by both male and female for 21 or 22 days. Northernmost populations migrate south in winter.

Corncrake *Crex crex* **VU**

RANGE Europe, Asia, Africa

HABITAT Grassland, cultivated land

SIZE 10¼ in (26.5 cm)

The small, slender corncrake seldom flies, although it migrates thousands of miles to winter in tropical Africa. It is a land-dweller and runs swiftly. It eats seeds, grain and insects. Dawn and dusk are the Corncrake's main periods of activity but in spring males make rasping calls day and night. Corncrakes are seen alone or in pairs except when migrating.

The female builds the nest on the ground from grass and weeds. She incubates the 8 to 12 eggs for 14 to 21 days. The young are fed for a few days by the female or by both parents.

SANDGROUSE, SEEDSNIPE, PLAINS-WANDERER, PAINTED SNIPE AND JACANAS

ORDER CICONIIFORMES

A large and diverse order, the Ciconiiformes contains 1,027 species in two suborders. Suborder Charadrii (shorebirds) has 10 families: Thinocoridae (seedsnipe), Pedionomidae (plains-wanderer), Scolopacidae (woodcock and sandpipers); Rostratulidae (paintedsnipe), Jacanidae (jacanas), Chionididae (sheathbills), Burhinidae (thick-knees), Charadriidae (oystercatchers, avocets, and plovers), Glareolidae (crab plover, pratincoles), and Laridae (Skuas, skimmers, gulls and auks). Suborder Ciconii (waders) consists of 18 families: Accipitridae (osprey, birds of prey), Sagittariidae (secretarybird), Falconidae (falcons), Podicipedidae (grebes), Phaethontidae (tropicbird), Sulidae (boobies), Anhingidae (anhingas), Phalacrocoracidae (cormorants), Ardeidae (herons), Scopidae (hammerhead), Phoenicopteridae (flamingos), Threskiornithidae (ibises), Pelecanidae (shoebill, pelicans), Ciconiidae (storks and New World vultures), Fregatidae (frigatebirds), Spheniscidae (penguins), Gaviidae (loons), and Procellariidae (petrels and albatrosses).

PTEROCLIDIDAE: SANDGROUSE FAMILY

The 16 species of sandgrouse are all terrestrial birds, found in the deserts and open plains of south Europe, Asia and Africa. They are not related to grouse. Sandgrouse are sturdy with short necks, small heads and long, pointed wings and short legs. They cannot run, but move fast with a waddling gait. Most are sandy colored, with spotted and barred feathers, which provide good camouflage. Females are usually smaller than males.

Pallas's Sandgrouse
Syrrhaptes paradoxus

RANGE C. Asia, S. Siberia, S. Mongolia
HABITAT High-altitude semidesert, steppe
SIZE 13¾–15¼ in (35–40 cm)

Pallas's sandgrouse is a rounded, short-legged bird about the size

of a small pigeon. It is a strong, fast flier with a long and pointed central tail and outer wing feathers. It is distinguished from other sandgrouse by the black patch on the belly. Adults eat hard seeds and shoots of desert plants and also take much hard grit.

These sandgrouse nest in large colonies from April to June, laying 3 or 4 eggs in a scrape on the ground. Both parents incubate the eggs for 22 to 27 days and feed the young by regurgitation. There are probably two or three clutches a year.

THINOCORIDAE: SEEDSNIPE FAMILY

The 4 species of seedsnipe all live in South America. The common name derives from the fact that all are seed-eating birds that have the rapid zigzagging flight of the snipes.

Seedsnipes are rounded, groundfeeding birds which range in size from 6¾ to 11 in (17 to 28 cm). The wings are long and pointed, the tail short and the bill strong and conical. The plumage is cryptic and partridgelike. The sexes show some differences in plumage.

Least Seedsnipe
Thinocorus rumicivorus

RANGE Andes: Ecuador to Tierra del Fuego; east to Patagonia and Uruguay; Falkland Islands
HABITAT Dry plains, coastal and inland
SIZE 6¾ in (17 cm)

The smallest of the seedsnipes, the least seedsnipe has typical mottled camouflaging plumage. The male bird's black markings give a "necktie" effect. Primarily a ground-living bird, the seedsnipe runs rapidly, despite its short legs. It blends well with its surroundings and, if threatened, it stays still and almost invisible, flying off at the last minute.

The nesting season varies according to latitude. The 4 eggs are laid on the ground in a shallow hollow and are incubated by the female. If she has to leave the eggs for a time she will half bury them in the sand. The young are able to run about soon after hatching.

PEDIONOMIDAE: PLAINS-WANDERER FAMILY

The single species in this family resembles the buttonquail, but it has four toes on each foot and lays pointed, not oval, eggs. The plains-wanderer is found in inland Australia.

Plains-wanderer *Pedionomus torquatus* **VU**

RANGE S.E. Australia

HABITAT Open grassland

SIZE 6–6¼ in (15–17 cm)

A small, compact bird with short, rounded wings, the female plains-wanderer has a chestnut-colored breast and a distinctive collar of black spots. Plains-wanderers seldom fly, but search for their food – which is insects, seeds and plants – on the ground.

The nest is a simple hollow in the ground, lined with grass. The female lays 3 or 4 eggs which are incubated by the male.

ROSTRATULIDAE: PAINTED SNIPE FAMILY

There are only 2 species in this family, one in the Old World and the other, the lesser painted snipe, *Rostratula semicollaris*, in South America. It is an unusual family in that the normal sexual roles are reversed.

Greater Painted Snipe *Rostratula benghalensis*

RANGE Africa, south of the Sahara; Madagascar, S. Asia, Australia

HABITAT Marshes

SIZE 9½ in (24 cm)

The greater painted snipe is a secretive crepuscular bird, which is

rarely seen in the open. It feeds on insects, snails and worms, (most of which it finds in muddy ground with its sensitive bill) and some plant food.

The female bird is the showily colored partner of breeding pairs, the male is smaller with brownish plumage. The female performs an impressive courtship display, spreading her wings forward and expanding her tail in order to show the spots on the feathers. Females will fight over males.

The male bird makes a pad of grass as a nest and, when the female has laid the 3 or 4 eggs, he incubates the clutch and cares for the chicks.

JACANIDAE: JACANA FAMILY

The 8 species of jacana, which are also known as lily-trotters, are all longlegged water birds found in tropical and subtropical areas worldwide. The jacanas have extraordinary feet, which are an adaptation for their habit of moving over floating vegetation. Their toes and claws are so exceedingly elongated that their weight is well distributed over a large surface area, and they are able actually to walk over precarious floating lily pads. Males and females look alike, with mainly brown plumage and black and white on the head. Females are slightly larger than males.

American/Northern Jacana *Jacana spinosa*

RANGE Central America, Greater Antilles, USA: S. Texas

HABITAT Lakes, ponds

SIZE 9¼ in (25 cm)

American jacanas feed on insects and other aquatic life and on the seeds of water plants, all of which they take from the water surface or vegetation. They swim and dive well, but fly slowly.

A nest is made of aquatic plants and the clutch of 3 to 5 (usually 4) eggs is incubated by both of the parents for a total of 22 to 24 days.

SANDPIPERS, WOODCOCK AND SNIPE

SCOLOPACIDAE: SANDPIPER FAMILY

There are 88 species which make up this diverse family of typical shorebirds. Under a wide range of common names, such as sandpiper, curlew, turnstone, snipe, woodcock and redshank, species are found worldwide, on every continent and on almost every island of any size. Most species are ground-living wading birds, which find much of their food in water. Males and females generally look alike, but some species develop special breeding plumage.

Whimbrel *Numenius phaeopus*

RANGE Breeds in Canada, Alaska, Asia, N. Europe; winters in S. America, Africa, S.E. Asia, Australasia

HABITAT Breeds on moors, tundra; winters on muddy and sandy shores, estuaries, marshes

SIZE 15¾ in (40 cm)

One of the group known as curlews, the whimbrel has a distinctive striped crown and a long, curving bill. It eats small invertebrates, including crabs, which it often partially dismembers before swallowing. It also eats insects and berries.

Whimbrels breed in subarctic and subalpine tundra and arrive at breeding grounds in the spring, often returning to the same territory year after year. As the snows disperse, males begin their courtship displays. The nest is made on the ground, usually in the open, and the female bird lays 4 eggs, which are incubated for 27 or 28 days by both parents. Once the chicks are fully fledged, at 5 or 6 weeks, the adults leave almost immediately, starting the migration south to wintering areas. The young birds follow a few weeks later.

American Woodcock *Scolopax minor*

RANGE N. America: breeds from Manitoba to Louisiana and Florida; winters from southern part of breeding range to Gulf Coast

HABITAT Woodland, young forest

SIZE 11 in (28 cm)

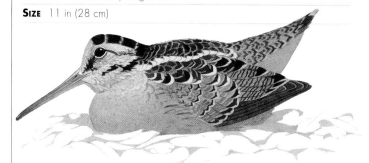

Woodcocks are inland wood and forest birds. The American woodcock is a shy, chunky bird with rounded wings. It probes the soil in search of worms and fly larvae with its long, slender bill, the tip of which is flexible and can open underground.

Males arrive at breeding grounds in March and April. They establish territories and make courtship flights. Females are attracted by the males' calls. A male will mate with several females. The female nests under a small tree or bush and lays 4 eggs which she incubates for 21 days. The female can fly the chicks to safety one at a time by carrying them between her legs.

Common Redshank *Tringa totanus*

RANGE Breeds in Europe, C. and E. Asia; winters in S. Europe, N. Africa, S. Asia

HABITAT Breeds on moorland, marshes; winters on mud flats, meadows, estuaries, shores

SIZE 11 in (28 cm)

An abundant and widespread sandpiper, the redshank adapts well to almost any habitat near water. It has red legs and dark stripes on its head and neck, which fade in winter. It eats mainly insects and also mollusks and crustaceans. Redshanks arrive at breeding grounds from March to May and pair off after courtship displays. The 4 eggs, laid in a nest on the ground, are incubated for 23 days.

Common Snipe *Gallinago gallinago*

RANGE Breeds in Canada, N. USA, Europe to N.E. Asia; winters in Central and South America, Africa, India, Indonesia

HABITAT Marshes, wet meadows, moors

SIZE 10 in (25.5 cm)

A shy bird, the common snipe has pointed wings, a long bill and striped, barred plumage, which provides effective camouflage among vegetation. Insects are the snipe's most important food items, but it also eats earthworms, small crustaceans, snails and plant material.

Males arrive at breeding grounds before females and establish territories for display. In the most common display the male dives through the air at great speed, causing a drumming sound as air rushes through his outer tail feathers. The nest is made on dry ground when possible and near clumps of grass, which the birds pull down over it. The 3 or 4 eggs are incubated for 17 to 19 days, usually by the female alone.

Ruff *Philomachus pugnax*

RANGE Breeds in N. Europe, Asia; winters in Europe, Africa, S. Asia, Australia

HABITAT Tundra, grassland, marshes

SIZE 9–12 in (23–30.5 cm)

Male ruffs perform complex communal displays to attract mates. In the breeding season, males develop large frills of feathers around their heads and necks and gather at a traditional display ground, called a lek. There is great individual variation in the color of frills. Each older, dominant male holds an area within the lek and may be attended by several males, who must display with him and pay court to him in the hope of a chance to mate with one of his females.

Once mated, the female bird, called a "reeve", leaves the display ground and makes a nest in long grass. She incubates her 4 eggs for 20 to 23 days.

Ruddy Turnstone *Arenaria interpres*

RANGE Circumpolar: breeds on Arctic coasts; winters south of breeding range

HABITAT Breeds on marshes, tundra; winters on rocky shores

SIZE 7–9 in (18–23 cm)

In the breeding season, the turnstone has bold black, white and reddish-brown markings, which dulls in winter. Insects, particularly midges, and some plant material are its main food in summer. In winter it forages on seashores, turning over stones and debris with its bill to find mollusks, crustaceans and carrion.

Breeding birds arrive from wintering areas in late May or early June. The 4 eggs are laid in a grass-lined hollow on the ground and incubated by both parents for 21 to 23 days.

Red Phalarope *Phalaropus fulicarius*

RANGE Breeds in N. America: Alaska to Hudson Bay and Arctic islands; winters off W. Africa and Chile

HABITAT Breeds in tundra and wet meadows; winters at sea

SIZE 7 in (18 cm)

The only swimming bird in its family, the toes of the phalarope are adapted for swimming, with flattened fringing scales. It comes ashore only to breed. In the breeding season the female is is brightly colored with a reddish throat and underparts. The male is smaller and duller. In winter both sexes have grayish plumage. Phalaropes eat beetles, flies, crustaceans and fish.

Normal sexual roles are reversed. Females take the initiative in courtship and mating and the male incubates the clutch of 4 eggs for about 19 days and cares for the young.

SHEATHBILLS, THICK-KNEES AND PRATINCOLES

CHIONIDIDAE: SHEATHBILL FAMILY

The 2 species of sheathbill are medium-sized – 14 to 17 in (35.5 to 43 cm) – white plumaged, shore-living birds, found on the islands of the far southern oceans. They are squat and heavy-bodied, resembling pigeons in build, and have a comblike covering over the upper beak, which gives them their common name. Their legs are short and stocky and their feet powerful. Male and female sheathbills look alike, but females are usually smaller.

Snowy Sheathbill *Chionis alba*

RANGE Subantarctic islands of the S. Atlantic Ocean, extending to Graham Land and S. South America when not breeding.

HABITAT Coasts

SIZE 15¼ in (39 cm)

Snowy sheathbills are gregarious and pugnacious birds and, except during the breeding season, they live in small flocks, feeding together and often fighting. Although they fly well and will make long journeys, even over sea, they spend most of their time on the ground. They swim well although their feet have only rudimentary webs. Sheathbills are avid scavengers and haunt seal and penguin colonies to seize afterbirths or weak young. They also search the shore for all kinds of fish, invertebrates, carcasses and almost any other debris that they can eat. They consume quantities of seaweed for the invertebrates that it harbors.

Sheathbills nest in isolated pairs in a crevice or among rocks. The 2 or 3 eggs are laid on feathers, seaweed and other soft material. Both parents incubate the eggs for 28 days, but it appears that only 1 chick is actually reared as a general rule.

In winter, sheathbills in the extreme south of the range migrate north, but those on subantarctic islands usually remain there. The other species in this family, the black-billed sheathbill, C. *minor*, is found in the subantarctic sector of the Indian Ocean.

BURHINIDAE: THICK-KNEE FAMILY

The 9 species in this family have a variety of common names, including thick-knee, stone curlew and dikkop. All have thickened joints between tarsus and shin and three partially webbed toes on each foot. Thick-knees are active at dusk and at night and their large yellow eyes are an adaptation for this. The sexes look alike. The family is widely distributed in the Old World and 2 species occur in Central and South America.

Beach Thick-knee

Burhinus giganteus

RANGE S.E. Asia and Australasia

HABITAT Coasts and rivers

SIZE 20 in (50 cm)

A sturdy, large headed bird, this thick-knee has a strong, slightly upturned bill and large yellow eyes. It feeds mostly at night on insects, worms, mollusks and crustaceans, and some small vertebrates. It runs fast, in short dashes, and is a reluctant but strong flier. To avoid danger, it may crouch or flatten itself on the ground.

The great shore plover lays 2, sometimes 3, eggs in a shallow hollow in the ground. They are incubated by the female, with some help from the male. Both parents care for the chicks which are able to fend for themselves almost immediately.

Stone Curlew *Burhinus oedicnemus*

RANGE S. England, Europe, N. Africa, S.W. Asia; winters to the south of its range

HABITAT Open country, heath, farmland

SIZE 16 in (41 cm)

Although some populations migrate, the stone curlew is the only migratory thick-knee, northern birds wintering in East Africa. Like all its family, the stone curlew's plumage camouflages it well. The two bold wing bars are conspicuous in flight. Its bill is short and straight, and it eats mainly invertebrates, snails and worms. The female lays her 2 eggs on the ground in a hollow and incubates them with some help from her mate.

GLAREOLIDAE: PRATINCOLE FAMILY

This family contains 18 species – pratincoles, coursers and the crab plover. All are fairly small ploverlike birds with sharply pointed bills. Pratincoles have short beaks, narrow, pointed wings, forked tails, short legs and feet with four toes. Coursers have longer bills, broader wings and tails and longer legs with three-toed feet. Birds of both groups eat insects, mollusks, leeches, small lizards and seeds. They inhabit warmer areas of the Old World, including Australia. Males and females have similar plumage but may differ in size.

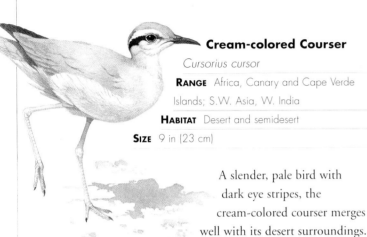

Cream-colored Courser

Cursorius cursor

RANGE Africa, Canary and Cape Verde Islands; S.W. Asia, W. India

HABITAT Desert and semidesert

SIZE 9 in (23 cm)

A slender, pale bird with dark eye stripes, the cream-colored courser merges well with its desert surroundings. Its flight is rapid, but it tends to run rather than fly, often crouching on the ground between bursts of movement.

Cream-colored coursers do not make regular migrations, but do wander out of their range, often flying to Europe, although they do not breed there. The female lays 2 or 3 eggs on the ground. She incubates them at night, when the temperature falls, but may need to stand above them by day to shade them.

Egyptian Plover *Pluvianus aegyptius*

RANGE N.E., W. and W. C. Africa

HABITAT Shores and sandbanks of rivers and lakes

SIZE 7¾ in (20 cm)

The Egyptian plover has more striking plumage and rather shorter legs, than the related coursers. It is usually found near water, and has long been known as the crocodile bird because of the belief that it feeds on the food particles remaining in the mouths of basking crocodiles. Though this is unconfirmed, the bird often feeds near crocodiles and on their body parasites. Its main food is insects.

The female lays 2 or 3 eggs which she covers with sand while they incubate. She may cover chicks temporarily, to hide them from danger.

Collared/Common Pratincole *Glareola pratincola*

RANGE S. Europe, S.W. Asia, Africa

HABITAT Open land, sun-baked mud-flats, freshwater banks

SIZE 9¾ in (25 cm)

The collared pratincole, with its deeply forked tail, is ternlike in its swift, agile flight, but can run easily on the ground like a plover. It has a characteristic creamy, black-bordered throat, but the border is less distinct in winter.

Pratincoles are gregarious birds, and flocks gather at dusk to feed on insects, which they chase and catch in the air, often in the vicinity of water. They breed in colonies of anything from a few pairs to hundreds of birds and generally breed after the rainy or flood season in their area.

Their 2 to 4 eggs are laid on the ground and are well camouflaged by their blotched, neutral coloration, which blends with the background, whether soil, sand or rock. Both parents incubate the eggs for a total of 17 or 18 days. The young are able to run around immediately after hatching. After breeding, European collared pratincoles migrate to Africa, south of the Sahara.

Crab Plover *Dromas ardeola*

RANGE Breeds on islands from E. Africa to the Persian Gulf; winters on coasts and islands of the W. Indian Ocean

HABITAT Estuaries, reefs

SIZE 15 in (38 cm)

A stocky bird with a heavy, compressed bill, the crab plover flies strongly and runs swiftly. Its black and white markings are striking and distinct in flight. The legs are long and the toes are partially webbed. Crabs are, indeed, the main item of its diet, but it also feeds on other crustaceans and on mollusks, which it breaks open with its strong, pointed bill.

Crab plovers are noisy, gregarious birds and they nest in colonies. The female lays her single egg at the end of a burrow in a sandbank, often in a crab burrow. Although it is able to run about soon after hatching, the chick is cared for by both parents and is fed in the burrow.

OYSTERCATCHERS, AVOCETS AND PLOVERS

CHARADRIIDAE: PLOVER AND AVOCET FAMILY

The 89 species of wading birds in this family are placed in
2 subfamilies – Recurvirostrinae (Oystercatchers, Avocets, Stilts),
and Charadriinae (Plovers and Lapwings).

RECURVIROSTRINAE: OYSTERCATCHER, AVOCET AND STILT SUBFAMILY

Oystercatchers are large, noisy, coastal birds found throughout
the world, except on oceanic islands and in polar regions. The
11 species show only slight sexual and seasonal plumage
differences. The 11 species of avocets and stilts are long-billed,
long-legged wading birds found throughout much of the world,
except in northernmost regions. These birds fly and sometimes
swim well and generally live near water. Their feet are usually at
least slightly webbed. Aquatic insects, mollusks, fish, frogs and
some plant food are the main items of their diet. Many species
have black and white plumage, and the sexes look more or less
alike. The ibisbill differs from other avocets and stilts because of
its downcurving beak and its high altitude habitat.

Common/Eurasian Oystercatcher *Haematopus ostralegus*
RANGE Breeds Eurasia; winters S. to Africa, India and South China
HABITAT Coasts, estuaries
SIZE 18 in (46 cm)

The common oystercatcher has a typical long, blunt, flattened
bill which it uses to pry shellfish off rocks. Mollusks and
crustaceans are its main food, but it
also seeks insects and worms on
farmland farther inland.
Oystercatchers are
gregarious and live and
move in large flocks.
The nest is a hole in the
ground, often lined with
grass or decorated with
moss. The female lays
2 to 4 eggs and
both partners
incubate them
for 24 to 27 days.

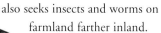
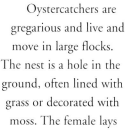

Pied Avocet *Recurvirostra avosetta*
RANGE Europe, W. and C. Asia; northern populations winter in Africa,
S. Asia, China
HABITAT Mud flats, estuaries, sandbanks
SIZE 16½ in (42 cm)

The avocet has striking black
and white plumage and a
long upward curving
bill. In flight, the long
legs usually project beyond the tail. Avocets
eat insects, small aquatic animals and some
plant matter, all of which they find by
sweeping their bills from side to side
at the surface of mud or shallow water. In deeper water, the
avocet dips its head below the surface and will swim and
"up-end" like a duck.

Avocets breed colonially; pairs mating after displays
involving both partners. The nest is usually a scrape near water
in which the female lays 3 to 5 eggs. Both parents incubate the
eggs and later guard their chicks against predators. Juveniles have
some brownish plumage but are similar to adults. The American
avocet, *R. americana*, resembles this avocet, but has cinnamon
plumage on head, neck and breast in the breeding season.

Black-winged Stilt *Himantopus himantopus*
RANGE Eurasia and Africa: tropical, subtropical and temperate latitudes
HABITAT Mainly freshwater swamps, marshes, lagoons
SIZE 15 in (38 cm)

The stilt has long pink legs, longer
in proportion to its body than those
of any bird except the flamingo. In
flight, its legs project far beyond
the tail. Stilts walk quickly, with long
strides. They wade in water to pick insects
and small aquatic animals off plants and the water
surface with their long slender bills.

Stilts nest in colonies near water.
Nests are large, built in shallow water
from sticks and mud or small flimsy
ground nests. Between April and
June females lays 3 to 5 eggs which
both parents incubate for 26 days.

Ibisbill *Ibidorhyncha struthersii*

RANGE High plateaux of C. Asia; Himalayas

HABITAT Shingle banks, shingle islands in mountain streams

SIZE 15 in (38 cm)

The ibisbill uses its down curving bill to probe for food under stones in the shingly river beds it frequents. It often wades into the water and submerges its head and neck. Small groups of ibisbills generally live and feed together. The female bird lays 4 large eggs in a ground nest, and the clutch is incubated by both parents.

CHARADRIINAE: PLOVER AND LAPWING SUBFAMILY

The members of this subfamily are found worldwide apart from Antarctica. The 67 species of plovers, lapwings, and dotterels are small to medium-sized, fairly plump wading birds. The typical plover has a short, straight bill, round head and short legs. Males and females are alike, or nearly so, but some species have seasonal differences in plumage. Plovers occur in sparsely vegetated areas, from sandy shores to semideserts, and eat insects and small invertebrates.

Ringed Plover *Charadrius hiaticula*

RANGE Breeds Arctic E. Canada and Eurasia; winters in Africa, S. Europe

HABITAT Seashore

SIZE 7½ in (19 cm)

A common northern shorebird, the ringed plover has distinctive head and breast markings in its summer plumage. It feeds on mollusks, insects, worms and some plants.

The female lays 3 to 5 eggs and will defend eggs or young with a distraction display technique used by many plover species. If a predator approaches the nest, the parent bird flaps awkwardly away as if injured and unable to fly, all the time leading the enemy away from the young. Once the predator is well away from the nest, the plover flies up suddenly and escapes, to return to the nest later.

Northern Lapwing *Vanellus vanellus*

RANGE Europe, W. and N. Africa, Asia

HABITAT Grassland, farmland, marshes

SIZE 12 in (30 cm)

A distinctive bird with a crested head and broad, rounded wings, the lapwing is also known as the peewit after the cry it makes in flight. Lapwings feed mostly on insects but also on worms, snails and some plant matter. The male makes a ceremonial nest scrape to initiate breeding behavior in the female. She completes the nest and lays 3 to 5 eggs. The clutch is incubated for 24 to 31 days.

American Golden Plover

Pluvialis dominica

RANGE Northern N. America, Asia; winters in South America

HABITAT Tundra, marshes, fields, open country

SIZE 9–11 in (23–28 cm)

This plover flies to wintering grounds 8,000 miles (12,800 km) south of its breeding grounds on the tundra of North America and Siberia. American golden plovers eat insects and some mollusks and crustaceans. They lay 3 or 4 eggs in a shallow dip in the tundra, lined with moss and grass. Both parents incubate the eggs for 20 to 30 days. In winter this plover loses its distinctive facial markings, and its head and breast are a speckled golden color.

Wrybill *Anarhynchus frontalis* **VU**

RANGE New Zealand

HABITAT River beds, open country

SIZE 8 in (20 cm)

The wrybill is a small plover with a unique bill, the tip of which turns to the right. To find its insect food, it tilts its head to the left and sweeps the tip of its bill over the mud with a horizontal scissoring action. Wrybills winter in North Island and travel to South Island to breed. They nest in large estuaries on a particular type of shingle, the stones of which are a similar color to the wrybill and its eggs. The female lays 2 or 3 eggs among the shingle in October.

SKUAS, GULLS AND SKIMMERS

LARIDAE: GULL AND AUK FAMILY

Most of the 129 species in this family are seabirds. There are two subfamilies.

LARINAE: SKUA, SKIMMER, GULL, AND TERN SUBFAMILY

There are four groups, or tribes, in this subfamily. The 8 species of skuas, or jaegers as they are called in North America, are dark-plumaged seabirds characterised by their practical method of obtaining food – they chase other seabirds, such as gulls and terns, in the air and force them to disgorge their prey.

Skuas are widespread throughout tundra and polar regions, where they breed, and the open seas, where they range at other times. Males and females are outwardly alike, but the females are sometimes larger.

The 3 species of skimmers resemble large terns. Two are tropical freshwater birds, 1 in Africa and the other found from India to South China. The third, from the Americas, is coastal in its habits. Skimmers have eyes with slit-like pupils, unique among birds.

Gulls are solidly-built seabirds with long, broad wings and long legs with webbed feet. Most are white with black or gray markings. They are the classic shoreline birds; they seldom dive and few species catch fish. Most are opportunist feeders, scavenging, stealing food from others birds, or killing small prey. The 50 species of gulls are found along sea coasts worldwide, although they are more predominant in the cooler regions.

Terns are gulllike but smaller with long, narrow wings, a narrow bill, and forked tail. They dive for fish and most species also catch insects in the air or on water. The 45 tern species are found worldwide at sea, near coasts, and on inland waters.

Great Skua *Catharacta skua*

RANGE N. Atlantic Ocean: Iceland, Faeroes, Shetland and Orkney Islands; winters as far south as the Tropic of Cancer

HABITAT Oceanic, coastal waters

SIZE 20–22 in (51–56 cm)

A strongly built bird with a hooked bill and sharply curved claws, the great skua not only attacks other birds to steal their prey, but also kills and eats ducks and gulls and preys on eggs and young at breeding grounds. It also follows ships to feed on scraps thrown overboard and takes carrion.

An otherwise solitary bird, it nests in colonies. A shallow scrape is made on a rocky slope or at the foot of a cliff, and 1 to 3 eggs, usually 2, are laid. Both partners incubate the eggs for 26 to 29 days and care for the chicks.

Black Skimmer *Rynchops niger*

RANGE USA; winters in S. USA, Central and South America

HABITAT Coastal waters, rivers and lakes with sandbanks

SIZE 16–20 in (41–51 cm)

Skimmers possess a unique structural modification – the lower half of the bill, which is laterally flattened and longer than the upper half, is an adaptation for a special method of fishing. The skimmer flies just above a smooth water surface, with its bladelike lower bill cleaving a furrow through the water. When the bill strikes a small fish or crustacean, the skimmer clamps down its upper bill and pulls its head back to swallow the prey, while flying.

Black skimmers breed in spring in colonies of up to 200 pairs. The female lays 2 to 4 eggs in a hollow scraped in the sand.

Ivory Gull *Pagophila eburnea*

RANGE Arctic coasts and islands; winters among ice floes, sometimes south of the Arctic Circle·

HABITAT Coasts, pack-ice

SIZE 14–17 in (35.5–43 cm)

The only gull with all-white plumage, the ivory gull is a striking, plump-bodied bird with black legs. It seldom swims but can run over ice. It feeds on fish and invertebrates and scavenges on carrion and refuse. It breeds in colonies and lays 2 eggs on the ground or on a cliff ledge.

Herring Gull

Larus argentatus

RANGE Most of northern hemisphere

HABITAT Coasts, estuaries; inland water and fields

SIZE 21¼–26 in (55–66 cm)

The commonest coastal gull in North America and Europe, the herring gull has a varied diet. It eats small surface-dwelling fish, scavenges on waste and sewage, steals eggs and preys on young birds and small mammals. It also flies inland to feed on worms and other invertebrates on farmland.

Herring gulls nest in colonies on cliff slopes, islands or beaches. The nest is usually made of weeds and grass in a hollow in the ground. It is sometimes built in a tree or on a building. The 2 or 3 eggs are incubated for 25 to 27 days by both parents. In their first year, the young have dark-brown plumage. They do not attain full adult plumage for 3 years. Male and female adult birds look alike, but males are often larger.

Black-headed Gull *Larus ridibundus*

RANGE Iceland, N. Europe and Asia; winters south of range to N. Africa, S. Asia and Philippines

HABITAT Coasts, inland marshes

SIZE 14–15 in (35.5–38 cm)

This small, active gull is often seen inland in winter (when it is not black-headed), and thrives in freshwater habitats, where it feeds on insects and invertebrates. It scavenges, especially on refuse tips, and feeds on the coast.

Black-headed gulls breed colonially on marshes, moors and coasts in the spring. A pair builds a nest, usually on the ground and made of plant material, and the female lays 3 eggs, which are incubated for 20 to 24 days.

Black-legged Kittiwake *Rissa tridactyla*

RANGE N. Pacific, N. Atlantic Oceans, parts of Arctic Ocean

HABITAT Oceanic

SIZE 16–18 in (41–46 cm)

The kittiwake is much more oceanic in its habits than the *Larus* gulls and normally comes ashore only to breed. It seldom walks, so its legs are much shorter than those of most gulls and it has only three toes on each foot. It

feeds on fish, small mollusks and crustaceans and also scavenges on the waste dumped from fishing boats.

Kittiwakes nest in huge colonies of thousands of birds, normally on high cliffs. A pair builds a nest from plants, seaweed and guano, cementing it to the cliff ledge with mud. The usual clutch of 2 eggs is incubated for 23 to 32 days by both parents.

Common Tern *Sterna hirundo*

RANGE E. N. America, N. Europe, Asia; winters south of range to the tropics

HABITAT Coastal islands, coasts; inland rivers and lakes

SIZE 13–16 in (33–41 cm)

A common and widespread coastal bird, the common tern feeds on small fish and other marine creatures, which it catches by hovering over the water and then diving rapidly to seize the prey it with its bill.

Terns nest in colonies of hundreds of thousands on isolated beaches, islands or cliffs. A pair scrapes a hollow in the ground which is then lined with vegetation. Both parents take turns at incubating the 2 or 3 eggs for 21 to 26 days.

Brown Noddy *Anous stolidus*

RANGE Tropical oceans

HABITAT Offshore waters, islands

SIZE 16–17 in (41–43 cm)

The 5 species of noddy tern are all inhabitants of tropical seas. The noddy seldom dives, but it will float on the surface of the water or perch on buoys, driftwood or reefs, watching out for prey. It often flies just above the water and snatches small fish when they are driven to the surface by larger fish.

Brown noddies make their untidy twig nests in bushes or on the ground. Both parents incubate the single egg.

AUKS

ALCINAE: AUK SUBFAMILY

The auks are a small family of short-tailed, short-necked diving seabirds found in the North Pacific, North Atlantic and Arctic Oceans, and along their coasts. They are truly marine birds, only coming to land to breed. The 23 species include the guillemots, razorbills, auklets, puffins, murres and auks. All have dark-brown or black plumage, usually with white underparts. Auks swim well and dive from the surface to pursue prey underwater, propelling themselves with their short, narrow wings. They stand upright on land and this, combined with their general body shape and marine habits, makes them the northern equivalents of the penguins, found in the southern hemisphere.

Indeed, the name penguin was first applied by early mariners to the largest member of the family, the great auk; it was only later used for the similarly adapted birds that we know today as penguins. The great auk was flightless – its short, powerful wings were of use only for underwater propulsion. Because of this it could not easily escape from man, so great auks were constantly slaughtered for food and have now been extinct for more than a century.

Auks are not, however, closely related to penguins evolutionarily: the resemblance is an example of two groups of birds adapting in a similar way to fill the same niche in northern and southern hemispheres.

Auks nest in colonies of hundreds or thousands of birds on cliff tops and rocks. They fly fast, with rapid wing beats, but some of the small species are better adapted for swimming than flying. Some species migrate south in winter. Males and females look alike but there are some seasonal plumage changes. In their annual molt, most species lose all the flight feathers at once and are temporarily flightless.

Guillemot/Common Murre

Uria aalge

RANGE N. Atlantic, N. Pacific Oceans

HABITAT Offshore waters, oceanic

SIZE 16–17 in (41–43 cm)

One of the most common auks, the guillemot has a longer, narrower bill than is usual for auks and a less bulky body. In breeding plumage, the head, neck and upperparts are dark brown, but in winter, the throat and front and sides of face and neck are white, with dark stripes extending back from the eyes. Guillemots feed on fish, mollusks and worms which they catch underwater.

At the end of May, colonies of guillemots gather in breeding areas on top of rocks or on cliffs. Each female lays 1 egg on bare rock; the egg is pear-shaped and this led to the long-held belief that, if it moves, it rolls round in a circle, rather than off the ledge. However, this is probably not so and the reason why the egg is this shape may well be related to its large size and the narrow pelvis of the female guillemot. The eggs vary enormously in color and pattern and this may help the birds to recognize their own eggs in the crowded breeding colony. Both parents incubate the egg for 28 to 30 days. In winter guillemots migrate south of their normal breeding range.

Atlantic Puffin *Fratercula arctica*

RANGE N. Atlantic Ocean: Arctic coasts of E. N. America and W. Eurasia

HABITAT Open sea, rocky coasts

SIZE 11¼–14¼ in (29–36 cm)

A small, round-bodied auk with a large head, the Atlantic puffin has a spectacular striped bill, which it uses to catch food and for display. In summer the puffin's bill is colorful, the upper parts of the body and collar are black and the underparts white. In winter, the face is grayish and the bill smaller and duller. Young birds resemble adults in winter plumage, but have smaller, darker bills. The puffin feeds on fish and shellfish and can carry several items at a time in its capacious bill as it flies back to its nest. Its flight is strong and fast but, like all auks, it has short legs set well back on the body and waddles along clumsily on land.

Atlantic puffins breed from late May in colonies on turfed cliff tops or on islands. The female lays 1 egg, rarely 2, in a burrow abandoned by a shearwater or rabbit, or in a hole which she digs herself with her feet. Both parents incubate the egg for 40 to 43 days. After breeding, most puffins spend the winter at sea, offshore from the breeding range, but some populations migrate southward.

Crested Auklet
Aethia cristatella

RANGE N. Pacific Ocean,
Bering Sea

HABITAT Ocean, sea cliffs

SIZE 9¼–10½ in (24–27 cm)

In the breeding season the crested auklet develops a dark crest of long plumes that fall forward over its bright bill, and white plumes behind the eyes. In winter, the crest and eye plumes are smaller, and the bill becomes a dull yellow. Young birds have no crests. These small auklets feed mainly on crustaceans.

Colonies of crested auklets gather on cliffs in order to breed, and the female lays a single egg in a rock crevice or among stones.

Razorbill *Alca torda*

RANGE N. Atlantic Ocean

HABITAT Coasts, open sea

SIZE 15¼–16½ in (40–42cm)

A well-built auk, with a heavy head and a thick neck, the razorbill has a stout, compressed bill with distinctive white markings. In summer, the razorbill's head, neck and upper parts are black, with prominent white lines running from bill to eyes. In winter, the auk's cheeks and forehead are white. Razorbills feed on fish, crustaceans and mollusks.

Colonies of razorbills nest on sea cliffs and rocky shores on the Atlantic coasts of Europe and North America often near guillemot colonies. The breeding season starts about mid-May, and the female lays 1 egg, rarely 2, in a hole or crevice. Both parents incubate the egg for about 25 days, and the young leaves the nest after about 15 days.

Little Auk/Dovekie *Alle alle*

RANGE Arctic Ocean; winters in N. Atlantic Ocean

HABITAT Coasts, open sea

SIZE 7¼ in (20 cm)

The smallest auk, the little auk is a squat, rounded bird, with a short thick neck and a stout, strong bill. In winter the throat and breast, which are dark in summer plumage, become white. The little auk feeds on crustaceans, small fish and mollusks. An excellent swimmer, it dives rapidly if alarmed.

From mid-June, thousands of little auks gather in crowded colonies on Arctic coasts and cliffs. They do not make nests, and the female lays 1 egg, occasionally 2, in a crack in the rock. Both sexes take it in turns to incubate the egg for 24 to 30 days.

Little auks spend the winter at sea, moving as far south as Iceland and Norway. They may even appear inland in particularly bad weather. This species occurs in vast numbers in its Arctic habitat and is believed to be one of the most abundant birds in the world.

Marbled Murrelet *Brachyramphus marmoratus*

RANGE N. Pacific Ocean

HABITAT Coasts, islands

SIZE 9½–9¾ in (24–25 cm)

In the breeding season, the marbled murrelet has distinctly barred and speckled underparts, which become white in winter. It feeds, like the rest of the auks, on fish and other marine animals and, when on water it holds its slender bill and tail pointing upward.

Unusually for an auk, it flies inland to breed in mountains or forest areas and lays 1 egg on a twig platform, on moss, or in a nest abandoned by another species of bird.

HAWKS

ACCIPITRIDAE: HAWK FAMILY

This is the largest family in the Falconiformes order and contains about 239 species of diverse predatory and carrion-eating birds. Representatives occur in almost all regions of the world except Antarctica, northern parts of the Arctic and small oceanic islands.

The accipiter family contains many different types and sizes of bird. The family includes the 14 or so carrion-feeding Old World vultures, the "true hawks" (including buzzards and eagles), harrier eagles and serpent eagles, harriers, kites and fish eagles, honey-buzzards and a few other specialized types.

Females tend to be significantly larger than the males in almost every case, excluding the vultures. Characteristic physical features of this family are the down-curved pointed beak, the base of which is covered with a fleshy cere carrying the external nostrils, and large wings with rounded tips and often barred or streaked underparts. All the birds have widely spaced toes and long, sharp, curving claws. On the soles of the feet are roughened, bulging pads to facilitate the seizing of prey.

Most species nest in trees, while some of the larger eagles and buzzards use cliff ledges. These large species are long-lived birds which reach breeding maturity slowly. They have small clutches of only 1 or 2 eggs. There are 2 subfamilies – one contains the single osprey species, the other the remaining hawk species.

Osprey *Pandion haliaetus*

RANGE Almost worldwide

HABITAT Lakes, rivers, coasts

SIZE 21–24 in (53–62 cm)

The osprey, or fish hawk, feeds almost exclusively on fish, but it will take small mammals and wounded birds. When hunting, it flies over water and may hover briefly before plunging into the water, feet forward. Grasping the fish in both feet, the soles of which are studded with spikes to aid its grip, it returns to feed at its perch.

A breeding pair makes a large nest on the ground, using sticks, seaweed and other debris. The same nest may be repaired and used year after year. A clutch of 2 to 4 eggs, usually 3, is incubated mainly by the female. The male feeds her during incubation and for the first 4 weeks of the chicks' fledgling period. Northern populations migrate south for the winter.

Egyptian Vulture *Neophron percnopterus*

RANGE S. Europe, Africa, Middle East, India

HABITAT Open country

SIZE 23½–27½ in (60–70 cm)

The Egyptian vulture is a small species. It defers to larger vultures at a carcass and must often be content with scraps. It also eats insects and ostrich and flamingo eggs. It is one of the few creatures to use a tool. In order to break into an ostrich egg the vulture drops rocks on it to crack it open. This vulture scavenges on all kinds of refuse, including human excrement.

Display flights of swoops and dives precede mating, and the pair builds a nest on a crag or a building. The parents incubate 1 or 2 eggs for about 42 days.

Lammergeier/Bearded Vulture *Gypaetus barbatus*

RANGE S. Europe, Africa, Middle East to C. Asia

HABITAT Mountains

SIZE 37–41 in (95–105 cm)

An uncommon and magnificent bird, the lammergeier descends from the mountains only to forage for food. It spends most of its day on the wing, soaring with unequaled grace. It feeds on carrion of all sorts, including human, but defers to larger vultures at carcasses. As one of the last in line, the lammergeier is often left with the bones, and it has developed the knack of dropping them on rocks to split them and reveal the marrow.

Each breeding pair holds a large territory, and the birds perform spectacular diving and swooping flight displays. They nest in cliff niches or on ledges and lay 1 or 2 eggs which are incubated for 53 days. Normally only 1 chick is reared.

Lappet-faced Vulture

Torgos tracheliotus

RANGE Africa, Israel, parts of Arabian peninsula

HABITAT Bush, desert

SIZE 39–45 in (100–115 cm)

The lappet-faced vulture is a typical Old World vulture with perfect adaptations for scavenging. The powerful hooked bill cuts easily into the flesh of carrion. Its bare head and neck save lengthy feather-cleaning after plunging into a messy carcass. The immense broad wings, with widely spaced primary feathers, are ideal for soaring and gliding for long periods, using few wing beats. No real mating display has been observed. A huge stick nest is made at the top of a tree or on a crag, and the female lays 1 egg.

European Honey-buzzard *Pernis apivorus*

RANGE Eurasia; winters south to S. Africa

HABITAT Woodland

SIZE 20–24 in (52–61 cm)

The honey-buzzard has broad, barred wings, a long tail and specially adapted feathers to protect it from the stings of bees and wasps whose nests it attacks. Larvae and honey are a major food source and it also feeds on live wasps, nipping off the sting before swallowing them. Small vertebrates and flying termites also feature in the honey-buzzard's diet.

A mating pair holds a home territory and the male performs a distinctive display flight, striking his wings together above his head. They make a tree nest of sticks and leaves. Both parents incubate the clutch of 1 to 3 eggs for 30 to 35 days and feed the young. Northern Eurasian populations migrate south to Africa in winter.

Red Kite *Milvus milvus* **LR:lc**

RANGE Europe, Middle East, N. Africa

HABITAT Woodland, open country

SIZE 24–26 in (61–66 cm)

The red kite is a large bird with long wings and a distinctive, deeply forked tail. It

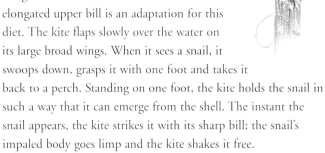

breeds in woodland but hunts in open country. As it flies low over fields, it searches for prey. It can hover briefly and pursues its quarry with great agility. Small mammals up to the size of a weasel, birds, reptiles, frogs, fish, insects and carrion are all eaten, and red kites also kill domestic poultry.

A breeding pair nests in a tree, often adding sticks and oddments to an old nest. Between 1 and 5 eggs, usually 3, are laid. It is mainly the female that incubates the eggs for 28 to 30 days. The male feeds her and takes over from time to time.

Brahminy Kite *Haliastur indus*

RANGE India, S. China, S.E. Asia, Australasia

HABITAT Near water, coasts

SIZE 18 in (46 cm)

The brahminy kite feeds on frogs, crabs, snakes, fish, insects and some carrion. It also scavenges around human habitation for all kinds of scraps and refuse. At the breeding site the birds perform display flights before starting to build a nest. The nest is made of sticks and lined with leaves and is sited in a tree or among mangroves. The female lays 1 to 4 eggs which she incubates for 26 or 27 days, while her mate keeps her supplied with food.

Everglade/Snail Kite *Rostrhamus sociabilis*

RANGE USA: Florida; Caribbean, Mexico, Central and South America

HABITAT Freshwater marshes

SIZE 15 in (8 cm)

The Everglade kite feeds solely on water snails of the genus *Pomacea*; the elongated upper bill is an adaptation for this diet. The kite flaps slowly over the water on its large broad wings. When it sees a snail, it swoops down, grasps it with one foot and takes it back to a perch. Standing on one foot, the kite holds the snail in such a way that it can emerge from the shell. The instant the snail appears, the kite strikes it with its sharp bill; the snail's impaled body goes limp and the kite shakes it free.

Breeding pairs build nests which are simple structures in marsh grass or bushes. The female lays 3 or 4 eggs, and both parents incubate the clutch and care for the young. This unusual bird is now rare, particularly in Florida, and is protected by conservation laws.

HAWKS CONTINUED

Bald Eagle

Haliaeetus leucocephalus

RANGE N. America

HABITAT Coasts, rivers and lakes

SIZE 32–40 in (81–102 cm)

The national symbol of the USA, the bald eagle is one of 8 species of eagle in the genus *Haliaeetus*, all of which have a liking for fish. Most of the others are called "sea" or "fish" eagles and are coastal birds. Dead and dying fish are the staple diet of the bald eagle, but it also takes live fish from the water and catches some birds and mammals. Groups of these impressive birds gather together where food is available, particularly by rivers near the Alaskan coast, where they prey on exhausted salmon which are migrating upriver to their breeding grounds.

Bald eagles breed in northern North America on inland lakes, migrating south, if necessary, in the winter to find food. Pairs remain together and reestablish bonds each year with spectacular courtship displays, when the birds lock talons in mid-air and somersault through the air together. The nest is made of sticks and sited in a large tree or on rocks. It is added to, year after year, and can be as large as 8 ft (2.5 m) across and 11½ ft (3.5 m) deep, one of the largest of all birds' nests. Most of the time the female incubates the 1 to 3 eggs, but the male takes an occasional turn. The young remain in the nest for 10 or 11 weeks and are aggressive and competitive. Often the youngest of the brood is starved or killed.

All populations of this fine eagle have declined, seriously in some areas. It has suffered from the contamination of its habitat and prey by toxic chemicals and, with its slow breeding rate, it is hard for the species to recover.

Palm-nut Vulture

Gypohierax angolensis

RANGE Africa, south of the Sahara

HABITAT Forest, mangroves, savanna

SIZE 28 in (71 cm)

This curious bird resembles both vultures and sea eagles, and some authorities believe it to be a link between them. It feeds almost exclusively on the husk of the fruit of the oil palm *Elaeis guineensis*, and its distribution coincides with that of the plant. The diet is supplemented with fruit of the raphia palm, crabs, mollusks, snails and locusts, but all are rejected in favour of oil palm. A sedentary bird, the palm-nut vulture tends to stay around the same haunts and may remain near its breeding grounds all year. A pair builds a nest in a tree, using sticks and pieces of oil palm, or repairs an old nest. The female lays 1 egg which is incubated for about 44 days.

Bateleur *Terathopius ecaudatus*

RANGE Africa, south of the Sahara, S.W. Arabia

HABITAT Savanna and plains

SIZE 22–28 in (55–70 cm)

Wingspan: 67–71 in (170–180 cm)

The most interesting bird in a group of birds of prey known as snake eagles or snake hawks, the bateleur has an unmistakable flight silhouette, with its exceptionally long wings and very short tail; its feet project beyond the tail tip in flight. Unlike other snake eagles, the bateleur feeds mostly on carrion, but also kills for itself. It makes fierce attacks on other carrion-feeding birds, robbing them of their spoils. A spectacular bird in flight, it soars effortlessly for hours and probably travels about 200 miles (320 km) every day. Once it gets aloft by means of rapid flapping, the bateleur makes scarcely a wing beat, and it performs aerobatic feats such as complete rolls.

Breeding pairs nest in trees and make compact, cup-shaped nests of sticks. A third adult is often present throughout the whole breeding cycle – an unusual occurrence in the bird world that has not been fully explained. The third adult does not incubate or visit the actual nest, but roosts nearby with the male and appears at the nest if an intruder troubles the parents. This habit may be a development of the tendency of juvenile and sub-adult birds to stay near the parents' nest during breeding. The single egg is normally incubated by the female for about 42 days. The young bird is particularly weak at first but has a long fledgling period, during which it is fed by both parents.

Crested Serpent Eagle

Spilornis cheela

RANGE India to S. China; S.E. Asia, Indonesia, Philippines

HABITAT Forest

SIZE 20–28 in (51–71 cm)

The crested serpent eagle is a variable species and the many races differ in size and plumage tones. The birds soar above the land, calling occasionally, but do not hunt in the air; they generally catch prey by dropping down on it from a perch. Like other snake eagles, the crested serpent eagle feeds mainly on reptiles, particularly tree snakes; its feet, with short, strong, roughsurfaced toes, are adapted for grasping its slippery prey.

A pair often remains together all year. In the breeding season, The birds perform flight displays, then build a small nest of sticks in a tree. The female incubates her 1 egg for about 35 days during which period the male supplies her with food.

African Harrier Hawk *Polyboroides typus*

RANGE Africa, south of the Sahara

HABITAT Forest, savanna, open grassland

SIZE 25 in (63 cm)

The African harrier hawk is a long-tailed, long-legged bird with a bare-skinned face. The young of other birds are its main source of food, although it also eats other creatures and the fruit of the oil palm. It clambers about on trees with great agility, searching for nests, and even hangs upside-down, with wings flapping, to attack pendulous weaverbird nests. The hawk's own nest is built in a tree, and both parents incubate the clutch of 1 to 5 eggs for about 40 days.

Hen/Northern Harrier *Circus cyaneus*

RANGE N. America, Eurasia

HABITAT Moors, marshes, plains

SIZE 17–20½ in (44–52 cm)

A widely distributed bird, the hen harrier breeds in North America, Europe and Asia, then migrates south of its breeding grounds in winter. There are 14 species of harrier, all in the genus *Circus*. All hunt by flying low over the ground, carefully searching the area for prey. Once a creature is spotted, the harrier drops down on it and kills it on the ground.

Hen harriers feed on small mammals, birds, including those wounded by hunters, and some reptiles, frogs and insects. A nest is made on the ground in marshy land or among low vegetation, and the average clutch contains 4 to 6 eggs. The female incubates the eggs and the male brings food, both during this period and after the chicks hatch.

Dark Chanting-goshawk *Melierax metabates*

RANGE W.C. and E. Africa; S. Arabia

HABITAT Bush, scrub

SIZE 15–19 in (38–48 cm)

The handsome dark chanting-goshawk perches on a vantage point in a tree or bush ready to glide swiftly down on a prey animal on the ground. The bird's long legs enable it to pursue quarry on the ground too, where it runs quickly, like a small secretary bird. Lizards, snakes and insects are the chief prey animals, but small mammals and ground birds are also caught.

At the onset of the breeding season, the male bird chants his melodious song in order to attract the female and the pair fly together over the breeding site. A small nest of sticks and mud is built in a tree, and the female lays 1 or 2 eggs.

The habits of the closely related pale chanting-goshawk, *M. canorus*, are almost identical.

HAWKS AND SECRETARY BIRD

Northern Goshawk

Accipiter gentilis

RANGE N. America, Europe, N. Asia, Turkey, Iran, Tibet, C.S. China, Japan

HABITAT Forest, woodland

SIZE 20–26 in (51–66 cm)
Wingspan: 47¼ in (120 cm)

These aggressive hawks are the largest birds in the genus *Accipiter* and are efficient killers. They fly through the forest, weaving skilfully in and out of trees, and sometimes soar over the treetops. They kill prey with a vicelike grip of the powerful talons, then pluck it (if a bird) and eat it on the ground. A goshawk is capable of killing birds as large as pheasant and grouse and mammals the size of rabbits and hares. The birds are often trained for falconry.

Goshawk pairs usually mate for life. They winter alone and in the spring meet at the breeding grounds where they perform flight displays. A new nest is made in a tree or an old nest is repaired. The pair roost together while nest-making and perform a screaming duet each day before sunrise. They mate about 10 times a day during the egg-laying period which lasts 6 to 8 weeks.

The clutch contains from 1 to 5 eggs, usually 3, but the number is affected by the availability of suitable prey. The female incubates the clutch for 36 to 38 days; the male brings her food and takes over occasionally. Some northern populations of goshawks migrate south after breeding.

Cooper's Hawk *Accipiter cooperii*

RANGE S. Canada, USA, N. Mexico

HABITAT Woodland

SIZE 14–20 in (36–51 cm)

Cooper's hawk is a medium-sized bird with rounded wings and tail. It is a typical *Accipiter* in its habits. It lives in the cover of woodland and ventures out to find prey. When hunting, Cooper's hawk usually perches to watch for prey, which it quickly swoops down and seizes unawares. Bobwhite quail, starlings, blackbirds, chipmunks and squirrels are common prey. The hawk also

pursues creatures on the ground, half running and half flying.

At the breeding site, the male defends a territory and, when a female appears he feeds her. Both then perform courtship flights. The clutch is usually 4 or 5 eggs, sometimes 6, and the female does most of the incubation. She helps the chicks to emerge from their shells and feeds and guards them closely in the first weeks of life. Some northern populations migrate south after breeding.

Black-collared Hawk *Busarellus nigricollis*

RANGE Tropical lowlands, Mexico to Paraguay and Argentina

HABITAT Open country near water

SIZE 18–20 in (46–51 cm)

A specialized hawk, the black-collared hawk has long, broad wings, a short, broad tail and a slightly hooked bill. The bottoms of its toes are covered with tiny prickly spines – an adaptation for catching and holding fish. In open areas the fishing buzzard can swoop down and catch its prey while scarcely wetting its plumage; elsewhere it will plunge into the water to fish, then sit drying its wings.

Common Buzzard *Buteo buteo*

RANGE Breeds in Europe, Asia to Japan; winters in E. Africa, India, Malaya and S. China

HABITAT Woodland, moorland

SIZE 20–22 in (51–56 cm)

The buzzard is not a bold hunter and spends more time perching than on the wing. Once aloft it soars well. It eats mainly small ground mammals, reptiles, insects, carrion and some ground birds. It kills most of its prey by dropping on it from its perch or from hovering flight and nearly always kills on the ground.

The size of the buzzard's breeding territory varies from year to year according to food supplies. The courtship flights are uncharacteristically energetic and the birds dive and swoop with great vigour. A nest is built on a tree or crag, and the female lays 2 to 6 eggs.

Red-tailed Hawk *Buteo jamaicensis*

RANGE North and Central America, West Indies

HABITAT Varied, deserts, forest, mountains

SIZE 18–24 in (46–61 cm)

A powerful, thickset, aggressive bird with a loud voice and a distinctive chestnut tail, the red-tailed hawk occupies a wide variety of habitats. It is an opportunistic hunter. Although its staple diet is rodents and rabbits, it also eats snakes, lizards, birds and insects. It hunts on the wing or from a perch, swooping down on prey.

Pairs display in the breeding territory. A nest is made of twigs high in a tree or cactus plant. The female stays on or near the nest for some weeks before laying 1 to 4 eggs. Her mate feeds her during this period. The pair share the incubation for 28 to 32 days.

Harpy Eagle *Harpia harpyja* **LR:nt**

RANGE S. Mexico to N. Argentina

HABITAT Lowland rain forest

SIZE 35½ in (90 cm)

The harpy is the world's largest eagle. It has huge feet (each the size of a man's hand), equipped with sharp talons. Its broad wings are relatively short. The harpy flies from tree to tree in search of prey, and can give chase through the branches with agility. Arboreal mammals, such as monkeys and opossums, are its main food. It may also catch large birds.

The harpy's nest is a platform of sticks high in the tallest trees, perhaps 150 ft (45 m) above the forest floor. The bird is believed to lay 2 eggs. The young birds stay with their parents for as long as a year, and pairs probably breed every other year. Now rare, harpy eagles have declined in numbers, largely due to destruction of their habitat and hunting by man.

Golden Eagle *Aquila chrysaetos*

RANGE Holarctic, as far south as N. Africa and Mexico

HABITAT Moor, mountain forest

SIZE 30–35 in (76–89 cm)

Golden eagles are probably the most numerous large eagles in the world. They have huge talons with long curved claws, a hooked bill and exceptionally sharp-sighted eyes. When hunting the golden eagle soars for long periods then dives to seize and kill the animal with its talons. Mammals such as hares and rabbits are the chief prey. Grouse and other birds are also caught, and carrion is an important food source.

Golden eagles perform spectacular flight displays over the nest site which is high on a ledge or tree. Some pairs have several nests, used in rotation. The 2 eggs are usually incubated by the female, but the male takes an occasional turn. In most cases, the first chick to hatch killed the younger one.

SAGITTARIIDAE: SECRETARY BIRD FAMILY

This family contains only 1 species, an eaglelike bird with a distinctive crest, long tail feathers and long legs.

Secretary Bird *Sagittarius serpentarius*

RANGE Africa, south of the Sahara

HABITAT Open, grassy country

SIZE 59 in (150 cm)

The secretary bird spends most of its time on the ground, walking with long strides, and may cover 30 km (20 miles) or so every day. It can run to catch prey which it takes with a swift thrust of its head; it kills larger animals by stamping on them. Small mammals, insects, some birds and eggs, reptiles, in fact almost anything crawling on the ground, are the secretary bird's prey.

In the breeding season, pairs are strongly territorial and chase intruders from their breeding range. The nest is usually on top of a tree and is made of sticks and turf, lined with grass and leaves. The female incubates the 2 or 3 eggs.

FALCONS

FALCONIDAE: FALCON FAMILY

The 63 species of falcon are all daytime-hunting birds of prey. They are found nearly all over the world. In appearance they are close to similar-sized accipiters, having sharp curved claws and powerful hooked beaks. Most species, however, have long pointed wings in contrast to the more rounded, slotted outlines of accipiters. There are also specific skeletal differences between the groups, such as details of skull structure and breastbones. Many falcons have so called "tomial" teeth – cutting edges on the upper bill with corresponding notches in the lower bill. Males and females look similar, but females are generally larger.

The family includes caracaras, laughing falcons, forest falcons, falconets, pygmy falcons and the typical falcons of the genus Falco, of which there are some 39 species. Falcons (except caracaras) do not build nests.

Crested Caracara
Polyborus plancus
RANGE S. USA; Central and South America
HABITAT Open country
SIZE 22–24 in (56–61 cm)

Caracaras are a group of neotropical birds quite unlike the rest of the falcons. They eat all kinds of animal food, from insects to mammals, and also scavenge on carrion.

Both members of a pair build the nest, usually in a tree or on the ground. The female lays 2 to 4 eggs, and both parents incubate them for 28 days and care for the young. The young remain in the nest for two or three months, being fed by their parents.

Barred Forest Falcon *Micrastur ruficollis*
RANGE S. Mexico to N. Argentina
HABITAT Forest
SIZE 13–15 in (33–38 cm)

One of a group of 6 neotropical forest falcons, the barred forest falcon is adapted for life in dense jungle. A long-legged, short-winged bird, it flies deftly through the trees and waits in cover to attack prey. It feeds on small mammals, lizards and birds and often hunts the birds that follow army ants. Little is known of its breeding habits.

Collared Falconet
Microhierax caerulescens
RANGE Himalayas, N. India, S.E. Asia
HABITAT Forest
SIZE 7½ in (19 cm)

The 5 species of falconet are the smallest birds of prey. All species have similar habits. The collared falconet hunts for its food more in the manner of a flycatcher than that of a true falcon; it makes short flights from a perch to catch insects and, occasionally, small birds. The female lays a clutch of 4 to 5 eggs in a hole in a tree.

Common Kestrel *Falco tinnunculus*
RANGE Europe, Asia, Africa
HABITAT Open country, plains, cultivated land
SIZE 13¼–15 in (34–38 cm)

Kestrels hunt over open ground and are the hovering specialists in the hawk family. They fly some 30 to 50 ft (10 to 15 m) above ground in order to search for prey over an area. They hover and watch and, if something is sighted, drop gently down on it. The staple diet of kestrels consists of small mammals, but they will also catch small birds, reptiles and insects.

The clutch of 4 to 9 eggs is laid on a ledge, in a hole in a tree or in the abandoned nest of another bird. The female does the greater share of the incubation which lasts between 27 and 29 days. She remains with the chicks when they are first hatched and the male brings food to her and the brood, but later she leaves the nest in order to assist her mate with hunting and feeding duties.

Eurasian Hobby

Falco subbuteo

RANGE Britain to China; winters in Africa and the Far East

HABITAT Open country, bush, savanna

SIZE 12–14 in (30–36 cm)

Hobbies are small, long-winged falcons found all over the world. All are exceedingly swift in flight and catch almost all of their prey on the wing. They are specialists in taking flying prey (such as birds, insects and bats) from among a swarm or flock and can even catch the aerially acrobatic swallows and swifts.

In the breeding season, pairs perform mutual aerobatic displays with great speed and agility. The 2 or 3 eggs are laid in an old abandoned nest of another bird and while the female does most of the incubation, her mate feeds her.

Brown Falcon *Falco berigora*

RANGE Australia, New Guinea, Tasmania, Dampier Island

HABITAT Open country

SIZE 15¾–20 in (40–51cm)

The brown falcon is one of the commonest birds of prey in Australia. Its appearance and behavior are more like those of an Accipiter hawk than a falcon, hence its name. Less active than other falcons, it spends much time perching, but is capable of swift flight. It kills prey on the ground, mammals such as rabbits, young birds, reptiles, insects and some carrion making up its diet. The female lays 2 to 4 eggs in the abandoned nest of another bird and both parents incubate the eggs.

Gyrfalcon *Falco rusticolus*

RANGE Arctic Europe, Asia, N. America, Greenland, Iceland

HABITAT Mountains, tundra, sea cliffs

SIZE 20–25 in (51–63 cm)

This impressive bird is the largest of the falcons. The gyrfalcon has a stockier build than the peregrine falcon. Plumage can be dark, white or gray. Most breed north of the treeline and remain in the Arctic all year, but some populations migrate south for the winter.

When hunting, the gyrfalcon flies swiftly near to the ground. It can make rapid dives in order to catch its prey, like the peregrine, but this is less characteristic in this species. Birds make up the majority of its prey, although it also feeds on some mammals, particularly in winter. Ptarmigan and willow grouse account for the bulk of the gyrfalcon's diet and as a consequence their numbers can in turn affect its breeding rate. In years when these prey birds are abundant, gyrfalcons produce large clutches, but in years of scarcity the female will lay only a couple of eggs or pairs will not breed at all.

Gyrfalcons perform display flights when courting. The female lays 2 to 7 eggs on a ledge or in an old cliff nest. She incubates the clutch for 27 to 29 days during which her mate supplies her with food. When the young hatch, both parents bring food to them.

Peregrine Falcon

Falco peregrinus

RANGE Almost worldwide

HABITAT Varied, often mountains and sea cliffs

SIZE 15–20 in (38–51 cm)

The 17 races of this widespread bird vary greatly in plumage color. The peregrine's wings are tapered and pointed and its tail is slim and short. The peregrine falcon is virtually without equal in the speed and precision of its flight. Birds are its chief prey. The peregrine makes a dramatic, high-speed, near-vertical dive at its prey, then kills it outright with its talons, or seizes it and takes it to the ground in order to feed. The peregrine can also chase prey through the air, changing direction with supreme ease. Because of its skills it is the most highly prized bird for falconry.

At the onset of the breeding season, peregrines perform spectacular flight displays as part of their courtship ritual. The 2 to 6 eggs are laid on a ledge site, on the ground or even on a city building. The female does most of the incubation, but the male takes an occasional turn and brings food for his mate.

When the young are about 2 weeks old the female begins to leave them alone in the nest in order to help the male to hunt for food for them. The young chicks begin to fly at about 40 days old.

These birds are seriously declining in numbers, partly because of poisoning through the incidental ingestion of pesticides, which reach them via the insect-feeding birds on which they in turn feed.

GREBES, TROPIC-BIRDS AND GANNETS

PODICIPEDIDAE: GREBE FAMILY

Twenty one species of these satin plumaged water birds are found scattered around the world; some species are widespread. They all breed in fresh water, usually making a nest of floating decaying vegetation. Like penguins, grebes are built as fast swimmers, with legs set well back on the body. Large grebes are highly streamlined birds which chase and catch fish under water with their long pointed beaks. Other species feed on bottom-feeding mollusks and are smaller and more compact with stubby thick bills. Males and females look similar in most species, while juveniles have striped heads and necks.

Little Grebe *Tachybaptus ruficollis*

RANGE Europe, Africa and Madagascar, Asia, Indonesia, New Guinea

HABITAT Lakes, ponds, rivers

SIZE 10½ in (27 cm)

The little grebe is one of the smaller grebes and is rotund and ducklike in shape. It feeds on insects, crustaceans and mollusks. In winter its plumage is gray brown and white, but in the breeding season it has a reddish throat and foreneck. The female lays 2 to 10 eggs in a floating clump of vegetation in shallow water or among aquatic plants. Both parents incubate the clutch for a total of 23 to 25 days.

Great Crested Grebe *Podiceps cristatus*

RANGE Europe, Asia, Africa, south of the Sahara; Australia, New Zealand

HABITAT Lakes, ponds, rivers, coastal waters

SIZE 20 in (51 cm)

Easily recognized on water by its long slender neck and daggerlike bill, the great crested grebe is rarely seen on land

(where it moves awkwardly) or in flight. It feeds mainly on fish, which it catches by diving from the surface of the water. The great crested is one of the largest grebes; adults are particularly striking in their breeding plumage, when they sport a double horned crest on the head and frills on the neck. In winter the crest is much reduced, the frills lost and the head largely white. The sexes look alike, but males generally have longer bills and larger crests and frills. Before mating, the grebes perform an elegant courtship dance. Both partners perform head-wagging and reed-holding displays and other ritualized movements. They mate on a reed platform near the nest, which is among the reeds. The female lays 2 to 7 eggs which are incubated by both parents for 27 to 29 days.

PHAETHONTIDAE: TROPICBIRD FAMILY

Tropicbirds are elegant seabirds easily distinguished by their two long central tail feathers. The 3 species in the family occur in tropical oceans, where they fly far out to sea and breed on islands. They are poor swimmers and tend to hunt by hovering above the water, then plunging down to seize the prey. Fish, squid and crustaceans are their main food. The sexes look alike.

Red-tailed Tropicbird
Phaethon rubricauda

RANGE Indian and Pacific Oceans

HABITAT Oceanic

SIZE Body: 16 in (41 cm) Tail: 20 in (51 cm)

The red-tailed tropicbird, with its dark red tail feathers, is a particularly striking species; in the breeding season, the bird's white plumage takes on a rosy tinge. Tropicbirds move awkwardly on land, so they tend to nest on ledges or cliffs where they are in a position for easy takeoff.

Although usually solitary at sea, they are numerous at breeding grounds and fight over nest sites and partners. No actual nest is made; the single egg is laid on the ground. Both parents incubate the egg for about 42 days and feed the downy chick until it leaves the nest at 12 to 15 weeks.

SULIDAE: GANNET FAMILY

The 9 birds in this family fall into two distinct groups – the 6 species of booby and the 3 species of gannet. They occur in all the oceans of the world: the boobies in tropical and subtropical areas, and the gannets generally in temperate zones. All are impressive marine birds that feed by plunge-diving for prey. Most have stout bodies, long pointed wings and short legs.

Male and female generally look alike, occasionally differing in bill and foot color. Juveniles have brownish feathers at first and develop the adult plumage over a few years.

Brown Booby *Sula leucogaster*

RANGE Tropical Atlantic and Pacific Oceans

HABITAT Mostly coastal

SIZE 29½–31½ in (75–80 cm)

Boobies were apparently given their common name because of their folly in allowing sailors to approach and kill them for food. Like gannets, boobies plunge-dive for fish and squid but specialize in feeding in shallow water and in the catching of flyingfish. The brown booby stays nearer to the coast than the gannet and breeds on cliffs and rocks or even on beaches and coral reefs. The female lays 1 or 2 eggs in a hollow on the ground or among rocks and both parents share the incubation and feeding duties.

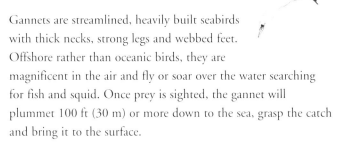

Northern Gannet *Morus bassanus*

RANGE North Atlantic Ocean

HABITAT Coastal waters

SIZE 34–39½ in (87–100 cm)

Gannets are streamlined, heavily built seabirds with thick necks, strong legs and webbed feet. Offshore rather than oceanic birds, they are magnificent in the air and fly or soar over the water searching for fish and squid. Once prey is sighted, the gannet will plummet 100 ft (30 m) or more down to the sea, grasp the catch and bring it to the surface.

The bird's stout bill and specially adapted skull, with resilient, air-filled spaces, take much of the initial impact of these expert dives. Other adaptations perfect gannets for marine life. First, there are no external nostrils. The nostril openings are covered by bony flaps so that water cannot be forced into them when the bird dives. The rear edge of the upper bill bows outward so that the gannet can breathe. Second, salt glands above the eye orbits produce a concentrated salt solution which enters the mouth by the internal nostrils and drips away from the beak, and this enables the gannet to feed on salty fish and to drink seawater without having to excrete vast quantities of urine in order to eliminate the salt.

Gannets are extremely gregarious birds, breeding in colonies of thousands of birds on rocks and islands. Attempts to breed gannets in small groups have failed, and it could be that the social stimulation of the colony is a crucial factor for breeding success. The birds display to establish and maintain pair bonds, and each pair occupies and defends a breeding territory. Nests are so closely packed that incubating birds can reach out and touch one another. The female lays 1 egg which both parents incubate for 43 to 45 days.

ANHINGAS AND CORMORANTS

ANHINGIDAE: DARTER FAMILY

These superb underwater fish-hunters look much like streamlined cormorants, but they have longer more slender necks and sharply pointed bills. Also known as anhingas, the 4 species of darter are found in a variety of freshwater habitats throughout the tropics.

There are some differences in the plumage of males and females, and males have light plumes on head and neck in the breeding season.

anhinga often swims with all but its head and sinuous neck submerged – hence its other common name "snake bird". Crustaceans, amphibians and insects also form part of the anhinga's diet.

Anhingas are colonial breeders, often nesting near other large water birds. They build nests in a tree near or overhanging water. The female lays 3 to 6 eggs which both partners incubate.

Anhinga *Anhinga anhinga*

RANGE S. USA to Argentina

HABITAT Lakes, rivers

SIZE 35 in (90 cm)

Anhingas dive deep in pursuit of fish, keeping their wings in at their sides and paddling with their feet. While under water, the bird keeps its long neck folded in, ready to dart out and impale prey on its sharp beak. The edges of the beak are serrated providing a firm grip on the fish. At the water surface, the

PHALACROCORACIDAE: CORMORANT FAMILY

There are about 38 species of these mainly black, medium-sized water birds. Typically, cormorants have long necks and bodies, wings of moderate length, short legs and large webbed feet. Male and female resemble each other with small plumage differences in the breeding season. All cormorants are specialist fish-eaters and are found in marine and freshwater habitats. They are coastal birds, rarely seen over open sea. They swim well and dive from the surface to catch prey. In flight, their necks are fully extended, and they often fly in lines or V-formations.

Cormorants are gregarious birds. They nest colonially and defend small nest territories. After feeding excursions they rest on rocks, trees or cliffs, often with their wings, which quickly become waterlogged when diving, spread out to dry.

Great Cormorant *Phalacrocorax carbo*

RANGE E. North America, Europe, Africa, Asia, Australia

HABITAT Coasts, marshes, lakes

SIZE 31–39¼ in (80–100 cm)

Also sometimes known as the black cormorant, this bird is the largest species in its family and the most widely distributed. Habitats and nesting sites vary greatly over its enormous range. Male and female birds look alike, but the breeding male acquires some white feathers on his head and neck and a white patch on each flank. Immature birds have brownish plumage with pale underparts.

Cormorants feed primarily on fish, but they will also eat crustaceans and amphibians. Prey is caught underwater during dives which last between 20 and 30 seconds. This bird swims by using its webbed feet for propulsion and its long tail as a rudder. Most prey is brought back up to the surface and shaken before being swallowed.

Breeding pairs make their nests in trees or on the ground, inland or on the coast, depending on the situation in their particular range. The usual clutch is 3 or 4 eggs. Both parents incubate the eggs and feed the chicks. The chicks make their first flight about 50 days after hatching, but are not completely independent for another 12 to 13 weeks.

Long-tailed Cormorant *Phalacrocorax africanus*

RANGE Africa, Madagascar

HABITAT Rivers, lagoons

SIZE 23 in (58 cm)

One of four small, long-tailed, shorter necked cormorants, the reed cormorant is primarily an inland water bird but it is also found on the west coast of southern Africa. The male and female generally look alike, but in the breeding season the male's plumage darkens and he develops a tuft of feathers on the forehead and white plumes on face and neck. Young birds are brown and yellowish-white.

Reed cormorants feed on fish and some crustaceans, which they catch under water by diving from the surface. Like other cormorants, they return to the surface in order to consume their prey. During the breeding season, reed cormorants build their nests on the ground or in trees, and the female lays a clutch of 2 to 4 eggs.

Flightless Cormorant *Phalacrocorax harrisi* **VU**

RANGE Galápagos Islands

HABITAT Coastal waters

SIZE 36–39 in (91–99 cm)

This species occurs only on two islands in the Galápagos islands. It is a large bird and moves clumsily on land, but is superbly agile in the water. It has lost all power of flight and its wings have shrunk to tiny, useless appendages with only a few flight feathers remaining.

There are no mammalian predators in the Galápagos so, unlike its fellow cormorants, this species has no need to fly in order to escape from danger. The stable climate of their habitat also means that there is no need for these birds to move south in winter or to travel great distances in search of food. The flightless cormorant is able to catch all of the food that it needs in the nutrient-rich waters around the island coasts and octopus make up a large part of its diet.

The flightless cormorant breeds all year round with a peak between March and September. Both partners share the incubation duties, making a ritual presentation of a strand of seaweed as they swap over on the nest. Birds may produce several clutches of young each year. However, the population of the flightless cormorant is small and they are now rare.

HERONS

ARDEIDAE: HERON FAMILY

The 65 species of heron, bittern and egret in this family are all moderate to large birds with slim bodies, long necks and legs, and large, broad wings. Male and female look alike in most species. All herons have patches of powder-down feathers on the breast and rump – a feature probably associated with their mucus-laden diet of fish and amphibians. The powder produced by these specialized feathers is utilized in preening in order to remove slime from the plumage.

Herons hunt in water of varying depth, either while standing motionless or while wading. Prey is grasped (rather than impaled) with the powerful, dagger-shaped beak. Herons usually breed in colonies. During the breeding season, many species undergo changes of plumage color and develop long plumes on the head or back.

American Bittern *Botaurus lentiginosus*
RANGE C. North America; winters in S.USA, Central America
HABITAT Marshland
SIZE 26 in (66 cm)

The American bittern has a distinctive cry, which is rather different from the characteristic boom of other bittern species. This strange, three-syllable cry has inspired one of the bird's common names – "thunder pumper".

This bittern feeds alone, moving slowly and deliberately with bill always at the ready to jab quickly at fish, crabs, snakes, frogs, insects or small mammals.

It is a migratory species; although birds in milder areas do not actually migrate, they do disperse after breeding.

The clutch of between 4 and 6 eggs is laid in a nest platform on land or in water, and the female bird seems to perform most of the parental duties.

Black-crowned Night Heron *Nycticorax nycticorax*
RANGE Europe, Asia, Africa, North and South America
HABITAT Varied, usually near marshes
SIZE 24 in (61 cm)

Probably the most numerous of all herons, the night heron is a stocky bird with white ribbonlike plumes extending from the back of its head; these are erected in courtship display. This bird feeds mainly at night and at dusk, it preys on fish, reptiles, frogs and insects and also raids the nests of other birds.

At the beginning of the breeding season, the male finds a nest site, usually among reeds or in a bush or a tree which he then uses as a base for his displays. His mate finishes the building of the nest and lays 3 to 5 eggs. Both parents feed and care for the chicks.

Gray Heron *Ardea cinerea*
RANGE Europe, Asia, Africa
HABITAT Varied, near shallow water
SIZE 36 in (92 cm)

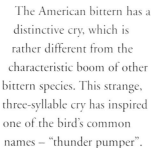

A large, long-legged, long-billed bird, the gray heron is familiar throughout most of the Old World except Australia. Its New World equivalent, the great blue heron, *A. herodias*, is similar, but slightly larger, with reddish coloring on neck and thighs. The gray heron eats fish, eels, young birds, eggs, snakes and plants. It fishes from the land, with its head stretched forward, or wades in shallows. The bird grasps its prey with a swift, lethal thrust of the bill.

Gray herons breed in colonies, the female lays 3 to 5 eggs, and both parents feed the young.

Cattle Egret *Bubulcus ibis*

RANGE Iberia, Africa, Asia, Indonesia,
North and South America, Australia
HABITAT Open land,
drier than the habitat of most herons
SIZE 19⁄ in (50 cm)

The cattle egret is an extremely successful species and has expanded its range all over the world. Its success is partly due to its association with herbivorous animals. The birds follow large grazing animals, wild or domesticated, and catch the insects, particularly grasshoppers, disturbed by them. Cattle egrets feeding in this way gain about 50 per cent more food for less effort than birds feeding by other methods. The cattle do not really benefit from the association, since cattle egrets do not remove parasites; they may, however, be warned of approaching danger by the birds. Cattle egrets have now learned that the same results can be achieved by following farm machinery. In water the egrets feed on frogs and fish.

The male gathers material for the nest and the female builds it, usually in a small tree. The pair copulate on the nest and the female lays a clutch of between 2 and 5 eggs.

Black Heron *Egretta ardesiaca*

RANGE Africa, south of the Sahara,
Madagascar
HABITAT Swamps,
mangroves, mud-flats
SIZE 18⁄–19⁄ in (48–50 cm)

Physically, the black heron is much like a black-plumaged version of an egret, but it is well known for its odd feeding method. The heron stands in shallow waters, bill pointing downward, and spreads its wings in a circle, forming a canopy over its head. Specialized broad flight feathers aid the effectiveness of the canopy. The exact purpose of this behavior is not known, but it has been suggested that fish are attracted to the apparent shelter of the patch of shade that is formed, thus making them easy prey for the heron. Fish must also be more easily visible within the canopy's shade. When young birds first begin to fish they make one-winged canopies. The canopy posture is also used in the courtship display. Black herons build a nest from twigs above the water in a tree or bush. The clutch usually contains 3 or 4 eggs.

Great Egret

Casmerodius alba
RANGE Almost worldwide;
absent from much of Europe
HABITAT Shallow water
SIZE 35–47 in (90–120 cm)

This egret, also sometimes known as the American egret, is one of the most widespread of its family. Non-breeding and immature birds have yellow bills, but as the breeding season approaches, the adult's bill becomes mostly black. It finds its food – fish, mollusks, insects, small mammals, birds and plants – either by standing and waiting in the water or by slowly stalking its prey. The nest is made in a tree or reed bed, and the female lays 2 to 5 eggs. Both parents incubate the clutch in shifts for a total of 25 or 26 days.

Boat-billed Heron *Cochlearius cochlearius*

RANGE Mexico to Bolivia, N. Argentina
HABITAT Swamps and wetlands
SIZE 17⁄–19⁄ in (45–50 cm)

The only important distinction of the boat-billed heron from other herons is the broad, scooplike bill. Boat-billed herons generally feed at night on fish and shrimps. The bill seems to be extremely sensitive and opens at the merest touch, drawing in water and prey; it is also used with a scooping action.

These birds perform bill-clattering and preening displays, accompanied by vocal signals, at mating time. They nest alone or in groups in trees and bushes. The female lays a clutch of 2 to 4 eggs which both parents incubate.

HAMMERKOP, FLAMINGOS, IBISES AND PELICANS

SCOPIDAE: HAMMERKOP FAMILY

The single species in this family has been the subject of much dispute as to its classification.

Hammerkop *Scopus umbretta*
RANGE Africa, Madagascar, Middle East
HABITAT Tree-lined streams
SIZE 19½ in (50 cm)

The hammerkop gets its common name from the resemblance of its head in profile – with its long, heavy, slightly hooked bill and backward-pointing crest – to a hammer. In flight the hammerkop holds its neck slightly curved back. Male and female birds look alike.

Hammerkops are generally active at dusk and feed on amphibians, fish, insects and crustaceans. They live in pairs and build remarkable nests – elaborate roofed structures of sticks and mud, measuring up to 6 ft (1.8 m) across placed in the branches of trees. The female lays 3 to 6 eggs, and both parents care for the downy young.

PHOENICOPTERIDAE: FLAMINGO FAMILY

There are 5 species of flamingo. All are tall, pinkish-white birds with long necks, large wings and short tails. Their toes are short and webbed. All swim and fly well; the neck and legs are extended in flight. Males and females look alike. Huge numbers of flamingos live and breed in colonies: in Africa, a colony of lesser flamingos, *P. minor*, may number a million or more individuals. They are irregular breeders and may only breed successfully every two or three years.

Flamingos feed in the water, filtering out minute food particles with their highly specialized bills.

Greater Flamingo *Phoenicopterus ruber*
RANGE Caribbean, Galápagos Islands, S. Europe, S.W. Asia, E., W., and N. Africa
HABITAT Lagoons, lakes
SIZE 49–57 in (125–145 cm)

The greater flamingo has an air of frivolous fantasy, but in fact, it is perfectly adapted for its way of life. The long legs enable it to stand in shallow water while it filter-feeds with the strangely shaped bill. The flamingo holds its bill so that it lies horizontally beneath the water, the upper half below the lower. Water flows into the bill and, by movements of the large, fleshy tongue, is pushed through hairlike lamellae which sieve out food particles before the water is expelled again at the sides of the bill. Flamingos feed on mollusks, crustaceans, insects, fish and minute aquatic plants.

The nest is a mound of mud which the female scrapes together with her bill. She lays 1 or 2 eggs in a shallow depression at the top of the mound. The young birds are dependent on their parents for food until their filtering mechanism develops and they are able to fly – about 65 to 70 days.

THRESKIORNITHIDAE: IBIS FAMILY

Ibises and spoonbills are medium-sized wading birds. The typical family member has a moderately long neck, long wings, short tail and toes webbed at the base. Male and female look more or less alike. In some species the face or even the whole head and neck is unfeathered. All ibises fly well, with neck extended. There are about 28 species of ibis, all with long curved bills, and 6 species of spoonbill, with broad spatulate bills. Most are gregarious birds. Northern species are migratory.

Glossy Ibis *Plegadis falcinellus*
RANGE Temperate and tropical Eurasia, Indonesia, Australia, Africa, West Indies, Caribbean
HABITAT Marshes, lakes
SIZE 21¼–25½ in (55–65 cm)

The glossy ibis is the most widespread member of the family. It feeds on insects and small aquatic life. The female lays 3 or 4 eggs in a nest in a tree or reed bed. Both parents incubate the eggs and care for the young. The range and numbers of this species have been reduced by the drainage of marshland.

PELECANIDAE: PELICAN AND SHOEBILL FAMILY

The pelicans, which give this order its name, comprise 8 species found in large lakes and on sea coasts; there is a single species of shoebill in a separate subfamily. Pelicans are gregarious, strong-flying birds which feed on fish, caught while the birds are swimming in shallow water or, in one case, by diving from the air. The most dramatic anatomical feature is the huge gular pouch beneath the long broad bill. Males and females look alike.

Shoebill *Balaeniceps rex* **LR:nt**
RANGE E. C. Africa
HABITAT Marshes
SIZE 46 in (117 cm)

The shoebill was formerly placed in a family of its own, but is now included with pelicans. It is a large bird, its most obvious feature being a large shovellike bill with a hooked tip. The bird seems to use this bill for searching out food – fish, frogs, snakes, mollusks and carrion – in the mud of its marshland home.

A solitary, nocturnal bird, the shoebill can fly well and even soar, holding its neck drawn in, pelican-fashion. It lays 2 eggs on the ground in a nest made of rushes and grass.

Great White Pelican *Pelecanus onocrotalus*
RANGE S.E. Europe, Asia, Africa
HABITAT Inland lakes, marshes
SIZE 55–69 in (140–175 cm)

The pelican is well adapted for aquatic life. The short strong legs and webbed feet propel it in water and aid takeoff from the water surface. Once aloft pelicans are powerful fliers and often travel in spectacular V-formation groups. The pelican's bill pouch is simply a scoop. As the pelican pushes its bill under water the lower bill bows out, creating a large pouch which fills with water and fish. As the bird lifts its head the pouch contracts, forcing out the water, but retaining the fish. A group of 6 to 8 pelicans will gather in a horseshoe formation in the water to feed together. They dip their bills in unison, creating a circle of open pouches, ready to trap every fish in the area.

Pelicans breed together in large colonies. The female lays 2 to 4 eggs in a nest of sticks in a tree or on the grass. The young are cared for by both parents.

Brown Pelican *Pelecanus occidentalis*
RANGE USA, Caribbean, S. America, Galápagos Islands
HABITAT Coasts
SIZE 50 in (127 cm)

The brown pelican is the smallest pelican and is rather different from the rest of its family. It is a seabird and catches fish by diving into the water from as high as 50 ft (15 m). When it dives, it holds the wings back and the neck curved into an S-shape, so that the front of the body, which is provided with cushioning air sacs, takes some of the impact of the plunge into the water. The bird generally returns to the surface to eat its catch.

The female brown pelican lays 2 or 3 eggs in a nest built in a tree or on the ground.

NEW WORLD VULTURES AND STORKS

CICONIIDAE: NEW WORLD VULTURE AND STORK FAMILY

This order contains two subfamilies – the New World vultures and the storks.

CATHARTINAE: NEW WORLD VULTURE SUBFAMILY

There are 7 species of New World vultures and condors, with a geographical range from Tierra del Fuego and the Falkland Islands to as far north as southern Canada. The cathartid vultures are superficially similar to Old World vultures, but are in fact, a quite distinct group with close affinity to the storks. None the less, like the Old World vultures, these birds feed on carrion and their unfeathered heads and necks enable them to plunge into messy carcasses without soiling their plumage. The feet, with long toes and weakly hooked claws, are adapted for perching rather than grasping. Vultures and condors are solitary birds, although some do roost in colonies. Nests are usually made in hollow trees. Males and females look alike.

King Vulture
Sarcoramphus papa
RANGE Mexico to Argentina
HABITAT Tropical forest, savanna
SIZE 31 in (79 cm)

The king is a medium-sized vulture with broad wings and tail. The featherless skin on its head is marked with extraordinary, garish patterns. The king vulture is reputed to kill live animals, but it feeds mainly on carrion. As its name suggests, this large, big-billed bird takes precedence over other vultures at carcasses. Carrion can be hard to spot in the dense tropical forest so the king vulture is one of the few birds that relies heavily on its sense of smell in order to detect food. Stranded fish on river banks are an important food item.

The breeding habits of this vulture are poorly known, but in one observation an egg was laid in a hollow tree stump and incubated by both parents. Young king vultures in their first full plumage have black feathers. The brilliant facial markings and creamy plumage develop over the first 2 years.

California Condor *Gymnogyps californianus* **CR**
RANGE USA: California
HABITAT Mountains
SIZE 45–55 in (114–140 cm)

One of the largest birds in the world this immense vulture is also one of the heaviest flying birds at over 25 lb (11 kg). The range of this bird was once much larger, but the population has declined drastically because of the destruction of its habitat and the onslaught of hunters, and the species is now probably on the verge of extinction. The condor is fully protected under the United States Endangered Species Act and by California law. There is a captive breeding program as a last attempt to save the species.

A spectacular bird in flight, with its extremely long, broad wings, the California condor soars at great heights and can glide as far as 10 miles (16 km) without wing movements. It must have the right air conditions for soaring and may stay at its roost in bad weather or on calm days. The California condor spends at least 15 hours a day at the roosting area, and out of the breeding season, roosting and foraging are its main activities. It feeds on carrion, mostly large animals, and is not known to attack living creatures.

At the start of the breeding season the male displays to his prospective mate. The female lays her egg on the ground in a cave or hole in a cliff. Both parents incubate in shifts. The young bird is fed and tended by the parents for over a year; thus California condors can breed only every other year.

Turkey Vulture *Cathartes aura*

RANGE Temperate and tropical North and South America, Falkland Islands

HABITAT Plains, desert, forest

SIZE 26–52 in (66–132 cm)

Also known as the turkey buzzard, this most widespread New World vulture soars high over open country in search of carrion. It feeds on waste of all sorts, including sea lion excrement, rotten fruit and vegetables and small carrion. Turkey vultures have been trapped and destroyed by man in many parts of their range because they are mistakenly believed to carry anthrax and other diseases of livestock. They are, however, pests on some Peruvian guano islands where they take eggs and young birds.

At night groups of 30 or more birds roost together, but this is really the only time that turkey vultures are social.

No real nest is made at breeding time; the female lays her clutch of 2 eggs in a cave or in a hollow log on the ground. Both parents incubate the eggs and care for the young.

CICONIINAE: STORK SUBFAMILY

Storks are large, long legged birds with elongated necks and long broad wings. Although their feet are webbed at the base, a feature which tends to denote aquatic habits, storks feed in drier areas than most other members of their order. They are strong fliers and look particularly striking in the air, with neck and legs stretched out, the legs trailing down slightly. Males and females look alike. There are 19 species, all but 3 of which are found in the Old World. Northern populations are migratory.

White Stork *Ciconia ciconia*

RANGE E. Europe, W. and S. Asia; winters in Africa, India and S. Asia

HABITAT Forest and near human habitation

SIZE 39–45 in (100–115 cm); 4 ft (1.2 m) tall

Legend has it that the white stork brings babies, and for this reason these birds have always been popular and protected to some degree. They are gregarious birds and tolerant of human habitation. Storks feed mostly on frogs, reptiles, insects and mollusks. The nest is a huge structure of sticks which the stork builds up in a tree or on a building. The female lays a clutch of between 1 and 7 eggs which both parents incubate.

Although they are not vocal birds, white storks perform a greeting ceremony, making bill-clattering sounds as they change shifts at the nest. In doing so, they turn their heads round over their backs thus turning away their bills – or weapons. This action, in direct contrast to their bill-forward threat display, appeases any aggression between the partners.

In winter white storks migrate south. Most go to Africa by way of Gibraltar or Istanbul, so avoiding long journeys over open sea for which their particular type of soaring flight is not well-suited.

Asian Openbill *Anastomus oscitans*

RANGE India to S.E. Asia

HABITAT Inland waters

SIZE 32 in (81 cm); 24 in (61 cm) tall

The openbill, as its name suggests, has a remarkably adapted bill. There is a gap between the mandibles which meet only at the tips. This feature, which develops gradually and is not present in juvenile birds, seems to be an adaptation for holding the large, slippery water snails on which the birds predominantly feed.

Openbills are more aquatic than most storks but still make their nests in trees. The female lays 3 to 6 eggs which are incubated by both parents. The African openbill, *A. iamelligerus*, has the same bill shape.

FRIGATEBIRDS, PENGUINS AND DIVERS

FREGATIDAE: FRIGATEBIRD FAMILY

Frigatebirds are the most aerial of all water birds and are graceful and spectacular in flight. They soar over huge oceanic distances. These large birds have long, pointed wings and long forked tails. All 5 species inhabit tropical and subtropical areas. Females are generally larger than males and have white breasts and sides. Males have bright-red throat pouches which they inflate in their courtship displays.

Magnificent Frigatebird *Fregata magnificens*
RANGE Central America; South America; Galápagos Islands
HABITAT Coastal waters, islands, bays, estuaries
SIZE 37–43 in (95–110 cm) Wingspan: 85–96 in (215–245 cm)

The frigatebird has a particularly large and splendid throat pouch and the greatest wing area, relative to body size, of any bird. It eats chiefly fish, squid, crustaceans and jellyfish, which it catches by swooping down to the water surface. It rarely alights on the sea. Frigatebirds supplement their diet by stealing fish from other birds. Having spotted a homecoming booby or other seabird, the frigatebird gives chase and forces its quarry to regurgitate its catch, which it then grabs in midair.

The nest of the magnificent frigatebird is a flimsy construction of sticks. The female lays a single egg which both parents incubate. Both feed and care for the chick for about 7 weeks. Both parents feed the chick until it can fly at 4 or 5 months old and feed it occasionally for some weeks more.

SPHENISCIDAE: PENGUIN FAMILY

Penguins are primitive and highly specialized marine birds. All 17 species are flightless and exquisitely adapted for marine existence. Their wings are modified into flat unfoldable paddles, which are used to propel them rapidly underwater in pursuit of fish and squid. Feathers are short and glossy and form a dense furlike mat which is waterproof, streamlined and a superb insulating layer. Their short legs, with webbed feet, are set far back to act as rudders, but this position means that the birds must stand upright on land or slide along on their bellies.

Penguins usually come ashore only to breed and molt; the rest of the year is spent entirely at sea. All forms, except the Galápagos penguin, breed on the Antarctic continent, subantarctic islands or the southern coasts of South America, southern Africa and Australia, often in extremely harsh conditions.

Little Penguin *Eudyptula minor*
RANGE New Zealand, Tasmania, S. Australia
HABITAT Coastal waters
SIZE 15¼ in (40 cm) tall

The smallest penguin, the little blue penguin, lives around coasts and islands in its range, seeking food in shallow waters. Birds tend to return to the same nesting sites and to the same mates. A brief courtship re-establiscolore pair bond. This species nests in a crevice or a burrow. The females lays 2 eggs, which both parents incubate for between 33 and 40 days.

Emperor Penguin *Aptenodytes forsteri*

RANGE Antarctic coasts

HABITAT Ocean and pack ice

SIZE 4 ft (1.2 m) tall

Emperor penguins, largest of the penguin family, endure the worst breeding conditions of any bird. These penguins never come to land, but gather in huge colonies on the Antarctic pack ice in order to breed.

After pairing, the female lays 1 egg at the beginning of winter and returns to the sea. Her partner incubates the egg on his feet, where it is protected by a flap of skin and feathers. The males huddle together for warmth and protection during their vigil in the cold and dark. The male fasts for the 64-day incubation period.

When the chick is born, the male feeds it from secretions in his crop and the chick remains protected on his feet. By this time the ice is breaking up and the female returns in order to take over caring for the young while the male recovers and feeds.

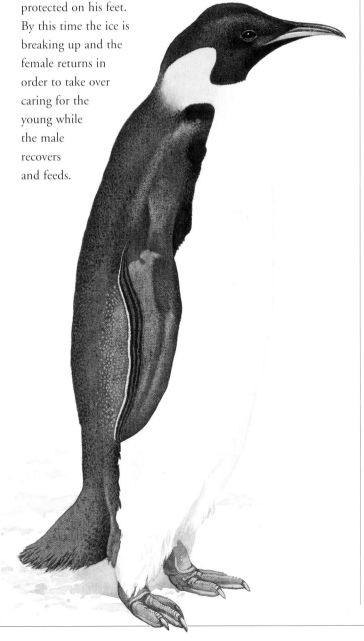

Galápagos Penguin

Spheniscus mendiculus **VU**

RANGE Galápagos Islands

HABITAT Coastal waters

SIZE 20 in (51 cm) tall

This rare penguin is the only species to venture near the Equator. The cool waters of the Humboldt Current bathe the Galápagos islands, making them habitable for a cold-loving penguin. The current is rich in nutrients, supplying plenty of food. The birds breed from May to July, making nests of stones in caves or crevices on the coast. Two eggs are laid.

GAVIIDAE: DIVER FAMILY

Divers, or loons, are foot-propelled diving birds. All 5 species live in the high latitudes of the northern hemisphere and are the ecological counterparts of grebes in those areas. The birds feed primarily on fish, which they chase and seize under water. Males and females look alike.

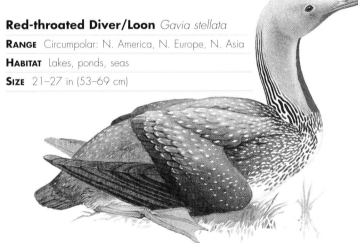

Red-throated Diver/Loon *Gavia stellata*

RANGE Circumpolar: N. America, N. Europe, N. Asia

HABITAT Lakes, ponds, seas

SIZE 21–27 in (53–69 cm)

The red-throated diver has a thin grebelike bill and a reddish throat patch at breeding time; in winter its back is spotted with white and its head is gray and white. The red-throated diver flies strongly and, because it is smaller than other species, takes off relatively easily. After a courtship display of bill-dipping and diving, 1 to 3 eggs are laid in a heap of moss or other vegetation, or in a shallow dip in the ground. The parents share the incubation of the clutch for 24 to 29 days and feed the young.

PETRELS

PROCELLARIIDAE: PETREL ALBATROSS AND STORM PETREL FAMILY

This family contains three subfamilies – petrels, albatrosses and storm petrels. All are totally marine birds with webbed feet and hooked beaks surmounted by elongated tubular nostrils. About 115 species of these "tubenoses" are distributed around the oceans of the world.

Most species store stomach oil as a long-distance food reserve, this oil can also be discharged from the mouth or nostrils as a foul-smelling chemical defence mechanism. Typical species in this order have low reproductive rates, long periods of immaturity and tend to be long-lived.

PROCELLARIINAE: PETREL SUBFAMILY

This family, with about 80 species, is the largest group of tubenoses and contains birds such as petrels, shearwaters, fulmars, prions and diving petrels. Most species have long slender wings and short tails. Males and females of the species look alike. Representatives of the family occur in all oceans; most species are migratory. Except when breeding, these birds rarely come to land and spend most of their lives flying over the ocean. They are expert at flying through the most severe weather.

Within the family, species have become adapted to different feeding methods. Fulmars feed on plankton and scavenge around fishing fleets; prions filter planktonic animals from the water; the gadfly petrels (such as *Pterodroma* sp.) catch squid and octopus at night, and shearwaters are surface predators on fish.

Most species nest in burrows or rock crevices, although a few nest on cliff ledges or open ground. The female usually lays a single egg which both parents incubate in shifts of between 2 and 12 days. Petrels usually nest in colonies.

Diving petrels form a highly distinctive group of 4 tubenose birds within the petrel subfamily, all classified in a single genus: Pelecanoides. All species have a compact body form, with short neck, wings, legs and tail, and their overall appearance is similar to that of the auks (Alcinae). The similarities are linked to their shared basic feeding method – they dive from the air into the sea and use their short wings in order to swim under water in search of prey. Food items include crustaceans and small schooling fish such as anchovies.

Diving petrels fly with rapid wing beats. All species are found in the southern oceans and along the west coast of South America as far north as Peru.

Broad-billed Prion/Whale Bird
Pachyptila vittata

RANGE	Southern oceans
HABITAT	Oceanic
SIZE	12¼ in (31 cm)

The 6 species of prion, all in the genus *Pachyptila*, are similar in appearance and size and virtually indistinguishable at sea. The broad-billed prion is slightly larger than the others and can be identified by its markedly broader bill. It feeds on small planktonic animals, which it filters from the water through the hairlike fringes of lamellae at the sides of the bill. The birds often form huge feeding flocks in areas of plankton-rich water. Colonies of broad-billed prions breed in summer on islands in the South Atlantic, southern Indian Ocean and off New Zealand.

Manx Shearwater *Puffinus puffinus*

RANGE	Atlantic and Pacific Oceans, Mediterranean Sea
HABITAT	Oceanic and coastal
SIZE	11¾–15 in (30–38 cm)

There are several geographically distinct races of the Manx shearwater with slight plumage differences. Shearwaters feed by day, seizing fish, squid, crustaceans and debris at the water surface or diving in pursuit of prey. They have complex migration routes between feeding grounds and travel long distances. A shearwater, removed from its burrow in Britain and taken to the USA, returned home, a distance of about 2,800 miles (4,500 km) in 13 days. The birds nest in huge colonies on offshore islands. The female lays her egg in a burrow, and both parents care for the chick.

Northern Fulmar *Fulmarus glacialis*

RANGE N. Atlantic, N. Pacific Oceans

HABITAT Oceanic

SIZE 17¾–19½ in (45–50 cm)

Fulmars exploit the waste from commercial fishing and, with the spread of this industry, these large, robust petrels have dramatically increased their numbers. They swim but seldom dive, catching most of their food at the water surface. Male and female birds look alike, but the males have bigger bills. They nest on cliff ledges on coasts or islands; the female lays 1 egg, incubated by both parents. The adults feed the chick and defend it by spitting stomach oil at predators.

Mottled Petrel *Pterodroma inexpectata*

RANGE South and North Pacific to 55°N

HABITAT Oceanic

SIZE 14¼ in (36 cm)

The mottled petrel is a fairly small species with long narrow wings. Its flight is fast and it swoops and dives with great ease. Primarily a nocturnal bird, it feeds largely

on squid and octopus. It breeds on Stewart and Snares Islands near New Zealand and migrates north in winter to the western North Pacific. Like most petrels it lays only 1 egg.

Common Subantarctic Diving Petrel *Pelecanoides urinatrix*

RANGE S. Atlantic, Indian and Pacific Oceans

HABITAT Coastal waters

SIZE 7–8¼ in (18–21 cm)

This diving petrel, like its fellows, is a coastal rather than an oceanic seabird. It breeds, sometimes colonially, on South Atlantic islands, from the Falklands east to Australia and New Zealand. Breeding birds dig a burrow nest several feet long. The parents take turns incubating their 1 egg for a total of about 8 weeks, and they share the feeding of the chick. The chick leaves the nest when it is about 7 or 8 weeks old.

ALBATROSSES AND STORM PETRELS

DIOMEDEINAE: ALBATROSS SUBFAMILY

The 14 species of albatross are all large pelagic birds, noted for their spectacular gliding flight over vast ocean distances. Most occur in the southern hemisphere, but a few do live in the North Pacific. The birds have an unmistakable body form with extremely long narrow wings. The albatross bill is large and hooked. Male and female look alike in all species except the wandering albatross. Albatrosses feed on fish, squid and other marine animals which they catch at the surface of the water or just below it. Most species are migratory.

Wandering Albatross *Diomedea exulans* **VU**

RANGE Southern oceans, approximately 60°S to 250°S

HABITAT Oceanic

SIZE 43–54 in (110–135 cm) Wingspan: 114–127½ in (290–324 cm)

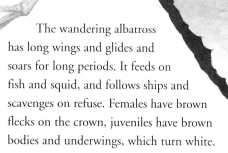

The wandering albatross has long wings and glides and soars for long periods. It feeds on fish and squid, and follows ships and scavenges on refuse. Females have brown flecks on the crown, juveniles have brown bodies and underwings, which turn white.

Wandering albatross land on subantarctic islands in the South Pacific, Indian and South Atlantic Oceans only to breed. The birds rattle their bills, touch bill-tips and spread their huge wings. The female lays 1 egg which is incubated for about 80 days by both parents then the chick is fed intermittently for about a year. This means that the birds can breed only every other year.

Light-mantled Sooty Albatross *Phoebetria palpebrata*

RANGE Southern oceans to about 330°S

HABITAT Oceanic

SIZE 28 in (72 cm)

The small, graceful light-mantled sooty albatross is able to maneuver well in the air. It breeds on Antarctic and subantarctic islands and makes a neat cup-shaped nest of plant material. The female lays 1 egg, and both parents care for the chick for a few months.

HYDROBATINAE: STORM PETREL SUBFAMILY

These small seabirds occur in most oceans, mainly south of the Arctic Circle. There are about 21 species which divide into 2 groups – those of the northern and southern hemispheres. Their ranges overlap in the tropics. Northern birds have short legs, long pointed wings and forked tails. They feed by swooping and skimming low over the water. Southern birds have long slender legs, short rounded wings and square tails. They feed by "stepping" over the surface of the water with wings spread to seize food items.

All have black, or black and brown, plumage with white rump feathers. Males and females look alike and all have a distinctive musky smell. Most storm petrels are deep-water birds and come to land on remote islands only to breed. Breeding usually takes place in colonies and long-term pair bonds are the rule. Pairs return to the same nest year after year. They nest in crevices and burrows. Most migrate after breeding.

Black Storm Petrel

Oceanodroma melania

RANGE N.E. Pacific Ocean: California to Peru

HABITAT Coastal and offshore waters

SIZE 8–9 in (21–23 cm)

With its deeply forked tail, the black storm petrel is characteristic of the northern group of storm petrels, It is one of several species inhabiting the Pacific and eats plankton and the larvae of the spiny lobster. The black storm petrel breeds on islands off the coast of Baja California. A single egg is laid in a nest in a burrow or rock crevice.

European Storm Petrel

Hydrobates pelagicus

RANGE N.E. Atlantic Ocean, W. Mediterranean Sea

HABITAT Oceanic

SIZE 5½–7 in (14–18 cm)

This is the smallest European seabird and one of the 3 Atlantic species of storm petrel. It eats fish, squid and crustaceans and often follows ships to feed on their waste. It lands only in the breeding season, to nest in remote coastal areas. The female lays 1 egg in a burrow or in a hole on a cliff-face. Both parents incubate the egg. In winter storm petrels fly south to the Red Sea and the west coast of Africa.

Wilson's Storm Petrel *Oceanites oceanicus*

RANGE Antarctic, Atlantic and Indian Oceans

HABITAT Oceanic

SIZE 6–7½ in (15–19 cm)

Wilson's petrel is typical of the southern group of storm petrels. Its legs are long and toes short, and it hops and paddles over the surface to pick up prey. This species eats mostly plankton and the oil and fat debris at whaling stations. Breeding is usually on islands off the tip of South America. The single egg is incubated by both birds. In winter the birds migrate north, to the tropics or north of the Equator, and can sometimes be seen off the Atlantic coast of North America. Some ornithologists believe this to be the most abundant bird species in the world.

Ringed Storm Petrel *Oceanodroma hornbyi* **DD**

RANGE Pacific coast of South America

HABITAT Oceanic

SIZE 7¼–8½ in (20–22 cm)

The ringed storm petrel has a white collar around the neck and a dark band across the chest. This species flies inland to breed in the Chilean Andes.

White-faced Storm Petrel

Pelagodroma marina

RANGE Atlantic, Indian and S. Pacific Oceans

HABITAT Oceanic

SIZE 8 in (20.5 cm)

This southern species has black and white plumage. It splashes down on the surface of the sea to feed on plankton and squid. Colonies breed on islands in the Atlantic and on the coasts of Australia and New Zealand. A single egg is laid in a burrow in the ground. This bird is vulnerable to attack by cats and birds during its breeding season.

NEW ZEALAND WRENS, PITTAS, BROADBILLS AND ASITIES

ORDER PASSERIFORMES

Usually known as the perching birds, or songbirds, this is the largest of all bird orders. It includes about half of the 9,000 or so bird species. There are about 47 families in the order and the most advanced 35 or so of these are grouped together in the suborder Passeri – the oscine perching birds or songbirds. The other families – the suborder Tyranni – are known as the suboscines; these birds have a simpler organ of song. Perching birds are usually small – the lyrebirds are the largest species – but they have adapted to almost all types of land-based habitat.

The group as a whole is identified by a number of structural and behavioural features. The foot is particularly characteristic and is excellently adapted for grasping any thin support, such as a twig or grass stem. There are always four toes all on the same level, with the hallux (big toe) pointing backward. The toes are not webbed. Male perching birds normally sing complex songs and give voice when courting or defending territory.

SUBORDER TYRANNI: PRIMITIVE PASSERINES

ACANTHISITTIDAE: NEW ZEALAND WREN FAMILY

This family of 4 species of small wrenlike birds is confined to forest and scrubland in New Zealand.

Rifleman *Acanthisitta chloris*

RANGE New Zealand and neighboring islands

HABITAT Forest and modified habitats with remnants of forest

SIZE 3–4 in (7.5–10 cm)

The tiny rifleman feeds mainly in the trees, searching trunks and branches for insects and spiders; occasionally it comes down to the forest floor. The female has dark and light-brown striped upperparts; the male is yellowish-green. Nests are made in a crevices in trees. Both parents incubate the clutch of 4 or 5 eggs and feed the young.

PITTIDAE: PITTA FAMILY

The 31 species of pitta occur in Africa, Asia and Southeast Asia to Australia. They are thrushlike, stout birds, with long legs and short tails and most species have brightly colored plumage. Male and female look alike in some species but differ in others. Nests are usually large domed or oval-shaped constructions in branches or bushes.

Indian Pitta *Pitta brachyura*

RANGE N. and C. India; winters in S. India and Sri Lanka

HABITAT Varied, including semi-cultivated land and forest

SIZE 7 in (18 cm)

This brightly plumaged little bird forages on or close to the forest floor, searching among fallen leaves and debris for food such as insects and spiders. It will also eat worms and maggots at excrement sites.

If alarmed the Indian pitta flies up into a tree with a whirring sound and then sits still, with only its tail moving slowly up and down.

The nest, built in a tree, is a domed, globular structure, made of moss and covered with twigs. It is lined with plant material and has a side entrance. Both parents incubate the clutch of 4 to 6 eggs and feed the helpless, naked young. Large flocks of Indian pittas migrate south in winter.

Garnet Pitta *Pitta granatina*

RANGE Malaysia, Sumatra, Borneo

HABITAT Lowland forest, swamps

SIZE 6 in (15 cm)

Both male and female garnet pittas have brilliant, jewellike plumage, while the juveniles are a dull brownish hue and acquire the bright adult coloration only gradually. The adults make a prolonged whistling call.

Much of the garnet pitta's life is spent running about on the ground, foraging for ants, beetles and other insects, as well as snails, seeds and fruit. It will fly short distances.

Its nest, typical of the pitta family, is made on the ground and is a domed structure of rotting leaves and fibers, roofed with twigs and leaves. There is a small entrance to the chamber in which the female lays her clutch of 2 eggs.

The numbers of this species are declining, due mainly to the destruction of its forest habitat.

EURYLAIMIDAE: BROADBILL FAMILY

There are about 14 known species in the broadbill family, all of which are found in Africa and south and Southeast Asia in forest and wooded land.

The broad-bills are rather rotund little birds, with bright plumage, heavy, flattened, wide bills, large eyes and short legs and tails. Male and female look unalike, with differences in size and coloration in most species.

Broadbills feed on insects, fruit, seeds and other plant material. Most build oval or pear-shaped nests, which are suspended from branches or twigs, often over water. Clutches of between 2 and 8 white or pinkish eggs are usually laid.

Green Broadbill *Calyptomena viridis*

RANGE Malaysia, Sumatra, Borneo

HABITAT Forest on lowland and hills

SIZE 7½ in (19 cm)

The green broadbill spends much of its life foraging for fruit, its main food, high in the forest trees, where it is hard to spot among the leaves. The male is bright and iridescent, but the female is a duller green and often larger than the male.

The nest is made of coarse, matted plant fibers and is suspended from thin twigs just above the ground. It is wider at the top than at the bottom and there is an entrance hole near the top. The female bird lays 2 eggs, which both parents are believed to incubate.

PHILEPITTIDAE: ASITY FAMILY

The 4 species in this family are divided into two distinct groups – the asities and the false sunbirds. They are plump, tree-dwelling birds, all found in Madagascar. Males and females of the species differ in plumage.

Wattled False Sunbird *Neodrepanis coruscans*

RANGE E. Madagascar

HABITAT Forest

SIZE 3½ in (9 cm)

The long, downward-curving bill of the wattled false sunbird gives it a strong superficial resemblance to the true sunbirds (*Nectariniidae*), hence the common name. The bill is used for the same purpose, that is, to drink nectar from flowers. The false sunbird also feeds on fruit, insects and spiders.

TYRANT FLYCATCHERS

TYRANNIDAE: TYRANT FAMILY

The 537 species in the large and diverse family are found only in the Americas. There are five subfamilies – Pipromorphinae (mionectine flycatchers), Tyranninae (tyrant flycatchers), Tityrinae (tityras and becards), Cotinginae (cotingas) and Piprinae (Manakins).

PIPROMORPHINAE MIONECTINE: FLYCATCHER SUBFAMILY

The 53 species of small, dull-colored birds are found in the forests and open woodlands of tropical Central and South America. Most, as their name suggests, are insect eaters although species belonging to the genus Mionectes also eat small fruits.

Ocher-bellied Flycatcher

Mionectus oleaginus

RANGE S. Mexico, through Central and South America to Peru and Brazil

HABITAT Forest, clearings

SIZE 4¼ in (12 cm)

The slender, long-tailed ocher-bellied flycatcher is mainly olive-green, with grayish plumage on the throat and ocher underparts. Its bill is long and slender, with a hooked tip.

This active little bird, constantly twitches its wings above its back, one at a time. Unlike other flycatchers, this species does not make aerial dashes after prey, but seizes insects and spiders from foliage as it flits from tree to tree. It also feeds on fruit and berries, particularly mistletoe berries. An extremely solitary bird, it never gathers in flocks or even pairs, except during the brief period of courtship and mating.

Normally silent, in the breeding season male ocher-bellied flycatchers take up territories in which they perch and sing tirelessly to attract mates. Several males may sing within hearing of each other. They do not assist females in nest-building or rearing of young.

A pear-shaped nest, covered with moss, is suspended from a slender branch or vine or from the aerial root of an airplant. It takes the female about 2 weeks to build this nest. She incubates the 2 or 3 eggs for 19 to 21 days and feeds the young for between 2 and 3 weeks.

Common Tody-flycatcher

Todirostrum cinereum

RANGE S. Mexico, Central and South America to Bolivia and Brazil

HABITAT Open country, plantations, parkland

SIZE 4 in (10 cm)

The long, straight bill and the narrow, graduated tail feathers make up over half of this bird's body length. Avoiding closed woodland, it feeds wherever there are scattered trees, making short darts from branch to branch and seizing insects and berries from foliage and bark. It hops sideways along branches, continuously wagging its tail as it goes. Male and female look alike and live in pairs throughout the year.

Both partners of a pair help to make the nest, which is suspended from a slender twig or vine. They mat together plant fibers and then excavate an entrance hole and central cavity in the resulting mass. The female lays 2 or 3 eggs, which she incubates for 17 or 18 days, and both parents feed the young.

TYRANNINAE: TYRANT FLYCATCHER SUBFAMILY

The 340 species of tyrant flycatchers constitute one of the largest subfamilies of perching birds. These small to medium-sized birds are found in most habitats through the Americas where they replace, and are in several respects similar to, the Old World Flycatchers, Muscicapinae. The rain forests of the Amazon hold the greatest density of species, but they have spread wherever food is available. Most species catch insects on the wing, but some eat fruit, small mammals, reptiles, amphibians and fish too. The insect-eaters' beaks are flattened and slightly hooked, with well-developed bristles at the base. The sexes look alike in most species.

Scissor-tailed Flycatcher *Tyrannus forficata*

RANGE Southcentral USA; winters S. Texas, Mexico to Panama

HABITAT Open grassland (prairie), ranchland

SIZE 11–15 in (28–38 cm) including tail of up to 9 in (23 cm)

When these elegant birds fly, the black feathers of their remarkably long tails open and close like the blades of a pair of scissors, but when they perch, the birds close up the blades. The female is smaller than the male, with a shorter tail. Scissor-tailed

flycatchers spend much of their time perched on fences, telephone wires and trees. They catch insects in the air or on the ground. Grasshoppers and crickets are the main food, but bees, moths, caterpillars, spiders, berries and seeds are also eaten.

The bulky nest is made from weeds, rootlets and cotton. It is lined with hair and rootlets. The female lays 4 to 6 eggs, and incubates them for about 14 days.

White-headed Marsh Tyrant *Arundinicola leucocephala*

RANGE South America, east of the Andes, to N. Argentina; Trinidad

HABITAT River banks, marshes, wet grassland

SIZE 4½ in (11.5 cm)

Sociable birds, these marsh tyrants live in pairs or family groups and feed on insects, which they catch on the wing. They make their nests in low bushes or clumps of grass, using boll cotton in their construction. The female lays 2 or 3 eggs.

Eastern Phoebe *Sayornis phoebe*

RANGE Eastern N. America; winters in S. USA and Mexico

HABITAT Woodland near water, rocky ravines, wooded farmland

SIZE 6¼–7¼ in (16–18.5 cm)

This flycatcher has an erect posture and appears to wag its tail when it alights. Its name is derived from its two-note call. In summer phoebes can be seen on farmland and wooded country roads, searching for beetles, ants, bees, wasps and invertebrates. Their cup-shaped nests are made from mud and moss and sited on rocky ledges, or in farm buildings. The 3 to 8 eggs are laid and incubated for 16 days.

Great Kiskadee

Pitangus sulphuratus

RANGE S.E. Texas, Central and South America to C. Argentina

HABITAT Groves, orchards, wooded banks of streams

SIZE 9–10½ in (23–26.5 cm)

A large bird with a big head, the great kiskadee is active and noisy, with a loud "kis-ka-dee" call. It is conspicuous at dawn and dusk and behaves much like a kingfisher, perching quite still above water and then plunging into it after fish and tadpoles. Its plumage needs to dry out after three dives, so it turns to catching flying insects such as beetles and wasps. In winter, when these are scarce, it feeds on fruit and berries.

Kiskadees make their large, oval nests about 20 ft (6 m) up in trees. The female lays 2 to 5 eggs, usually 4.

Eastern Kingbird *Tyrannus tyrannus*

RANGE C. Canada, through USA to Gulf of Mexico. Winters in Central and South America to N. Argentina

HABITAT Open country with trees, orchards, gardens

SIZE 8–9 in (20.5–23 cm)

The eastern kingbird is a noisy and aggressive bird and will attack other birds, such as hawks, vultures and crows, sometimes landing on the other bird's back. It has even been known to occasionally attack low-flying aircraft.

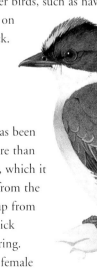

The kingbird has been observed to eat more than 200 types of insect, which it takes in the air or from the ground or scoops up from water. It will also pick berries, while hovering.

Both male and female kingbirds incubate the clutch of 3 to 5 eggs for about 2 weeks and both help to feed the young.

TYRANT FLYCATCHERS CONTINUED

Willow Flycatcher *Empidonax traillii*

RANGE S. Canada, USA: Maine to Virginia, west to Arkansas and California

HABITAT Open country near water to 7,900 ft (2,400 m)

SIZE 5¼–6 in (13.5–15 cm)

True to its common name, this bird is most frequently encountered where willow trees abound – on islands in rivers, in shrubs along streams and in beaver meadows. In appearance it is similar to the alder flycatcher (*E. alnorum*), but it has a slightly longer bill and more rounded wings. It is a prodigious insect eater, known to catch at least 65 species of beetle, as well as aphids, bees, wasps, crane flies, caterpillars, spiders and millipedes, all of which it takes in flight. It also eats some berries.

Traill's flycatchers usually build their nests about 8 ft (2.5 m) above the ground in the upright fork of a bush or tree, in an area where willows or plants of the rose family grow. The shredded bark of milkweed, cat tail and the silky catkins of aspen and willow are used in its construction, and it is softly lined with grass and feathers. The female lays 3 or 4 eggs, which are incubated for about 12 days. The young leave the nest when they are about 2 weeks old.

Many-colored Rush-tyrant

Tachuris rubrigastra

RANGE South America: Peru, S.E. Brazil, Paraguay, Uruguay, Argentina, Chile

HABITAT Fields, meadows near water, swampy ground

SIZE 4¼ in (10.5 cm)

There are seven colors visible in the plumage of these pretty little birds –

yellow, blue, white, bronze, black, carmine and green. They are sprightly and flit about constantly among the stems of tall grasses, particularly cat tails, searching for small insects to eat. Although they are so active, many-colored tyrants are seldom seen and often can be located only by their frequently repeated, sharp, ringing calls.

The cone-shaped nest is attached to the stalk of a cat tail or a reed, 20 to 30 in (50 to 80 cm) above the water. It is intricately woven from small pieces of dry reed, with the point of the cone at the bottom, and the reeds are cemented with a sticky substance, which gives the nest a smooth, shiny surface. The female lays her eggs in multiples of three – 3, 6 or 9.

Royal Flycatcher *Onychorhynchus coronatus*

RANGE C. and S. America: Mexico south to Guianas, Bolivia, Brazil

HABITAT Rain and cloud forest, forest edge

SIZE 6½ in (16.5 cm)

The royal flycatcher has a rather dull brown body, but a spectacular large crest of crimson feathers on its head that end in discs with a metallic blue lustre. In the female the crest is orange or yellow. Normally the crest lies flat, but in display it is opened and closed like a fan.

The bill is broad and flat and quite wide, a shape that is well suited to the birds' diet of insects which are caught on the wing.

These flycatchers are usually found singly or in pairs in secondary growth or at the forest edge where they perch on low branches.

The long, loose, bag-shaped nest, which can be up to 6 ft (1.8 m) long, is built in a tree, often near a stream, and the female lays 2 eggs.

Eastern Wood Peewee
Contopus virens

RANGE Breeds S.E. Canada, E. USA;
winters Central America, N. South America

HABITAT Deciduous or mixed woodland, tall shade trees in gardens

SIZE 6–6¼ in (15–17 cm)

The eastern peewee is so similar in appearance to the western species (*C. sordidulus*) that in western Manitoba and Nebraska, where their ranges overlap, it is possible to distinguish it only by its plaintive, whistling call. It perches in the deep shade of tall trees, darting out to catch flying insects, beetles and treehoppers.

Eastern peewees build thick-walled, cup-shaped nests high up on the horizontal branches of trees. The nest is made of weeds and fibers, lined with wool, grass and hair, and well covered with lichen, which makes it invisible from the ground. Normally 3 eggs are laid, which are incubated until they hatch after about 13 days.

Short-tailed Pygmy-tyrant *Myiornis ecaudatus*

RANGE N. South America, east of the Andes,
Amazonian Brazil; Peru, Bolivia, Trinidad

HABITAT High open rain forest, clearings in forest, plantations

SIZE 2½ in (6.5 cm)

The smallest of the tyrants, this tiny bird has an exceptionally short tail, scarcely longer than the tail coverts. Male and female look alike. Alone or in pairs, the birds dart about in the forest trees, from the bottom branches to the canopy, looking for insects to feed on.

Pygmy-tyrants are not shy, but because they live in such dense vegetation, they are hardly ever seen, and no information is available about their breeding or nesting behavior.

White-crested Spadebill
Platyrinchus platyrhynchos

RANGE N. South America to Amazon basin

HABITAT Rain forest, forest edge

SIZE 3 in (7.5 cm)

A tiny, stout-bodied bird, with a round head and a wide, short bill, the white-crested spadebill is distinguished by the white feathers on its head. Pairs stay together throughout the year, flitting busily through the bushes and the lower branches of forests searching for insects and spiders to eat. Occasionally they are seen among the many birds that follow columns of army ants.

The female spadebill builds a bulky, cup-shaped nest, rather like a hummingbird's, using tree fern, plant fibers and cobwebs. The nest is usually in the vertical fork of a tree about 6½ ft (2 m) from the ground. Two eggs are laid, two days apart, and are incubated for about 17 days by the female. Both parents feed the young, which can fly at about 2 weeks old.

Yellow-bellied Elaenia *Elaenia flavogaster*

RANGE Central and South America:
S. Mexico to N. Argentina;
Trinidad, Tobago

HABITAT Shady pasture,
savanna, parks, plantations,
to 6,000 ft (1,800 m)

SIZE 6¼ in (16 cm)

The most remarkable characteristic of this flycatcher is the double crest of stiff gray feathers that stands up on each side of the head, revealing the white patch between. The bird's breast and belly are pale yellow, the tail is long and the bill short. Male and female look alike. Elaenias live in pairs all year round, always in open country with trees, where they eat insects taken on the wing and on many different types of berries.

Both birds help to build the nest in the fork of a tree, generally about 6½ to 15 ft (2 to 4.5 m) above the ground. It is a shallow, open structure, made from rootlets, plant fibers and cobwebs covered with lichen and moss and lined with feathers. The female lays 2 eggs, which she incubates for about 15 days. The chicks are fed by both parents and leave the nest at 17 or 18 days old. There are often two broods produced in a year.

TYRANT FLYCATCHERS, SHARPBILL AND PLANTCUTTERS

Cliff Flycatcher
Hirundinea ferruginea

RANGE N. South America to Brazil and N. Argentina

HABITAT Arid hillsides, ravines, cliffs, open woodland

SIZE 7¼ in (18.5 cm)

A mainly brown and black bird, this flycatcher has bright chestnut underparts and wing patches, which are conspicuous in flight. Its wings are long and swallowlike, and it catches much of its insect prey in skilful aerial dashes.

The nest is made in a crevice in a rock or cliff.

Great Shrike Tyrant
Agriornis livida

RANGE South America: S. Argentina, Chile

HABITAT Open scrub, fields

SIZE 11 in (28 cm) including Tail: 4¼ in (11 cm)

This silent bird avoids woodland and populated regions and frequents lonely, open areas. It has a powerful beak and eats insects, other birds' eggs and small animals, such as newts, and mice.

On the coast, the birds begin nesting in October, but farther inland, in the Andean foothills, breeding does not start until November. A bulky nest, made of grass and sticks and lined with sheeps' wool, is built in a thick bush. The female lays 2 to 4 eggs, usually 3.

Vermilion Flycatcher *Pyrocephalus rubinus*

RANGE S.W. USA, Mexico, Central and South America to Argentina; Galápagos Islands

HABITAT Scrub, savanna, riparian woodland

SIZE 5½–6¾ in (14–17 cm)

The male vermilion flycatcher has a bright red head and underparts. The female is brownish above, with a lighter, streaked belly and breast. These flycatchers eat flying insects, particularly bees, darting into the air from a high perch in pursuit of their prey. They also feed on the ground on grasshoppers and beetles, especially in areas of sparse vegetation.

The courting male flies up from a tree, singing ecstatically, his vermilion crest erect and his breast feathers puffed out. He hovers briefly, then flutters down to the female. A flattish, cup-shaped nest, made of twigs, grass and rootlets, is built on a horizontally forked branch. The female incubates the 2 to 4 eggs, and the male defends the nest. Chicks leave the nest at about 2 weeks old.

Piratic Flycatcher *Legatus leucophaius*

RANGE S. Mexico, Central and South America to N. Argentina

HABITAT Open woodland

SIZE 5¾ in (14.5 cm)

A dull bird, the piratic flycatcher makes itself conspicuous by being one of the noisiest flycatchers, with a wide range of calls. It eats insects, especially dragonflies, and berries.

Piratic flycatchers appear to be the only members of the tyrant flycatcher family to depart from normal nest-building habits, and this earns them their common name. They do not build their own nests but usurp the freshly built nests of other birds, often other species of flycatcher. Having chosen their victims, the pair of piratic flycatchers perches nearby to watch the building progressing. They chatter noisily and make their presence felt, but do not usually attack until the nest is complete. Then they harass the rightful owners until they abandon the nest. Any eggs are thrown out, and the female piratic flycatcher lays 2 or 3 eggs, which she incubates for about 16 days. Both parents feed the nestlings on berries and insects until they leave the nest almost 3 weeks after hatching. Central American and northern South American populations migrate south after breeding.

Torrent Tyranulet *Serpophaga cinerea*

RANGE Central and South America: mountains of Costa Rica and Panama, Andes from Venezuela to Bolivia

HABITAT Rocky streams

SIZE 4 in (10 cm)

The torrent tyranulet lives amid the fast flowing waters of mountain streams, and its gray and black plumage echoes its rocky habitat. It plucks insects, not only from the air, but also from slippery boulders surrounded by foaming water, often becoming drenched in the process. It also alights on wet rocks to search for tiny invertebrates. Male and female look alike and live together all year, holding a stretch of river as their territory.

A cup-shaped nest, covered with moss, is made in vegetation overhanging water, rarely over the bank. The 2 eggs are incubated by the female for 17 or 18 days, but the male stays nearby. Both parents feed the young on insects for 2 or 3 weeks, and even after leaving the nest, the young birds stay with their parents for a further 5 or 6 weeks before seeking their own territory.

COTINGINAE: COTINGA SUBFAMILY

This subfamily of 69 species, which includes the sharpbill, plantcutters, and the cotingas, is found from southern Mexico south to Brazil. The single species of small, conical-billed sharpbill is found in the upper layers of humid forests from Costa Rica south to

Paraguay. The plantcutters, of which there are three species, are found in the more open areas of western South America. Despite their close relationship with the cotingas, plantcutters, with their strong, conical beaks, bear more resemblance to the finches of the Old world. The edges of their bills are finely serrated and used for cropping the buds, fruit, and leaves that make up much of their diet. The 65 species of cotingas constitute a colorful and varied group of birds, some with common names such as bellbird, umbrellabird, fruiteater and cock-of-the-rock. This variety of nomenclature mirrors the diversity in body form and habit. Cotingas are non-migratory birds in forested areas and often spend most of their time in the canopy layers, feeding on fruit and insects.

Sharpbill *Oxyruncus cristatus*

RANGE Patchy distribution in Costa Rica, Panama to Paraguay, Amazonian Brazil

HABITAT Humid tropical forest from 1,300–6,000 ft (400–1,800 m)

SIZE 6½–7 in (16.5–18 cm)

The sharpbill has a straight, pointed beak, which gives it its common name. It is a strong flier, with rather rounded, long wings. Male and female look similar, but the male has a black and scarlet crest, bordered with black, while the female may have a pale crest. Sharpbills are secretive birds, which forage actively for fruit in the middle to canopy layers of the forest.

Rufous-tailed Plantcutter *Phytotoma rara*

RANGE Central Chile, W. Argentina

HABITAT Open scrub, orchards, gardens, mountain valleys

SIZE 8 in (20.5 cm)

These short-legged birds have bright reddish-orange eyes and stout, serrated beaks. The male has reddish-chestnut underparts and tail; the female is paler with a buff throat and underparts. Plantcutters usually occur singly or in small groups, flying sluggishly among fruit trees. They eat the buds, shoots and young leaves and often destroy fruit.

In spring plantcutters move to high mountain valleys, where they mate between October and December. A clutch of 2 to 4 eggs is laid in a cup-shaped nest, made of twigs and lined with fine twigs and rootlets.

COTINGAS AND MANAKINS

Andean Cock-of-the-Rock *Rupicola peruviana*

RANGE Andes, N. Venezuela to N. Bolivia

HABITAT Forest along river gorges 1,640–1,875 ft (500–2,400 m)

SIZE 15 in (38 cm)

The male of this species is one of the most brilliantly colored of all birds, with its flashing orange or red plumage and strong, golden-colored beak. On its head is a crest of feathers that almost conceals the beak. Both male and female have powerful legs and sharp claws.

The Andean cock-of-the-rock lives in the lower levels of the forest, where its swift, weaving flight and maneuverability enable it to move about easily as it searches for fruit to eat. Females also catch frogs and lizards to feed to their young.

Males roost alone at night, and forage in pairs and display in pairs at dawn and dusk at traditional leks, where each has his own place near to that of his paired male. Only the dominant male of the lek mates with females. The female builds the nest on a rocky cliff face. Often several nests are grouped together. The nest is a large truncated cone, made of mud, with a deep, 2½ in (6.5 cm), lined nest cup in which 2 eggs are laid.

Barred Fruiteater *Pipreola arcuata*

RANGE Andes, N.W. Venezuela to C.W. Bolivia

HABITAT Cloud forest at 4,000–11,000 ft (1,200–3,350 m)

SIZE 8½ in (21.5 cm)

The heavy-bodied barred fruiteater is the largest fruiteater. It is found at higher altitudes than any other. Males have striking coloration, but females are mostly olive-green. Both sexes have rather weak, slightly hooked beaks and red legs and feet. They live in the middle and lower layers of the forest and eat mainly fruit and some insects. No breeding information is available.

Bearded Bellbird *Procnias averano*

RANGE Parts of Colombia, Guyana, Venezuela, N. Brazil; Trinidad

HABITAT Forest to 5,250 ft (1,600 m)

SIZE 10 in (25.5 cm)

The fringe of black wattles hanging from the throat of both male and female gives this species its common name. They are shy birds, feeding singly or in pairs on large, single-seeded berries, particularly laurel, which they take on the wing and then sit on a branch to eat.

In the breeding season, male bearded bellbirds display to other males and to females on special "visiting" perches in the lower forest layers. They jump as high as 4 ft (1.2 m) into the air and land crouched, on another perch, with tail spread. After mating, the female builds a light, thin, cup-shaped nest of twigs from specific trees, about 8 to 50 ft (2.4 to 15.25 m) up, in the horizontally forked outer branch of a tree. She lays 1 egg, which she incubates for about 23 days.

Spangled Cotinga *Cotinga cayana*

RANGE S. America, E. of Andes from Colombia and Guianas south to Bolivia and Amazonian Brazil

HABITAT Forest, woodland, savanna

SIZE 8½ in (21.5 cm)

The blue plumage of the male spangled cotinga is iridescent, hence the name. These are gregarious birds, usually

feeding in groups, sometimes with birds of other species, on large berries.

The female alone builds the flimsy, shallow nest, using twigs and rootlets and coating the whole structure in white fungal threads. She lays and then incubates 1 large egg, sometimes 2.

Amazonian Umbrellabird

Cephalopterus ornatus

RANGE N. South America to Amazonian Brazil, N. Bolivia

HABITAT Virgin forest to 4,600 ft (1,400 m), islands in larger rivers

SIZE 16–19 in (40.5–48 cm)

The largest of the cotingas, the ornate umbrellabird is distinguished by its erect crest of long, silky feathers and by the wattle at the base of the neck. The female is much duller than the male, with a smaller wattle and "umbrella". The wings are short. These strange birds live in the forest canopy and spring noisily through the branches, looking for fruit and insects.

Males have their preferred calling trees, where they perch, spread their umbrellas and, filling two specially modified sacs in the trachea with air, make loud booming noises. The shallow, open nest is built of twigs in the fork of a fairly low tree, and the female lays 1 egg, which she incubates alone.

PIPRINAE: MANAKIN SUBFAMILY

This intriguing and showy family contains 52 species, all of which are found in the tropical forests of Central and South America. They are small, colorful birds, rarely more than 5 to 6 in (12.5 to 15 cm) in length. Males and females are dramatically different in appearance. Males, typically, have a solid background plumage color, commonly black, brilliantly counterpointed with areas of contrasting primary colors. Females are generally olive-green. The decorative males utilize their plumage in intricate courtship dances.

Blue-backed Manakin

Chiroxiphia pareola

RANGE N. South America to S.E. Brazil, N. Bolivia; Tobago

HABITAT Rain forest, secondary growth

SIZE 4 in (10 cm)

These lively, agile little birds forage in pairs or small groups for insects and fruit in low bushes, often near wet ground or streams. They are square tailed, with the male showing dazzling patches of pale blue and red feathers on back and crown.

Male manakins have display perches or "bowers", which they keep clear by plucking at the surrounding leaves from flight and pecking at the bark while perching. They wear the perch smooth by continually moving around. Before display the dominant male summons a subordinate male by calling and then duets with him, the subordinate following a fraction of a second behind. The males dance together, but the dance only becomes fully developed if a female appears. The other bird drops out, leaving the dominant male to mate with the female after a quite different solo display. She lays 2 eggs in a nest, made of fine plant fibers, so cobwebby and transparent that eggs and young can be seen through it.

Wire-tailed Manakin *Pipra filicauda*

RANGE S. America E. of Andes from Columbia and Venezuela S. to N.E. Peru, W. Brazil

HABITAT Rain forest, plantations

SIZE 4½ in (11.5cm)

The male wire-tailed manakin has dramatic black, red and yellow patches typical of the family, and the tails of both male and female end in long wiry filaments, from which the common name is derived. These birds prefer humid areas and are found from the middle story to the forest canopy, as well as in clearings and cocoa plantations. Solitary birds, they forage alone for insects and fruit.

TYPICAL ANTBIRDS, AND GROUND ANTBIRDS

THAMNOPHILIDAE: TYPICAL ANTBIRD FAMILY

Antbirds are found exclusively in Central and South America, mostly on the floor and in the lower vertical levels of the tropical rain forests of the Amazon basin, as well as in some drier and more open habitats. About 240 species of small to medium-sized birds are known in two families: Thamnophilidae (typical antbirds) and Formicaridae (ground antbirds). The 188 species of typical antbirds are found mainly in tropical forest and scrub. Many do actually feed on ants and other social insects; some eat the invertebrates disturbed by columns of army ants which they follow through the forest, while others, although insectivorous, have no particular predilection for ants.

The plumage is usually dull, and there are usually differences between that of male and female birds. Little is known of their breeding biology, but open, cup-shaped nests seem to be the rule.

Ocellated Antbird *Phaenostictus mcleannani*

RANGE Tropical Nicaragua to Panama; S. Colombia, N.W. Ecuador

HABITAT Undergrowth of humid, lowland forest

SIZE 7¼–7¾ in (19–20 cm)

The dark markings in the plumage of the ocellated antbird give it a spotted appearance. It's tail is relatively long and the eyes are surrounded with an area of bright-hued bare skin, and it is these two colored circles, one within the other, that give the bird its common name. Males and females of the species look alike.

It is an uncommon, timid species and often found in association with bicolored antbirds. It is seldom seen away from the columns of army ants that march through the forests, for it feeds on the invertebrates, such as cockroaches and spiders, which are disturbed by the ants' progress. The call is a fast series of whistles.

Ocellated antbirds form lasting pair bonds, and before mating, the male feeds the female with titbits.

White-cheeked Antbird *Gymnopithys leucaspis*

RANGE S. E. Colombia, E. Ecuador, N. Peru, Amazonian Brazil

HABITAT Forest undergrowth up to 6,600 ft (2,000 m)

SIZE 5½ in (14 cm)

Although there is some disagreement, this bird is generally considered conspecific with the bicolored antbird, *G. bicolor*, of Central America, north Colombia and west Ecuador. The plumage of male and female are alike, and there are patches of bare skin around the eyes. It is a fairly common species and usually the most numerous and noisy of the birds that follow army ants. It spends much of the time on the ground but will perch just above the forest floor, watching for insects, spiders and other invertebrates which are driven out of the leaf litter as the ants advance.

The nest of the bicolored antbirds is usually a few feet from the ground in the stump of a decaying palm tree. It is made from small pieces of leaf, especially palm leaf, and lined with rootlets and plant fibers. The female lays 2 eggs, which both parents incubate for about 15 days.

Streaked Antwren *Myrmotherula surinamensis*

RANGE Amazonian Brazil, west to Pacific coast of South America

HABITAT Clearings in rain forest, forest edge, woodland, swampy areas

SIZE 4 in (10 cm)

The male of this species is largely black and white, while the female has a bright orange-red head and nape and pale orange-buff underparts. Both sexes have two white bars on the wings. Streaked antwrens are fairly common birds, often found near rivers and on wet ground, where they can generally be seen in pairs, busily searching for grasshoppers and spiders among the undergrowth, vines and leaves. They have a fast, rising, chipping call.

The nest is made in a tree, and the female lays 2 eggs.

Great Antshrike *Taraba major*

RANGE Tropical S. Mexico, Central and South America to N. Argentina

HABITAT Undergrowth in humid forest, brush and grassland up to 6,600 ft (2,000 m)

SIZE 7¼ in (20 cm)

The great antshrike is a fairly large bird with a thick, hooked bill and a crest; males and females have quite dissimilar coloration. These common but shy birds are usually found only in pairs or, occasionally, alone. They move stealthily through the bushes and low branches of small trees, searching for beetles, grasshoppers, bees and even small lizards to eat. When disturbed the male performs a threat display, pointing his bill straight upward and raising his crest so that the dorsal patch shows clearly.

The flimsy nest is cup shaped, made of dried grass and roots, sometimes lined with leaves, and is about 2½ in (6.5 cm) deep. The female lays 2 or 3 eggs, which both parents incubate for 2 to 3 weeks; they then feed the young until they are ready to leave the nest, about 2 weeks after hatching.

Barred Antshrike *Thamnophilus doliatus*

RANGE Tropical Mexico, Central and South America to N. Argentina; Trinidad and Tobago

HABITAT Varied, forest, brush, savanna, gardens; rarely above 6,600 ft (2,000 m)

SIZE 6 in (15 cm)

The plumage of this antshrike is conspicuously barred and streaked. The male is mainly black and white, while the female is chestnut, shading to buff, with black barring. Both birds have a crest, which the

male always carries partially erect, and a toothed beak. Barred antshrikes are common birds, usually found in pairs. They are always on the move through bushes and branches in thickets and forest edge about 15 ft (4.5 m) up, they are usually heard calling to one another before they are seen. Insects, such as beetles and caterpillars, and berries make up their diet.

There seems to be no clearly defined mating season, but the male feeds the female during courtship and they may form a permanent pair bond. The female lays 2, rarely 3, eggs in a deep cup-shaped nest, made of grass and plant fibers and suspended by the rim in the fork of a low branch of a tree. Both parents incubate the eggs for about 14 days; only the female incubates at night. The young leave the nest 2 to 3 weeks after hatching.

FORMICARIIDAE: GROUND ANTBIRD FAMILY

This family of 56 species of mainly terrestrial antbirds are found from Mexico to northern Argentina, mainly on the forest floor of forests and bamboo thickets. The family includes antthrushes and antpittas.

Chestnut-crowned Antpitta

Grallaria ruficapilla

RANGE Tropical and subtropical areas, Venezuela to N.W. Peru

HABITAT Dense cloud forest, damp woodland and open grassland

SIZE 7¼ in (20 cm)

The chestnut-crowned antpitta is a long-legged bird, with a short tail and a noticeably large head. The feathers on head and neck are reddish brown, hence its common name. It is a groundliving bird, usually found alone, looking for the insects that make up its diet. Even though difficult to see, it is not shy, and its three-note call is often heard. In fact, it will respond to imitations of its call and has a number of local names that suggest it, such as "Seco estoy".

OVENBIRDS

FURNARIIDAE: OVENBIRD AND WOODCREEPER FAMILY

The family of small to medium-sized birds, found in Central and South America, consist of two subfamilies – the ovenbirds and the woodcreepers.

FURNARIINAE: OVENBIRD SUBFAMILY

The 231 or so known species in this family occur from southern Mexico through Central and South America, in a wide variety of habitats. As well as the ovenbirds proper, the family includes birds such as spinetails and foliage-gleaners.

All the birds in the family have gray, brownish or russet plumage and are between 4¾ and 11 in (12 and 28 cm) long. They tend to be quick-moving, yet skulking, birds, which generally remain well hidden within vegetation.

The diversity of this family is best shown by their breeding behavior. The true ovenbirds, for which the family is named, construct ovenlike mud nests, which are baked hard by the sun. Others build domed nests of grass or sticks, while some make well-lined nests in holes in the ground or in trees. Females generally lay from 2 to 5 eggs, and both parents care for the young. In most species, male and female look more or less alike.

Rufous Hornero

Furnarius rufus

RANGE Brazil, Bolivia, Paraguay, Uruguay, Argentina

HABITAT Trees, often near habitation

SIZE 7½–8 in (19–20.5 cm)

There has been an increasing tendency to refer to the ovenbirds by their South American name (hornero), to avoid confusion with a North American wood warbler which is also called the ovenbird. The rufous hornero is a dignified bird, which walks with long, deliberate strides, holding one foot aloft as it hesitates between steps. It feeds on insect larvae and worms and is vocal throughout the year.

Pairs stay together all year round, often for life, and breed during the wettest months. Each year they build a domed, ovenlike nest on a branch, post or building, using clay, with a little plant material mixed into it, which is then baked hard by the hot sun. A small entrance leads to the interior chamber, lined with soft grass, where up to 5 eggs are laid. Both parents incubate the clutch, and, after leaving the nest, the young birds stay with their parents for a few months.

Plain Xenops *Xenops minutus*

RANGE S. Mexico, through Central and South America to N. Argentina

HABITAT Humid forest, forest edge

SIZE 5 in (12.5 cm)

One of several species of xenops, the plain xenops is distinguished by its unstreaked back. An active little bird, it forages in shrubs and thin branches of trees in search of insects to eat.

The nest is made by both partners of a breeding pair in a hole in an old, decaying tree and is lined with fine pieces of plant material. Alternatively, the birds may take over a hole abandoned by another bird. The 2 eggs are incubated by both parents for about 16 days.

Stripe-breasted Spinetail *Synallaxis cinnamomea*

RANGE Venezuela, Colombia; Trinidad and Tobago

HABITAT Forest, undergrowth, open woodland

SIZE 6½ in (16.5 cm)

Distinguished by its streaked cinnamon breast, this spinetail moves jerkily and makes low, short flights as it forages for small insects and spiders. It may also jump into the air in order to catch flying ants.

Both partners of a breeding pair help to build the nest, which is a round structure, made of twigs and placed in the fork of a branch in low scrub or on the ground. The nest is lined with soft plant material and has an entrance tunnel. The 2 or 3 eggs are incubated by both parents.

Red-faced Spinetail *Cranioleuca erythrops*

RANGE Costa Rica to Ecuador
HABITAT Humid mountain forest
SIZE 5/–6/ in (14–16.5cm)

Adult red-faced spinetails have reddish markings on the crown
and sides of the head; juveniles have brownish crowns. They are
active, acrobatic birds and much of their life is spent in the low
levels of the forest, foraging in thickets and undergrowth for
insects and other small invertebrates. They tend to move alone
or in pairs but sometimes join in a flock of other highland birds.

The bulky, ball-shaped nest is made from vines and hangs
from the end of a slender branch, well above ground. Both sexes
incubate the 2 eggs and feed the young.

Larklike Bushrunner *Coryphistera alaudina*

RANGE S. Brazil, Bolivia, Paraguay, Uruguay, N. Argentina
HABITAT Dry scrub regions
SIZE 6 in (15 cm)

Identified by its prominent crest and streaked breast plumage,
the larklike bushrunner generally moves in groups of 3 to 6,
which are possibly family groups. Active both on the ground
and in bushes and low trees, they stride along in the open but,
if alarmed, take to the trees.

A rounded nest is made in a low tree from interwoven
thorny twigs. A small entrance tunnel leads to the central
chamber, where the eggs are laid.

Point-tailed Palmcreeper *Berlepschia rikeri*

RANGE Amazonian Brazil, also Venezuela, Guyana,
HABITAT Palm groves, often near water
SIZE 8/ in (21.5 cm)

An elegant little bird, the pintailed palmcreeper has distinctive
black, white and chestnut plumage and pointed tail feathers. In
pairs or small groups, it frequents palm trees of the genus
Mauritia and forages for insects on the trunks and leaves of the
trees. When it catches an insect, the palm creeper bangs it
sharply against the trunk or branch before swallowing it.

Des Murs' Wiretail *Sylviorthorhynchus desmursii*

RANGE W. Argentina, adjacent Chile
HABITAT Humid forest with thick undergrowth
SIZE 9/ in (24 cm)

Over two-thirds of the length of this species is taken up by its
long and decorative tail, which consists of only two pairs of
feathers, plus a vestigial pair. Otherwise this spinetail is an
inconspicuous little
bird, revealed only
by its persistent calls.
The wiretail frequents
the most dense parts of the
forest and seems to be on the
move ceaselessly in search
of food.

A globular nest is made
just off the ground amid
twigs and grass. It is
constructed from dry plant material, lined with soft
feathers, and has a side entrance. Usually 3 eggs are laid.
The bird holds up its tail when it is in the nest.

WOODCREEPERS, GNATEATERS, TAPACULOS AND AUSTRALIAN TREECREEPERS

DENDROCOLAPTINAE: WOODCREEPER SUBFAMILY

The 49 species of woodcreeper found in wooded areas of Central and South America, from Mexico to Argentina, are in many ways the New World equivalent of the treecreepers of the Old World. These birds also known as woodhewers, vary in length from 6 to 15 in (15 to 38 cm). Their laterally compressed beaks, range from short and straight to long and curved.

Woodcreepers are insectivorous and peck their food from crevices in the bark as they climb up the trunks of trees, with the aid of their sharp claws and the strong shafts of their tail feathers. They are usually solitary but may join mixed flocks.

and secondary growth of the rain forest. They are not timid and can be seen alone or in twos and threes often following army ants and feeding on the insects disturbed by their progress.

The female lays 2 eggs, in a hole or crevice in a tree, which are incubated for 14 or 15 days.

Red-billed Scythebill

Campylorhamphus trochilirostris

RANGE E. Panama to N. Argentina

HABITAT Swampy and humid forest, woodland

SIZE 8–12 in (20.5–30.5 cm)
including Bill: 3 in (7.5 cm)

These shy, arboreal birds live in the middle to upper stories of forest trees. They are usually found alone, although they may feed among other types of insectivorous birds. Their strong legs and stiff tail feathers help them to climb quickly. They probe for insects with their long, thin, curved bills, under the bark of trees and inside bromeliads. The female lays 2 or 3 eggs in a hole in a tree or in a crevice, and incubates them for about 14 days.

Barred Woodcreeper *Dendrocolaptes certhia*

RANGE Tropical S. Mexico, through Central America to Bolivia, Amazonian Brazil

HABITAT Lowland rain forest to 4,600 ft (1,400 m), forest edge

SIZE 10½ in (26.5 cm)

Both male and female barred woodcreepers are strongly built and have light olive-brown, barred plumage. The medium-length beak is heavy and slightly curved. These birds live in the undergrowth

Long-billed Woodcreeper

Nasica longirostris

RANGE Tropical N. South America to Brazil and Bolivia

HABITAT Rain forest at 330–650 ft (100–200 m)

SIZE 14 in (35.5 cm)
including Bill: 2½ in (6.5 cm)

The solitary, agile long-billed woodcreeper climbs about in the trees, looking for insect food under the bark and in bromeliads. It has a long, slightly curved bill, and the sexes look similar. The female lays 2 eggs in a nest in a tree hole. They are incubated for about 2 weeks.

Olivaceous Woodcreeper

Sittasomus griseicapillus

RANGE Tropical and subtropical Mexico, through Central and South America to N. Argentina

HABITAT Deep forest, forest edge, open woodland, to 7,500 ft (2,300 m)

SIZE 6–6½ in (15–16.5 cm)

The buff bands on the wings of these active little birds are conspicuous in the air. The sexes look alike. They are more or less solitary, but may associate with other types of birds. They forage for insects on the trunks of trees with soft bark and may catch insects in the air. Only one nest has ever been found, in a hole in a tree.

CONOPOPHAGIDAE: GNATEATER FAMILY

The gnateaters, or antpipits, are a small group of forest-dwelling birds, quite closely related to the antbirds and ovenbirds. Eight species are recognized, all in Central and South America. Most are long-legged brown birds with round bodies and short tails. They live largely on the forest floor, capturing insect food on the ground with their flycatcherlike bills.

Black-cheeked Gnateater
Conopophaga melanops

RANGE E. Brazil

HABITAT Rain forest

SIZE 5 in (12.5 cm)

These neat little birds have long legs and appear almost neckless. Females are more olive-brown than males. They are quite tame, but are not often seen because they forage in the undergrowth.

Black-cheeked gnateaters make an open, cup-shaped nest on the ground, using big leaves, and line it with plant fibers. The female lays 2 eggs which both parents incubate. The nesting bird protects the eggs by feigning injury to lure predators away.

RHINOCRYPTIDAE: TAPACULO FAMILY

The approximately 28 described species of tapaculo are found among low-growing plants in habitats as varied as dense forest, grassland and semiopen arid country in Central and South America. They are ground-living birds, with poor powers of flight, but can run fast on their strong legs. Tapaculos vary in size from 5 to 10 in (12.5 to 25.5 cm) and have rounded bodies; they often cock their tails vertically. They have curious movable flaps covering the nostrils; the exact function of these is not known, but they presumably protect the openings against dust. Males and females look alike, or nearly so.

Elegant Crescentchest *Melanopareia elegans*

RANGE W. Ecuador to N.W. Peru

HABITAT Arid scrub, deciduous forest undergrowth

SIZE 5½ in (14 cm)

These small birds seldom fly, but they have long legs and large feet and run about rapidly, gathering up insects; when excited, they cock up their tails.

Elegant crescentchests are shy birds that are not often seen, although their calls can be heard. No information is available about the breeding biology of these birds.

Chestnut-throated Huet-huet *Pteroptochos castaneus*

RANGE Chile

HABITAT Forest

SIZE 10 in (25.5 cm)

This is a medium-sized bird with a rounded body, long legs and a relatively long tail – about 4 in (10 cm). The upperparts are mostly blackish-brown, but the throat and underparts are a dark reddish-brown, with some black and buff bars. Male and female look alike. These huet-huets are ground-dwellers which rarely fly, and they run, rather than hop, about looking for their insect food.

The nest is made from roots and soft grasses in a hole in the ground or in a tree stump, and the female lays 2 eggs.

CLIMACTERIDAE: AUSTRALIAN TREECREEPER FAMILY

The 7 species of Australian treecreeper resemble the treecreepers of the family Certhiidae. With the aid of their long curved bills, they eat mainly bark-dwelling insects. Some species also come to the ground to feed. They occur in New Guinea and Australia. The plumage of the sexes differ slightly.

Brown Treecreeper *Climacteris picumnus*

RANGE Australia: Queensland to Victoria

HABITAT Forest, woodland

SIZE 6 in (15 cm)

The brown treecreeper feeds largely on insects, which it picks from crevices in the bark of a tree trunk as it climbs upward in a spiral path; it makes short, fluttering flights from tree to tree. It also occasionally feeds on the ground. Male and female look more or less alike, but the female has a chestnut, not black, patch on the throat.

A cup-shaped nest is built in a hole, low down on a tree or in a rotting stump or post, and the female lays 3 or 4 eggs.

LYREBIRDS, BOWERBIRDS, FAIRY WRENS AND GRASS WRENS

SUBORDER PASSERI: ADVANCED PASSERINES

MENURIDAE FAMILY

This small family of Australian birds include 2 subfamilies – the lyrebirds and the scrub-birds.

MENURINAE: LYREBIRD SUBFAMILY

The 2 species of lyrebird live in the mountain forests of southeast Australia. Both sexes have brownish plumage, but males have long and elaborate tails.

Superb Lyrebird *Menura novaehollandiae*

RANGE Australia: S.E. Queensland to Victoria; introduced in Tasmania

HABITAT Mountain forest

SIZE Male: 31½–37½ in (80–95 cm) Female: 29–33 in (74–84 cm)

Although male and female lyrebirds are similar in body size and general appearance, the male's tail is up to 21½ in (55 cm) long and is a flamboyant mix of boldly patterned, lyre-shaped feathers and fine, filamentous feathers. The lyrebirds are mainly ground-living and rarely fly but hop and flap up into trees to roost. They search on the ground for insects and larvae, scratching around with their large, strong legs and feet.

Prior to mating, the male makes several earth mounds and displays near them before the female, spreading his shimmering tail right over himself and dancing. The nest is a large, well camouflaged dome, made of grass and plant fiber and lined with rootlets. It is built on the ground near rocks or logs or sometimes in a tree. The female incubates her 1 egg for about 6 weeks and cares for the nestling.

PTILONORHYNCHIDAE: BOWERBIRD FAMILY

The 20 bowerbird species all occur in New Guinea and Australia and are closely related to the birds of paradise. Bowerbirds have stout bills, straight or curved, and strong legs and feet. Much of their life is spent on the ground, but they feed and nest in trees. Females have duller plumage than males, usually brownish and gray.

The family gets its common name from the "bower-building" activities of all but a few species – the males build ornate bowers on the ground, which they decorate with colorful objects in order to attract females.

MacGregor's Bowerbird

Amblyornis macgregoriae

RANGE Mountains of New Guinea (not N.W.)

HABITAT Forest

SIZE 10 in (25.5 cm)

The male MacGregor's bowerbird is distinguished by his spectacular crest, but otherwise has sober plumage. The female looks similar but lacks the crest. They are common, but shy, birds and feed on fruit. The male's bower consists of a saucer-shaped platform of moss with a central column of twigs. The column and the outer rim of the saucer are both decorated. The bird repairs and cleans his bower daily. Once he has attracted a mate, he displays and then chases her before mating. The female builds a cup-shaped nest in a tree and incubates her single egg herself.

Satin Bowerbird *Ptilonorhynchus violaceus*

RANGE Australia: Queensland to Victoria

HABITAT Forest

SIZE 10½–13 in (27–33 cm)

The male satin bowerbird has a violet sheen to his black plumage – hence the common name. The female is mainly olive-green, tinged with yellow. Noisy, gregarious birds outside the breeding season, they feed on fruit and insects and often raid orchards. They make a variety of calls and also mimic other sounds. The male's display bower is of the "avenue" kind, which sweeps upward at both ends and is decorated with berries, flowers and other bright objects. This bird is particularly attracted to blue items, such as bits of blue glass, paper or plastic. If a female shows interest, the male dances in his bower, alternately drooping and raising his wings and puffing up his feathers.

The female builds a nest of twigs and leaves in a tree and lays 2 eggs, which she alone incubates for 19 to 23 days.

MALURIDAE: FAIRY WREN AND GRASS WREN FAMILY

There are 26 species in this family of Australasian wrens. There are two subfamilies. The subfamily Malurinae includes the fairywrens, found in Australia and New Guinea, and the emu wrens, found in Australia. These small birds are mainly insect-eaters whose habitats range from tropical forests to semidesert. Male fairy wrens are brightly or boldly plumaged, with long, slender tails. Some have unusual social and reproductive habits, which may be their way of dealing with the often harsh conditions of their habitat. Groups of birds hold a territory together, which they defend from other birds, and each group builds

a single, spherical nest, in which one dominant female lays her eggs. All other adult members of the group then assist in the incubation and care of the young. Sometimes pairs nest alone, but they tend to have a high failure rate. The subfamily Amytornithinae consist of 8 species of grasswrens that live on rocky outcrops and in ground vegetation in the drier parts of Australia. Grasswrens rarely fly, and forage on the ground for seeds and insects.

Superb Fairywren

Malurus cyaneus

RANGE Australia: Victoria to Queensland; Tasmania

HABITAT Woodland, savanna, parks

SIZE 5 in (13 cm)

The breeding male has shiny blue plumage around the head and neck, contrasting with some bold black markings. Older, dominant males tend to keep this plumage all year. Nonbreeding males and females are mainly brownish and dull white. The birds live in groups, ruled by a dominant pair, and together defend a territory from intruders. Hopping about with tails cocked, they forage for insects on the ground and among the vegetation.

All members of the group combine to build the dome-shaped nest, which is situated near the ground in a bush or on a tussock and is made of grass, rootlets and bark, bound with spiders' webs. The dominant female lays 3 or 4 eggs, and again, all the group members assist with the 14-day incubation and the rearing of the young.

Eyrean Grasswren *Amytornis goyderi* **LR:lc**

RANGE Parts of C. Australia

HABITAT Canegrass on sandhills, spinifex grassland

SIZE 5½ in (14 cm)

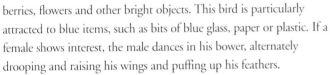

The Eyrean grass wren is a rare bird. In 1976, it was recorded in some numbers in the sandhills of Simpson Desert, in South Australia, but by the following year, the habitat had deteriorated, and the birds had largely gone. Prior to 1976, it had been recorded only at its discovery in 1874, in 1931 and in 1961. This furtive bird stays hidden as it forages among vegetation. Little is known of its breeding habits, but the observed nests were partly domed, made of interwoven grass and stems.

SCRUB BIRDS AND HONEYEATERS

ATRICHORNITHINAE: SCRUB-BIRD SUBFAMILY

There are 2 species of scrub-bird, both found in Australia. They have small wings, long, broad tails and strong legs. Male and female differ slightly in coloration and females are smaller.

Noisy Scrub-Bird *Atrichornis clamosus* **VU**
RANGE Extreme S.W. of W. Australia
HABITAT Coastal scrub, vegetated gullies
SIZE 9 in (23 cm)

The noisy scrub bird is extremely rare and is protected by law. It was thought to be extinct for over 70 years until it was found again in 1961 at Two People's Bay. Noisy scrub birds live among dense vegetation on or near the ground and feed on insects and seeds. They usually live alone and rarely move far afield. The female builds a domed nest of dried rushes in which she lays 1 egg. She incubates the egg for 36 to 38 days.

MELIPHAGIDAE: HONEYEATER FAMILY

The 182 species of honeyeater occur in Australia and New Guinea and Southwestern Pacific islands from Samoa to Bali. The honeyeaters eat nectar from flowers in a similar manner to sunbirds. They are usually larger than sunbirds however, and most have duller, green or brownish plumage. They are diverse, having adapted to a variety of habitats. Honeyeaters have remarkable specializations for nectar feeding. Despite the variation in body size and beak shape all species have a highly modified, long, protrusible tongue. At its base, the tongue can be curled up to form two long, nectar-transporting grooves. At its tip, it splits into four parts, each of which is frilled, making the entire end of the tongue an absorbent brush for nectar collection. Honeyeaters also eat insects, for protein, and fruit.

Generally tree-dwelling, honeyeaters are gregarious birds, aggressive to other species. Male and female look alike in some species, unalike in others.

Kauai O-o *Moho braccatus* **CR**
RANGE Hawaiian Islands: Kauai
HABITAT Montane rain forest
SIZE 7½–8½ in (19–21.5 cm)

Thought to be extinct, like the 2 other species of Hawaiian O-o, the Kauai species was rediscovered, in 1960, in the Alaka`i Swamp. Its relatives were hunted to extinction for their yellow feathers, but this species' sober coloration saved it. It is, however, intolerant of any alteration in its rain forest habitat. The present population is protected but very small.

The Kauai O-o eats nectar berries, spiders, insects and snails. It makes its nest in a cavity in an ohia tree and lays 2 eggs on a bed of dead plant material. Both parents feed the young.

Brown Honeyeater *Lichmera indistincta*
RANGE Australia, New Guinea, Aru Islands
HABITAT Forest, woodland, mangroves, cultivated land, gardens
SIZE 4¾–6 in (12–15 cm)

A restless, active brown honeyeater feeds among flowering trees and bushes on nectar and insects. It is always found near water and has a beautiful voice. The nest is cup-shaped and made of tightly packed bark shreds and grass, bound with cobwebs. It is suspended from a twig or placed among the foliage of a bush or tree. The female lays a clutch of 2 eggs.

Strong-billed Honeyeater
Melithreptus validirostris

RANGE Tasmania,
islands in Bass Strait

HABITAT Open forest, woodland

SIZE 5½ in (14 cm)

Popularly known as the bark-bird, this honeyeater hops about on tree trunks, stripping off the bark in its search for insects. It is often seen on *Eucalyptus* trees. Nectar forms only a small part of this bird's diet. The sexes look alike. The nest, suspended from a branch is made of bark strips and grass. The female lays 2 or 3 eggs.

Cardinal Honeyeater
Myzomela cardinalis

RANGE Islands of Vanuatu, Samoa, Santa Cruz and Solomon

HABITAT Forest, open woodland, cultivated land

SIZE 5 in (13 cm)

This is one of the smallest honeyeaters. With its bright coloration, it resembles a sunbird. It forages for small insects and nectar and will often form large groups at favored feeding sites. Its flight is fast and direct. Male and female differ in appearance; the male has vivid red and black plumage, while the female is mainly olive gray, with some red on her rump and lower back.

A small, cup-shaped nest, made of grass stems, is built on a forked branch. The female lays 1 or 2 eggs.

Fuscous Honeyeater
Lichenostomus fusca

RANGE Australia from N.E. Queensland to S.E. south Australia

HABITAT Open forest

SIZE 6 in (15 cm)

The fuscous honeyeater forages busily among the foliage at various heights searching for nectar and insects. It also catches insects on the wing. It is a fairly common bird and generally lives alone or in small parties. The sexes look alike, with olive brown plumage with touches of yellow and dark markings on the cheeks. The female lays 2 or 3 eggs in a cup-shaped nest, made of plant fiber and grass and hung in a tree.

Little Friarbird *Philemon citreogularis*

RANGE E. and N. Australia, S. New Guinea, islands in Banda Sea

HABITAT Open forest, woodland

SIZE 9¾–11 in (25–28 cm)

Like all friarbirds, the little friarbird has an area of bare skin on its head, the origin of its common name. Male and female look similar and, despite the name, are not much smaller than other friarbirds. The little friarbird forages in all kinds of trees and bushes for fruit, insects and nectar. It makes a variety of harsh cries, particularly when feeding in a squabbling flock, but also has a more attractive musical song. In the south of Australia, these birds are thought to make regular seasonal movements.

The cup-shaped nest is made of bark strips and plant fiber and is built on a forked branch or suspended from a branch, often overhanging water. The female lays 2 to 4 eggs.

Long-bearded Melidectes *Melidectes princeps*

RANGE New Guinea

HABITAT Mountain forest, alpine grassland

SIZE 10½ in (26.5 cm)

Distinguished by the white "whiskers" on its throat, the long-bearded melidectes has largely black plumage, with some light-colored bare skin around the eyes. Less arboreal than other honeyeaters, this bird spends much of its time on the ground, probing the leaf litter with its long, curved bill to find insects and sedge seeds. It also flies jerkily from tree to tree and will climb trees occasionally in order to feed on berries and fruit. A bulky nest, made of moss and fungal threads, is built in a bush or tree a meter or so above the ground. The female lays 1 egg.

PARDALOTES, AUSTRALASIAN ROBINS AND LEAFBIRDS

PARDALOTIDAE: PARDALOTE FAMILY

The birds in this family occur in Australia, New Guinea, Indonesia, and the western Pacific islands. There are 68 species of these small birds, found in a range of habitats including forest, heathland, scrub, and semidesert. Most are insect eaters. There are three subfamilies – pardalotes; bristlebirds; and scrubwrens and thornbills (a group which also includes the gerygones).

Spotted Pardalote *Pardalotus punctatus*

RANGE Australia, Tasmania
HABITAT Forest, woodland
SIZE 3½ in (9 cm)

The colorful spotted pardalote has characteristic spots on its plumage that are mostly white in the male and yellow in the female. It feeds on insects, which it finds on the ground and in trees. An agile climber, it clings to twigs in almost any position as it makes a thorough search of the foliage. Outside the breeding season, these pardalotes live alone or in small flocks, sometimes including other species.

A breeding pair excavates a tunnel in a bank or slope and makes a globular nest of bark and grass in a chamber at the end of it. There are usually 4 eggs, incubated by both parents for 14 to 16 days.

White-browed Scrubwren *Sericornis frontalis*

RANGE E. and S.E. and S.W. Australia, islands in Bass Strait
HABITAT Dense forest undergrowth, bushy coastal vegetation
SIZE 40 in (11 cm)

The white-browed scrubwren lives on or near the ground, keeping hidden in the thick undergrowth while it hops about in search of insects and other small invertebrates. The domed nest is built in the undergrowth on or near the ground. It is made of leaves and fibers and has a side entrance. The female lays 3 eggs.

Yellow-rumped Thornbill *Acanthiza chrysorrhoa*

RANGE Australia, south of Tropic of Capricorn
HABITAT Open woodland, savanna
SIZE 4 in (10 cm)

The male and female of this species both have somewhat sober plumage but with deep-yellow rump feathers, the origin of their common name. They eat insects and plant matter, such as seeds, which they find on the ground and by foraging in bushes and trees.

The large, untidy nest is made of grass and plant fibers and has a hooded brood chamber with a low, overhung entrance. It is usually situated in a low bush or other foliage. The female lays 3 eggs, which she incubates for 18 to 20 days; both parents then tend the young. The birds produce up to four broods a season, and young from earlier broods assist in the care of subsequent nestlings. This unusual habit is common to many members of this subfamily.

White-throated Gerygone *Gerygone olivacea*

RANGE S.E. New Guinea, coastal N. and E. Australia
HABITAT Open forest, woodland
SIZE 4¼ in (11 cm)

An arboreal bird, the white-throated warbler forages for insects on bark and foliage and occasionally chases prey on the wing. It usually occurs alone or in scattered, loosely knit groups. Male and female look alike, both with grayish-brown upperparts and yellow underparts.

The long, oval shaped nest is suspended from twigs up to 50 ft (15 m) above the ground. It is constructed from plant fiber and strips of bark, interwoven with spiders' webs and lined with feathers or plant down. The nest has a hooded entrance near to the top. The female lays 2 or 3 eggs.

EOPSALTRIIDAE: AUSTRALASIAN ROBIN FAMILY

This family of small, arboreal birds is found mainly in Australia and New Guinea, but 1 species is found in Malaysia and another in the Himalayas and south China. Most of the 46 species occupy the lower vegetation in forests or woods and eat insects.

Flame Robin *Petroica phoenicea*
RANGE Tasmania, S.E. Australia
HABITAT Dry forest, woodland, open country
SIZE 5–5¼ in (13–14 cm)

The male flame robin has a bright red throat and belly, reminiscent of those of the European robin. The female has pale buff underparts, with occasionally a touch of orange-red on the belly. It eats insects, taken on the ground and in trees. Normally solitary birds, they may form flocks outside the breeding season.

The nest is made of grass and bark strips, bound with spiders' webs. It may be in a tree fork or hollow on a bank or among tree roots. The female lays 3 eggs.

Citrine Canary Flycatcher *Culicicapa helianthea*
RANGE Philippines, Greater Sunda Islands
HABITAT Forest, woodland
SIZE About 4 in (10 cm)

Also called the sunflower flycatcher, the plumage of this bird is largely yellow of various shades; the upperparts of juveniles tend to be darker and greener than those of adults. It perches on the outer branches of trees and makes short aerial dashes after insects in true flycatcher fashion. It sometimes feeds in mixed flocks.

IRENIDAE: LEAFBIRD FAMILY

The leafbird family consists of 10 species divided into 2 groups – leafbirds and fairy bluebirds. All occur in southern and Southeast Asia, generally in forest, but sometimes in orchards. Leafbirds are bright green and eat fruit and berries, as well as insects, pollen, and nectar. They are gregarious, moving in flocks. The 2 species of fairy bluebirds are brilliant blue, highly arboreal and gregarious birds. They gather in small flocks and feed on fruit. In all species females are usually duller than males.

Gold-fronted Leafbird *Chloropsis aurifrons*
RANGE India, Sri Lanka, S.E. Asia, Sumatra
HABITAT Forest fringe, open country, gardens, damp hill country to 3,000 ft (900 m)
SIZE 7 in (18 cm)

These brightly colored arboreal birds are seldom seen, except when they fly briefly from clump to clump of trees or attract attention by calling or imitating other birds. The male is brilliant green, with a blue throat patch and a bright orange crown. With this primarily green plumage, leafbirds blend well with foliage. They are agile and acrobatic in the trees even swinging from the branches as if on a trapeze. They live in pairs or small groups, feeding among the leaves on insects, particularly caterpillars, spiders, berries and the nectar of the flowers of the coral tree (*Erythrina*), loranthus and the silk cotton tree. As they search for nectar, they pollinate plants.

The small, cup-shaped nest is built among thick foliage at the outer end of a branch, high up in a tree. The female lays 2 or 3 eggs and is thought to incubate them alone.

Asian Fairy Bluebird *Irena puella*
RANGE India to S.E. Asia, Greater Sunda and Andaman Islands, Philippines: Palawan
HABITAT Hill forest to 5,600 ft (1,700 m)
SIZE 10 in (25.5 cm)

Fairy bluebirds are almost totally arboreal, preferring to spend their time high up in the branches of evergreen trees near running water. Males, particularly, are shy birds, not often clearly seen except when they come down to drink or bathe, when their striking coloration – bright ultramarine upperparts, with velvety black below and red eyes – make them conspicuous. Females are duller, with peacock-green and blackish-brown plumage. These birds feed mainly on the nectar of the flowers of the coral tree (*Erythrina*), and on fruit, especially ripe figs, often in the company of hornbills and pigeons.

The nest is built 10 to 21 ft (3 to 6.5 m) up in a small tree, in the darkest part of the forest, and is made of roots and twigs, covered with moss. Usually 2 eggs are laid.

SHRIKES AND VIREOS

LANIIDAE: SHRIKE FAMILY

The 30 species in this family are found in North America and Eurasia south to Indonesia, New guinea, and the Philippines. Shrikes are small to medium-sized songbirds that feed mainly on large insects, but will also take small reptiles, birds, and mammals. They have a large head, and a strong, hooked-tip beak used to pull prey apart. They inhabit savanna, scrub, bush, and open woodland, All habitats that have a mixture of tall vegetation and open spaces.

Typically shrikes keep watch from a high vantage point, swooping down to the ground to take prey or else catching it flycatcher fashion, on the wing, then returning to the perch. Some species impale prey on thorns before eating it.

Great Gray/Northern Shrike *Lanius excubitor*

RANGE Widespread in N. America, Asia, Europe, N. Africa; winters south of breeding range

HABITAT Varied, woodland, open country, marsh, tundra, savanna, desert

SIZE 9½ in (24 cm)

Great gray shrikes perch in a prominent position and from there fly out to capture their prey – mainly insects, although small birds, mammals, reptiles and frogs are also sometimes taken. Normally the birds return to the perch to eat, but they will sometimes store food in a kind of larder. Great gray shrikes defend their territory strongly against all intruders, even hawks, and like hawks, they hover when hunting. The female looks similar to the male, but she is duller, with crescent-shaped markings on the underparts; the juvenile is even more heavily marked.

The bulky nest is constructed by both birds from twigs, moss and grass and is usually placed about 40 ft (12 m) from the ground. In the north, the female lays 5 to 7 eggs, which she incubates for 14 to 16 days. Fewer eggs are laid at a time in the southern area of the range, but there may be two clutches in a year.

The great gray shrike is one of only 2 species found in North America; the other is the loggerhead shrike, *Lanius ludovicianus,* which is fairly similar to the great gray shrike both in its physical appearance and its habits.

Magpie Shrike *Corvinella melanoleuca*

RANGE Africa: Kenya, Tanzania, Mozambique across to S. Angola

HABITAT Open country with scattered trees and bush, neglected cultivation

SIZE 17½ in (45 cm)

The black and white plumage of this large bird resembles that of a magpie, and it is also known as the magpie shrike. Male and female look alike, the juvenile is duller. Despite its striking coloration and its habit of sitting conspicuously on the tops of trees, this shrike is a rather shy bird. It usually moves in pairs or small parties, often with other bird species, and feeds on insects, which it catches on the ground by dropping down on them from a high perch. Long-tailed shrikes often skewer their prey on a thorn before eating it.

The nest is a bulky, untidy structure, sited among thorny branches, and is usually made of thorny twigs. There are normally 3 or 4 eggs.

VIREONIDAE: VIREO FAMILY

There are about 51 species in this family, all found in the New World. The true vireos dominate the group – there are about 45 species. All feed on insects among the foliage in forested and wooded areas. Similar to the wood warblers in appearance, vireos are more stoutly built, have heavier bills and tend to be more deliberate in their movements.

The remaining birds in the family are divided into two groups – 2 species of peppershrikes and 4 shrike-vireos. All are slightly larger birds than vireos and have heavy, hooked bills; they feed in the trees, mainly on insects and fruit. In all species of this family, male and female look alike, or nearly so.

Red-eyed Vireo *Vireo olivaceus*

RANGE Canada, much of USA (not S.W.), Central and South America to Argentina; West Indies

HABITAT Deciduous forest and woodland, gardens, parks, orchards

SIZE 5½–6¾ in (14–17 cm)

This widespread vireo is distinguished by its ruby-red eyes; immature birds have brown eyes. It occurs almost anywhere that there are deciduous trees and moves slowly through the lower

levels and undergrowth, foraging for insects and berries. It sings more than any other bird on hot summer days.

The neat, cup-shaped nest is suspended between the twigs of a horizontal fork in a tree or bush. There are usually 4 eggs in a clutch, which the female incubates for between 11 and 14 days. The young leave the nest some 10 to 12 days after hatching.

Tawny-crowned Greenlet *Hylophilus ochraceiceps*
RANGE S. Mexico, Central and South America to Bolivia

HABITAT Rain forest, woodland

SIZE 4¼ in (11 cm)

This little vireo has predominantly yellowish and brown plumage, with a tawny forehead and crown. It forages among the leaves of bushes and saplings for insects and other small invertebrates. It usually moves in small groups, often in mixed flocks with other forest birds.

The female lays 2 eggs in a strongly built, cup-shaped nest, which is attached by its rim to a forked twig. Both parents feed their young with insects and larvae until they leave the nest at about 14 days old.

Rufous-browed Peppershrike *Cyclarhis gujanensis*
RANGE N.E. Mexico, through Central and South America to N. Argentina; Trinidad

HABITAT Forest, woodland, cultivated land

SIZE 6 in (15 cm)

A heavy-bodied bird, with a large head and strong legs and feet, this peppershrike is a good climber and forages in trees, but it is weak in flight. It is slow and deliberate in its movements as it

searches for insects and berries, particularly at the ends of branches and twigs. If a large insect is caught, the bird holds it down with its foot and tears it apart with its strong, hooked bill.

A secretive bird, this peppershrike rarely comes out into the open, but it can often be heard singing loudly and persistently from a perch. It usually lives alone or in pairs.

The nest is woven from bark and grasses and suspended in the fork of a branch in a bush or tree. Both parents incubate the clutch of 2 or 3 eggs and feed the young.

Chestnut-sided Shrike-vireo *Vireolanius melitophrys* **LR:nt**
RANGE Mexico to Guatemala

HABITAT Forest

SIZE 7 in (18 cm)

All 4 species of shrike-vireo are more brightly plumaged than typical vireos, and the chestnut-sided shrike-vireo is particularly attractive, with its green back, chestnut flanks and boldly striped head. It has a stout, hooked bill and strong legs and feet.

Seldom seen, this bird lives high up in the forest canopy and rarely flies in the open or perches in exposed spots. It feeds on insects, holding down large ones with its foot and tearing them apart with its bill, and it also eats some fruit.

The nest is suspended from a forked branch of a tree, but the breeding habits of this shrike-vireo are not known.

WHIPBIRDS, QUAILTHRUSH, APOSTLEBIRDS, SITELLAS, SHRIKE TITS AND WHISTLERS

CORVIDAE: CROW FAMILY

Members of this large and diverse family are found worldwide. There are 647 species in 7 subfamilies.

CINCLOSOMATINAE: QUAIL THRUSH AND WHIPBIRD SUBFAMILY

There are 15 species of quail thrush and whipbird. All but the 1 in Southeast Asia, occur in Australia and New Guinea.

Eastern Whipbird *Psophodes olivaceus*

RANGE Australia: Queensland to Victoria

HABITAT Thickets in or near forest

SIZE 9¾–11 in (25–28 cm)

The eastern whipbird has mainly dark plumage, with some white, and a long, broad tail. The sexes look alike.

It lives on or near the ground, but usually stays in dense undergrowth, searching for insects, larvae and spiders among the leaf litter. It hops and runs swiftly and climbs into bushes, but flies rarely and only for short distances.

The nest of twigs and rootlets is made near the ground in dense undergrowth. The female lays 2 eggs.

Cinnamon Quail Thrush

Cinclosoma cinnamomeum

RANGE Australia: drier areas, Western Australia to Queensland and Victoria

HABITAT Semidesert, scrub

SIZE 7¼ in (20 cm)

Alone or in small family groups, the cinnamon quail thrush skulks among bushes or hides in holes and burrows to escape predators and the heat of the day. It usually feeds at dawn and dusk, on seeds and insects. It also hunts for insects over open country, flying low with noisy, whirring wings. The female lacks the male's characteristic black markings.

The nest is sited in a shallow dip in the ground or under a bush or fallen branch and is made of grass and twigs, lined with bark and leaves. The female lays 2 or 3 eggs.

CORCORACINAE: AUSTRALIAN CHOUGH AND APOSTLEBIRD SUBFAMILY

The two species in this subfamily are gregarious birds that inhabit scrub and open woodlands of eastern Australia. Both forage on the ground for insects, invertebrates, and seeds. They rarely fly, but roost, and build communal nests, in trees.

Apostlebird *Struthidea cinerea*

RANGE Australia: Victoria, New South Wales, Queensland

HABITAT Open woodland, scrub, cultivated land

SIZE 13 in (33 cm)

The apostlebird usually lives in groups of about 12 birds – hence its common name – which stay together even in the breeding season. The group may be led by a dominant pair. The birds feed mainly on the ground on insects and seeds, but they also jump from branch to branch and fly for short distances.

The bowl-shaped mud nest is lined with grass and made in a tree, usually near other nests. The female lays 4 or 5 eggs which are incubated for 19 days. More than one female may lay in one nest. The chicks are fed by the group.

PACHYCEPHALINAE: SITELLA, MOHOUA, SHRIKE-TIT AND WHISTLER SUBFAMILY

A diverse group of 59 species, sitellas and their relatives are small, mainly arboreal birds found in New Zealand, Australasia and Southeast Asia. There are 4 groups within the subfamily – sitellas, mohouas, shrike-tits, and whistlers or thick-heads.

Varied Sitella *Daphoenositta chrysoptera*

RANGE Australia

HABITAT Open forest, woodland

SIZE 4–4¼ in (10–12 cm)

The agile varied sitella runs up or down tree trunks with ease. Most of its life is spent in the trees and it flits from place to place, probing crevices in the bark for insects. It is gregarious and usually moves in small groups. There are many forms, all included in this one species, which differ greatly in coloration.

The cup-shaped nest is made on a forked branch and camouflaged with pieces of bark. Both parents incubate the 3 or 4 eggs and feed the young.

Crested Shrike-tit

Falcunculus frontatus

RANGE Australia (patchy distribution)

HABITAT Dry forest, woodland

SIZE 6¾–7½ in (17–19 cm)

The crested shrike-tit has a rather unusual bill for an insect-eater – it is deep, laterally compressed and slightly hooked. The bird often clings to tree trunks and uses its bill to strip off bark in its search for insects and larvae. It also forages among foliage for insects and is beneficial to mankind in that it eats many larvae of the codlin moths that attack orchards.

The deep, cup-shaped nest is built in a fork of a tree, such as a eucalyptus sapling, and the male often clears the area around it by breaking twigs above the nest. The female lays 2 or 3 eggs.

Golden Whistler *Pachycephala pectoralis*

RANGE Indonesia: Java to the Moluccas; Bismarck Archipelago to Fiji and Tonga; E., S. and S.W. Australia, Tasmania

HABITAT Forest, woodland, mallee (eucalyptus) scrub

SIZE 7 in (18 cm)

Divided into 70 or 80 races distributed among the many islands in its range, the golden whistler may have more subspecies (some of which are as distinct as species) than any other bird. Races vary enormously, particularly the head plumage. The male bird is generally olive-green, yellow and black or gray. Females usually have olive-brown to olive-gray upperparts, with grayish throat and breast and whitish belly plumage.

A tree-dwelling bird, the golden whistler feeds in the trees on insects and sometimes on berries. It perches for long periods and is rather inactive compared to most flycatchers.

Both partners of a breeding pair help to build the nest, which is usually in a fork of a small tree or bush. It is made of grass, bark and leaves, lined with fine grass. Both birds incubate the 2 or 3 eggs and tend the young.

Gray Shrike-thrush *Colluricincla harmonica*

RANGE Australia, Tasmania, islands in Bass Strait, S.E. New Guinea

HABITAT Forest, woodland, grassland, suburban parks

SIZE 9 in (23 cm)

The gray shrike-thrush is a wide-spread species, common in Australia but found only in a restricted area of New Guinea. A solitary bird, it feeds in undergrowth, on the ground and among lower branches of trees. It sings with clear, musical notes. The female differs slightly from the male in plumage, having a touch of brown on the upperparts, less distinct white facial markings and streaks on the breast.

The bowl-shaped nest is built on the ground, in a tree or bush or on a rock ledge, from bark strips and grass. The birds may take over an old nest of another species. The female lays 2 or 3 eggs, and there may be more than one brood.

Rusty Pitohui

Pitohui ferrugineus

RANGE New Guinea area, Aru Islands

HABITAT Lowland forest

SIZE 10–11 in (25.5–28 cm)

One of the largest whistlers, the rusty pitohui is gregarious and lives in pairs or small parties. It moves slowly through the low levels of the forest, feeding on insects and fruit and often uttering soft calls. The sexes look alike, with mainly brown and rufous plumage.

The deep, cup-shaped nest is built on a multiple-forked branch, high in a tree. It is made of twigs, vine and fiber, lined with leaves and fine plant material. The female lays 1 egg.

CROWS

CORVINAE: CROW, BIRDS-OF-PARADISE, CURRAWONG AND ORIOLE SUBFAMILY

The 297 species of this subfamily make up 4 tribes.

The 117 species of crows, jays and magpies are successful, intelligent, and adaptable birds. They occur worldwide, apart from the polar regions. All species are large with powerful, often hooked bills. The jays are most brightly colored; nutcrackers are spotted, and crows are mainly black.

Birds-of-paradise are medium to large arboreal birds found in the rain forests of New Guinea, north east Australia, and the Moluccas. There are 45 species, and this group probably contains the most visually spectacular of all birds. Males have colorful plumage, often with long, decorative tail and head feathers, which is used to attract females. Females have dull, usually brown, plumage.

The third tribe in the subfamily contains 24 species in 2 groups – the currawongs, Australian butcherbirds and Australian magpies (which resemble crows) and the wood swallows (which resemble martins). Currawongs and their relatives include arboreal species and ground-feeders, and are found in Australia and New Guinea. Magpies have been introduced to New Zealand and Fiji. Most eat insects and other small invertebrates. Wood swallows are found from Australia and Fiji to South China and India. They have stocky bodies and long, pointed wings and are skilled fliers.

The oriole and cuckoo-shrike tribe consists of two groups. The 29 species of orioles are found from temperate Eurasia to Australia, and in tropical Africa. They are noted for their clear, melodious calls. Orioles are arboreal and feed in trees on insects and fruit. The 82 species of cuckoo-shrikes and minivets occur from northern India to Australia and the islands of the western Pacific, and in Africa. Most are arboreal, drab birds, with strong, notched beaks, long pointed wings, and bristles round the base of the bill. Minivets are colorful. Many cuckoo-shrikes and minivets have erectile feathers on the back and rump.

American Crow *Corvus brachyrhynchos*
RANGE S. Canada, USA
HABITAT Open country, farmland, open woodland, woodland edge, parks
SIZE 17–20¾ in (43–53 cm)

This stocky, black crow is abundant and widespread and adapts well to most habitats. Almost omnivorous, it feeds largely on the ground, but also in trees, on insects, spiders, frogs, reptiles, small mammals, birds and their eggs, and carrion. It also eats grain, fruit and nuts and scavenges on refuse. They usually forage in pairs, although lone males are seen in the breeding season. In winter, huge flocks gather to fly to communal roosts. A nest of sticks and twigs is made in a tree, bush or, on a telegraph pole. The 3 to 6 eggs are incubated for about 18 days, probably by the female. Northern populations migrate south in winter.

Rook *Corvus frugilegus*
RANGE Europe, Middle East, C. and E. Asia
HABITAT Open country and farmland with clumps of trees, small woods
SIZE 17¾ in (45 cm)

The glossy black rook is distinguished by the patch of bare skin on its face in front of the eyes and the shaggy, loose feathers on its thighs. It feeds largely on grain and earthworms, which it obtains by driving its bill into the earth and forcing it open to seize the worm. Insects and other invertebrates, small mammals, young birds, eggs, nuts and fruit are also included in its diet. Primarily a groundfeeder, the rook will fly up into trees to take nuts or other specific items. Rooks live in pairs but in autumn and winter gather in large, communal roosts.

Colonies nest at the tops of tall trees, each pair making a nest of sticks and twigs. The male feeds the female while she incubates the 3 to 5 eggs for 16 to 18 days. Both parents feed the young. Northern birds migrate south in winter.

Tibetan Ground Jay *Pseudopodoces humilis*
RANGE W. China, Tibet, N.E. India
HABITAT Open, sandy country
SIZE 7¾ in (20 cm)

One of a group of ground-living corvids, the Tibetan ground jay runs speedily on its long legs and has a heavy bill, with which it probes and digs in the ground for its insect food. It digs its own nest in the earth, and the female lays 4 to 6 eggs.

Black-billed/Common Magpie
Pica pica

RANGE Europe to N. Africa; Asia to Himalayas and just into S.E. Asia; Alaska, W. Canada and USA to Utah

HABITAT Open country with trees, woodland edge, grassland

SIZE 17¼–22½ in (44–57 cm)

This sprightly magpie has black and white plumage and a long tail; the many subspecies show slight variations in plumage, some having a pronounced green, purple or golden sheen. Insects, snails, slugs and spiders are the main foods, but grain, small mammals and carrion may also be taken. The magpie will fly up into a tree to take fruit, nuts and young birds. Some magpies remain in their breeding territory all year round usually in pairs or small groups, while others gather in communal roosts out of the breeding season.

The large, domed nest is made in a tree or bush by both members of a pair. The male feeds the female while she incubates the 5 to 8 eggs for 17 or 18 days.

Blue Jay *Cyanocitta cristata*

RANGE S.E. Canada, E. USA to Gulf of Mexico

HABITAT Woodland, city parks, gardens

SIZE 11¾ in (30 cm)

This noisy, colorful jay is mainly blue with black and white plumage on the wings and tail and black markings on the face. It feeds on the ground and in trees on nuts, seeds, grain, fruit, berries, insects and invertebrates, and the eggs and young of other birds. Seen in family parties in summer, blue jays gather in large groups in autumn, which often mob predators or intruders.

They nest in a tree or bush, and the female incubates the 2 to 6 eggs for 16 to 18 days. The male feeds her and the brood.

Eurasian Jay *Garrulus glandarius*

RANGE Europe to N. Africa; C. Asia to E. and S.E. Asia

HABITAT Forest, woodland, orchards, towns

SIZE 13¼ in (34 cm)

An extremely variable species over its range, the European jay generally has a pinkish-brown body, with brilliant wing patterns of blue and black bars. Alone or in pairs, it feeds in trees and on the ground on insects and small invertebrates and also on acorns, berries and grain.

The female lays 3 to 7 eggs in a nest made in a tree. The male feeds her while she incubates them for 16 to 19 days and feeds the brood until she can leave the nest to help him.

Green Jay *Cyanocorax yncas*

RANGE USA: S. Texas; through Mexico and Central and South America to Brazil and Bolivia

HABITAT Forest, woodland, thickets

SIZE 11¾ in (30 cm)

This bright green, yellow and blue bird has green tail feathers. The many subspecies show slight variations in plumage. Green jays live in pairs or small groups and eat mainly insects as well as acorns and seeds and the eggs and young of other birds.

The 3 to 5 eggs are laid in a nest in a tree or bush and are incubated by the female. Both parents tend the young.

Ceylon Magpie *Urocissa ornata*

RANGE Sri Lanka

HABITAT Forest, gardens

SIZE 18 in (46 cm)

The Ceylon magpie lives alone, in pairs or in small groups. It feeds in trees and on the ground on insects, invertebrates and fruit. The nest is made in a small tree. The female lays a clutch of between 3 and 5 eggs.

Piapiac *Ptilostomus afer*

RANGE Africa: Senegal to Nigeria, east to Ethiopia

HABITAT Open country, palm groves

SIZE 18 in (46 cm)

A slender, long-tailed bird, with a thick bill, the piapiac lives in flocks of 10 or more. It feeds mainly on the ground on insects and invertebrates, often following herds of large animals in order to pick up the insects they disturb; it also takes insects from the backs of large mammals and eats the fruit of the oil palm.

The nest is made in a palm or other tree, and the female lays a clutch of between 3 and 7 eggs.

BIRDS OF PARADISE, BUTCHERBIRDS, AUSTRALIAN MAGPIE AND CURRAWONGS

King of Saxony's Bird of Paradise

Pteridophora alberti

RANGE Mountains of New Guinea

HABITAT Rain forest up to 9,500 ft (2,850 m)

SIZE 9 in (23 cm)

The male King of Saxony's bird of paradise has two plumes, one extending from each side of its head, that are unique to it. These plumes are two or three times the body length and consist of wirelike shafts, bearing a series of horny plates The bird chooses a display site on a high branch, holds his head plumes up, and bounces up and down, while expanding and retracting his back feathers and hissing. The whole effect is quite spectacular. As the female approaches, the male sweeps the long head plumes in front of her and then follows her, and they mate.

The female bird is brownish-gray, with black-barred white underparts. The birds live in the middle and upper layers of the forest and feed on fruit.

Crinkle-collared Manucode *Manucodia chalybata*

RANGE New Guinea, Misoöl Island

HABITAT Rain forest

SIZE 14½ in (37 cm)

The crinkle-collared manucode is a glossy purplish-black bird, with curly green feathers adorning its head and neck. Male and female look alike and have none of the spectacular adornments which are associated with the other species of birds of paradise. They live in the middle to upper stories of the forest and feed on fruit.

These manucodes form monogamous pairs and nest on forked branches. The female is thought to lay 1 egg.

Blue Bird of Paradise *Paradisaea rudolphi* **VU**

RANGE Mountains of S.E. New Guinea

HABITAT Rain forest

SIZE 11 in (28 cm) excluding tail, which is 13½ in (34 cm) long

The male blue bird of paradise has a velvety black breast, long, lacy, flank plumes and distinctive tail feathers. These are narrow and straplike and play an important part in the display dance he performs to attract the much plainer female. The male hangs upside-down from a branch, with the flank plumes spread out and the tail straps held in curves. In this position, he swings to and fro making a grating call.

A nest is made by the female in a low tree, and she is thought to lay 1 egg.

King Bird of Paradise *Cicinnurus regius*

RANGE New Guinea; Yapen, Misoöl, Sulawati and Aru Islands

HABITAT Lowland rain forest

SIZE 12 in (30.5 cm) including tail (male)

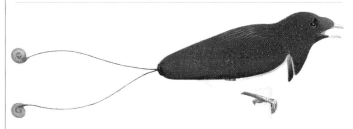

A spectacular crimson bird, the king bird of paradise has two wirelike, lyre-shaped tail feathers, tipped with metallic green, and a fanlike plume at each shoulder. The female lacks the tail wires and has brown plumage, edged with chestnut and olive. These birds eat mainly on fruit at all levels of the forest. The male uses a horizontal branch as his display ground and spends much time there adopting display postures to attract a mate. He raises his tail wires, hangs upsidedown, and vibrates his wings.

The female makes her nest in a hole in a tree – the only bird of paradise to do so. She lays 2 eggs, which she is thought to incubate for about 12 days.

Ribbon-tailed Astrapia

Astrapia mayeri **VU**

RANGE Mountains of
C. New Guinea

HABITAT Rain forest

SIZE 4 ft (1.2 m) including tail of up
to 36 in (91.5 cm)

The spectacular ribbonlike central tail
feathers are the main identifying feature of
the male of this species, which is mainly black, with
patches of green iridescencent plumage on the head and
throat. The tail feathers play a central role in the male's
courtship display, when they are twitched from side to side
to attract the attention of a female.

The female bird has a much shorter tail and glossy black,
green and brown plumage.

This species was one of the last birds of paradise to be
discovered, and was first described in 1939 and then only on
the basis of a pair of the tail feathers that were found in a
tribal headdress. It lives in a very restricted area of the
central highlands of New Guinea. It frequents the
branches of tall trees and feeds on fruit, insects, spiders
and small mammals and reptiles. The shallow, cup-
shaped nest is constructed on a base of leaves
from moss and vine tendrils.

Pied Currawong *Strepera graculina*

RANGE Australia: Queensland to Victoria; Lord Howe Island

HABITAT Forest, clumps of trees in parks, suburban land

SIZE 17¾ in (45 cm)

Primarily an arboreal bird, the pied
currawong climbs trees
in search of insects,
larvae and fruit, it
will also eat the young and
eggs of other bird species. It
sometimes searches for insects on the
ground. These noisy, gregarious birds,
live in flocks. The name is derived from
their call. The female lays
3 or 4 eggs in a nest in a tree.

Black Butcherbird

Cracticus quoyi

RANGE Australia:
Queensland, coast
of Northern Territory; New
Guinea, Yapen and Aru Islands

HABITAT Forest

SIZE 12½–14¼ in (32–36 cm)

A bold, often aggressive bird, the black
butcherbird feeds mostly on the ground, where
it hops along on its short legs. Using its sharp,
hooked bill, it tears up prey too large to be swallowed
whole, such as large insects (particularly grasshoppers)
and small vertebrates. Male and female look alike and
live alone or in small family groups.

A nest of twigs is made on a forked branch, and the
female lays 3 or 4 eggs.

Australian Magpie *Gymnorhina tibicen*

RANGE S. New Guinea, Australia, Tasmania;
introduced in New Zealand

HABITAT Open woodland, grassland, parks, gardens

SIZE 14¼–15¾ in (36–40 cm)

Although it roosts and nests in trees, the Australian magpie does
much of its feeding on the ground, searching for larvae, beetles
and grasshoppers. Fruit and vegetation also make up part of its
diet. Australian magpies are gregarious birds, and live in groups
consisting of two pairs of adults or a larger number of
birds, led by a dominant, polygamous male.
Males and females look more or less alike.

The nest is made in a tree,
and the female lays 3 eggs,
which she incubates for 20 to
21 days. She also does most of
the feeding of the young.

CUCKOO SHRIKES AND MINIVETS

Ground Cuckoo-shrike *Coracina maxima*

RANGE Australian interior

HABITAT Dry, open country

SIZE 13 in (33 cm)

The ground cuckoo-shrike is far more terrestrial than other cuckoo shrikes which only occasionally forage on the ground. A stout-legged bird, it walks and runs well as it searches for insects to eat. It usually lives in family groups.

The nest, usually placed in the fork of a tree, is made of grass, stems and rootlets, and spiders' webs may be used to bind the plant material together. It may sometimes be built on top of the old nest of another bird species. The female usually lays 2 or 3 eggs; more than one female may lay eggs in the same nest.

Slender-billed Cicadabird *Coracina tenuirostris*

RANGE Sulawesi to Solomon Islands, New Guinea, Australia

HABITAT Forest edge, grassland, mangroves

SIZE 10 in (25.5 cm)

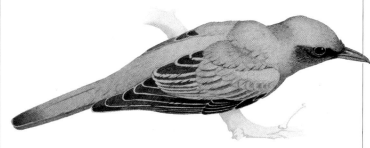

Known as a cicadabird because of its high, shrill song, this bird is rather shy and is more often heard than seen; it is usually silent, however, outside the breeding season. Insects, such as beetles, caterpillars and cicadas, are its main foods, and most are caught up in the trees.

The nest of the cicadabird is about 3 in (7.5 cm) across. It is made of twigs and spiders' webs, camouflaged with lichen and is usually placed on a horizontal, forked branch. The female lays 1 egg, and the male defends the nest and his territory against intruders. He feeds his mate while she incubates the egg.

Black-faced Cuckoo-Shrike *Coracina novaehollandiae*

RANGE India to S.E. Asia and Australia

HABITAT Light forest, gardens, suburbs, plantations

SIZE 13 in (33 cm)

A heavily built, largely gray bird, the male large cuckoo shrike has some black, shrikelike markings on its head. The female looks similar in most respects, but the markings on her head are dark gray.

Small groups of cuckoo shrikes forage for food, mainly fruit such as figs, insects and insect larvae high in the treetops. They sometimes dive to pick up food from the ground, or take insects in the air. Their flight is undulating and they land with a characteristic shuffling of wings. They maintain contact as they move with a rolling call and make a high-pitched, trilling call during displays.

Large cuckoo shrikes tend to return to the same breeding site, even the same branch, year after year. The nest is saucer-shaped and constructed from twigs and spiders' webs and is usually sited in the fork of a branch. The female lays a clutch of 2 or 3 eggs.

Bar-winged Flycatcher-Shrike *Hemipus picatus*

RANGE India, Sri Lanka, S.E. Asia, Sumatra, Borneo

HABITAT Woodland, forest, forest edge

SIZE 5 in (12.5 cm)

The bar-winged flycatcher shrike is a small cuckoo shrike, which pursues insects in the air as skilfully as a true flycatcher. It also finds food by hopping around the branches, gleaning insects from leaves, and may sometimes feed on the ground, although it is primarily a tree-living bird.

Small groups of about 6 birds usually live together out of the breeding season and may also join in mixed flocks. The male and female look similar, but the black plumage of the male is replaced by dark brown in the female in some races.

The shallow, saucer-shaped nest is built on a branch of a tree and is constructed from grass and rootlets, bound together with spiders' webs. Lichen is used to camouflage the outside of the nest, and the sitting bird appears to be on a clump of lichen rather than a nest. The female lays 2 or 3 eggs. Once hatched, the young birds sit still, with their eyes closed and their heads raised together, and can easily be mistaken by the casual observer for a spur of dead wood.

Red-shouldered Cuckoo-shrike

Campephaga phoenicea

RANGE Africa, south of the Sahara

HABITAT Forest, woodland

SIZE 8 in (20.5 cm)

Some races of this species have the distinctive red markings they are named for, but others have small yellow shoulder patches or none at all. Males have glossy black plumage, while females are predominantly olive-brown or gray with yellow-edged wings and tail. Restless, active birds, red-shouldered cuckoo shrike are always on the move in pairs or in parties of several species. They feed on caterpillars and insects, gleaned from foliage or found on the ground. Some insects may even be taken in the air.

A cup-shaped nest, constructed from moss and lichen bound together with spiders' webs, is built in the fork of a tree and the female lays a clutch of between 2 and 3 eggs. She incubates the eggs for about 20 days, and both parents then feed the newly hatched nestlings.

White-winged Triller

Lalage sueurii

RANGE Java, Lesser Sunda Islands, Sulawesi, Australia, New Guinea

HABITAT Open forest, woodland

SIZE 7 in (18 cm)

The white-winged triller makes its melodious calls as it flies from tree to tree taking insects from leaves and branches. Male and female differ in plumage, the female being largely brown, while the male is glossy black, gray and white.

Both partners of a breeding pair help to build a nest of plant material, usually situated in the fork of a branch. They both incubate the 1 to 3 eggs for about 14 days and feed the young.

Scarlet Minivet *Pericrocotus flammeus*

RANGE India, Sri Lanka, S. China, S.E. Asia to Philippines, Bali and Lombok

HABITAT Forest, woodland

SIZE 9 in (23 cm)

One of the 13 species of minivet, the scarlet minivet, with its bright plumage, is typical of the group. The male is red and black, while the female has dark gray and yellow plumage, distributed in the same manner. Both can be identified by the oval patch on each wing that is red in males and yellow in females. Strictly arboreal, scarlet minivets search among the treetops for large, soft-bodied insects to eat, often catching them in flight.

The shallow, cup-shaped nest is constructed on the branch of a tree from twigs, roots and grass stems, bound together with spiders' webs. A covering of lichen and fragments of bark camouflages the nest from predators. The female lays a clutch of 2 or 3 eggs and incubates them alone. Both parents feed and tend the young.

WOOD SWALLOWS, ORIOLES AND FANTAILS

White-breasted Wood Swallow

Artamus leucorynchus

RANGE Australia and New Guinea, Philippines, Andaman, Palau and Fijian Islands

HABITAT Woodland, mangroves

SIZE 6¾ in (17cm)

The white-breasted wood swallow lives in groups of 10 or more birds, which often huddle together on a branch, waiting for insect prey. They return to the perch to eat a catch. If there is a shortage of flying insects, these birds eat ground insects and larvae.

Both members of a pair help to build a cup-shaped nest in the fork of a tree, in a hole in a tree or in an old magpie-lark's nest. Both parents incubate the 3 or 4 eggs for about 19 days.

White-browed Wood Swallow

Artamus superciliosus

RANGE Australia: breeds Victoria, New South Wales to S.E. Queensland; winters throughout continent

HABITAT Arid scrub, savanna

SIZE 7–7¾ in (18–20 cm)

The nomadic white-browed wood swallow disperses over much of the continent out of the breeding season, often moving in mixed flocks with other species of wood swallow. They perch in groups on branches and fly out to catch insects in the air. Females have less distinct "eyebrow" streaks than males.

The nest is built from sticks and grass in a tree or on a tree stump. Both parents incubate the 2 or 3 eggs for about 16 days.

Bornean Bristlehead *Pityriasis gymnocephala* **LR:nt**

RANGE Borneo

HABITAT Lowland forest to 4,000 ft (1,200 m), peat swamp, forest

SIZE 10 in (25.5 cm)

This rare bird has a large, extremely heavy, hooked bill and relatively short tail feathers, which gives it a top-heavy look. These self-confident birds are ponderous fliers, which keep to the middle layers of the forest. They eat insects and their larvae, mainly beetles, grasshoppers and cockroaches, noisily snapping them up with their large bills.

Golden Oriole *Oriolus oriolus*

RANGE Breeds in Europe, as far north as S. Finland, Sweden and Britain, N. Africa, Asia; winters in Africa and N.W. India

HABITAT Forest, woodland, orchards

SIZE 9½ in (24 cm)

The golden oriole frequents the treetops, feeding on insects and fruit. Even the brightly plumaged male is seldom seen. Females and juveniles are duller with yellowish-green upperparts and lighter, grayish-white underparts. Golden orioles rarely descend to the ground, and their flight is swift and undulating. Although they may remain in family groups for a while after breeding, they usually live alone or in pairs.

The courting male chases the female at top speed through the branches. She does most of the work of building the hammocklike nest, which is suspended by its rim from a forked branch. It is mainly the female partner that incubate the 3 or 4 eggs for 14 to 15 days.

Figbird *Sphecotheres viridis*

RANGE Lesser Sunda Islands, S.E. New Guinea, Cai Islands, W., N., and E. Australia

HABITAT Forest, savanna, fruiting trees

SIZE 11 in (28 cm)

Although they differ strikingly in appearance, all forms of *Sphecotheres*, from Timor to southern New Guinea and New South Wales, are now regarded as conspecific under the name *S. viridis*. Females have duller plumage than males. An arboreal bird, the figbird moves in noisy flocks, eating figs and other fruit and insects caught in the air.

The saucer-shaped nest is built of twigs and plant tendrils on a high branch. Usually 3 eggs are laid.

DICRURINAE: FANTAIL, MONARCH AND DRONGO SUBFAMILY

This subfamily of insect-eating birds has three distinct groups or tribes. The 42 species of fantails are arboreal birds found mainly in Australasia but with some species in Asia. Their common name comes from their habit of continually spreading and wagging their tails as they move through low vegetation. They catch insects either on the wing or by flushing out prey using the fantail when moving through vegetation and holding it down using a foot.

Monarchs are boldly plumaged birds of forest areas that occur from central Asia and northern China, south to Australia and the western Pacific islands, and in Africa. The 98 species also include paradise flycatchers, Australian flycatchers, magpie-larks and the silktail. Most species are arboreal flycatchers, some species dart out from perches to catch insect prey, while others search the foliage of the trees.

Drongos occur in Africa and from south Asia to Australia. The 24 species are tree-dwellers with dark plumage, pointed wings and square or forked tails, often with long, decorative feathers. Drongos spend much of their time perched, on the look out for insect prey, which they catch in the air. They are skilful, but not sustained, fliers. Males and females look alike, but females are usually slightly smaller.

Yellow-bellied Fantail
Rhipidura hypoxantha

RANGE Himalayas to S.W. China; northern S.E. Asia: Myanmar, Thailand, Laos

HABITAT Forest, rhododendron thickets

SIZE 5 in (13 cm)

The yellow-bellied fantail has bright yellow underparts and distinctive white tips to some of the tail feathers. Male and female birds look similar, but the male has black, masklike markings on the face, which are dark olive-brown in the female.

A lively, restless little bird, this fantail frequents the undergrowth up to the lower levels of the forest canopy, where it prances around with its tail fanned out, foraging for insects. It also feeds on tiny insects, which it takes in the air during brief, aerobatic flights, and may flush insects out of vegetation with its spread wings.

The nest is made the same width as the horizontal branch on which it is sited, which provides a measure of camouflage. It is built from moss covered with lichen and spiders' webs and lined with hair and feathers. The female lays 3 eggs.

Willie Wagtail *Rhipidura leucophrys*

RANGE Australia, Tasmania, New Guinea, Solomon Islands, the Moluccas

HABITAT Forest edge to desert edge, parks, gardens, cultivated land

SIZE 7¾ in (20 cm)

A common, adaptable bird, the willie wagtail has learned to take advantage of man-made environments. Male and female birds look alike, and their black and white plumage gives them a resemblance to the European pied wagtail, hence the common name. The willie wagtail generally lives alone, outside the breeding season, and finds food on the ground as well as in flight. It also sometimes sits on the backs of cattle and feeds on the insects disturbed by their hoofs.

The nest is made of grass bark strips or plant fiber bound tightly with spiders' webs. It is usually built on a horizontal branch, but may be made almost anywhere above ground. The female lays 4 eggs.

Rufous Fantail *Rhipidura rufifrons*

RANGE Lesser Sunda and W. Papuan Islands, N. and E. Australia, coastal areas of New Guinea, Louisiade Archipelago, Solomon and Santa Cruz Islands, Micronesia

HABITAT Forest, mangroves

SIZE 6½ in (16.5 cm)

With its tail fanned out, this flycatcher flies with great speed and dexterity through the undergrowth, catching insects in flight and picking them off the foliage. Although it is mainly a tree-living bird, it also feeds on the ground.

A pear-shaped nest, made of coarse plant material bound together with spiders' webs, is built on a thin, forked branch as much as 30 ft (9 m) from the ground. Both parents incubate the clutch of 2 eggs for about 15 days and feed the young. The young fantails are able to fly about 15 days after hatching out. Breeding birds may produce two to five broods a year, depending on the abundance of food.

MONARCH, MAGPIE-LARK AND SILKTAIL

Black-naped Monarch

Hypothymis azurea

RANGE India, S. China, S.E. Asia to Lesser
Sunda Islands and Philippines

HABITAT Forest, scrub, bamboo, cultivated land

SIZE 6½ in (16.5cm)

The male black-naped monarch has bright blue
plumage, with a little patch of black feathers
on the nape of the neck that are erected when
the bird is excited. There is also a narrow black
band across his chest. The female looks similar to the male
but has grayish brown plumage on the upperparts and lacks
the black nape and chest markings.

This flycatcher tends to perch in higher trees than other
species and makes agile looping flights after insect prey; it also
forages in undergrowth and on the ground. When a large insect
is caught the bird holds it down with its foot and tears it apart
before eating it. Usually seen alone or in pairs, the black-naped
monarch is an active bird, constantly on the move.

The neat, cup-shaped nest is built on a forked branch, to
which it is bound with spiders' webs, or in a bush, sapling or
bamboo clump. The female bird does most of the work, using
grass and bark for the cup and covering the outside with moss,
spiders' webs and egg-cases; the male attends her closely
throughout the nest-building. She lays 3 or 4 eggs, which she
incubates for 15 or 16 days. Both parents tend the young.

White-tailed Crested
Flycatcher *Trochocercus albonotatus*

RANGE Africa: Uganda, W. Kenya
to Malawi, Zambia, Zimbabwe

HABITAT Highland forest

SIZE 4 in (10 cm)

The white-tailed crested flycatcher has black,
gray and white plumage. The sexes look
alike. The bird eats insects, making short,
jerky flights after prey or foraging over
foliage. The male displays to his mate,
hopping around her with his tail raised
and wings trailing. The nest is moss, bound with cobwebs,
woven around a fork of a low tree. The female lays 2 eggs.

Asian Paradise Flycatcher *Terpsiphone paradisi*

RANGE Turkestan to N.E. China; S.E. Asia, Indonesia

HABITAT Open forest, mangroves, gardens, cultivated land

SIZE 8¾ in (22.5 cm)

The male Asian
paradise flycatcher is a
beautiful bird, with
extremely long central
tail feathers, which
add 10 in (25.5 cm) or more to
his length. Males occur in two color
phases – white and rufous. The white
male has white body and tail plumage, with
a black head, crest and throat, the rufous
male is more variable, according to race, but
has rufous tail, back and wings. The female is
similar to the rufous male, but lacks the crest
and long tail feathers.

Alone, or sometimes in pairs or mixed hunting
parties, the paradise flycatcher frequents the higher
branches of trees, flitting from perch to perch. Its
flight is swift and it makes brief sallies from a perch to
catch insect prey, returning to the same tree or to
another to consume the item. It may also flush out
insects on the ground. Flies, dragonflies, beetles, moths
and butterflies are its main prey.

The courting male displays to his mate by arching his tail
streamers gracefully, while singing and beating his wings.
Both sexes help to build the nest, which is a deep, inverted
cone, made in a horizontal forked branch of a tree often near or
overhanging water. The 3 or 4 eggs are incubated mostly by the
female for 15 or 16 days; unusually for such a decorative bird,
the male may sometimes assist and sits with his long tail hanging
out behind him. The male bird also helps to tend the nestlings.

Yellow-breasted Boatbill

Machaerirhynchus flaviventer

RANGE Australia: N.E. Queensland;
New Guinea and adjacent islands

HABITAT Rain forest

SIZE 4¾ in (12 cm)

The broad, flat bill is the
distinctive feature of this
flycatcher and the reason for its
common name. Male and female
differ slightly in appearance – the
female has yellowish-olive upperparts,
with areas of brownish-black. She has
fewer yellow and more white markings
than the male.

A tree-living bird, the yellow-
breasted boat-bill gleans insects from the foliage,
moving busily from branch to branch, mainly keeping to the top
of the tree canopy, and making soft trills to maintain contact.
Short flights may be made in order to catch prey on the wing.

The shallow, cup-shaped nest is constructed from strips of
bark, which are bound together with spiders' webs and decorated
with lichen to provide camouflage. The interior of the nest is
lined with vine tendrils. It is usually built fairly high up in the
forest canopy on a slender, forked branch. The female lays a
clutch of 2 eggs.

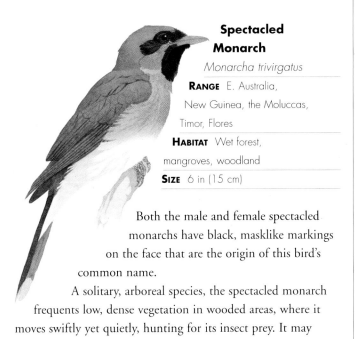

Spectacled Monarch

Monarcha trivirgatus

RANGE E. Australia,
New Guinea, the Moluccas,
Timor, Flores

HABITAT Wet forest,
mangroves, woodland

SIZE 6 in (15 cm)

Both the male and female spectacled
monarchs have black, masklike markings
on the face that are the origin of this bird's
common name.

A solitary, arboreal species, the spectacled monarch
frequents low, dense vegetation in wooded areas, where it
moves swiftly yet quietly, hunting for its insect prey. It may
sometimes feed on the ground.

The cup-shaped nest is constructed from bark strips, lined
with spiders' webs, and is usually situated low in a bush or
sapling. The female lays a clutch of 2 eggs.

Magpie-Lark

Grallina cyanoleuca

RANGE Australia,
S. New Guinea

HABITAT Open woodland,
parks

SIZE 9¾–11 in
(25–28 cm)

A distinctive black and
white bird, the magpie-lark
spends much of its time on the ground, feeding on insects. It
is not shy and is common near human settlements and by
roadsides. Many of the insects it consumes are considered pests
by man, and it also feeds on the freshwater snails that harbor
the liver fluke, so often transmitted to cattle and sheep.

The female differs from the male in having a white throat
and forehead and lacks the male's patches of white plumage
above or below her eyes.

Magpie-larks pair for life and tend to nest in the same tree
year after year, several pairs nesting near one another. The
bowl-shaped nest is made from mud lined with grass and is
situated on a branch. The female lays 3 to 5 eggs, which are
incubated by both parents. The young are also fed by both
parents and are independent at 4 weeks.

Silktail *Lamprolia victoriae* **VU**

RANGE Fiji

HABITAT Mature mountain forest

SIZE 4¾ in (12 cm)

The silktail is a striking bird, with dark velvety plumage,
scattered with metallic blue spangles, and a white rump. It
forages for its insect prey on the foliage of the forest understory
and also goes down to the ground in order to find food. This
bird is swift and agile in flight, it darts between the trees and
may also pursue slow-flying insects.

The nest is made in a tree, of fibers, rootlets, vines and
slivers of bark and is lined with feathers.
The female lays a single egg.

DRONGOS, IORAS AND BUSH-SHRIKES

Fork-tailed Drongo *Dicrurus adsimilis*
RANGE Africa, south of the Sahara
SIZE 9–10 in (23–25.5 cm)

A typical drongo, with its black plumage and deeply forked tail, this bird is a common inhabitant of almost any type of woodland, including coconut plantations. It darts out from a perch to catch insects and then returns to the same perch; a wide range of insects is eaten, including butterflies. This drongo is fast and highly maneuverable in flight.

The nest, woven from plant stems, is made on a forked branch of a tree, and there are usually 3 eggs. Like all drongos, this bird is extremely aggressive in defence of its nest and will chase away even much larger birds.

Greater Racquet-tailed Drongo
Dicrurus paradiseus
RANGE India, Sri Lanka, Andaman and Nicobar Islands, S.W. China, Hainan, S.E. Asia, Sumatra, Java, Borneo
HABITAT Forest, cultivated land
SIZE 13 in (33 cm)

The elongated, racquet-tipped, outer tail feathers may add another 12½ in (32 cm) or more to the total length of this bird. The female has slightly shorter tail streamers, but otherwise resembles the male. This drongo is also identified by its prominent crest which is smaller in young birds.

A bold, noisy bird, it hunts for its insect prey mainly at dusk, when it darts out from the treetops to seize creatures, such as moths termites and dragonflies. It also picks larvae off tree trunks and branches and sometimes eats lizards and even small birds. Nectar from flowers is another important item of diet.

The nest is a loosely constructed cup, made on a forked branch of a tree. There is usually a clutch of 3 eggs, and both parents are believed to incubate the clutch and feed the young. The parents are extremely pugnacious in their defence of the nest and their young.

Pygmy Drongo *Chaetorhynchus papuensis*
RANGE New Guinea
HABITAT Forest on mountain slopes
SIZE 8 in (20.5 cm)

Rather different from other drongos and the only species in its genus, the pygmy drongo has a heavier, more hooked bill than other species and twelve, instead of ten, tail feathers. It perches to watch for insect prey and then darts out to seize it in the air. This unusual drongo can be mistaken for a monarch flycatcher, which it resembles.

AEGITHININAE: IORA SUBFAMILY

The 4 species of ioras are small, arboreal birds. They are found from south Asia to Indonesia and the Philippines. Ioras feed mainly on insects but may also eat nectar.

Common Iora *Aegithina tiphia*
RANGE India, Sri Lanka to S.E. Asia, Java, Sumatra, Borneo
HABITAT Open country and gardens up to 5,600 ft (1,700 m)
SIZE 5 in (12.5 cm)

There are considerable variations in coloration in this species, according to sex and season. The male, in winter, tends to lose almost all of his black feathers, and the yellow ones become paler. The female is green above and yellow below throughout the year, merely becoming paler in winter. Both sexes have soft, abundant feathers on their rumps. Ioras are often found in gardens, hopping about among the branches of trees and shrubs. They eat insects (such as ants and beetles) and seeds.

In the breeding season, the male displays by fluffing out his feathers, particularly those on the rump, so he looks like a ball, then spiralling down to a perch making a croaking noise, rather like a frog. The nest is made from soft grass covered in spiders' webs, in which 2 to 4 eggs are laid.

Malaconthinae: Bush-shrike, Helmet-shrike and Vanga Subfamily

There are two groups or tribes within this subfamily of insect-eaters – the first is the bush-shrikes and the second is helmet-shrikes and vangas.

Bush-shrikes are found in a wide range of habitats throughout Africa and the southern Arabian peninsula. They generally hunt for their insect prey among leaves and other vegetation. The 48 species in this tribe include puffbacks, gonoleks and tchagras.

The second tribe includes 58 species of helmet-shrikes and vangas. Helmet-shrikes are arboreal shrikes that occur in open forests, savanna and scrub in southern and Southeast Asia. They include batis and wattle-eyes. Some hunt in vegetation for insects, while others catch insects on the wing. Vangas are found in Madagascar and include the coral-billed nuthatch.

Black-backed Puffback *Dryoscopus cubla*

Range Africa: Kenya, west and south to Angola and South Africa

Habitat Open woodland, gardens, scrub

Size 6 in (15 cm)

There are 4 races of black-backed puffback. The race that is illustrated here is found in South Africa, and the other 3 occur in the rest of the range. The female is duller and paler than the male, with pale yellow eyes.

When excited this bird puffs up the feathers on its back and rump until it looks like a ball. These sociable little birds are usually found in pairs or in small parties along with other bird species, hunting among the leaves of shrubs and trees for insect larvae. They often catch insects in flight and, during the breeding season, will also eat the eggs and young of small birds.

The cup-shaped nest is constructed from bark fiber and rootlets. It is well hidden and tightly bound to the fork of a tree with spiders' webs. The female lays a clutch of 2 or 3 eggs.

Crimson-breasted Gonolek *Laniarius atrococcineus*

Range Parts of southern Africa

Habitat Thorn veld, acacia bush

Size 8 in (20.5 cm)

Surprisingly these strikingly marked birds are not easy to see in the dense cover of the thornbushes where they prefer to perch,

but they are not timid by nature and as soon as they come out into the open, they are conspicuous. Male and female look alike, but the juvenile is duller in appearance, with distinct crimson feathers found only under the tail.

Crimson-breasted shrikes usually travel in pairs, keeping in touch by calling, the male with a clear, deep whistle that the female answers with a throaty, growling sound. They feed mainly on insects.

The nest is a shallow cup, made from grass, plant fibers and dry bark, and is sited in the forked branch of a thorn tree. The female lays a clutch of 2 or 3 eggs.

Gray-headed Bush-shrike *Malaconotus blanchoti*

Range Africa, south of the Sahara (not extreme south)

Habitat Woodland, acacia trees, often near water (East Africa)

Size 10 in (25.5 cm)

Despite their size and quite bright coloration, these birds are not easily seen in the thick foliage of the trees and bushes they frequent. Most often they can be located by their calls – either a brisk, chattering sound or a two- or three-note whistle. They have big hooked bills and, in South Africa, are known to take prey as large as mice and lizards, which they find among leaf litter on the ground. Male and female look alike.

The conspicuous nest is built close to the ground. It is either a rough heap of grass and leaves or a platform of twigs with an inner cup, in which 2 or 3, or, rarely 4, eggs are laid.

HELMET SHRIKES, VANGAS, AND NEW ZEALAND WATTLE BIRDS

White/Long-crested Helmet Shrike *Prionops plumata*

RANGE Africa: S. Ethiopia to Angola, Namibia, N. South Africa

HABITAT Open bush country, woodland

SIZE 8 in (20.5 cm)

The tame and gregarious white helmet shrikes live in small flocks of 8 to 12 birds. They move close together through the lower branches of trees and bushes, where they forage for insects often with birds of other species. The sexes look alike. A number of birds will share the brooding and feeding at a single nest and 3 or 4 eggs are laid.

Black-headed Batis *Batis minor*

RANGE Africa: Sudan to Somalia, south to Cameroon and Angola

HABITAT Open woodland, bush

SIZE 4 in (10 cm)

A small, rather stumpy flycatcher, the batis can erect the plumage on its back, making itself appear round and fluffy. The sexes look alike in most respects, but the female lacks the male's black head plumage and has a dark chestnut band on the chest. These birds move in pairs, searching foliage for insects or making brief hunting flights.

The nest is made of fibers and lichen, bound with spiders' webs, and is usually placed in a forked branch of a tree. The female lays 2 or 3 eggs.

Common/Brown-throated Wattle-eye *Platysteira cyanea*

RANGE W., C. and N.E. Africa

HABITAT Forest, woods, crops

SIZE 5 in (13 cm)

Distinctive red wattles over the eyes make the common wattle-eye easily recognizable. Wattle-eyes behave more like warblers than flycatchers, foraging in pairs over foliage for insect prey. In noisy, chattering flocks they make some seasonal migrations.

The cup-shaped nest is made of fine grass, plant fibers and lichen and is bound to a forked branch with spiders' webs. The female lays 2 eggs.

Maroon-breasted Philentoma

Philentoma velata

RANGE Malaysia, Sumatra, Java, Borneo

HABITAT Forest

SIZE 8 in (20.5 cm)

A noisy, active bird, the maroon-breasted philentoma frequents the lower to middle layers of the forest, often perching on low branches, vines and creepers. It catches all its prey on the wing and does not forage on foliage. It normally lives in pairs, and both sexes have loud, harsh calls. Male and female differ slightly in plumage: the female is a darker blue than the male and lacks his maroon chest patch. Nearly always found near water, these flycatchers love to bathe.

The nest is made on a forked branch of a tree.

Coral-billed Nuthatch

Hypositta corallirostris

RANGE E. Madagascar

HABITAT Humid forest

SIZE 5 in (13 cm)

The coral-billed nuthatch has been a taxonomical problem for ornithologists. It feeds like a treecreeper and looks somewhat like a nuthatch, but more recently it has been regarded as a close, but highly aberrant, relative of the vangas. A brightly colored little bird, it clings with its feet to the bark on the upper part of tree trunks, while it searches diligently in cracks and crevices for insects to eat. The female and young are blue above, with gray underparts.

Hook-billed Vanga

Vanga curvirostris

RANGE N.E. and S.W. Madagascar

HABITAT Forest and secondary brush to 6,000 ft (1,800 m), mangroves

SIZE 9¾ in (25 cm)

These birds are usually seen alone or in pairs among the larger branches of trees where they move about slowly and deliberately, searching for their prey. Their strong beaks, with sharply hooked tips, and the fact that they respond to squeaks and cheeping sounds, suggest that they may eat small mammals and young birds, in addition to the chameleons, lizards, frogs and insects that are known to be part of their diet.

Sickle-billed Vanga/Sicklebill *Falculea Palliata*

RANGE W. Madagascar

HABITAT Woodland, dense savanna, forest edge, mangroves

SIZE 12½ in (32 cm) including bill

This vanga is more like the woodhoopoe *Phoeniculus*, in appearance and habits than it is like the vangas with which it is classed. A party of up to 25 birds will suddenly appear in a patch of woodland, where, like woodhoopoes, they run about on the tree trunks and branches. They even hang upside down by their claws while they poke their long, curved beaks into crevices in the bark in search of large insects to eat.

The female builds a well-hidden nest from twigs, some 40 ft (12 m) up in a tall, isolated tree. It is not known how many eggs are laid, since none has yet been found.

CALLAEATIDAE: NEW ZEALAND WATTLEBIRD FAMILY

The wattlebirds, named for the fleshy, colorful wattles at the sides of the bill, live in the forests of New Zealand. They have large, strong legs and are thought to be related to starlings. There are 2 species, with a further species, the huia, *Heteralocha acutirostris*, which became extinct at the beginning of the 20th century. Like many island birds, the wattlebirds suffered from the colonization of New Zealand and the resulting introduction of foreign animals. The remaining species need careful conservation if they are to survive.

Kokako *Callaeas cinerea* **EN**

RANGE New Zealand

HABITAT Forest

SIZE 15 in (38 cm)

The kokako has suffered severely from the introduction into New Zealand of predators, such as rats, mustelids and cats, all of which are likely to prey on the birds and their eggs and nestlings. The race on South Island is critically endangered and may even be extinct, but on North Island kokakos, although vulnerable, are still fairly well distributed. They are under continued pressure from predators and the destruction of the forest, however, and must be actively conserved. Competition for food from introduced herbivores may also be a factor in their decline. The South Island race of kokako has orange wattles, and the North Island race, blue wattles.

Kokakos, like all wattlebirds, rarely fly but feed on the ground and in trees, hopping energetically from branch to branch. They do occasionally glide from one tree to another. They feed on leaves, flowers, fruit and insects. Usually in pairs or small flocks, kokakos reveal their presence by their varied musical calls.

The nest is made of sticks, lined with plant material, on a forked branch of a tree. The female incubates the 2 or 3 eggs for about 25 days, and both parents feed the young until they leave the nest some 27 or 28 days after hatching.

ROCKFOWL, WAXWINGS, AND DIPPERS

PICATHARTIDAE: ROCK-JUMPER AND ROCKFOWL FAMILY

The 2 species of rockfowl, which are also called picathartes or bald crows, are large, long-tailed birds. They are found in the forests of West Africa, and are similar in their biology and habits. Both species have a characteristic bare patch on the head.

Rock-jumpers, of which there are also 2 species, are found in open rocky habitats in southern africa. Like rockfowls, rock-jumpers have strong legs and hop vigorously across the ground when searching for insects and other prey.

White-necked Rockfowl *Picathartes gymnocephalus* **VU**

RANGE W. Africa: Guinea and Sierra Leone to Togo

HABITAT Forest

SIZE 15–16 in (38–41 cm)

Recognizable by the bare, yellow head, with two black patches at the back, both male and female rockfowls have gray and white plumage and powerful legs and feet. Rockfowls spend much of their life on the forest floor, where they move with graceful hops, searching for insects, snails, crustaceans and small frogs. When alarmed the rockfowl utters a repeated gutteral call.

The species is becoming rare, partly because of forest clearance and partly because of trapping to fulfil the demands of zoos and private collectors. It is now protected by law in Ghana.

Rockfowls are sociable and nest in colonies in caves, in nests built from mud and fibrous plant materials which are attached to the walls and ceilings of the caves. Unfortunately, this habit of colonial nesting in often easily identified sites makes the birds easy prey for collectors.

Both parents incubate the clutch of 2 eggs for about 21 days and then feed their young with insects.

BOMBYCILLIDAE: WAXWING FAMILY

This complex family of songbirds is divided into 3 tribes.

The waxwings proper, with 3 species, are found in high latitudes of the northern hemisphere, but they do occasionally migrate south to Europe, central China, Japan and even to Central America for the winter months.

The male and female are almost alike, with soft, silky plumage and crested heads. They are gregarious mainly tree-dwelling birds and feed on fruit and berries and insects.

The silky flycatchers of the New World are a group of 4 species, which also have prominent crests and eat berries.

The single species of palmchat is found in the Caribbean. These sociable birds roost, feed, and nest together.

Gray Silky Flycatcher

Ptilogonys cinereus

RANGE N. Mexico to Guatemala

HABITAT Oak and pine forest at 4,000 to 10,000 ft (1,200–3,000 m)

SIZE 8¼ in (21 cm)

With their soft, silky plumage, these flycatchers resemble the waxwings, but their long, narrow tails are like those of the flycatchers, and it is this that gives them their common name.

In fact, silky flycatchers live largely on fruit and berries, especially mistletoe berries, although they do also sometimes capture flying insects in the air. Silky flycatchers are usually found in small flocks outside the breeding season.

The female constructs the nest from twigs and fibers bound together with spiders' webs, quite high up in a tree and lays her clutch of 2 or 3 eggs.

Bohemian Waxwing

Bombycilla garrulus

RANGE Circumpolar regions of
N. America, Europe and Asia

HABITAT Tall coniferous forest of
the taiga

SIZE 7 in (18 cm)

This bird's common name is derived from the drop-shaped and waxlike tips of the secondary wing feathers. The tips are, in fact, elongations of the feathers' shafts. The sexes look much alike, except that the female's plumage is duller. Waxwings normally live on fruit and berries, although they will catch insects on the wing during the breeding season. In winter months they sometimes migrate south of their range.

During his courtship display, the male presents the female with a berry or ant pupa, which the birds then pass back and forth from beak to beak as part of their courtship ritual, but do not swallow.

The bohemian waxwing's bulky nest is made from twigs, moss and plant fibers, mainly by the female, who lays a clutch of 3 to 7 eggs, which she alone incubates.

Palmchat *Dulus dominicus*

RANGE West Indies: Hispaniola, Gonave

HABITAT Open country with Royal Palms (Roystonea)

SIZE 6¾ in (17.5 cm)

The plumage of the palmchat is thick and rough, and quite different from that of the waxwings. The male and female look alike, but the juvenile has a dark throat and neck and a buff-colored rump.

Palmchats are sociable birds, which live in pairs or in groups of 2 to 5 pairs in a large communal nest about 3¼ ft (1 m) in diameter. The nest is loosely constructed from dry twigs, woven around the trunk and the base of the fronds of a royal palm tree. Within this structure, each pair of birds has a separate breeding area, divided off from the others and with its own entrance. Here the birds roost and, in an inner chamber, raise their family of 2 to 4 young.

Palmchats feed on berries from the palms and other plants and also eat flowers.

CINCLIDAE: DIPPER FAMILY

The 5 species of dipper live in Europe, Asia and North and South America, usually in upland country close to swift flowing mountain streams.

These are the only passeriform birds to have adopted a truly aquatic way of life, yet they have no webs on their feet and few obvious special adaptations other than movable flaps which close off the nostrils when the bird is underwater. Propelling themselves with their wings, the dippers can swim and dive underwater, and they also appear to be able to walk on the bottoms of streams. Males and females look alike in all species.

American Dipper *Cinclus mexicanus*

RANGE Alaska, through N.W. America to Panama

HABITAT Mountain streams

SIZE 7–8½ in (18–22 cm)

A wren-shaped bird, the dipper has a compact body, long, stout legs and a short, square-tipped tail. Its bill is hooked and is notched at the tip. Like all dippers the American dipper frequents mountain streams and walks or dives into the water. It can swim underwater and can even walk on the bottom of the stream, in order to obtain insect and invertebrate prey, especially caddis fly larvae.

A bulky, domed nest, made of moss and grass, is built by the female on a rock in the stream or beside the stream among tree roots or rocks; it has a side entrance. The female lays a clutch of 3 to 6 eggs, which she incubates for 15 to 17 days.

THRUSHES

MUSCICAPIDAE: THRUSH, OLD WORLD FLYCATCHER, AND CHAT FAMILY

This large family of songbirds has 449 species in 2 subfamilies – Turninae (thrushes) and Muscicapinae (Old World flycatchers and chats).

TURDINAE: THRUSH SUBFAMILY

There are 179 species in this subfamily, found almost all over the world except on the polar ice caps and some Pacific islands; formerly absent from New Zealand, they have now been introduced there. The group contains not only the thrushes proper, in the genus Turdus, but also bluebirds and solitaires. Male and female look alike in some species, but differ in others.

Most members of the subfamily are small to medium-sized songbirds with slender beaks. They are strong fliers, many forms making regular, long migrations. Insects and other invertebrates, such as slugs, snails, worms and crustaceans, make up the bulk of the diet for most thrushes, but berries and other plant foods are also eaten.

Cape Rock-thrush *Monticola rupestris*

RANGE South Africa: Transvaal to Cape Province

HABITAT Scrub, rocky country

SIZE 8½ in (22 cm)

The male Cape rock-thrush is recognized by his blue-gray head, neck and throat, while the female's head is mottled brown and black. They are fairly common birds, seen in pairs or small groups, often perching on rocks, boulders or the tops of bushes. Insects and small mollusks are their main foods, mostly found on the ground.

The shallow, cup-shaped nest is made of grass, small twigs and plant fibers, lined with rootlets. It is usually situated in a rock crevice or even under a roof. The female lays 3 to 5 eggs.

White's Thrush

Zoothera dauma

RANGE E. Europe, Russia (stragglers as far west as Britain), India, China, Taiwan, Philippines, Sumatra and Java, south to Australia, N. Melanesia

HABITAT Forest, woodland

SIZE 4¼ in (11 cm)

White's thrush is characterized by the crescent-shaped, scalelike markings on its back and underparts. Juveniles have barred, rather than scaly, markings.

A shy, retiring bird, white's thrush spends much of its life on the ground, feeding on insects and berries. Some populations migrate in winter, and vagrants may even stray into Europe.

The nest is rather different from that of most thrushes. Situated up to 13 ft (4 m) above ground in a tree, it is large and flat and is constructed mostly from pine needles, with a base of mud and moss to fix it to the branch. The female lays a clutch of between 3 and 5 eggs.

Veery

Catharus fuscescens

RANGE S. Canada; USA: Oregon to New Mexico, Great Lakes area and New England, south to Georgia; winters in South America

HABITAT Moist woodland

SIZE 6¼–7 in (16–18 cm)

More often heard than seen, the veery is an inconspicuous little bird with a beautiful, musical song. It feeds on insects, spiders and earthworms, as well as on fruit and berries, which it finds by foraging in the trees and by searching under leaves on the woodland floor.

The bulky, cup-shaped nest is constructed from weed stems, grass, pieces of bark and twig, and lined with dry leaves and rootlets. It is situated on or near the ground either in a bush or a clump of plants.

The female lays a clutch of 3 to 6 eggs, usually 4, which she incubates for 11 or 12 days. Both parents care for the young, which leave the nest about 10 to 12 days after hatching.

American Robin *Turdus migratorius*

RANGE N. America, Mexico, Guatemala

HABITAT Open woodland, forest edge, gardens, city parks

SIZE 9–11 in (23–28 cm)

The American robin lives in urban areas. The coloration varies. In the breeding season, the male is gray above, with a black head and tail and reddish breast. The female is duller, with a gray head and tail. Robins feed on insects, earthworms, fruit and berries.

Some robins winter in the northern states, but generally they are migratory, breeding north of the Gulf Coast. The nest is a cup of mud, enclosed by twigs, and stems and lined with grass. The 3 to 6 eggs are incubated for 12 to 14 days.

Eurasian Blackbird *Turdus merula*

RANGE Europe, N. Africa, parts of Asia, introduced in New Zealand, Australia

HABITAT Forest, woodland, scrub, gardens, parks

SIZE 10 in (25.5 cm)

The blackbird finds the short grass of lawns and parks ideal for foraging for insects and worms. It also eats many kinds of fruit and berries. It spends a lot of time on the ground, but it finds a prominent perch from which to sing. The male is black, with a yellowish-orange bill and eye-ring. The female has dark brown plumage with paler underparts.

A variety of nest sites is used. The female builds the nest, which has an outer layer of plant stems, twigs and leaves covering the inner cup of mud and plant material and is lined with fine grass or dead leaves. She lays up to 9 eggs at daily intervals and incubates them for 12 to 15 days. Both parents feed the young in the nest and for a further 3 weeks.

Olive Thrush *Turdus olivaceus*

RANGE Africa, south of the Sahara

HABITAT Forest, cultivated land

SIZE 9½ in (24 cm)

Several races of olive thrush, which vary in coloration, occur over its range. Male and female look alike, but juveniles have streaked upperparts and dusky spots on underparts. This thrush has taken well to life in urban gardens. Much of its food is found by scratching around on the ground to uncover insects and invertebrates such as snails and worms. It also eats fruit.

The courting male puffs himself up, spreads his tail, then shuffles around the female with his wings trailing. The nest is made of grass, on a foundation of twigs, roots and earth, and is situated on a branch, tree stump or bush. The 2 or 3 eggs are incubated for about 14 days.

Austral Thrush *Turdus falcklandii*

RANGE S. America: S. Argentina, S. Chile; Falkland and Juan Fernandez Islands

HABITAT Open country with shrubs

SIZE 11–11¼ in (28–29 cm)

The southern counterpart of the robin of North America, the austral thrush is common on both sides of the Andes up to about 6,600 ft (2,000 m). It digs for earthworms and other invertebrates on grassland and in damp places. It also eats fruit.

The cup-shaped nest is made of twigs, bound with grass and mud, and is usually concealed in dense vegetation. Females produce two or three clutches a season, each of 2 or 3 eggs.

Island Thrush *Turdus poliocephalus*

RANGE Islands from Christmas Island through Indonesia, New Guinea to New Caledonia, Fiji and Samoa

HABITAT Forest edge

SIZE 9–10 in (23–25.5 cm)

There may be 50 or more forms of island thrush, all varying slightly in appearance, some found on only one island or on a small group of islands. Most males have largely black plumage, and females look similar, but usually duller, in color. Generally a shy, solitary bird the island thrush takes refuge in trees but feeds on the ground in the open, on plant matter, such as seeds and fruit, and on a few insects.

The female normally lays 1 egg in a nest on a bush or rocky ledge.

THRUSHES, OLD WORLD FLYCATCHERS AND CHATS

Eastern Bluebird *Sialia sialis*

RANGE N. America: S. Canada, east of the Rockies to Gulf coast, USA; Mexico, Central America

HABITAT Open country, farmland, gardens, parks

SIZE 6½–7½ in (16.5–19 cm)

A beautiful bird, the male eastern bluebird has distinctive, bright blue plumage on its upperparts and a chestnut breast and a melodious song. The female looks similar, but has paler, duller plumage. The juvenile is mainly brown with a mottled white and brown chest.

This bluebird often perches in a hunched posture on wires and fences, but takes most of its insect prey on the ground. Berries are also an important component of its diet, particularly in winter. Flocks often form in autumn and winter and several birds may roost together.

The male bluebird performs flight displays in order to court his mate and once a pair bond is made both partners build a nest from grass, twigs and other plant material, lined with hair, fine grass and feathers. The nest is situated in a natural hole in a tree or stump, in an abandoned woodpecker hole, or even in a bird box. Competition for nest sites has caused some decline in recent years and nest boxes are increasingly important for conservation of bluebird numbers.

The female lays between 3 tand 7 eggs, usually 4 or 5, which she incubates for 13 to 15 days, sometimes with assistance from her mate. The young chicks are fed by both of the parents and leave the nest about 15 to 20 days after they hatch. There are usually two broods produced in a season. Some northern populations of bluebirds migrate south for the winter.

Andean Solitaire
Myadestes ralloides

RANGE South America: Colombia and Venezuela south through the Andes to Ecuador, Peru and Bolivia

HABITAT Mountain forest

SIZE 7 in (18 cm)

The shy, secretive Andean solitaire usually lives between altitudes of 3,000 and 15,000 ft (900 and 4,500 m). It is an excellent songster and sings more or less throughout the year in a pure, clear voice. True to its name, the solitaire tends to live alone for much of the time, but birds are also found in pairs. Its bill is rather short and wide, and it feeds on fruit and insects.

A nest is made on the ground or in a tree, and about 3 eggs are laid and incubated for 12 or 13 days.

White-browed/Blue Shortwing
Brachypteryx montana

RANGE E. Nepal to W. and S. China, south to S.E. Asia, Indonesia and Philippines

HABITAT Forest undergrowth

SIZE 6 in (15 cm)

The male of this species is a distinctive little bird, with dark blue plumage and conspicuous, long white eyebrows; females have brownish plumage, with rusty-red markings on the forehead and indistinct eyebrows. In some areas, males are colored like females but with white eyebrows. Shy, retiring birds they skulk around in the densest undergrowth, searching for insects, especially beetles, and usually staying on or close to the ground.

The globular nest is made on a tree trunk or rock face, and the female lays 3 eggs.

Fire-crested Alethe *Alethe castanea*

RANGE Africa: Nigeria to Zaire and Uganda

HABITAT Lowland forest

SIZE 7 in (18 cm)

One of 6 species of alethe living in Africa, the fire-crested alethe is a bird of dense forest and shady undergrowth. Although it does not eat ants, it follows army ants as they march through the forest in order to catch the other insects that flee from their path.

Male and female birds look alike, both with dark-brown plumage and an orange streak of feathers along the crown. When the bird becomes excited, it erects this crest, while spreading out its tail.

The cup-shaped nest is made of moss and roots, lined with soft rootlets, and is situated in a tree stump or among heaps of debris on the forest floor. The female lays 2 or 3 eggs.

MUSCICAPINAE: OLD WORLD FLYCATCHER AND CHAT SUBFAMILY

This large subfamily of the family Muscicapidae includes 270 species of insect-eating songbirds. The 115 species of flycatchers all occur in the Old World, with the greatest diversity in Africa, Asia and Australasia. Some are brightly plumaged, others are dull, and flycatchers have diversified into a wide range of body forms and habits to fit different niches. Males and females look alike in some species and differ in others.

The "typical" flycatchers, which include some examples that occur in Europe, have a flat, wide beak, the base of which is surrounded by prominent bristles. Their method of insect capture is extremely characteristic – the feeding bird sits on a perch in a good vantage position for observing prey. If an insect passes, the bird launches itself into the air for a brief, agile, hunting flight and deftly captures the prey in its bill; it takes the prey back to its perch to eat. Some birds, of course, do use other methods of catching prey and feed on the ground or on foliage.

The 155 species of chats are found in Eurasia south to Indonesia, New Guinea, and the Philippines, and in Africa. One species, the Northern wheatear, also occurs in Alaska and Canada. Chats are thrushlike birds that live in a wide range of habitats from woodland to the sides of rivers to semidesert. Most feed on insects which are caught with their thin bills in flight or on the ground after swooping down from a perch. The chat subfamily includes redstarts, wheatears, robins, and nightingales.

Spotted Flycatcher

Muscicapa striata

RANGE Europe: Scandinavia southeast to S.W. Siberia and south to Mediterranean countries; N. Africa to C. Asia; winters tropical Africa and S.W. Asia

HABITAT Forest edge, woodland, scrub, gardens, parks

SIZE 5½ in (14 cm)

The spotted flycatcher feeds in the manner which is typical of its group, perching in exposed spots and making swift aerial sallies after insects. While perched, it constantly flicks its wings and tail. Male and female look alike, both have mainly grayish-brown plumage.

The female does most of the work of nest-building, making a neat structure of moss, bark and fibers, lined with rootlets and feathers. The nest may be in a variety of sites, such as on a ledge, in a cavity or tree fork or on a wall or rock. Both parents incubate the clutch of between 4 tand 6 eggs for 12 to 14 days and tend the young. Breeding pairs often produce two broods of chicks in a season.

Rufous-tailed Jungle Flycatcher

Rhinomyias ruficauda

RANGE Philippines, Borneo

HABITAT Forest

SIZE 5½ in (14 cm)

A rather rare bird, the rufous-tailed jungle flycatcher frequents dense undergrowth, where it feeds on insects and spiders. Much of its food is gleaned from foliage, but it also makes swift flights into the air to catch winged insects.

The subspecies of this bird vary slightly in coloration, but all have the distinctive chestnut tail. The female looks similar to the male in most respects.

The breeding habits of this species are not known.

OLD WORLD FLYCATCHERS AND CHATS CONTINUED

Blue-throated Flycatcher *Cyornis rubeculoides*

RANGE Himalayas through northern S.E. Asia to China; winters south of range

HABITAT Forest, gardens

SIZE 5½ in (14 cm)

The blue-throated flycatcher lives in well-wooded areas with plenty of under-growth. It makes aerial dashes after insect prey, but hardly ever returns to the same perch, or even the same tree, to consume the catch. It may also drop down to the ground to find food and may flush out a concealed cricket or grasshopper with its open wings. Male and female differ in plumage, the female having mainly olive-brown and black feathers instead of the distinctive blue of the male.

The nest is made in a hollow in a mossy bank, in a rock crevice or in a hole in a tree or bamboo stem. The female lays 3 to 5 eggs, which both birds incubate for 11 or 12 days.

Pale Flycatcher *Bradornis pallidus*

RANGE Africa, south of the Sahara

HABITAT Woodland, coastal scrub, gardens, maize fields

SIZE 6–7 in (15–18 cm)

The pale flycatcher has largely grayish-brown plumage and is less conspicuous than many flycatchers. Juveniles have some streaked and spotted plumage. In pairs or small, loosely knit groups, they forage on the ground for much of their food, such as spiders and termites, but also catch flies and moths in the air. They are quiet, making only occasional twittering calls.

Breeding begins at the start of, or just before, the rainy season. The small neat, cup-shaped nest is made from rootlets and is sited on a forked branch of a tree or bush. The female lays a clutch of 2 or 3 eggs. Families remain together for a prolonged period, and there is some evidence that birds other than the parents help to rear broods.

Common Stonechat *Saxicola torquata*

RANGE Europe, Africa, W. and C. Asia

HABITAT Moors, fields, hill scrub, agricultural land

SIZE 5 in (13 cm)

The plump little stonechat is a lively, restless bird. It seldom moves on the ground, but flies fast and perches in exposed spots, such as on a post or on top of a bush, to watch for insect prey. It also eats plant matter and grain. The female has paler, browner plumage than the male and her white markings are less distinct.

The breeding season begins between late March and early June, depending on area. The male displays to the female by spreading his wings and tail to show off his markings. The nest is usually made by the female from coarse grass, moss and plant stems, lined with hair, fine grass or feathers. It is sited in an open area on the ground, under cover of a bush or actually in a bush. The female lays 5 or 6 eggs, which she incubates for about 14 days, sometimes assisted by the male. The young remain in the nest for 12 or 13 days, being fed on insects by both parents. Some northern populations may migrate south in winter.

Northern Wheatear *Oenanthe oenanthe*

RANGE Europe, N.W. Africa, W. and C. Asia, Arctic North America; winters mainly in Africa

HABITAT Open country, moors, tundra, heaths

SIZE 5½ in (14 cm)

A widely distributed species, this is the only wheatear to have become established in the New World. In summer breeding plumage, the male has a grayish crown, black marks on the cheeks and a white stripe above each eye. Both sexes have distinctive white rumps, but the female is brownish and buff. In winter the male resembles the female.

Primarily a ground dweller, the wheatear finds much of its food, such as insects, spiders, centipedes and small mollusks, on

the ground. It flits from one perch to another and may sometimes fly up to catch an insect on the wing.

In display, the male reveals his white rump to the female and dances with wings outspread. The nest is made in open country in a hole on the ground, in a rock or wall, or in debris such as a can or drainpipe. The female lays a clutch of 5 or 6 eggs, occasionally up to 8, which are incubated for about 14 days. She does most of the incubation, although the male may assist. Both of the parents feed the young, which remain in the nest for about 15 days.

Oriental Magpie Robin *Copsychus saularis*

RANGE India, S. China, S.E. Asia, much of Indonesia, east to the Philippines

HABITAT Brush, gardens, cultivated land

SIZE 8½ in (21.5 cm)

A widespread, common bird, the male magpie robin has distinctive black and white plumage. The female looks similar but she has dark-gray instead of black plumage. This species

often lives near human habitation and feeds in the open, usually near or on the ground. The magpie robin is a good mimic, and it imitates other birds, but it also has a loud and melodious song of its own, which it uses to announce its presence. Insects, such as crickets, beetles and ants, are its main foods.

The large, cup-shaped nest is constructed from fine roots and is situated among tree roots or branches or in any protected hole. The female lays a clutch of between 3 and 6 eggs, usually 5, which both parents incubate for 12 or 13 days.

White-crowned Forktail *Enicurus leschenaulti*

RANGE Sikkim to S. China and Hainan, S.E. Asia to Bali

HABITAT Rocky streams in forest

SIZE 8–11 in (20.5–28 cm)

Both male and female white-crowned forktails have similar, sharply contrasting black and white plumage and long tails. These long-legged birds frequent streams and feed on aquatic insects, which they take from the water surface or the stream bed. They wade from stone to stone, searching for food and occasionally dipping under the water in pursuit of prey.

Their cup-shaped nest is built from moss and rootlets. It is always built in a damp area, often near a stream, and is generally sited on a rock, in a crevice or among stones or tree roots. The female lays a clutch of 2 eggs.

STARLINGS

STURNIDAE: STARLING AND MOCKINGBIRD FAMILY

This family of 148 species divides into two tribes: the starlings and the mockingbirds. Apart from the species introduced into other locations by humans, all 114 species of starling occur in the Old World, with the greatest diversity in Asia. As well as starlings, the tribe includes the mynas and 2 species of oxpecker. Starlings are medium-sized songbirds with a sturdy appearance and active habits. Most have long bills and strong legs and feet; wings may be rounded and short or long and pointed. Typically the plumage is dark, often enlivened with a beautiful iridescent sheen of blue, green or purple, particularly in the breeding season. Male and female look alike in some species and differ slightly in others. Many starlings live in open country and feed on the ground, although some occur in more wooded areas and are arboreal. They feed on almost anything, but largely on insects, fruit, grain, birds' eggs and lizards. Starlings fly swiftly and run or walk on the ground. Generally gregarious birds, they roost communally, often making characteristic loud whistles while flying to roosting sites in huge flocks. Most starlings nest in holes in trees or buildings, but some dig nesting burrows in river banks or build domed nests in trees.

The 34 species belonging to the mockingbird tribe are all found in the Americas. As well as the mockingbirds, this group of thrushlike birds also includes thrashers, tremblers and catbirds. Most live in wooded country or scrub, and feed on or near ground level on insects and other invertebrates, as well as on fruit and seeds. Typically they are slim-bodied birds, with long legs and tails, that are well known for their ability to mimic the songs of other birds and sounds such as piano notes, barking dogs and sirens. Male and female look alike or nearly so.

Starling *Sturnus vulgaris*

RANGE Europe, Asia; introduced almost worldwide

HABITAT Near habitation, cultivated land

SIZE 8½ in (21.5 cm)

One of the most familiar birds in city areas, starlings roost in huge numbers on buildings, often performing spectacular massed flights over the site prior to settling. In breeding plumage both male and female are blackish, with a green or purple iridescent sheen. In winter, the plumage is heavily spotted with white, particularly in the female. Juveniles are grayish-brown with pale throats. Starlings are adaptable birds and take to a wide variety of habitats, although deciduous woodland and built-up areas are preferred in the breeding season. They feed on the ground on insects, larvae, earthworms, slugs, snails and centipedes, among other invertebrates, constantly probing the surface with their bills. Fruit, grain, berries and seeds are also included in their widely varying diet. Starlings may sometimes feed in the trees, and they also pursue insect prey in the air, with swift, wheeling flight.

Starlings breed in colonies or in separate pairs. The nest is usually built in a hole in a tree or building or among rocks, and is made of stems, leaves and other plant material. The female lays 4 to 9 eggs, usually 5 to 7, which both parents incubate for 12 or 13 days. They feed their young for about 3 weeks, but even after leaving the nest, the young starlings follow their parents and solicit food. There may be one or two broods a season. Northernmost populations migrate south in winter.

Red-winged Starling

Onychognathus morio

RANGE Africa: Senegal to Sudan, south through E. Africa to South Africa: Cape Province

HABITAT Rocky hills and cliffs, cultivated and city areas, woodland

SIZE 12 in (30.5 cm)

A noisy, conspicuous bird, the red-winged starling moves in pairs or small flocks, searching for its main foods – fruit and insects. Its flight is fast and dipping, and it makes a constant whistling call while in the air. The male bird is mainly blue-black, with brown-tipped, rufous flight feathers; the female has a gray head and neck and a gray-streaked breast but otherwise looks similar to the male.

The nest is made of grass and mud and is built in a hole in a cliff, cave or building or in the roof of a hut. The female lays 3 to 5 eggs, which she incubates for 12 to 23 days.

Hill Myna *Gracula religiosa*

RANGE India, Sri Lanka, Andaman and Nicobar Islands, S. China, Hainan, S.E. Asia, Indonesia; introduced elsewhere

HABITAT Forest

SIZE 12 in (30.5 cm)

A stockily built bird, the hill myna has glossy black plumage, with bright golden-yellow wattles on the head and a conspicuous white patch on each wing. Male and female look similar. A noisy, sociable bird, it lives in small groups of up to 6 outside the breeding season, occasionally gathering in larger groups at feeding trees. It spends most of its life in trees or bushes and feeds on fruit, particularly figs, berries, buds, nectar, and some insects and lizards. It rarely descends to the ground. Hill mynas have a wide repertoire of calls, but although "myna-birds" are first-rate mimics in captivity, they do not mimic sounds in the wild.

The nest is made in a hole in a tree trunk, often an old woodpecker hole. Both parents incubate the 2 or 3 eggs and feed the young.

Superb Starling *Lamprotornis superbus*

RANGE Africa: Ethiopia, Sudan to Tanzania

HABITAT Scrub, near habitation

SIZE 7 in (18 cm)

One of the most brilliantly plumaged starlings, the superb starling has metallic green and blue plumage. Male and female look alike, but juveniles have dull black plumage on head, neck and breast. The superb starling is a gregarious bird and is quite fearless of man where it occurs near villages and towns. It feeds on the ground on insects and berries.

The ball-shaped nest is made of grass and thorny twigs and is usually situated on a branch of a thorn tree or in a bush. A hole in a tree may sometimes be used or the old nest of another bird. There are usually 4 eggs in a clutch.

Metallic/Shining Starling *Aplonis metallica*

RANGE The Moluccas, across New Guinea region to Bismarck Archipelago and Solomon Islands; migrates to N. coast of Australia

HABITAT Rain forest

SIZE 9¾ in (25 cm)

The black plumage of the metallic starling has a purple and green sheen and the bird is also characterized by its long, sharply graduated tail and its red eyes. A gregarious, noisy bird, it is mainly tree-dwelling but does sometimes feed on the ground. Fruit and insects are its main foods.

Metallic starlings nest in large colonies of as many as 300 pairs. The large, domed nests are made of plant tendrils and suspended from branches. The usual clutch is 2 to 4 eggs.

Yellow-billed Oxpecker *Buphagus africanus*

RANGE Africa, south of the Sahara (not extreme south)

HABITAT Dry open country

SIZE 9 in (23 cm)

Common sights in African game reserves, the yellow-billed oxpecker and the similar, red-billed oxpecker, *B. erythrorhynchus*, both specialize in feeding on ticks, which they pull off buffalo, zebra and other large mammals. Their heavy bills are well suited to this, and they have strong, sharp claws with which they cling to the animal's skin. They clamber nimbly all over the body in their search, even probing ears and nostrils. Flies are also eaten. Oxpeckers give a warning call when alarmed, often alerting the mammal to danger. Male and female birds look alike.

The nest is made in a hole in a tree or rock, or under the eaves of a building. The female lays a clutch of 2 to 5 eggs, which are incubated for about 12 days.

MOCKINGBIRDS, NUTHATCHES AND WALLCREEPERS

Charles/Galápagos Mockingbird *Nesomimus trifasciatus* **EN**

RANGE Galápagos Islands

HABITAT Varied

SIZE 10 in (25.5 cm)

There are 4 species of Galápagos mockingbird, of which this one is rare and found only on Champion and Gardner islets. The birds appear to use all available habitats on the islands and to feed on anything they can find, mainly insects, fruit and berries, but also carrion and seabirds' eggs. The twig nest is built in a cactus or low tree and 2 to 5 eggs are laid.

Northern Mockingbird *Mimus polyglottos*

RANGE S. Canada, USA, south to Mexico; West Indies; introduced in Hawaii

HABITAT Open woodland, gardens, orchards

SIZE 9–11 in (23–28 cm)

This is one of the best-known American songbirds and is the state bird of five USA states. The male mockingbird sings night and day, often mimicking other birds and other sounds. Mockingbirds are aggressive and hold territories, which they defend vigorously against all enemies; in winter, female birds hold their own separate territories. They feed on insects, particularly grasshoppers and beetles, and also on spiders, snails and small reptiles. Fruit, too, is an important part of the diet.

At the onset of the summer breeding season, males court mates, flashing the white markings on the wings as they make display flights. Both partners help to build the nest, from twigs, leaves and bits of debris such as paper and wool which is placed in a low tree or bush. The female incubates the clutch of 3 to 6 eggs for 12 days, and both parents help to feed the young. There may be two or three broods produced a year.

California Thrasher *Toxostoma redivivum*

RANGE USA: California; Mexico: Baja California

HABITAT Chaparral, mountain foothills, parks, gardens

SIZE 11–13 in (28–33 cm)

This large thrasher has a distinctive downward-curving, sickle-shaped bill, which it uses to rake through leaves and dig in the soil for insects and berries. Its wings are rather short, and it is an awkward bird in flight, so it lives mainly on the ground, where it runs around with its long tail raised. The male bird sings for prolonged periods from a perch on a bush and is an excellent mimic. Females also sing.

Both parents help to build a large, cup-shaped nest of plant material three feet or so off the ground, in a low tree or bush. They incubate their clutch of between 2 and 4 eggs for about 14 days. When the young leave the nest 12 to 14 days after hatching out, the male continues to feed them for a few days longer, even while the second brood is being incubated in the nest by the female.

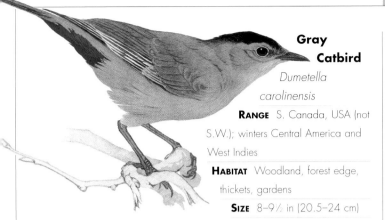

Gray Catbird

Dumetella carolinensis

RANGE S. Canada, USA (not S.W.); winters Central America and West Indies

HABITAT Woodland, forest edge, thickets, gardens

SIZE 8–9½ in (20.5–24 cm)

Named for its mewing, catlike call, the gray catbird usually lives in dense vegetation, where it forages for insects and berries, mainly on the ground. At the end of the winter, catbirds migrate north to breeding grounds in huge flocks, often at night.

The males arrive at breeding areas and sing to attract females. They display to, and chase, their mates. Both partners of a pair help to build a ragged nest of plant material in a low tree or bush. The 2 to 6 eggs, usually 4, are incubated for 12 to 15 days, mostly by the female, but the male helps to feed the newly hatched young. There are usually two broods a season.

Brown Trembler *Cinclocerthia ruficauda*

RANGE Lesser Antilles

HABITAT Rain forest, woodland

SIZE 9–10 in (23–25.5 cm)

Tremblers are identified by, and named after, their characteristic habit of violently shaking the wings and body. Their main foods are insects and invertebrates, most of which are found on the forest floor. A nest is made in a cavity in a tree or tree fern, and the female lays 2 or 3 eggs.

SITTIDAE: NUTHATCH FAMILY

There are 25 species in this family, found in North America, Europe and Asia. There are two subfamilies – the nuthatches and the single species of wallcreeper. They are all robust little birds, with strong legs and feet and sharp claws to help them climb. Nuthatches are the only birds to routinely look for food by walking down tree trunks head first. Their strong, pointed bills are ideal for probing crevices in bark or rocks for insects. The sexes look alike in many species, but differ slightly in others.

Red-breasted Nuthatch *Sitta canadensis*

RANGE Alaska, Canada, USA

HABITAT Coniferous or mixed woodland

SIZE 4¼–4¾ in (11–12 cm)

The male red-breasted nuthatch is identified by his white-edged black cap, black eye stripe and rusty-colored breast. The female has a dark-gray cap. The birds move rapidly over tree trunks and branches, searching for seeds and insects, and deftly investigate pine cones with their bills and extract any food items. Large insects may even be wedged into bark crevices so that the nuthatches can bite off pieces. They pursue insects in the air and collect seeds on the ground.

The breeding season begins in April or May. The nest is made in a tree hole, or a cavity is excavated in the stump or branch of a dead tree. Resin from coniferous trees is smeared around the entrance. Both parents incubate the 4 to 7 eggs for about 12 days.

Wallcreeper *Trichodroma muraria*

RANGE C. and S. Europe, across Asia to Mongolia and W. China

HABITAT Mountain cliffs

SIZE 6½ in (16.5 cm)

An unusual bird, with similiarities to both nuthatches and treecreepers, the wallcreeper is sometimes placed in its own monotypic family. It has a long curved bill and broad, rounded wings with distinctive red patches. In its search for insects to feed on, it climbs up cliff faces, investigating every crevice, and then flits down to the bottom and starts again on another section of rock. It also forages on the ground under stones but is rarely seen on trees.

The male courts the female with display flights, which show off his wing colors. He helps the female build a nest of moss, grass and rootlets in a rock crevice. The female incubates the 3 to 5 eggs, and both parents feed the young.

WRENS AND TREECREEPERS

CERTHIIDAE: WREN, TREECREEPER AND GNATCATCHER FAMILY

These small songbirds are found in the Americas and Eurasia, with one species in Africa. There are three subfamilies.

TROGLODYTINAE: WREN SUBFAMILY

There are 75 species of wren, all except one are confined to the Americas. The exceptional species is the bird known as the wren in Europe and the winter wren in North America. Most wrens are between 4 and 9 in (10 and 23 cm) long and are generally brown, with barred patterning. Wings are short and bodies plump. Some have stumpy tails. The sexes look alike or nearly so.

Wrens occur in a wide range of habitats, including rain forest, cooler wooded areas, marshes, deserts, moorland and mountains. They generally frequent dense, low vegetation, where they hunt for insects and other invertebrates with great agility and speed. They are excellent and varied songsters, often with loud voices for birds of their size. In many species the female also sings, and some tropical wrens perform "duets". Wrens generally produce two or more broods a season. Eggs are usually incubated by the female, but both parents care for the young.

Wren/Winter Wren *Troglodytes troglodytes*
RANGE Iceland, Europe, N.W. Africa, Middle East, east to E. China, Japan; S. Canada, E. USA and Pacific coast

HABITAT Undergrowth in coniferous forest, gardens, heaths and parks

SIZE 3¼ in (8 cm)

This is the only Old World wren. It is a plump bird with a short tail, (usually held cocked up), and a loud, vibrant song. The wren is extremely active and forages in undergrowth for insects, mainly larvae, and a few berries.

Breeding begins in April in most of the range. The male makes several nests, in which he installs various females. The bulky, domed nest is made of plant material and situated in a cavity in a bank, among tree roots or in a hollow stump. The male may also make "dummy" nests, which may help to divert potential predators.

Having lined her chosen nest with hair and feathers, the female lays 4 to 16 eggs, which she incubates for 14 to 16 days. The young are fed by the female and fly at 16 or 17 days. Some populations migrate south of the breeding range in winter.

House Wren *Troglodytes aedon*
RANGE S. Canada through USA and Central and South America; Trinidad and Tobago

HABITAT Woodland, gardens, parks

SIZE 4¼–5½ in (11–14 cm)

The common house wren is gray-brown with a faint stripe above each eye. It eats a variety of insects, such as crickets, flies and caterpillars, as well as spiders and snails. House wrens winter to the south of their range and migrate north in spring.

Males build nests of twigs, leaves and other plant material, usually in cavities in trees or rocks. When the females arrive, each selects a nest, which she lines with feathers, wool and hair. She lays up to 9 eggs, which she incubates for 13 to 15 days. The young leave the nest 12 to 18 days after hatching.

There are many subspecies of house wren; two Caribbean races are endangered and thought to be near extinction.

Cactus Wren *Campylorhynchus brunneicapillus*
RANGE S.W. USA to C. Mexico

HABITAT Desert, arid scrubland

SIZE 7–8½ in (18–22 cm)

The cactus wren has a distinctive white stripe over each eye and a long tail than many wrens, which it rarely cocks up. Cactus wrens frequent areas with thorny shrubs, cacti and trees and forage mostly on the ground for insects and occasionally lizards or frogs. Some cactus fruit and berries and seeds are also eaten. They run swiftly but usually fly over any distance. Nests are made for roosting at night and for shelter in bad weather.

The breeding season is March or April, and there may be two or three broods. The bulky, domed nest is made of plant material and lined with fur or feathers. It has a tubelike side entrance. It is sited on a prickly cactus or a yucca. The female lays 3 to 7 eggs and incubates them for about 16 days.

Long-billed Marsh Wren *Cistothorus palustris*

RANGE S. Canada, USA, Mexico

HABITAT Marshes

SIZE 4–5½ in (10–14 cm)

The marsh wren has a dark head, stripy marks on its back and a white streak over each eye. It inhabits dense vegetation in marshland and eats aquatic insects.

The male wren builds several "dummy" nests before the females arrive in the breeding area. She completes the building of the nest that she uses. It is a large coconut-shaped structure, lashed to bulrushes or other upright vegetation, and made of water-soaked sedges and grasses, woven with rootlets and stems. There is a tubelike side opening. The interior is lined with feathers and shredded plant material. The 3 to 10 eggs are incubated by the female for 13 to 16 days.

Bewick's Wren *Thryomanes bewickii*

RANGE S.W. and central Canada, USA, Mexico

HABITAT Open woodland, thickets, gardens, pastures

SIZE 5½ in (14 cm)

Bewick's wren has a long, slim bill, which it uses to forage on the ground and on vegetation for insects, as well as for spiders. It also delves into crevices in buildings for food.

The nest is made by both partners in almost any available cavity in a tree, rock or building, or in any hollow object, natural or manmade. It is cup-shaped and constructed with plant material and lined with feathers. The female incubates her 4 to 11 eggs for 14 days.

Rock Wren *Salpinctes obsoletus*

RANGE S.W. Canada, W. USA, south to Costa Rica

HABITAT Dry rocky valleys, cliffs

SIZE 5–6 in (13–15 cm)

The rock wren blends well with its arid, bare habitat. It moves with great agility over rocks, in search of insects and spiders.

Both partners build the nest in a crevice in a rock, a pile of stones or a burrow. It is made of plant

material and lined with fur and feathers. Although the nest is carefully concealed, there may be a path of small pebbles leading to it, and the entrance may be lined with stones bones and other debris. The female usually lays 5 or 6 eggs which she incubates.

CERTHIINAE: TREECREEPER SUBFAMILY

The 6 species of treecreeper occur throughout the northern hemisphere in North and Central America, Europe, North Africa and Asia; and 1 species, the spotted creeper, lives in Africa south of the Sahara. Treecreepers are arboreal and clamber up tree trunks searching for insects. Their sharp claws enable them to cling to bark. Their long, thin bills are used for probing insect holes. All but the spotted creeper have stiff tails, which help to support them as they climb. The sexes look alike, or nearly so.

Eurasian/Common Treecreeper *Certhia familiaris*

RANGE Europe and Asia, from Britain to Japan, south to the Himalayas

HABITAT Forest, parks

SIZE 4¾ in (12 cm)

Using its stiff tail feathers as a prop, the treecreeper slowly makes its way up a tree trunk in a spiral path, searching crevices in the bark for insects. When it reaches the top of one tree, it flies off to another and begins again at the base of that trunk. It also eats nuts and seeds. The sexes look alike, and both have long claws and slender, curved bills.

The nest is usually made behind a piece of loose bark and lined with moss and feathers. The female incubates her 5 or 6 eggs for 14 or 15 days, sometimes assisted by the male.

Spotted Creeper *Salpornis spilonotus*

RANGE Africa: irregular distribution south of the Sahara to Angola and Zimbabwe; N. India

HABITAT Forest, savanna, woodland

SIZE 5 in (13 cm)

The spotted creeper differs from other treecreepers – it has a soft tail, which it holds away from the tree trunk as it clambers up, searching for insects. With its long, curved bill, it probes every crevice in the bark for insects.

The cup-shaped nest is made in a vertically forked branch. Both parents incubate the 2 or 3 eggs.

GNATCATCHERS, PENDULINE TITS, TITMICE AND LONG-TAILED TITS

POLIOPTILINAE: GNATCATCHER SUBFAMILY

There are 15 species in this subfamily of the family Certhiidae, which are found in North, Central and South America. They are small, dainty birds, related to and resembling Old World warblers, but with more bluish-gray and white plumage. The sexes differ slightly.

Blue-gray Gnatcatcher *Polioptila caerulea*

RANGE   USA, Mexico, Cuba and Bahamas

HABITAT   Forest, woodland, swamps, inhabited areas

SIZE   4–5 in (10–13 cm)

The blue-gray gnatcatcher is a slender, lively little bird with a long tail often held cocked like a wren's. The male and female look similar, but the female tends to be less blue colored and lacks the black head markings of the breeding male. The birds search for insects, larvae and spiders in the trees, sometimes launching themselves into the air to catch prey.

The cup-shaped nest is usually sited on a horizontal branch of a tree and is made from plant fibers, lined with fine bark, grass and feathers. The parents incubate the clutch of 3 to 6 eggs in shifts for about 14 days and care for the young.

PARIDAE: TIT FAMILY

The birds in this family occur in Eurasia, Africa, and North and Central America. There are 65 species in two subfamilies.

REMIZINAE: PENDULINE-TIT SUBFAMILY

The 12 species of penduline-tit differ from other tits in possessing finely pointed beaks. Most live in Africa or Asia, but there is 1 species each in Europe and North America. They tend to inhabit more open country than other tits, which favour woodland. Male and female generally look alike.

Yellow Penduline-tit *Anthoscopus parvulus*

RANGE   Africa: Senegal to Sudan, Zaire and Uganda

HABITAT   Dry savanna and acacia woodland

SIZE   3 in (7.5 cm)

A rare, little-known species, the yellow penduline-tit is an active, but quiet, bird. It eats caterpillars and other insects and larvae, which it finds by foraging over foliage and large flowers.

The elaborate nest is suspended from a branch and takes some time to build. It is made of felted plant matter and has a short, tubelike opening near the top that is self-closing. The female usually lays 4 eggs.

Verdin *Auriparus flaviceps*

RANGE   S.W. USA: S.E. California to S. Texas; C. Mexico

HABITAT   Desert

SIZE   4–4¼ in (10–11 cm)

The verdin has a distinctive yellow head and throat and a chestnut patch at the bend of the wing, conspicuous only when the wings are open. The female's yellow plumage is slightly duller than the male's, and juveniles lack both yellow and chestnut plumage.

The verdin lives among the thorny bushes and cactus plants of its arid habitat and flits about in search of insects and their eggs and larvae. Berries and fruit are also eaten for moisture.

The globular nest is made of thorny twigs, lined with softer material, such as feathers and leaves, and has a tiny side-entrance. It is suspended from a prickly branch or a crotch of a tree or cactus and gains some protection both from its surroundings and the outward-facing thorns of the nest itself. The female lays 3 to 6 eggs, which are thought to be incubated for 10 days.

PARINAE: TITMOUSE SUBFAMILY

Titmice are small, stocky songbirds, found throughout the northern hemisphere and Africa, usually in wooded areas. There are 53 species. Many titmice live alongside humans. Their normal diet is insects and seeds. Active birds, tits are constantly on the move, flitting around the trees in search of food. Male and female may look alike or differ slightly in plumage.

Black-capped Chickadee
Parus atricapillus

RANGE Alaska, Canada,
S. to C. USA

HABITAT Coniferous forest,
woodland

SIZE 4¾–6 in (12–15 cm)

Identified by its "chickadee-dee-dee" call, the black-capped chickadee has a black throat and cap and a white face. It is always on the move, hopping over twigs and branches in search of insect larvae, spiders, snails, seeds and berries.

Both partners of a pair help to excavate the nest cavity in a soft, rotting stump or branch, and the female lines the nest with plant fibers, moss or feathers. Sometimes chickadees nest in an abandoned woodpecker hole or even in a nesting box. The 5 to 10 eggs are incubated for 11 to 13 days.

Sultan Tit *Melanochlora sultanea*

RANGE Himalayas, mountains of
S. China and S.E. Asia; Sumatra

HABITAT Forest on foothills,
trees near cultivated land

SIZE 7¾ in (20 cm)

The striking, showy sultan tit is large for its family and has a distinctive yellow crest. The sexes look similar, but the female has olive, not black, plumage on the throat and an olive tinge to her back plumage. Pairs or small parties search for insects, seeds and berries in foliage. Birds often hang upside down to peer into crevices or under leaves. The female lays 6 or 7 eggs on a thick pad of moss and plant material placed in a hole in a tree.

Red-throated Tit *Parus fringillinus*

RANGE Africa: S. Kenya, Tanzania

HABITAT Savanna with scattered trees

SIZE 4½ in (11.5 cm)

The agile, lively red-throated tit lives in pairs or small family groups, foraging on vegetation for insects and larvae. The female lays 3 eggs in a cavity in a tree, which is lined with down and plant fibers.

Great Tit *Parus major*

RANGE Europe, N.W. Africa, Asia (except N.), S.E. Asia, Indonesia

HABITAT Forest, woodland, cultivated land, parks, gardens

SIZE 5½ in (14 cm)

Many forms of great tit, with varying plumage, occur over its vast range. Typically, the plumage is blue and yellow with a black cap and a black stripe down the middle of the chest, which is broader on the belly of the male than of the female. A noisy, sometimes dominant and aggressive bird, the great tit lives in large family groups after the breeding season and may join mixed flocks. It feeds in trees and on the ground, eating insects, spiders, worms and small mollusks, as well as seeds, fruit, nuts and buds. It will use its strong bill to hammer at nuts.

The male courts and chases the female before mating. Both partners build the nest of moss and grass in a hole in a tree or wall, or in a nest box and line it with hair or down. The 5 to 11 eggs are incubated by the female for 13 to 14 days, and the male helps her to feed the young. There may be two broods in a season.

AEGITHALIDAE: LONG-TAILED TIT FAMILY

The 8 species of long-tailed tit are closely related to the true tits, Paridae, and occur in Europe, Asia and North and Central America. They are small, with tails often as long or longer than their bodies.

Long-tailed Tit *Aegithalos caudatus*

RANGE Europe (not N. Scandinavia or Iceland);
Asia to Japan

HABITAT Woodland, scrub, bushy heaths, hedgerows, parks

SIZE 5½ in (14 cm)

The plumage of the tiny long-tailed tit varies over its range, but is usually a mixture of black, white and pink feathers. The sexes look alike. This restless, active bird feeds in trees and undergrowth on insects and their larvae, spiders, seeds and buds. Both parents construct a long, oval nest, with a side entrance near the top, from moss, bound with spiders' webs and covered with lichen. The 8 to 12 eggs are incubated mostly by the female, but the male may help and does take a share in feeding the young.

SWALLOWS

HIRUNDINIDAE: SWALLOW FAMILY

The 89 species of swallow and martin are all swift-flying birds, which display great agility in the air. They are found almost worldwide, and many make regular migrations between breeding and wintering areas, sometimes travelling as far as 8,000 miles (13,000 km).

There are two subfamilies – the river martins (of which there are 2 species) and the swallows and martins themselves. There is little consistent difference between the swallows and martins. All forms have smallish bodies, short necks and long, pointed wings. They are fast, agile fliers and catch their prey on the wing in their wide, gaping beaks. Swallows and martins are the passerine equivalents of swifts. The two families have become alike by adapting to a similar way of life in the air; swifts, however, do have longer wings and tend to fly higher than swallows.

On the ground, their short legs and weak feet allow "little more than a feeble shuffle," but they do perch. They frequently nest close to or in human dwellings, or use natural hollows in trees, caves or cliffs in which to construct a burrow. Clutches of 3 to 7 eggs are laid, which both parents incubate.

Swallows and martins are generally gregarious birds and feed, nest and migrate in large flocks. Males and females look more or less alike, but in some species there may be minor differences, such as the male having longer tail feathers.

White-eyed River Martin
Pseudochelidon sirintarae **CR**

RANGE Winters central Thailand

HABITAT Reedbeds in marshes

SIZE 9½ in (24 cm) including tail streamers of 3½ in (9 cm)

The white-eyed river martin is identified by its distinctive white spectacles and rump and by the long streamers flowing from its rounded tail. It also has a large swollen, yellow bill, unusual for a swallow. The juvenile has a darker head and only very short tail streamers.

This rare species was discovered only in 1968 and is believed to be a migrant from the north. Its nearest relative, and the only other member of its subfamily, is *P. eurystomina*, which lives in Africa, in Zambia. The white-eyed river martin winters in central Thailand, at Bung Boraphet, where it roosts at night in large lakeside reedbeds in flocks with other species of swallows. By day, it perches on trees and wires and catches insects in flight.

The summer migration and breeding habits of this species remain a mystery, although it may breed in holes in river banks in Thailand or China.

Barn Swallow *Hirundo rustica*

RANGE Almost worldwide; breeds between 30°N and 70°N; winters in Southern hemisphere

HABITAT Open cultivated country with buildings, near water

SIZE 7¾ in (19.5 cm)

The barn swallow is absent only from very high latitudes and some oceanic islands. The male is a metallic blue hue, with a deeply forked tail covered in white spots, and a white breast. Females and young birds have shorter tails and less vibrant plumage. They feed on insects, which are caught on the wing or plucked from the surface of water.

In summer, barn swallows are often seen in pairs and small groups, but in autumn they form huge flocks and roost in reedbeds before migrating south for the winter. The Old World races spend the winter months in Africa, south of the Sahara, on the Indian subcontinent and in northern Australia. The North American birds fly down to Panama, central Chile and northern Argentina.

Both sexes help to build the open nest, using mud and straw and lining it with feathers. They now seem to prefer to use ledges on buildings to the original cave or cliff sites. The female lays a clutch of 4 or 5 eggs and incubates them for about 15 days, with some help from the male. Both parents feed the nestlings, which can fly at about 3 weeks old. There are two, sometimes three, broods a year.

Sand Martin/Bank Swallow *Riparia riparia*

RANGE Temperate regions of Eurasia, N. America; winters in S. America, Africa, N. India, S.E. Asia

HABITAT Steep sand or gravel banks, near water

SIZE 4¾–5½ in (12–14 cm)

The tiny sand martin is the smallest swallow in North America, with a wingspan of only 10 to 11 in (25.5 to 28 cm). This energetic little bird darts, twists and zigzags in the air, snapping up a variety of winged insects, including termites, leafhoppers and mosquitoes.

Sand martins live in burrows, which they dig straight into sand or gravel banks, often by water, or alongside roads and railway tracks. The birds start the burrow with their bills, and both male and female take turns to kick out the soil until the burrow is about 3¼ ft (1 m) long.

Each spring, the sand martins flock north, often returning to the previous year's nesting hole, and fights over ownership are not unusual. The nest is built at the end of the burrow from soft grass, feathers, hair and rootlets. The female lays a clutch of up to 8 eggs, usually 4 or 5, which are incubated alternately by both parents for 16 days. The young fly at 3 weeks old.

Purple Martin *Progne subis*

RANGE Breeds Canada to Mexico; winters south to West Indies, Venezuela, Brazil

HABITAT Suburban gardens and farmland

SIZE 7 in (18 cm)

The purple martin is one of the tamest birds of the family. The male's metallic blue plumage gradually fades out to brown on the wings and tail; the female is mainly brown, and the juveniles are a grayish-brown. The purple martin supplements its diet of insects, which are taken on the wing, with snails, which are probably a source of calcium.

These birds build their nests in trees or cliff holes, using grass, feathers and often green leaves, which may help to keep the nest cool and moist. The clutch of 3 to 5 eggs is incubated for 13 days, mainly by the female, and the young leave the nest within a month of hatching.

There are 2 races of purple martin; *P. s. subis* breeds in southern Canada down the west coast of the USA to central Mexico and east to the Gulf Coast and Florida. It winters in Venezuela and southeast Brazil. *P. s. hesperia* breeds in the lowlands of Arizona, Baja California and the Mexican coast, but it is not known where it winters.

Blue Saw-wing

Psalidoprocne pristoptera

RANGE Africa: Ethiopia

HABITAT High plateaux

SIZE 7 in (18 cm)

The blue saw-wing swallow has glossy blue-black plumage above, with an oily green look to its wings and tail. The tail is broad and not as deeply forked in the female as in the male. The juvenile is a dull, dark brown and blue.

These birds are often seen in pairs, making swooping flights over streams in search of insects, which they take on the wing.

The nesting hole is at the end of a tunnel, chiseled into a river bank or cliff face, and is padded with layers of soft grass. The female lays 3 eggs, which are glossy white and thin shelled.

Golden Swallow

Tachycineta euchrysea **LR:nt**

RANGE Jamaica, Hispaniola

HABITAT Dry, wooded, limestone hills

SIZE 5 in (12.5 cm)

This delicate, graceful bird earns its common name from the bright golden gloss over its olive-green plumage. The juvenile keeps its duller colors and gray chest band until maturity. The Jamaican race is now believed to be rare, although there is insufficient information available at present to classify it as such.

Golden swallows feed entirely on the wing and nest in tree holes or under the eaves of houses. The female lays 3 eggs.

BULBULS

PYCNONOTIDAE: BULBUL FAMILY

The bulbuls are a family of 137 species, found in forest, orchards and cultivated land in the tropical regions of Africa in particular, but also in Madagascar, southern and Southeast Asia.

With only a few exceptions, they are noisy, gregarious birds of medium size, with shortish wings and comparatively long tails. Beaks are long and notched, with stiff bristles at the base. Some forms possess a crest. Males and females look alike, although occasionally the male is larger.

Their food consists mainly of fruit, berries, buds, flower nectar and insects removed from vegetation.

Yellow-bellied/Yellow-breasted Greenbul

Chlorocichla flaviventris

RANGE Africa: Tanzania to Namibia

HABITAT Forest, woodland with heavy undergrowth, coastal scrub

SIZE 8½ in (22 cm)

Unexpectedly shy and skulking birds for their family, the greenbuls are generally found only in pairs or small parties, although they are widespread throughout their range. The male and female of the species look alike, with yellowish underparts and olive green plumage on the back, wings and head; in juveniles, the head and mantle are the same color.

These birds creep through undergrowth and dense vegetation in search of seeds and berries to eat and they will also cling to the trunks of trees like woodpeckers, looking for insects underneath the bark.

The flimsy nest is neatly constructed from tendrils, grass and some stems and it is well hidden in dense cover. The female lays a clutch of 2 eggs.

Leaflove *Phyllastrephus scandens*

RANGE Africa: Senegal to Sudan, Uganda, Tanzallia

HABITAT Forest

SIZE 8½ in (22 cm)

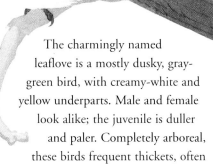

The charmingly named leaflove is a mostly dusky, gray-green bird, with creamy-white and yellow underparts. Male and female look alike; the juvenile is duller and paler. Completely arboreal, these birds frequent thickets, often near streams, climbing among the foliage, looking for insects to eat. They move about in small parties, chattering incessantly; when disturbed they become extremely noisy.

The cup-shaped nest is made from fine grass and leaves and is often slung between the stems of a vine or creeper. There are normally 2 eggs in a clutch.

Garden Bulbul

Pycnonotus barbatus

RANGE Africa

HABITAT Gardens, woodland, coastal scrub, open forest

SIZE 7 in (18 cm)

Both male and female garden bulbuls have grayish-white plumage on breast and belly and white under-tail coverts. In fact, albinism is not uncommon in this species. The head appears slightly crested when the feathers are raised on the nape. They are tame, lively birds and have a habit of warbling briefly and slightly raising their wings when they land. They seem to eat equal quantities of fruit and insects.

The nest is a neat cup shape, lightly made from grass and a few dead leaves, and is often suspended in the fork between two twigs. The female normally lays a clutch of 2 or 3 eggs.

Red-whiskered Bulbul
Pycnonotus jocosus

RANGE India, S.E. Asia, S. China, Andaman Islands; introduced in USA, Australia, Nicobar Islands, Mauritius

HABITAT Low scrub, cultivated land near villages, gardens, orchards

SIZE 8 in (20.5 cm)

This widespread bird is locally abundant throughout its range. It is named for the tufts of deep-red feathers that sprout, like a mustache, on each side of the head; it also has red undertail feathers. Male and female look alike, but the tufts are white in the juvenile. It is a sprightly, cheerful bird, with a musical call, and in the summer, dozens can be seen feasting together in fruit trees. They do a great deal of damage to the crop, since they eat both green and ripe fruit; they also eat the insects they come across when feeding.

The cup-shaped nest is made from grass, roots and stalks, lined with fine grass, and some dry leaves and pieces of fern are woven into the bottom of it. The female lays 2 to 4 eggs.

Crested Finchbill *Spizixos canifrons*

RANGE Assam to S.W. China, Myanmar, Laos, Tonkin

HABITAT Deciduous and evergreen forest

SIZE 8 in (20.5 cm)

This handsome bird has a black crest, which, when erected, hangs forward like Punch's cap, and a thick, finchlike beak: noticeable characteristics that give it its common name. Male and female look alike. Also known as the crested finchbilled bulbul, this bird is a typical bulbul in its habits, traveling in flocks of up to 100 through the trees and undergrowth and calling constantly with a typically chattering note. It feeds on seeds and fruit and on insects, which it often takes in the air, flycatcher-fashion. It is one of the few birds to profit by the slash-and-burn agricultural methods of the seminomadic tribes in its habitat, for it flourishes where scattered low trees grow through dense undergrowth.

The distinctive cup-shaped nest is always made from corkscrew tendrils of a vine, sometimes with a few twigs added, and is placed low in a tangle of bushes and brambles. There are 2 or 3, rarely 4, eggs.

Black/Madagascar Bulbul *Hypsipetes madagascarensis*

RANGE Madagascar, Aldaboa, Glorieuses and Comoro Islands

HABITAT Forest up to 6,560 ft (2,000 m)

SIZE 10 in (25.5 cm)

The bold, noisy black bulbul lives entirely in the trees. Its flight is swift and agile, but its legs and feet are weak, so it does not hop about in the branches but flies everywhere. It feeds on berries – preferring mulberries and bukain berries – and may catch flies or other insects, which it snaps up when they visit flowers for their nectar.

The nest is cup-shaped and made of coarse grass, dry leaves and moss, bound with spiders' webs and lined with fine grass, moss roots and pine needles. Partners seem to be very attached to each other – the male stays close to the female as she incubates their 2 to 4 eggs.

White-throated Bulbul *Alophoixus flaveolus*

RANGE Himalayas in India, China: Yunnan Province, Myanmar, Thailand

HABITAT Humid forest with thick undergrowth

SIZE 9 in (23 cm)

These large, crested bulbuls are usually found in rowdy parties of 6 to 15 birds. They chatter to each other as they climb about in the trees and bushes, or fly in a stream from one dense patch of undergrowth to another. They are seldom found more than about 10 ft (3 m) from the ground, where they forage for berries, wild figs and insects, which they sometimes take on the wing. Their flight is strong and direct, and when they perch they fan out their tails.

Both male and female help to build a substantial nest from fine roots, bamboo leaves and dead leaves, which is concealed in the cover of vines or brambles about 3¼ ft (1 m) from the ground. The 3 or 4 eggs are incubated by both parents for 13 days.

BULBULS, KINGLETS, HYPOCOLIUS AND AFRICAN WARBLERS

Common Bristlebill *Bleda syndactyla*

RANGE Africa: from Senegal to S. Sudan, Kenya, Uganda, Zaire

HABITAT Dense forest

SIZE 8½ in (21.5 cm)

The bristlebill is a large heavily built bird, with olive-brown plumage on the upperparts and a yellow throat and belly. Like all bulbuls, it has tufts of bristles near the bill base. Male and female look alike; the juvenile is duller and more rusty colored. The bill of the male is larger and more hooked than that of the female. These uncommon birds are shy and alert and difficult to observe as they move around in small trees and forest undergrowth, consequently little is known of their habits.

They are known to build a shallow, cup-shaped nest from leaves, sticks and plant fibers and to lay 2 eggs.

Common/Yellow-spotted Nicator *Nicator chloris*

RANGE W. and C. Africa

HABITAT Tropical forest, thick woodland, scrub

SIZE 8½ in (21.5 cm)

This shy forest bird is inconspicuous, often revealing itself only by a burst of clear, chattering song or by grunting, almost squirrellike calls. It lives among the lower branches of trees or in dense undergrowth, feeding on plant matter and insects. Male and female look alike, but the juvenile has paler plumage on the upperparts and narrower, more pointed tail feathers.

Normally 2 eggs are laid in a nest that is either a shallow grass cup or a flat platform of stalks and tendrils, sited in the cover of thick vegetation.

Hook-billed Bulbul

Setornis criniger **LR:nt**

RANGE Borneo, Sumatra, Bankga Island

HABITAT Primary lowland forest

SIZE 7½ in (19 cm)

This bold and busy bird moves about among the branches, searching for beetles, dragonfly nymphs, and small, stoneless berries. Usually seen alone, sometimes in pairs, hook-billed bulbuls are silent, only occasionally making loud, harsh cries. Males, females and juveniles look alike, but the plumage of young birds is duller. No information is available on mating and nesting behavior.

REGULIDAE: KINGLET FAMILY

The 6 species in this family are very small, insect-eating arboreal birds. They include the firecrests and the goldcrests. Kinglets occur in the coniferous and mixed woodlands of Eurasia and North America.

Golden-crowned Kinglet *Regulus satrapa*

RANGE Alaska, S. Canada, USA; winters Mexico and Central America

HABITAT Forest, usually coniferous

SIZE 3–4 in (8–10 cm)

This tiny bird's plumage is restrained for the most part, but there is a conspicuous black-bordered crown, which is orange in the male and yellow in the female, hence the common name. Juveniles develop the crown patch as they mature. Kinglets join mixed flocks to forage in the trees and bushes for insects and larvae.

The birds nest high in a conifer, usually spruce. The female builds a globular nest of moss, lichen, pine needles and grass, bound together with spiders' webs and lined with fine rootlets, fibers and feathers. This structure has an opening at the top and is suspended from twigs, to which it is bound with spiders' webs. The female alone is thought to incubate the 8 to 10 eggs for 14 to 17 days, but both parents tend the young.

HYPOCOLIIDAE: HYPOCOLIUS FAMILY

The gray hypocolius, the single member of this family, is a shrikelike bird found in Iraq, Iran and North India.

Gray Hypocolius *Hypocolius ampelinus*

RANGE S.W. Asia: Iran, Iraq to Arabian Peninsula and to India

HABITAT Semidesert

SIZE 9 in (23 cm)

The unique gray hypocolius is sociable, and outside the breeding season small parties are to be found foraging for fruit and berries. They also eat some insects. Females look like males, lacking only the black feathers on the head that can be erected into a crest. Juveniles are a buffy-brown, with no black on the tail. They are shy, slow-moving birds, like the waxwings, but their flight is strong and straight. Both sexes help to build the large, cup-shaped nest, which is usually well hidden among the leaves of a palm tree. It is roughly constructed from twigs and lined with soft plant matter and hair; the female lays 4 or 5 eggs. When disturbed, the pair desert the nest and reputedly return to destroy it, then build a new one a week or so later.

CISTICOLIDAE: AFRICAN WARBLER FAMILY

This family of warblers includes apalises, camropterans, and cisticolas. Most of the 119 species of African warblers occur in Africa, although two species of cisticolas extend to Eurasia and Australia. The scrub-warbler also occurs in Afghanistan and Iraq.

Zitting Cisticola *Cisticola juncidis*

RANGE Africa, south of the Sahara; S. Europe; India, China, Japan; S.E. Asia to N. Australia

HABITAT Grassland, scrub, ricefields, cultivated land

SIZE 4 in (10 cm)

This bird skulks in grass, feeding on insects. It flies only when disturbed or during courtship. The sexes look similar, but breeding males have more strongly defined streaks on the head.

In the breeding season, males perform various courtship displays, including a jerky, dipping flight, accompanied by a particular song. The unique nest is built amid grass taller than itself, for camouflage. It is pear-shaped, with the entrance at the top, and is made of soft grass stems, bound together with spiders' webs and lined with plant down. Some blades of the surrounding grass are woven into the nest for support. The 3 to 6 eggs are incubated by both parents for about 10 days.

Graceful Prinia *Prinia gracilis*

RANGE E. Africa: Egypt to Somalia; east across S. Asia to N. India

HABITAT Scrub, bushy areas

SIZE 4 in (10 cm)

As much as half the length of this little warbler is accounted for by its tail of graduated feathers, the outer ones of which are tipped with white. The graceful prinia tends to frequent sandy ground near rivers, where there is some grass and bushy cover. It forages for insects in the vegetation and comes into the open only to fly clumsily from one patch of cover to the next.

The courting male sings a somewhat monotonous song from a perch on a tall grass stem. The tiny, domed nest is made of fine grass and is woven into a thick clump of grass stems, three feet or so above ground; there is an entrance at one side. Both parents incubate the 3 or 4 eggs for about 12 days. There are usually two broods a year.

Yellow-breasted Apalis *Apalis flavida*

RANGE Africa, south of the Sahara to South Africa: Transvaal

HABITAT Forest, bush

SIZE 4¼ in (11 cm)

The yellow-breasted apalis occurs in a variety of well-vegetated areas. It usually moves in pairs or small family groups, carefully searching through the foliage for insects.

The domed, pear-shaped nest is constructed from moss, lichen and spiders' webs and is bound to a twig of a low bush with spiders' webs; there is a side opening. Alternatively, this apalis may take over an old domed nest abandoned by another bird species. The female lays 2 or 3 eggs.

WHITE-EYES AND LEAF WARBLERS

ZOSTEROPIDAE: WHITE-EYE FAMILY

The 96 species of white-eye are a remarkably uniform group of birds. Most are small, with rounded wings and short legs, and have a greenish back, yellow underparts and characteristic rings of white feathers around the eyes. Some exceptions are larger in size with duller in plumage. The center of their distribution is Indonesia, but they also extend into Africa, New Zealand, Japan and the Pacific islands. They tend to live in wooded country and gardens, and eat insects, fruit and nectar. The sexes look alike.

Japanese White-eye *Zosterops japonicus*

RANGE Japan, E. and S. China, Taiwan, Hainan, Philippines, Korea

HABITAT Woodland, scrub

SIZE 4½ in (11.5 cm)

The Japanese white-eye has some gray plumage on the lower part of its belly; its beak is slender and pointed. A small, active bird, it forages in flocks over trees and bushes, searching for insects, particularly ants, and their eggs and larvae; it also feeds on buds, seeds and fruit. It flits from tree to tree, constantly making its faint, plaintive call, and never comes to the ground.

A cup-shaped nest is made of grass stems and fiber, lined with moss, and is placed in the fork of a thin branch. The female lays 3 or 4 eggs.

Gray-backed White-eye/Silver-eye *Zosterops lateralis*

RANGE E., S.E., S. and S.W. Australia, Tasmania, New Zealand, Vanuatu, Fiji

HABITAT Varied, with trees

SIZE 4¾ in (12 cm)

An adaptable bird, the gray-backed white-eye tolerates almost any habitat at any altitude, particularly on the islands in its range. It forages at any

level of trees, on agricultural land or in gardens, feeding on fruit, insects and nectar from flowers. It occasionally comes to the ground to feed and even into open country. Male and female look alike both with sharply pointed and slightly curved bills.

The nest is made of plant fiber and grasses, bound together with cobwebs and is attached to twigs of a tree or bush by its rim. The female lays 2 to 4 eggs, which are incubated by both parents for about 11 days.

Príncipe Island Speirops *Speirops leucophoeus* **VU**

RANGE Príncipe Island (Gulf of Guinea)

HABITAT Forest

SIZE 5¼ in (13.5 cm)

One of the few African species of white-eye, this speirops has largely buff-gray plumage, with some white on throat and belly. In small parties, these restless, active little birds feed in the trees, searching the foliage for insects and also consuming seeds. Their movements are quick and agile, with much flicking of the wings. The nest is made of grass and bound to a branch with cobwebs or fine plant fiber. The female lays 2 eggs.

SYLVIIDAE: WARBLER FAMILY

This large family of songbirds has 552 species in 4 subfamilies – Acrocephalinae (Leaf-warblers), Megalurinae (Grass-warblers), Garrulacinae (Laughingthrushes), and Sylviinae (babblers, wrentit, and the typical warblers). Warblers are small, often dull-colored birds, some of which are noted for their melodious songs. Most species occur in Europe, Asia, and Africa but there are several in Australia and 1 species, the wrentit, in North America. Most warblers are active, quick-moving birds, found in woodland, moorland, marshes and reedbeds feeding on insects and fruit. Male and female generally look alike.

ACROCEPHALINAE: LEAF-WARBLER SUBFAMILY

This subfamily contains 221 species and includes the grasshopper warbler, reed-warblers, tailorbirds, and the willow warbler, as well as the leaf-warblers. Leaf-warblers are found from Eurasia south to New Guinea and the Solomon Islands, and in Africa.

Long-billed/Tahiti Reed-warbler *Acrocephalus caffer* **VU**

RANGE Society and Marquesas Islands

HABITAT Woodland bordering rivers, hillside forest

SIZE 8½ in (22 cm)

One of the largest warblers, the long-billed reed-warbler has a distinctive beak that can be 1½ in (4 cm) long. Subspecies on the different islands vary in coloration, and on Tahiti alone, there are some birds with olive upperparts and yellow underparts, and others that are blackish-brown all over.

Long-billed reed-warblers forage in trees and bushes for insects; they do not feed on the ground. They have a musical varied song, performed from a high perch. The nest is usually made in a bamboo thicket, 30 ft (9 m) or more above ground.

Chestnut-headed/Chestnut-crowned Warbler *Seicercus castaniceps*

RANGE Himalayas, S. China, S.E. Asia, Sumatra

HABITAT Forest

SIZE 4 in (10 cm)

An attractive little bird, the chestnut-headed warbler has a reddish-brown crown, with dark bands at the sides of the head, and

yellow underparts. Male and female look alike. They live in dense forest and, outside the breeding season, move in mixed flocks, searching for insects in the middle to canopy layers of the forest. In the Himalayas, the warblers breed at between 6,000 and 7,900 ft (1,800 and 2,400 m), moving down the mountains during the winter months.

The compact, oval nest is situated on the ground. It is well hidden by moss or creepers in a hollow at the base of a tree or bush or in a bank or hillside. Both partners help to build the nest, which is constructed from densely woven moss. They both incubate the clutch of 4 or 5 eggs.

The emerald cuckoo, *Chrysococcyx maculatus*, often lays its eggs in the nests of this warbler.

Grasshopper Warbler *Locustella naevia*

RANGE Europe: Britain and S. Sweden, south to N. Spain and Italy, east to S. Siberia, W. China, S. Russia and C. Asia; winters in Africa and Asia

HABITAT Marsh edge, open woodland

SIZE 5 in (13 cm)

The grasshopper warbler is a retiring, secretive bird species, which quickly disappears into thick cover when it is disturbed. It feeds on insects and larvae. Male and female birds have similar streaked plumage.

The male warbler performs courtship displays to attract the female, spreading his tail and flapping his wings. The nest, which is built by both birds, is placed in thick cover on the ground or just above it in grasses or rushes and is made of plant stems and grass on a base of dead leaves.

The female lays a clutch of between 4 and 7 eggs, usually 6, which both parents incubate for 13 to 15 days. The young then spend 10 to 12 days in the nest, tended and fed by both parents. Birds in the south of the range produce two broods, and those in the north usually only one. In autumn, the birds migrate south for the winter.

LEAF WARBLERS, GRASS WARBLERS AND LAUGHING THRUSHES

Willow Warbler *Phylloscopus trochilus*

RANGE N. Europe and Asia: Britain and Scandinavia, south to C. France, east to Russia; winters in Africa and S. Asia

HABITAT Open woodland, cultivated land with scattered trees and bushes

SIZE 4¼ in (11 cm)

Typical of the many species in the genus *Phylloscopus* in appearance, the willow warbler is extremely hard to distinguish from the chiffchaff, *P. collybita*, except by its song. It is said to look "cleaner" than the chiffchaff, and its eyebrow streak is more marked. Male and female birds look similar, but juveniles have much more yellow on their underparts. Willow warblers search in the vegetation for insects and also sometimes catch prey in the air. In autumn, they feed on berries, before migrating south for the winter. Some northern birds travel as far as 7,500 miles (12,000 km) to winter in African forest and savanna.

Willow warblers nest on the ground, in vegetation under a bush, tree or hedge, or sometimes a little above ground in a bush or on a creeper-covered wall. The female builds the domed nest from grass, moss, stems and roots, lined with finer stems and feathers. She lays 6 or 7 eggs, which she incubates for 13 days. Both parents tend the young, which spend 13 to 16 days in the nest. Birds in the south of the range may produce two broods.

Ceylon Bush Warbler *Bradypterus palliseri* **LR:nt**

RANGE Sri Lanka

HABITAT Montane forest undergrowth, dwarf bamboo

SIZE 6¼ in (16 cm)

Ceylon bush warblers live at altitudes of over 3,000 ft (900 m). In pairs, they skulk in dense undergrowth, searching under leaves and among stems for insects and worms, and rarely climb more than 6½ ft (2 m) above ground.

The male performs a sketchy courtship, climbing a little farther than usual up a stem to sing a brief song and then flying

from one patch of vegetation to another. The nest is relatively large for the size of the birds and is made of moss, grass and bamboo leaves, lined with fine fibers. It is situated in a bush, close to the ground. The female lays 2 eggs.

Brownish-flanked Bush Warbler *Cettia fortipes*

RANGE Himalayas, S. China and S.E. Asia

HABITAT Open forest, swamp-jungle, gardens

SIZE 4 in (10 cm)

A small, skulking warbler, the brownish-flanked bush warbler has a distinctive whistling call, culminating in a loud, explosive phrase, but it is rarely seen. It is a solitary bird and forages for insects in the dense undergrowth which is found in its habitat. It may hop up into bushes but rarely climbs trees. Mountain birds make seasonal movements, descending to lower altitudes in winter and breeding between 6,600 and 10,000 ft (2,000 and 3,000 m).

The untidy nest is built in a bush usually less than a meter or so above ground. It may be a cup-shaped or sometimes a domed structure, with an entrance near the top. Both parents incubate the 3 to 5, usually 4, eggs.

Longtailed/Common Tailorbird
Orthotomus sutorius

RANGE India, S. China,
S.E. Asia to Java

HABITAT Scrub,
bamboo, gardens

SIZE 4¾ in (12 cm)

Both sexes of this
species have similar
plumage, but in the breeding season, the male's two central tail
feathers grow much longer than the others, adding about 1½ in
(4 cm) to his length. The tailorbird is a common, widespread
species. It spends much of its time hopping about in bushes
and low trees, searching for insects, larvae and small spiders.
It also eats nectar.

Pairs mate for life and nest on a bush or low
branch. The nest is made in a cradle, formed by
sewing together the edges of a large leaf or two
smaller leaves. A series of small holes is made in the
edges of the leaf with its beak and strands of wool, spiders' web
or cocoon silk, are used to draw them together. The 2 or 3 eggs
are laid inside the cradle, on a nest of soft fibers. Both parents
incubate the eggs and tend the young.

MEGALURINAE: GRASS-WARBLER SUBFAMILY

The 21 species in this subfamily include songlarks and fernbirds.
They occur in a variety of habitats ranging from forest to
semidesert in south and Southeast Asia, the western Pacific
islands, Africa and Madagascar. Most are slender birds with
short wings that skulk in reeds, tall grass, or other vegetation.

Little Grassbird
Megalurus gramineus

RANGE Australia (except N.); Tasmania

HABITAT Swamps

SIZE 5½ in (14 cm)

The little grassbird lives amid
the vegetation of coastal and inland
swamps. This furtive bird stays in
cover as it creeps about, foraging for
insects and small aquatic animals. It seldom
flies, but it occasionally makes long flights to
find a new home, if its swamp dries out.
The sexes look alike, with streaked
brownish plumage and white eye

stripes. The tail accounts for almost half of the bird's length.
The cup-shaped nest is made in thick vegetation, sometimes
over water. It is made of grass, lined with feathers. The female
lays 3 or 4 eggs.

GARRULACINAE: LAUGHINGTHRUSH SUBFAMILY

These sociable birds communicate with shrieking calls that give
the group its name. The 54 species of laughingthrushes are found
from Pakistan to Borneo, and most species live in forest or scrub.

White-crested Laughing thrush
Garrulax leucolophus

RANGE Himalayas, S.W. China,
S.E. Asia, W. Sumatra

HABITAT Forest

SIZE 12 in (30.5 cm)

The white-crested laughing thrush has an erectile crest on
its white head, a white throat and breast and characteristic
black masklike markings on its head. The several races within
the range differ slightly in the shade of the darker areas of
plumage. They are sociable and move in small flocks, foraging in
dense undergrowth and on the ground and communicating by
chattering calls often followed by wild, cackling sounds, which
resemble laughter and are the origin of the common name.
Insects, berries and seeds are their main foods, but they take
nectar and small reptiles as well. Large items of prey are held
down with the foot while being torn to pieces with the bill.
The cup-shaped nest is hidden in a low tree or
bush. It is made of grass, bamboo leaves, roots
and moss, bound with tendrils of vine
and lined with rootlets. The
female lays 3 to 6 eggs and both parents incubate the clutch for
about 14 days. The chestnut-winged cuckoo, *Clamator
coromandus*, is known to lay its eggs in the nest of this species.

BABBLERS

SYLVINAE BABBLER, WRENTIT AND TYPICAL WARBLER SUBFAMILY

This large and diverse subfamily contains 256 species in three tribes – babblers, the wrentit, and typical warblers.

The 233 species of babblers are all found in the warmer parts of the Old World, with the greatest diversity of species occuring in Africa and south Asia. As their name suggests, most are extremely vocal, noisy birds, and some are fine songsters.

Babblers are either warblerlike or thrushlike birds that tend to have short, rounded wings. They are poor fliers and spend much of their time on the ground or clambering around in trees and bushes. Their feathers are soft, and the plumage varies from dull browns to bright colors, often with bold markings on the head and neck. Most babblers have thickset bodies and fairly long tails. Their legs and feet are strong which enables them to probe and dig in thick vegetation and ground litter in search of invertebrate prey, such as slugs and snails. They also eat small berries and some fruit.

Feeding activity is generally accompanied by the loud and varied "babbling" calls that give the group its common name. Much of this calling behavior may be linked to keeping the small feeding flocks together as they move through the dense vegetation. The babbler tribe also includes parrotbills, yuhinas, fulvettas, and rhabdornis.

The single species of wrentit is a warblerlike North American babbler.

The 22 species of typical warblers, that include the blackcap and whitethroats, are found in Eurasia, Africa, the middle East and northern India. Most warblers are slender arboreal birds that inhabit areas of shrubs or woodland where they feed on insects and fruits. Many warblers are migratory and winter in the southern part of their range.

Brown-cheeked Fulvetta *Alcippe poioicephala*

RANGE India to S.W. China, S.E. Asia

HABITAT Forest, scrub, bamboo

SIZE 6 in (15 cm)

The brown-cheeked fulvetta is a rather plain little bird, with mainly buffy brown plumage. Both the male and female of the species have gray plumage on the top of the head.

In small groups of 4 to 20, these babblers forage among the forest undergrowth for insects. They rarely, if ever, descend to the ground but may climb farther up trees into the canopy layers. The birds keep in touch as they search for food by calling to one another and they are extremely wary of any possible danger that might arise.

The nest is constructed on a branch of a tree or bush a few meters above ground or it is suspended from a few twigs. It is cup-shaped and is built of moss and dead leaves, lined with fine moss and ferns. The female usually lays a clutch of 2 eggs, which are incubated by both parents.

Stripe-throated Yuhina *Yuhina gularis*

RANGE Himalayas to northern S.E. Asia and W. China

HABITAT Forest

SIZE 6 in (15 cm)

The stripe-throated yuhina is a distinctive little bird. It has a prominent head crest, dark streaks on its throat and an orange-rufous streak on the wings. The male and female of the species look alike.

Small parties of these active little birds forage in the trees for insects, such as beetles and wasps, calling to each other as they go. They will sometimes join in mixed flocks with other species of babbler. They also feed on seeds and nectar, and their crests become coated with pollen as they fly from flower to flower.

Little is known of the breeding habits of these birds, but nests made of roots and of moss have been described. The female is thought to lay a clutch of 4 eggs.

Brown Babbler *Turdoides plebejus*

RANGE Africa: Senegal, east to Sudan, Ethiopia and W. Kenya

HABITAT Bush, savanna

SIZE 9 in (23 cm)

Both male and female brown babblers have mainly grayish-brown plumage, with some white markings and light underparts. Typical babblers, they form noisy flocks flying from one bush to another while making chattering, babbling calls. They feed on insects and some fruit, which they find in the low levels of bushes or by scratching about on the ground.

The cup-shaped nest is made of rootlets, lined with fine plant material, and is situated in a dense bush. The female lays a clutch of 2 to 4 eggs.

Red-billed Leiothrix *Leiothrix lutea*

RANGE Himalayas, mountain areas of northern S.E. Asia and S. China; introduced in Hawaii

HABITAT Forest undergrowth, scrub, grass

SIZE 6 in (15 cm)

The male red-billed leiothrix is an attractive bird, with an orange-red bill and bright yellow and orange plumage on the throat, breast and wing feathers; his bill has a blackish base in winter. The female has duller plumage, with a paler throat and breast, and she lacks the bright wing feathers. The courting male perches on top of a bush and fluffs out his feathers to attract his mate, while delivering what has been described as "a delightful song."

These birds live in many different types of forest where they forage in the undergrowth for insects. They are lively, gregarious birds, usually seen in small groups, except in the breeding season when they form pairs.

The cup-shaped nest is made of leaves, moss and lichen, of moss only or of bamboo leaves, depending on what plant material is available, and it is lined with fine threads of fungal material. Usually rather conspicuous, the nest is placed on a horizontally forked branch or in an upright fork, or is bound to several twigs or stems. The female lays a clutch of 3 eggs and there is usually more than one brood. This leiothrix is a familiar cage bird, under the name of the Peking robin.

Fire-tailed Myzornis *Myzornis pyrrhoura*

RANGE Himalayas from Nepal to Myanmar; S.W. China

HABITAT Bush, forest

SIZE 5 in (12.5 cm)

An exquisite little bird, the fire-tailed myzornis has touches of black, white and red on its mainly green plumage. The female looks similar to the male, but her red plumage is duller, and the throat and belly tend toward buff brown.

Generally found in forest at altitudes above 6,000 ft (1,800 m), the myzornis lives either alone or in small groups of 3 or 4, which may sometimes join with mixed flocks of other babblers and warblers.

It is a most adaptable bird in its feeding techniques – it forages on foliage and flowers for insects and spiders, like other babblers, but can also run up mossy tree trunks to find prey or hover like a sunbird in front of flowers. Using its bristly tongue, it will probe the flowers of shrubs, such as rhododendrons, for nectar and also feeds on sap which it obtains from trees.

Little is known of the breeding habits of this bird, the only representative of its genus. The one nest that has ever been observed was in dense, mossy forest, and both parents appeared to be feeding the young.

BABBLERS, WRENTIT, AND TYPICAL WARBLERS

Blackcap Mountain Babbler/Bush Blackcap

Lioptilus nigricapillus **LR:nt**

Range South Africa: E. Cape Province, Natal, N.E. Transvaal

Habitat: damp forest

SIZE 6½–7 in (16.5–18 cm)

A rare, little-known babbler, the bush blackcap is a quieter, less conspicuous bird than many of its relatives. Alone or in pairs, it forages for berries and other fruit, much of which it finds on or near the ground in dense undergrowth.

Both the male and female of the species have characteristic black markings on the head, and the rest of the plumage is brownish and gray.

The neat, cup-shaped nest is made of twigs and moss, lined with rootlets, and is usually situated just above the ground in a bush. The female lays a clutch of 2 eggs.

Bearded Parrotbill/Reedling *Panurus biarmicus*

RANGE Scattered locations in S. and C. Europe, east across Russia and S. C. Asia to Manchuria

HABITAT Reedbeds, swamps, near lakes and streams

SIZE 6¼ in (16 cm)

This is the only babblerlike bird to occur in Europe. The bearded parrotbill has a long tail for its size

and a smaller, weaker bill than other parrotbills. The male has a distinctive gray head, with black mustachial markings, while the female has a brown head and no black markings.

This active little bird moves with agility through reed stems, often straddling two stalks as it picks off insects. It may also come to the ground in order to scratch for insects and in winter it feeds on seeds. Though their flight seems labored, bearded parrotbills do often wander great distances, and northern populations may migrate in winter.

The male displays in order to court his mate, raising his head feathers, puffing out his "mustaches" and spreading his tail. The pair builds a nest of reed and grass stalks, lined with flowering reed heads, which is concealed among reeds or aquatic vegetation. The female lays a clutch of 5 to 7 eggs, which are incubated for 12 or 13 days by both parents. The nestlings are fed by their parents for 9 to 12 days. There may be two or more broods produced a season.

Spot-breasted Parrotbill *Paradoxornis guttaticollis*

RANGE N.E. India (Assam), S.W. China, northern S.E. Asia

HABITAT Scrub, grass, bamboo

SIZE 8 in (20.5 cm)

The spot-breasted parrotbill can be identified by its yellow, parrotlike bill, the reddish-brown plumage on its head and the dark, arrowhead markings on its throat and breast. Male and female look alike. In noisy flocks, parrotbills forage in dense vegetation for insects, seeds and berries.

The cup-shaped nest is built from bamboo leaves and grass, bound with spiders' webs, and 2 to 4 eggs are laid.

Stripe-sided Rhabdornis *Rhabdornis mysticalis*

RANGE Philippines

HABITAT Forest

SIZE 6 in (15 cm)

The stripe-sided rhabdornis, or creeper, has strong legs and feet, which are well suited to climbing tree trunks. It uses its long, slightly curved bill to probe the bark for insects and feeds in the same manner as the treecreepers, gradually working its way up a tree. It also licks up nectar from flowers with its brush-tipped tongue and feeds on fruit.

The female has lighter plumage than the male and she is brown where he is black.

Little is known of the breeding habits of this bird other than that it makes its nest in a hole in a tree.

Wrentit *Chamaea fasciata*

RANGE USA: Pacific coast, Oregon to California; coast of Baja California

HABITAT Scrub, chaparral

SIZE 6–6¾ in (15–17 cm)

The single species of wrentit is included within the main babbler subfamily, although its relationships and classification have been the subject of much dispute.

The wrentit is an elusive, inconspicuous little bird, which spends all of its life within its selected territory, and which it defends throughout the year. It flies weakly and seldom takes to the air across any distance of open country. Pairs mate for life and once they have bonded they forage and roost together. Insects, including spiders, ants, caterpillars, flies and beetles make up the majority of its diet. It also eats berries and occasionally visits bird feeders.

The paired wrentits work together to construct a neat, cup-shaped nest from bark, plant fiber and grass, bound together with spiders' webs. The nest is usually above ground in a bush or small tree. The female lays a clutch of 3 to 5 eggs, generally 4, which are incubated for 15 or 16 days by the female, although the male may take a turn.

Blackcap *Sylvia atricapilla*

RANGE Breeds in Europe, Britain and Scandinavia to Mediterranean countries, east to Iran and Siberia; winters south of range and in Africa

HABITAT Woodland, gardens, orchards

SIZE 5½ in (14 cm)

The male blackcap is distinguished from other *Sylvia* (typical) warblers by his glossy black crown and gray neck. He has a rippling song and is also an accomplished mimic. Females and juveniles have rusty brown caps and are otherwise similar to males, but are browner. It is an active, lively bird and forages in trees and bushes for insects. This species eats more fruit than most other warblers.

The male courts his mate by raising his head and back feathers and drooping and flapping his wings. He builds several rough nests as part of his courtship ritual. She may reject them all and build her own or finish off one of his. The final nest is made in a low bush or other low cover and is constructed from dry stems, spiders' webs and is lined with wool. Both parents incubate the clutch of between 3 and 6 eggs for between 10 and 15 days. They both feed their newly-hatched young.

The species of blackcap *S.a. heineken* which is found on Madeira has darker plumage.

LARKS

ALAUDIDAE: LARK FAMILY

The larks, about 91 species in all, are concentrated in the Old World except for a single species, the shore lark, *Eremophila alpestris*, which also occurs in the Americas. Typically, the wings are fairly long and pointed and the beak rather long and slightly down-curved. Males and females look more or less alike, but the female is often smaller.

Most species favor an open habitat with low vegetation, such as tundra, meadowland or desert, where they are commonly seen walking or running along the ground. The diet consists of seeds, buds, insects and small underground invertebrates, obtained by bill-probing or digging.

Desert Lark *Ammomanes deserti*

RANGE Africa: Sahara; Middle East, through Iran to N.W. India

HABITAT Stony, hilly desert, dry wooded slopes

SIZE 6 in (15 cm)

The plumage of the desert lark matches the color of the desert soil. The dark subspecies, *A. d. annae*, blends with the black larval sand of central Arabia, while the pale race, *A. d. isabellina*, does not stray from areas of white sand.

The nest is usually built up against a rock or tuft of grass and is reinforced on the windward side by small decorative pebbles. In the harsh desert interior, 3 eggs are laid, while 4 or 5 may be produced at the desert edge.

Singing Lark *Mirafra cantillans*

RANGE W., C. and E. Africa, Middle East, Pakistan, India

HABITAT Open bush or scrub, rice fields

SIZE 6 in (15 cm)

The vibrant songs of the singing bush lark can often be heard issuing from bushes or the air, even on bright moonlit nights. Darker and more evenly colored than other larks, this plump

gregarious bird has a heavy, finchlike bill, which it uses to pick up grass seeds and insects. Its shape, strong rapid gait and weak flight suit the bush-lark to life on the ground.

The igloo-shaped grass nest is built in the shelter of a rock or a tuft of grass and has a side entrance and soft, grass lining. The female lays a clutch of 3 to 5 eggs.

Thick-billed/Clotbey Lark *Ramphocoris clotbey*

RANGE N. Africa to Syria

HABITAT Stony desert

SIZE 6¾ in (17 cm)

True to its name, this lark is distinguished by its large, powerful bill. The bird uses it to crush tough seed cases and hard-shelled desert insects, and carries its head very straight or thrown backward, to counteract the weight of the bill. The male is sandy colored, with black spots on the underparts, the female has a redder tinge and fewer spots.

Although this species is normally sedentary, some birds move away from the heat of the desert outside the breeding season.

The nest is sited up against a stone or grass tussock and starts out as a small hollow, filled with soft plant material. As it begins to overflow, the nesting material is supported by a collection of small pebbles. The female lays a clutch of between 2 and 5 eggs.

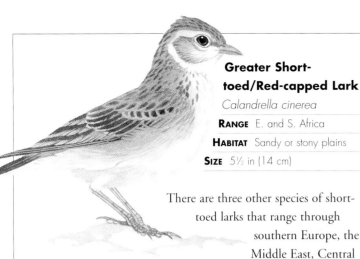

Greater Short-toed/Red-capped Lark

Calandrella cinerea

RANGE E. and S. Africa

HABITAT Sandy or stony plains

SIZE 5½ in (14 cm)

There are three other species of short-toed larks that range through southern Europe, the Middle East, Central and Eastern Asia and that are considered by some ornithologists to be conspecific with *C. cinerea*. The 14 or so races of short-toed larks vary in color throughout the range, from sandy to reddish – the South African race, for example, has a rufous cap on its head and reddish patches on the sides of its breast. This bird is a speedy runner and when alarmed it escapes by flying low, then landing abruptly and sprinting away. Short-toed larks feed on the ground on seeds and insects but perform long, undulating song flights at a height of about 50 ft (15 m).

Short-toed larks gather in large flocks out of the breeding season but disperse to mate, when they are seen singly or in pairs. The nest, deep and cup-shaped, holds two clutches of 3 to 5 eggs each in a year. Incubation lasts for 11 to 13 days.

Shore/Horned Lark *Eremophila alpestris*

RANGE N. America, Europe, N. Africa, Asia

HABITAT Varied, rocky alpine meadows up to 17,300 ft (5,275 m), stony steppe, tundra and desert, open grassland

SIZE 6¼ in (16 cm)

The only lark native to the Americas, the shore lark comprises 40 widespread races. The male has a black and yellow head with short black tufts of feathers. Females and juveniles are less black. In winter, northern groups migrate to southern breeding grounds. Most populations winter in lowland fields, and may form flocks with buntings. They eat seeds, buds and insects and their larvae, small crustaceans and mollusks.

The nest is a simple structure on the ground made from plant stems, lined with soft plant material. It is surrounded with sheep droppings, plant debris and pebbles. There are usually two broods of 4 eggs each, which are incubated for 10 to 14 days.

Eurasian/Common Skylark

Alauda arvensis

RANGE Europe, Asia, N. Africa; introduced in Australia, New Zealand, Canada, Hawaiian Islands

HABITAT Moorland, marshes, sand-dunes, arable and pasture land

SIZE 7 in (18 cm)

The skylark has dark wings and a long tail, both with a white fringe, a boldly streaked breast and a short, but prominent, crest. It is a terrestrial bird and roosts on the ground. It walks rather than hops and crouches when uneasy, emitting a liquid chirrup when flushed.

Skylarks enjoy dust baths and prefer to perch on low walls, fences or telephone wires. They usually sing early in the morning and have a characteristic song flight, fluttering high in the sky. Their diet consists of seeds and ground-living invertebrates.

The female builds a well-concealed grass nest in which she lays 3 to 5 eggs. She then incubates them for 11 days. Two or three broods are raised each year. Northern races migrate south of their range for the winter.

Greater Hoopoe Lark/Bifasciated Lark

Alaemon alaudipes

RANGE Cape Verde Archipelago, across the Sahara to Middle East, W. India

HABITAT Open sandy desert

SIZE 8 in (20.5 cm)

The greater hoopoe lark is long legged, long billed and distinguished by its white eyebrow tufts. It uses its down-curved bill to dig into the desert soil in search of grubs, locust pupae and seeds. This bold bird defends its territory. It has a long, melodious call, but its song is a series of pipes and whistles. It rarely flies except during its song flight. It nests on the ground, although in the hottest areas, the nest is placed a few inches off the ground in the shady lower

SUNBIRDS

NECTARINIIDAE: SUNBIRD, FLOWERPECKER, AND SUGARBIRD FAMILY

Some 169 species of nectar and insect feeders are found in this family. There are 2 subfamilies – Nectariniinae (sunbirds and flowerpeckers) and Promeropinae (sugarbirds).

Sunbirds are the Old World counterparts of the hummingbirds of the Americas, but they are less skilful fliers. There are 123 species of sunbird and more than half live in Africa, south of the Sahara. Others occur in southern Asia and Australasia. In all species (except for the spiderhunters, which are soberly colored) the males have more showy plumage than females. Typical sunbirds have short, rounded wings and a long, downward-curving bill. Most eat nectar and insects. The beak is inserted into the flower, and the nectar is sucked through the tubular, split-tipped tongue. Sunbirds can hover only briefly, but their sturdy legs and feet enable them to perch as they feed.

The 44 species of flowerpeckers live in Asia, from India to China, and south to Australasia. The greatest diversity is found in the New Guinea area and the Philippines. They are small birds with short legs and tails and their bills vary in shape but are partially serrated. The tongue is forked, with the edges rolled into almost complete tubes. Fruit and berries are the most important foods, but they do take some nectar and insects associated with the flowers. Some flowerpeckers have dull plumage, but in other species, however, the male is brightly colored.

The 2 species of sugarbirds resemble larger, drabber versions of the sunbirds and are found in South Africa, living on mountain slopes where Protea bushes grow.

Crimson/Yellow-backed Sunbird *Aethopyga siparaja*

RANGE India, S.E. Asia, Sumatra, Java, Borneo, Sulawesi, Philippines

HABITAT Forest, cultivated land

SIZE 4½ in (11.5 cm)

The metallic green tail of the male crimson sunbird has elongated central feathers. The female lacks his bright plumage and is olive-green, with yellowish underparts. Crimson sunbirds cling to stems and twigs as they suck nectar from flowers. Some insects and spiders are also eaten.

A pear-shaped nest, made of plant down, rootlets, moss and grass is hung from a branch or twig. The female lays 2 or 3 eggs.

Ruby-cheeked Sunbird *Anthreptes singalensis*

RANGE E. Himalayas to Myanmar, Thailand, Malaysia, Sumatra, Java, Borneo and adjacent islands

HABITAT Open forest, scrub

SIZE 4½ in (11.5 cm)

Both male and female ruby-cheeked sunbirds have pale orange throats and yellow bellies, but the female is otherwise less brilliantly colored than the male and has largely olive-green plumage. These sunbirds flit quickly around the foliage, searching for insects and probing blossoms for nectar.

The pear-shaped nest is suspended in a bush from twigs not far from the ground. It is made of fine plant fiber and stalks and has a side entrance, sheltered by an overhanging porch. The female lays a clutch of 2 eggs.

Long-billed Spiderhunter *Arachnothera robusta*

RANGE Thailand, Malaysia, Sumatra, Java, Borneo

HABITAT Forest

SIZE 7½–8½ in (19–21.5 cm)

The long-billed spiderhunter is a large sunbird, with an extremely long, thick bill. Like all spiderhunters, it has duller plumage than other sunbirds; male and female look similar, but the male has small orange-yellow tufts at each side of his breast. This spiderhunter usually forages at the tops of tall trees, darting from one to another in search of insects and spiders or perching on high branches. Its flight is strong and direct.

The nest is made under a large leaf such as banana, which forms the top of the nest. This structure of coarse plant fiber is neatly attached to the leaf by threads of fiber, which are passed through the leaf and twisted into knots on its upper surface. An entrance hole is left near the tip of the leaf. The female lays a clutch of 2 eggs.

Olive-backed Sunbird *Nectarinia jugularis*

RANGE S.E. China, S.E. Asia, Indonesia, New Guinea, Bismarck Archipelago, Solomon Islands; Australia: N.E. Queensland

HABITAT Forest, scrub, mangroves, gardens

SIZE 4¾ in (12 cm)

The only sunbird found in Australia, this species is common throughout its range. Darting from tree to tree, it searches flowers for insects and nectar, sometimes also catching insects in the air. It will hover briefly before a flower, but normally clings to the foliage.

The male and female of the species differ in appearance, the female having a bright yellow throat and underparts but the same olive back as the male. Non-breeding males are sometimes similar to females but have a blue-black band down the center of the throat and an orange tinge to the throat and upper breast.

The nest is made of plant fibers and bark, bound with cobwebs and suspended from a twig of a bush or low tree. The female lays a clutch of 2 or 3 eggs.

Purple-throated Sunbird
Nectarinia sperata

RANGE Assam, Bangladesh, Myanmar, Thailand, Laos, Malaysia, Sumatra, Java, Borneo, Sulawesi, Philippines

HABITAT Scrub, second growth forest, mangroves, gardens

SIZE 4 in (10 cm)

The colorful male purple-throated sunbird is distinguished by his glittering amethyst throat. The female has olive upperparts and a yellow belly.

This sunbird does eat small insects, but its main food is nectar, which it extracts from flowers with its slender, curved bill. It hops and climbs with ease around trees and bushes, but its flight is rather weak.

An oval nest is constructed from plant fiber and rootlets bound with spiders' webs. It is suspended from a branch or palm frond up to 20 ft (6 m) above the ground. The female lays a clutch of 2 eggs.

Scarlet-tufted Malachite/ Red-tufted Sunbird

Nectarinia johnstoni

RANGE Africa: mountain ranges in E. Zaire, W. Uganda, Kenya, Tanzania, Malawi, Zambia

HABITAT Alpine zone of mountains up to the limits of plant growth

SIZE Male: 10–12 in (25.5–30.5 cm) Female: 5½–6 in (14–15 cm)

The elongate central tail feathers of the male of this species account for much of the difference in length between the sexes. In non-breeding plumage the male's gleaming, metallic feathers are dark brown, but the long tail feathers are retained. The female is dark brown but, like the male, she has red tufts at each side of the breast.

This sunbird is attracted to the flowers of the protea bushes and giant lobelias found in its alpine habitat. Its main food, however, is insects, particularly flies, which it often catches on the wing.

Its oval nest is built in a low shrub from plant down, dried stems and rootlets. The female lays 1 or 2 eggs.

Superb Sunbird *Nectarinia superba*

RANGE Africa: Sierra Leone to Angola, Uganda

HABITAT Forest edge, clearings

SIZE 5½ in (14 cm)

The superb sunbird forages in the forest canopy for insects and also sucks nectar from flowers. It is partial to the flowers of *Erythrina* trees, which occur near forest, and also to the flowers of forest creepers. The male bird has multicolored plumage, some of it with a metallic sheen, while the female is olive-green with greenish-yellow underparts.

An untidy nest is made of grass, leaves and lichen and suspended from a branch. The female lays 1 or 2 eggs.

FLOWERPECKERS, SUGARBIRDS, BERRYPECKERS AND DUNNOCKS

Crimson-breasted Flowerpecker *Prionochilus percussus*

RANGE Malaysia, Borneo, Java, Sumatra and adjacent small islands

HABITAT Forest, secondary growth

SIZE 4 in (10 cm)

The male of this species has a red patch on the breast and one on the crown, a bright yellow belly and blue upperparts. The female is mainly olive-green, with some grayish plumage and an indistinct orange patch on the crown. An active little bird, the crimson-breasted flowerpecker flies with quick, darting movements and feeds high in the trees, mostly on berries.

The purse-shaped nest is suspended from a branch of a tree and is made of pieces of tree fern. Little is known of the laying habits of this species, but it is thought to produce 1 egg.

Mistletoebird *Dicaeum hirundinaceum*

RANGE Australia, Aru Islands

HABITAT Forest, scrub

SIZE 4 in (10 cm)

The handsome male mistletoebird has shiny, blue-black, red and white plumage, while the female is a duller, brownish-gray. A tree-dwelling species, the mistletoebird forages high in the trees for berries, particularly those of the mistletoe; the young

also feed on insects. The soft part of the berry passes to the stomach while the hard seeds bypass the specialized digestive system and are quickly expelled. Thus the bird is of great aid to the plant in dispersing its seeds. A solitary bird, this flowerpecker wanders wherever it can find mistletoe in fruit.

The female makes a nest the shape of an inverted cone, which hangs from a branch of a tree. She lays 3 eggs and incubates them for about 12 days. Both parents feed the young.

Cape Sugarbird *Promerops cafer*

RANGE South Africa: Cape Province

HABITAT Mountain slopes where protea bushes grow

SIZE Male: 17 in (43 cm); Female: 9–11 in (23–28 cm)

The male Cape sugarbird's extremely long tail feathers account for the difference in size between the sexes. Male and female look otherwise similar in plumage. Cape sugarbirds are generally associated with protea bushes, where they forage for insects and take nectar from the flowers. They do, however, visit many other trees and bushes and take some insects in the air. Their flight is swift and direct, the tail held straight out behind. Outside the breeding season, sugarbirds are gregarious and live in small groups.

Breeding takes place in the winter months, particularly April to June. The male bird establishes a territory and perches on top of a protea bush to sing and warn off other males. He performs a courtship display for the female over the nesting site, twisting and turning the tail feathers, which are held curved over his back, and clapping his wings. The female bird builds a cup-shaped nest of twigs, grass and stems, lined with fine plant material and the down from protea leaves. The nest is positioned in the fork of a bush, usually protea. She incubates the 2 eggs for about 17 days and does most of the work of feeding the young on insects, spiders and nectar. The young are able to fly about 20 days after hatching but are tended by their parents for another 2 weeks. There are usually 2 broods a season.

MELANOCHARITIDAE: BERRYPECKER AND LONGBILL FAMILY

The forests of New Guinea and nearby islands are home to the 10 species of small birds that make up this family. Berrypeckers forage among the trees and shrubs within the forest, and at the forest edge, in search of spiders and fruit.

The 4 species of longbills have longer and more curved bills than the berrypeckers. They feed at all levels in the forest and, like the berrypeckers, can hover briefly in order to take insects and other invertebrates from leaves and branches. They also eat some nectar.

Black Berrypecker *Melanocharis nigra*

RANGE New Guinea, other associated islands, including Aru Islands

HABITAT Lowland forest

SIZE 4½ in (11.5 cm)

An agile, quick-moving bird, the black berrypecker usually feeds in the lower levels of the forest, eating mainly berries and fruits but also spiders and insects; it will occasionally drink nectar. It may fly to an isolated tree outside the forest to feed.

Although usually solitary, black berrypeckers do sometimes congregate at feeding trees. Male and female differ in appearance: the male is all black or black and green, while the female is dull green and gray.

Pygmy Longbill *Oedistoma pygmaeum*

RANGE New Guinea and adjacent islands

HABITAT Forest

SIZE 3 in (7.5 cm)

One of the smallest of New Guinea birds, the male pygmy longbill has olive plumage with lighter underparts and an off-white throat. The female of the species is slightly smaller and has duller plumage. Both sexes have short tails and curved bills.

The pygmy longbill frequents the lower levels of the forest but it also forages in the tallest flowering trees. It feeds on nectar and insects and spiders.

PASSERIDAE: DUNNOCK, WAGTAIL, SPARROW, WEAVER, AND GRASS FINCH FAMILY

The passeridae family of small birds contains 386 species, which are found throughout the Old World. Some species have also been introduced elsewhere.

There are 5 subfamilies – Prunellinae (dunnocks), Motacillinae (wagtails), Passerinae (sparrows), Ploceinae (weavers), and Estreldinae (grass finches).

PRUNELLINAE: DUNNOCK SUBFAMILY

These are small, sparrowlike birds with inconspicuous plumage. They are found in Europe and Asia. There are 13 species, all in the genus *Prunella*. Male and female birds look similar.

Dunnock/Hedge Accentor *Prunella modularis*

RANGE Europe, Asia, east to Urals, south to Middle East

HABITAT Woodland, scrub, gardens

SIZE 6 in (15 cm)

The little brown dunnock is distinguished by its slender bill and gray underparts. Mainly ground-living, it forages among fallen leaves and other debris for insects, larvae and, particularly in winter, seeds.

The neat, cup-shaped nest is made of twigs, grass and roots and is situated in a bush. The female lays a clutch of 3 to 6 eggs which she incubates for between 12 and 14 days. The male partner of the pair helps to feed the young. There may be two broods produced by a pair in a season.

PIPITS AND WAGTAILS

MOTACILLINAE: PIPIT AND WAGTAIL SUBFAMILY

The family of longclaws, pipits and wagtails is absent only from the extreme north and small oceanic islands. Most of the 65 species are characterized by a long tail, which they wag up and down, and some by a long hind claw. All forms are essentially ground-living birds, with strong feet, and have narrow, pointed beaks and slender bodies, which, among the wagtails, have an elongated appearance. Males and females look alike in some species, unalike in others.

Yellow-throated Longclaw *Macronyx croceus*

RANGE Africa, south of the Sahara

HABITAT Wet grassland, open woodland, swamps, cultivated land

SIZE 8 in (20.5 cm)

The hind claw of this widespread species is nearly 2 in (5 cm) long. Male and female look alike, but the juvenile lacks the black chest marking of the adults and has only black spots. These confident birds live in pairs and are often seen, perching in trees or on farmland. In flight they flap, rather like the larks, and occasionally dive into the grass to rummage for insects.

The male's courtship flight is more leisurely, and he fans out his tail and sings at the same time. The loosely constructed nest, made of grass and roots, is usually hidden among long grass or under a tussock. The female lays 3 or 4 eggs.

Golden Pipit *Tmetothylacus tenellus*

RANGE Africa: Ethiopia, Somalia, Sudan to Tanzania

HABITAT Dry scrub

SIZE 6 in (15 cm)

The shy golden pipit is bright yellow, but the darker bars and mottling help it to blend with its arid scrub habitat. The female and juvenile are browner and paler than the male. All have a long hind claw. These birds are usually seen alone or in small family groups, wagging their tails as they perch above the ground, watching for the insects that form their food.

In his courtship display, the male flies down from a tree, with wings raised in a V-shape over his back, whistling as he goes. The female makes a grass nest, lined with rootlets, just off the ground in a clump of grass and lays 2 to 4 eggs.

Forest Wagtail *Dendronanthus indicus*

RANGE E Asia: breeds Siberia to N China; winters south from India and China to the Philippines

HABITAT Glades and clearings in montane forest, near water

SIZE 8 in (20.5 cm)

The forest wagtail can be identified by the loud chirruping sound it makes as it flies, perches or runs about looking for the snails, slugs, worms and insects on which it feeds. When standing, by rotating its body, it wags its tail from side to side, rather than up and down as other wagtails do. Bundles of plant material are bound together with spiders' webs to form a compact nest, which is usually built on a horizontal branch overhanging water. The female lays 4 eggs.

Meadow Pipit *Anthus pratensis*

RANGE Europe, Asia; winters in N. Africa, Middle East

HABITAT Tundra, grassland, heaths

SIZE 6 in (15 cm)

The meadow pipit has typical pipit plumage, with white outer tail feathers, although its body coloration is variable. In winter, meadow pipits gather in small, loose groups. In summer, individuals perch high – on telephone wires for instance – or on the ground in open grassland or alpine meadows. The diet is varied and generally includes flies, mosquitoes, spiders, worms and some seeds.

The male displays to court a mate by flying up and then, with wings stretched out and tail lifted, gliding down singing a simple song. The nest is made and lined with soft grasses and is often tucked into a tussock of heather or grass to hide it. The female lays two clutches of 4 or 5 eggs and incubates them for 2 weeks. The male helps to feed the young.

Water Pipit *Anthus spinoletta*

RANGE S. European mountains east to C. and E. Asia, winters in S. Asia

HABITAT Summers in marshy areas of tundra, mountain and coast; winters in plains and lowlands

SIZE 6–7 in (15–18 cm)

The water pipit has a slender body and thin, pointed bill. Both sexes have grayish-brown plumage and creamy-white underparts. When walking, the head nods and the tail swings from side to side. Water pipits eat aquatic worms and insects, which they obtain by wading in shallow pools and from mudflats and mats of seaweed. They also eat seeds and insects such as weevils and ants.

In spring, flocks of up to 500 birds feed together before flying to the breeding grounds. The female builds a nest of dried grass and twigs in the shelter of a rock, bank or grass tussock. The nest may be a scraped hollow on the ground. She incubates the 4 or 5 eggs for about 2 weeks.

Yellow Wagtail *Motacilla flava*

RANGE Europe, Asia to W. Alaska; winters in tropical Africa and Asia

HABITAT Marshy grassland, heaths, moors, steppe, tundra

SIZE 6½ in (16.5 cm)

All forms of yellow wagtail are greenish and black, with yellow underparts, but males display a variety of head colors. The female has a pale patch above the eye, and the juvenile has dark throat spots. Several races flock together to migrate to the tropics, where they winter by rivers and lakes. They eat insects on the ground or in the air.

During his courtship display flight, the male puffs up his feathers, fans out his tail, which he holds bowed, and vibrates his wings. The nest is made of plant fibers, lined with hair and wool, and is well hidden on the ground. The female lays 5 or 6 eggs, which she incubates for 13 days.

Pied/White Wagtail *Motacilla alba*

RANGE Europe, Asia, N. Africa; winters south to S. Africa, S. Asia

HABITAT River banks, steppe, tundra, alpine meadows, cultivated land, gardens, near water

SIZE 7 in (18 cm)

The two races of wagtail both have similar black and white markings and develop a white throat in winter. The mantle and rump of the white wagtail, *M. a. alba*, of continental Europe, are gray, while those of the pied wagtail, *M. a. yarrellii*, of the British Isles, are black, or dark gray in the female. These birds often roost in hundreds in trees and reedbeds and occasionally wade in shallow water. They take off from a fast run into undulating flight and catch insects in the air.

The cup-shaped, grassy nest is usually made in a hollow in a steep bank, on a building or on flat ground. The two, sometimes three, broods of 5 or 6 eggs, are incubated for 2 weeks.

SPARROWS AND WEAVERS

PASSERINAE: SPARROW SUBFAMILY

Sparrows and their relatives are found in Africa and Eurasia to Indonesia; some species have been introduced into other parts of the world. Sparrows are generally gregarious and roost, feed and breed together. Most of the 36 species are ground-feeders found in open habitats, though there are some woodland species.

Gray-headed Sparrow
Passer griseus

RANGE W. and C. Africa

HABITAT Bush, cultivated land, near human habitation

SIZE 6 in (15 cm)

A bold little bird, the gray-headed sparrow is common in towns and villages and is similar to the house sparrow in its behavior. It feeds on almost any grain, plant matter and insects and does some damage to crops. The male is slightly larger than the female, but the two look alike, both with distinctive gray heads and mottled wings.

An untidy nest, made of grass, is built in a tree, a thatched roof or any other suitable site, or the birds may use an old nest of another species. There are usually 2 to 4 eggs in a clutch.

House Sparrow *Passer domesticus*

RANGE Temperate Europe and Asia, Africa, north of the Sahara; introduced worldwide

HABITAT Cultivated land, human habitation

SIZE 5¼ in (14.5 cm)

An extremely adaptable and successful bird, the house sparrow lives in close association with humans all over the world and is one of the most familiar of all birds. House sparrows were first introduced into North America in 1850, when a few birds were released into Central Park, New York City. Since then, house sparrows have spread all over North and South America, and the birds seem to be able to adapt remarkably quickly to new environments.

House sparrows often perch on trees and buildings but they feed mainly on the ground. They eat almost anything – grain, weed seeds, insects, refuse and food scraps put out by people.

Gregarious birds, they usually move in flocks and roost in closely packed groups. The male bird is identified by his gray crown, edged with chestnut, his black bib and brown and black-striped back and wings. The female is a brownish-gray color, with gray underparts.

Both members of a breeding pair help to build the nest, although the male does most of the work. The nest is built in any hole or crevice in a building or wall, such as under eaves or in pipes, or sometimes in a tree or creeper. It is constructed from straw, plant stems, paper, cloth or any other available material. The 3 to 5 eggs are incubated, mostly by the female, for between 11 and 14 days. Both parents feed the young, mainly on insects. There may be two or three broods a year.

Rock Sparrow *Petronia petronia*

RANGE N. Africa, Madeira and Canary Islands; S.W. Europe, east through Balkans and central Asia to N. China

HABITAT Stony mountain slopes, ruined buildings, semidesert

SIZE 5½ in (14 cm)

Although they are not as bold with humans as the house sparrow, the rock sparrow often lives near villages and dwellings. It is a gregarious bird and moves in flocks, searching for seeds, insects and berries to eat. Males and females look alike.

The nest is made in a crevice in a rock, wall or building or sometimes in a tree or a rodent's burrow. The female lays a clutch of 4 to 8 eggs, usually 5 or 6. Both parents tend and feed the young, and there may be a second brood.

White-billed Buffalo Weaver
Bubalornsis albirostris

RANGE Africa, from Senegal to Ethiopia and S. to Uganda and Kenya

HABITAT Savanna, scrub, cultivated land

SIZE 9¼ in (24 cm)

Usually seen in small flocks, the buffalo weaver feeds mainly on the ground on a variety of grass seeds and insects. The male's plumage is black, but with white bases to the feathers, and he has a black and white or reddish bill. The female has mottled brown plumage and a blackish or red bill.

Up to 8 pairs of buffalo weavers make a huge communal nest in a tree; it is maintained all year round and used for years on end. The framework is made of thorny sticks, and each individual nest inside is lined with fine grass and rootlets. Females usually lay clutches of 2 to 4 eggs and feed their young on insects.

White-winged Snowfinch *Montifringilla nivalis*

RANGE S. Europe, across central Asia to W. China

HABITAT Barren, stony ground on mountains at 6,000–7,000 ft (1,800–2,100 m)

SIZE 7 in (18 cm)

Although it seldom leaves its mountain habitat, the snowfinch may descend to alpine valleys in bad winter weather. It perches on rocks and buildings and hops and walks quickly on the ground as it forages for insects and, in summer, the seeds of alpine plants. A bold little bird, it is often seen by skiers in alpine resorts and readily approaches to collect crumbs of food. The male is identified by his gray head, black throat and black and white wing and tail feathers. The female has a brownish head and less white on the wings and tail. Adults have black bills in the breeding season and orange-yellow bills in the autumn and winter.

The nest of feathers, dead grass and moss is made in a hole in a rock or building, where these exist, or in a mammal's burrow. The female lays 4 or 5 eggs on a warm lining of feathers and hair. Both parents incubate the eggs for 13 to 14 days and feed the young; a second brood may follow.

Sociable Weaver *Philetarius socius*

RANGE Africa: Namibia, South Africa

HABITAT Dry scrub

SIZE 5½ in (14 cm)

Sociable weavers move in flocks of up to a few hundred birds. They eat insects and seeds, all of which they take on the ground. Male and female look alike and are identified by their grayish-brown crowns, black bibs and the cream-edged dark feathers on the back that give the plumage a scaly look.

These birds build an enormous communal nest, usually made in a large *Acacia* tree, which may house up to a hundred pairs. The birds breed, live and roost in the nest all year round. Nests are constantly repaired and rebuilt and may be used for years. Sociable weavers are monogamous, and within the communal nest, each pair has its own chamber and entrance. A clutch contains 3 or 4 eggs.

PLOCEINAE: WEAVER SUBFAMILY

This subfamily of 117 species includes the weavers, queleas, bishops, and widowbirds. Weavers take their name from the intricate, often colonial, nests "woven" by members of the group. They are found in a range of habitats in the tropical and subtropical regions of Africa, Madagascar, and south and south-east Asia. Some species live in woodland and forest while others are ground-dwellers, found in grassland or scrub. Like the sparrow, they have short, stubby beaks which are used to feed on seeds, insects, flower parts, and nectar. During the breeding season, males are often brightly colored.

GRASS FINCHES AND PARASITIC WHYDAHS

ESTRILDINAE: GRASS FINCH SUBFAMILY

The 155 species of small, seed-eating birds in this subfamily occur in open habitats from Africa across southern Asia to Australasia and the western Pacific islands. Many species nest socially. Most are colorful, while some are drab with striking patches. The sexes look alike in some species, different in others. There are two tribes. One includes waxbills, firefinches, parrot-finches, the zebra finch, and the gouldian finch. The other contains 15 species of parasitic whydahs which lay their eggs in the nests of other grass finches.

Red-billed Firefinch

Lagonosticta senegala

RANGE Africa, south of the Sahara (not extreme south)

HABITAT Scrub, thickets, cultivated land

SIZE 3½ in (9 cm)

A widespread, common bird in Africa, the red-billed firefinch eats grass and seeds. The female is plainer than the male, with only a touch of red on the face and rump, her underparts are buff, with white spots on the breast.

Out of the breeding season, these birds gather in small flocks. The globular nest, usually made of dry grass, is built on a wall or in a bush or roof. Both parents incubate the 3 to 6 eggs.

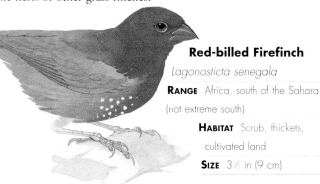

Red-cheeked Cordon-bleu

Uraeginthus bengalus

RANGE Africa, Senegal to Ethiopia, south through E. Africa to Zambia

HABITAT Open country, cultivated land

SIZE 5 in (12.5 cm)

The male of this species has crimson cheek patches. Females and juveniles are duller and lack the red markings. These common birds eat grass seeds.

Cordon-bleus live in pairs or family groups. The globular or oval nest is made of dry grass with an entrance hole at the side. It is built in a bush, tree or roof. Females lay 4 or 5 eggs.

Red Avadavat *Amandava amandava*

RANGE India, Pakistan, S.W. China, Hainan, S.E. Asia (introduced in Malaysia), Java, Lesser Sunda Islands

HABITAT Scrub, grassland, reedbeds, cultivated land

SIZE 3½–4 in (9–10 cm)

The male red avadavat has bright crimson plumage, dotted with many white spots, his dark wings, too, are spotted with white. Outside the breeding season, he resembles the female, with a grayish-buff throat and breast. Both sexes have red bills and a patch of red at the base of the tail. Often found in swampy land, the red avadavat feeds on grass seeds. It lives in pairs or groups of up to 30, often with other waxbill species.

The ball-shaped grass nest has an entrance at the side, it is built low in a bush or among rushes or grass. The female incubates the 6 to 10 eggs.

Java Sparrow *Padda oryzivora* **VU**

RANGE Java, Bali; introduced in India, Sri Lanka, China, S.E. Asia, Malaysia, Sumatra, Sulawesi, Lesser Sunda Islands, Philippines, Moluccas, Hawaiian Islands, Fiji, Florida, Puerto Rico

HABITAT Ricefields, scrub, mangroves, urban areas

SIZE 6¼ in (16 cm)

The Java sparrow is widely established outside its native range, in some places by deliberate introduction, in others due to the escape of caged birds. The sexes look alike, both with pinkish-red bills and black and white heads. This sparrow largely eats rice and is considered a pest. It also eats fallen seeds of other plants. It climbs with great agility on stalks and trees. A gregarious bird, it moves in flocks.

The domed nest is made of grass and built on a wall, under a roof or in a tree. The female lays up to 7 or 8 eggs, which are incubated for 13 or 14 days. The young are fed on insects until they can digest rice and seeds.

Blue-faced Parrot-finch *Erythrura trichroa*

RANGE Sulawesi, the Moluccas, New Guinea, Bismarck Archipelago, Solomon Islands, Guadalcanal, N.E. Australia, Caroline Islands, Vanuatu, Loyalty Islands

HABITAT Rain forest, mangroves

SIZE 4¾ in (12 cm)

The blue faced parrot-finch lives alone or in small groups and feeds on seeds on bushes, low trees and vegetation. The sexes look alike, both with blue, green, scarlet and black plumage.

The domed or pear-shaped nest is made of moss and plant fiber and has a side entrance, it is built in a tree or bush. There are 3 to 6 eggs in a clutch.

Zebra Finch *Taeniopygia guttata*

RANGE Australia, Lesser Sunda Islands

HABITAT Woodland, dry open country with bushes and trees

SIZE 3½ in (9 cm)

A common bird in Australia, the zebra finch is gregarious and sometimes occurs in large flocks. It feeds in the trees and on the ground on seeds and insects. The sexes differ in appearance: the female lacks the male's facial markings and chestnut flanks and has a grayish-brown throat, with no gray barring. The timing and frequency of the breeding depend on rainfall. A domed nest is made of grass and twigs low in a tree or bush. A clutch usually contains 4 to 6 eggs.

Gouldian Finch *Chloebia gouldiae* **EN**

RANGE Tropical N. Australia

HABITAT Savanna

SIZE 5½ in (14 cm)

The 3 forms of gouldian finch vary in the color of the forehead and face, which may be black, scarlet or yellow. The sexes look similar, but females have duller plumage. The gouldian finch mainly eats seeds and some insects. It seldom comes to the ground, but clings to grass stems or low twigs on bushes and trees within reach of grass heads. Outside the breeding season it lives in flocks.

The gouldian finch lays its 4 to 8 eggs in a hole in a tree or in a termite mound sometimes on a sketchy, globular nest.

Paradise Whydah

Vidua paradisaea

RANGE E. and S. Africa: Sudan to Angola; South Africa: Natal

HABITAT Dry open country

SIZE Male: 15 in (38 cm)
Female: 6 in (15 cm)

The elongated central tail feathers of the male account for the great discrepancy in size between male and female paradise whydahs. The female of the species has mottled brown and buff plumage similar to, but duller than, that of the male in his nonbreeding plumage. Often gathering in small flocks, paradise whydahs usually feed on the ground on seeds.

In his courtship display, the male bird flies with his spectacular, long central tail feathers raised almost at a right angle to his body, and may also hover near the female, slowly beating his wings.

Like all whydahs, this species is a brood parasite. It lays its eggs in the nests of other bird species, most usually the melba finches that belong to the same subfamily. The young of the melba finch have complex patterns on the lining of their mouths which stimulate their parents to feed them, and the association between this brood parasite and its host, the melba finch has become so strong that the young whydahs have similar mouth patterns. The whydah chicks are also able to mimic the calls and postures of their foster siblings.

FINCHES, BUNTINGS AND TANAGERS

FRINGILLIDAE: FINCH, BUNTING, AND TANAGER FAMILY

This large and diverse family of small to medium-sized songbirds contains 993 species in 3 subfamilies – Peucedraminae (the olive warbler), Fringillinae (finches and Hawaiian honeycreepers), and Emberizinae (buntings, wood warblers, tanagers, cardinals, and icterids).

FRINGILLINAE: FINCH AND HAWAIIAN HONEYCREEPER SUBFAMILY

Finches are a successful, widely distributed group of small, tree-dwelling, seed-eating songbirds. They are most numerous in Europe and northern Asia, but species occur in other parts of the Old World and in the Americas. The 139 species include the chaffinches and the cardueline finches, such as crossbills, grosbeaks, redpoll, and goldfinch. There is a great diversity of bill shapes in the tribe. The sexes usually differ in appearance.

It is likely that the 22 extant species of Hawaiian honeycreepers, as well as the extinct forms, are derived from a one-off colonisation by one type of wood warbler. Existing forms divide into 2 groups. The nectar feeders, which also eat insects and have reddish and black plumage. The second group of finchlike birds, which eat seeds and have yellowish-green plumage. Bill shape differs according to feeding habits. Sexes differ in some species and look alike in others. Most species are threatened.

Chaffinch
Fringilla coelebs

RANGE Europe, across Asia to Afghanistan, Mediterranean region, N. Africa, Canary Islands, Azores

HABITAT Forest, woodland, gardens

SIZE 6 in (15 cm)

The abundant, widespread chaffinch varies in coloration over its range, and its attractive song exists in many different dialects. The female has duller plumage than the male, being mostly grayish and olive-brown. The chaffinch searches for food in the trees and on the ground, where it hops or moves with short, quick steps, it flies in the undulating manner typical of the finches. Three-quarters of

its food intake is plant material, mostly seeds, fruit and corn, but it also eats insects, spiders and earthworms.

A neat, well-constructed nest is made in a tree or bush, and the female lays 4 or 5 eggs, which she incubates for 11 to 13 days. Northern populations migrate south for the winter.

Purple Finch *Carpodacus purpureus*

RANGE N. America: British Columbia, south to Baja California, east to Quebec, Newfoundland, Minnesota and New Jersey; winters in S. USA and Mexico

HABITAT Woodland, coniferous forest

SIZE 5½–6¼ in (14–16 cm)

The male purple finch is distinguished by his rich, reddish coloration, while the female's plumage is mainly brown and gray. Outside the breeding season, these finches form large feeding flocks and search out seeds of weeds and trees. In spring and summer, they also feed on beetles and caterpillars.

The male displays to the female, dancing around her and beating his wings and singing a warbling song. A nest is made of twigs and grasses, usually in a conifer. The female lays 4 or 5 eggs, which she incubates for 13 days.

Island Canary *Serinus canaria*

RANGE Canary Islands, Madeira, Azores; introduced in Bermuda

HABITAT Wooded areas, gardens

SIZE 5 in (12.5 cm)

All races of domestic canaries are descended from this species, which was first made popular as a cage bird by the Spanish conquerors of the Canary Islands. The female is generally brown and duller than the bright yellow and brown male. Canaries feed on seeds and usually remain hidden in the trees, but their attractive song is often heard.

A cup-shaped nest is made in a tree or bush, and the female lays 4 or 5 eggs, which she incubates for 13 or 14 days.

Red Crossbill
Loxia curvirostra

RANGE N.W. Africa, Europe, Asia, south to Himalayas; Japan, Vietnam, Philippines, N. America, south to Nicaragua

HABITAT Coniferous forest

SIZE 5–6¼ in (13–16 cm)

The crossbill feeds almost entirely on conifer seeds, which it extracts from the cones by using its crossed mandibles. The bird may hang upside down to feed or tear off the cone and hold it in its foot. It rarely comes down to the ground. In summer, it also eats insects. Male and female differ in plumage, the female being greenish-gray.

A cup-shaped nest is made in a conifer. The female lays 3 or 4 eggs, which she incubates for 13 to 16 days; both parents feed the young, which hatch with symmetrical bills.

Eurasian Goldfinch
Carduelis carduelis

RANGE Europe, N. Africa, Azores, Canary Islands, Madeira; Asia, east to Lake Baikal, south to Himalayas

HABITAT Open woodland, gardens, orchards, cultivated land

SIZE 4¼ in (12 cm)

Both male and female goldfinches have red faces and black and white heads. The wings are long and pointed and their bills almost conical. Outside the breeding season, they often fly to open country and feed near the ground on thistles and other weed seeds; they also eat some insects.

The female builds a nest on a branch of a tree in a wooded area and lays 5 or 6 eggs. The male feeds her while she incubates the eggs for 12 or 13 days.

Pine Grosbeak
Pinicola enucleator

RANGE N. Scandinavia, Russia, N. Asia; Alaska, Canada, N. USA

HABITAT Coniferous and mixed forest

SIZE 7¾ in (20 cm)

A large, long-tailed finch, the pine grosbeak uses its stout, heavy bill to crush the stones of fruit such as cherries and plums. It also eats seeds, buds and insects in summer. It finds its food in trees and on the ground and is a strong flier. The sexes differ in plumage, the female being largely a bronzy color.

The nest is usually made in a conifer or a birch tree, and the female lays 4 eggs, which she incubates for 13 or 14 days. The male feeds her during this period and helps to feed the young.

Common/Mealy Redpoll
Carduelis flammea

RANGE Breeds in Iceland, Ireland, Britain, Scandinavia, central European mountains, N. Asia to Bering Sea, northern N. America; winters south of breeding range

HABITAT Woodland, forest, tundra

SIZE 5–6 in (13–15 cm)

The redpoll can survive lower temperatures than any songbird except the Arctic, or hoary, redpoll, *C. hornemanni*. It eats seeds, particularly those of birch and alder, and will hang upside down to reach the catkins. It also scratches on the ground to find seeds and in summer feeds on insects.

At the start of the breeding season, males perform display flights. The female builds a nest on a forked branch and lays 4 or 5 eggs. She incubates the eggs for 10 or 11 days.

Eurasian Bullfinch
Pyrrhula pyrrhula

RANGE Scandinavia, Britain, south to Mediterranean regions (not S. Spain); Asia to Japan

HABITAT Coniferous forest, woodland, parks, gardens, cultivated land

SIZE 5½–6¼ in (14–16 cm)

The male bullfinch is identified by his black cap, rose-red underparts and black and white wings. The female looks similar but has pinkish-gray underparts. This shy bird usually perches in cover in a bush or tree and does not often come to the ground. In spring, it feeds largely on the buds of fruit trees and can cause considerable damage to crops; buds of other trees are also eaten, as well as berries and seeds.

A nest of twigs and moss is built by the female in a bush or hedge. She lays a clutch of 4 or 5 eggs, which she incubates for 12 to 14 days.

FINCHES, BUNTINGS AND TANAGERS CONTINUED

Palila *Loxioides bailleui* **EN**

RANGE Hawaii: Mauna Kea

HABITAT Forest

SIZE 6 in (15 cm)

The palila is now found only on the western slope of Mauna Kea and is a seriously endangered bird, largely due to the disturbance and destruction of its forest habitat. It feeds principally on the seeds and flowers of the mamane tree.

The female nests in a mamane tree. She lays 2 eggs, and incubates them for 21 to 27 days. Both parents feed the chicks.

Akepa *Loxops coccineus* **EN**

RANGE Hawaii, Maui, Kauai

HABITAT Forest

SIZE 4–5 in (10–12.5 cm)

Abundant in some areas of the Hawaiian Islands until the end of the 19th century, the akepa is in serious decline. The Oahu Island race is extinct. A sprightly bird, with a short, conical bill, it eats mainly caterpillars and spiders, which it finds on leaves and small twigs. It also drinks nectar. The female lays 3 eggs in a cavity in a tree.

Akiapolaau

Hemignathus wilsoni **EN**

RANGE Hawaii

HABITAT Forest

SIZE 5½ in (14 cm)

This bird is found only in small numbers in a few areas. It has declined due to the deterioration of its forest home and the introduction of predators, particularly arboreal rats. The akiapolaau forages on branches and tree trunks, which it creeps up and down with ease. Its unique bill – the upper mandible is long and curved and the lower short, straight and wedge-shaped is used to open out the burrows of woodboring insects. It uses its thin, brushlike tongue to extract its prey.

EMBERIZINAE: BUNTING, TANAGER, CARDINAL, WOOD WARBLER, AND ICTERID SUBFAMILY

This largest and most diverse subfamily of the finch family Fringillidae contains 823 species in 5 tribes.

The 156 species of bunting are small finchlike birds, usually with somber brown or black plumage, occasionally with patches of yellow and orange-brown. Their beaks are short and conical. Their diet includes seeds and insects. Buntings are found in a range of habitats in the Americas, Africa, and Eurasia.

The 413 species of tanagers occur through the Americas, apart from polar regions. They are vividly colored. In many species the sexes look alike, but in the 4 species in the temperate zones of North America they differ in appearance. Tanagers frequent the upper layers of forests and woods. The feet and legs are well developed. Their diet usually consists of fruit and insects.

Cardinals, which include the American grosbeaks, saltators, and dickcissels, are found in the New World, from Canada to Argentina. The 42 species are stocky with short, strong bills. Males are brightly colored and females are duller.

The 115 species of American wood warblers, or parulid warblers, are found from Alaska and northern Canada to the south of South America. Small, slender birds, with pointed bills, most are brightly colored, particularly in breeding plumage. The sexes look alike in some species and differ in others.

The 97 species of icterids are found throughout the Americas. Icterids include many groups such as oropendolas, caciques, and American blackbirds. The majority live in woodland or forest, but others occur in all types of habitat.

Reed Bunting

Emberiza schoeniclus

RANGE Europe, N. Africa, C. and N. and E. Asia

HABITAT Reedbeds, swamps; in winter, farmland and open country

SIZE 6 in (15 cm)

The male reed bunting has a black head and throat and white collar, while the female has a brown and buff head, with black and white mustachial streaks. The reed bunting

forages on low vegetation and reed stems and on the ground for seeds. In spring and summer, it also eats insects and larvae.

The female nests on the ground or in low vegetation and lays 4 or 5 eggs. She incubates them for about 14 days. The male helps to feed the young.

Yellowhammer

Emberiza citrinella

RANGE Europe, W. Asia to Urals

HABITAT Grassland, farmland, open country with bush and scrub

SIZE 6¼ in (16 cm)

The yellowhammer feeds for the most part on the ground eating seeds, grains, berries, leaves and some insects and invertebrates.

The male has a mainly yellow head and chestnut rump, while the female of the species is duller and has less yellow plumage.

After a courtship chase and display, a nest is made on or near the ground often in a hedge or under a bush. The female lays 3 or 4 eggs, which she incubates, mostly on her own, for 12 to 14 days. There may be two or three broods.

Dark-eyed Junco *Junco hyemalis*

RANGE N. America: Alaska, east to Newfoundland, south through Canada and USA to Mexico

HABITAT Clearings, woodland edge, roadsides, parks, gardens

SIZE 5–6¼ in (13–16 cm)

There are 4 subspecies of this junco, with considerable variations in color. Females of all races are less colorful than males. This junco feeds largely on the ground, eating mainly seeds in the winter and seeds berries, insects and spiders in summer.

The male establishes a breeding territory, and his mate builds a nest on the ground, near vegetation or tree roots or in the shelter of a bank or ledge. She lays 3 to 6 eggs and incubates them for 11 or 12 days. There are usually two broods. Northernmost populations migrate to southern USA in winter.

Savannah Sparrow *Passerculus sandwichensis*

RANGE Alaska, Canada, much of USA (does not breed in S.E.), Mexico, Guatemala

HABITAT Tundra, open grassland, marshes

SIZE 4¼–6 in (11–15 cm)

The many subspecies of savannah sparrow, differ slightly in coloration and song. This species hops about, while scratching and foraging, or runs, mouselike, through grass. Its main foods are seeds and insects, such as beetles, grasshoppers and ants.

The female makes a grassy nest on the ground, usually in a natural hollow, and lays 4 or 5 eggs. Both parents incubate the eggs for about 12 days. Northern populations migrate south to winter in southern USA and Central America.

Snow Bunting *Plectrophenax nivalis*

RANGE Breeds in Iceland, Scandinavia, N. Scotland, Arctic and subarctic Asia, N. America; winters south of breeding range

HABITAT Open stony country, tundra, mountains; winters also on coasts and open country

SIZE 6¼ in (16 cm)

In breeding plumage, the male snow bunting is almost pure white, except for his black back, central tail and primary wing feathers. In winter, his white plumage becomes mottled with rusty brown. The female has a gray-brown head and back in summer and is paler and duller in winter. The snow bunting feeds on seeds and insects on the ground.

The nest is made from dead grass, moss and lichen and is concealed among stones. The female lays 4 to 6 eggs, which she incubates for 10 to 15 days. The male bird feeds his mate during the incubation period and helps to feed the young.

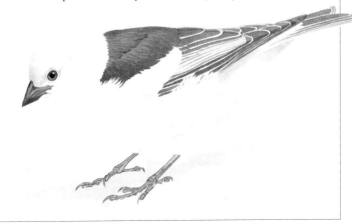

FINCHES, BUNTINGS AND TANAGERS CONTINUED

Chipping Sparrow *Spizella passerina*

RANGE Canada, USA, Mexico,
Central America to Nicaragua

HABITAT Open woodland, clearings in forest,
gardens, parks

SIZE 5–6 in (13–15 cm)

Both sexes of chipping sparrow have distinctive chestnut caps, edged by white eyebrow stripes. They are inconspicuous birds and often live in suburban and inhabited areas. Grass seeds are their main food, but they also eat weed seeds, insects and spiders.

The female bird makes a nest in a vine or on a branch of a bush or tree. She lays 3 to 5 eggs, and her mate feeds her while she incubates the eggs for 11 to 14 days. There may be two broods in a season.

White-naped Brush Finch *Atlapetes albinucha*

RANGE Mexico

HABITAT Forest edge, scrub

SIZE 7 in (18 cm)

Male and female of this species look alike, both with distinctive black and white heads. Basically terrestrial birds they flutter and hop about on the ground and up on to stems and low branches. They forage in the litter of the forest floor by flicking leaves aside with sweeps of the bill as they search for grass seeds and some insects.

A grassy nest is built by the female in a low bush. She usually lays 2 eggs.

Rufous-sided Towhee
Pipilo erythrophthalmus

RANGE S. Canada, USA, Mexico,
Guatemala

HABITAT Forest edge, woodland, parks,
gardens

SIZE 7–8½ in (18–22 cm)

The male rufous-sided towhee is recognized by his mainly black and white plumage and the distinctive rufous patches on each side of the belly. The female has a similar plumage pattern but is brown where the male is black. Both sexes have red eyes. The birds scratch around on the ground and under vegetation for a wide variety of food, including insects, small lizards, snakes, salamanders, spiders, millipedes, seeds and berries.

The courting male chases the female and fans his tail to expose the white markings; he sings to her from a perch in a bush or tree. The female builds the nest on or close to the ground, using grass, rootlets, leaves, bark shreds and twigs. She incubates the 3 to 4 eggs for 12 or 13 days. The young leave the nest 10 to 12 days after hatching, and there may be a second brood. Birds from the north and mountainous areas migrate south in winter.

Scarlet Tanager *Piranga olivacea*

RANGE Extreme S.E. Canada, E. C. states of USA;
winters in E. South America

HABITAT Woodland, parks and gardens

SIZE 7½ in (19 cm)

In his summer breeding plumage, the male scarlet tanager is unmistakable with his gleaming red head and body and black wings and tail; in winter, he is similar to the female, with mainly olivegreen plumage, but retains his black wings and tail. Despite

his brilliance, the scarlet tanager is hard to see when he moves slowly or perches high in the trees, eating berries and fruit. The scarlet tanager also eats insects, slugs, snails and spiders.

Male birds return from the wintering grounds a few days before females, and each establishes a territory in the trees. When the female birds arrive, they are courted by the singing males. The female builds a nest in a large tree, using twigs, rootlets, weed stems and grass. She lays 3 to 5 eggs, which she incubates for 13 or 14 days.

Magpie Tanager *Cissopis leveriana*
RANGE N. South America, south to Brazil and N.E. Argentina
HABITAT Rain forest, scrub, cultivated land, clearings
SIZE 11 in (28 cm)

As its common name suggests, this large tanager resembles a magpie and is certainly different from all other tanagers. It is a black and white bird, with long, graduated tail feathers, tipped with white. Male and female look alike, and both have black eyes. Little is known of this tanager, which inhabits areas up to 6,600 ft (2,000 m) in some parts of its range. In pairs or small groups of 4 or 5 birds, it frequents the middle layers of the forest, flying from tree to tree, feeding on insects and berries.

There is no information available about the breeding habits of this tanager.

Song Sparrow *Melospiza melodia*
RANGE N. America: Aleutian Islands, east to Newfoundland, south through Canada and USA to Mexico
HABITAT Forest edge, scrub with nearby water, cultivated and suburban areas
SIZE 5–7 in (13–18 cm)

The song sparrow has more than 30 subspecies, which vary in appearance from the small sandy-colored scrub and desert birds to the larger, dark-plumaged northern varieties. Song sparrows

eat insects, wild fruit and berries and seeds.

The male bird establishes a territory, and his mate builds a neat nest, concealed among vegetation on the ground or in a bush. She incubates her 3 to 6 eggs for 12 or 13 days. There may be two or three broods a season.

Black-capped Hemispingus *Hemispingus atropileus*
RANGE Andes, from N.W. Venezuela to Peru
HABITAT Forest at 7,500–10,000 ft (2,300–3,000 m)
SIZE 6½ in (16.5 cm)

The black-capped hemispingus inhabits the high-altitude cloud forests and the sparse, stunted woods above this zone. Alone or in small groups, it forages among the trees for fruit and insects. Male and female look similar, both with black crowns and largely olive plumage. The cup-shaped nest is made in a tree.

White-shouldered Tanager *Tachyphonus luctuosus*
RANGE Honduras to Panama, south to N. Bolivia, Amazonian Brazil
HABITAT Rain forest, open woodland, plantations, clearings
SIZE 5 in (13 cm)

The white-shouldered tanager varies slightly in coloration over its range – for example, males in western Panama have yellow or tawny crowns – but in most instances, males are bluish-black with the white shoulders of their common name, while females are gray, olive and yellow. These active, noisy birds live in pairs or small groups or may join in mixed flocks. They forage for fruit and insects from the treetops down to the undergrowth, calling to each other with harsh, loud calls.

The open, cup-shaped nest is made of leaves and grasses and is built in a tree not far from the ground. The female incubates the 2 eggs, and both parents feed the young.

FINCHES, BUNTINGS AND TANAGERS CONTINUED

Blue-crowned Chlorophonia

Chlorophonia occipitalis

RANGE S.E. Mexico to W. Panama

HABITAT Forest, usually over 5,000 ft (1,500 m)

SIZE 5½ in (14 cm)

The male blue-crowned chlorophonia has bright green and blue plumage set off by touches of yellow. The female is largely green, with less blue and yellow. Young males resemble females until they acquire full adult plumage at about a year old. Arboreal birds, these chlorophonias frequent the treetops, where they eat fruit; when fruit is scarce in their high-altitude habitat, they may sometimes descend to lower levels. For a few months after the end of the breeding season in July, the birds move in flocks of up to 12, but for the rest of the year, they live in pairs.

The breeding season begins in March. Both partners of a pair build a domed nest high in a tree, usually among camouflaging moss and epiphytic plants – which are profuse in these high forests. The nest is made of moss, roots of epiphytes and spiders' webs. There are believed to be 3 or more eggs in a typical clutch, and these are incubated by the female alone. Whenever she leaves the nest to feed, she drops almost to the ground before flying off, in order to confuse predators. Once hatched, the young are fed by both parents on regurgitated food, and they remain in the nest for 24 to 25 days. A second brood may follow.

Blue Dacnis *Dacnis cayana*

RANGE E. Nicaragua to Panama, tropical South America to N. Argentina

HABITAT Open forest, secondary growth, orange groves

SIZE 4½ in (11.5 cm)

The blue dacnis is one of the honey-creeper group of tanagers but differs from them in having a short, conical bill. The male bird is bright blue and black, while the female is bright green, with some blue, gray and black plumage. These active little birds forage in the treetops, alone or in small groups sometimes joining mixed flocks of tanagers and other honeycreepers. They eat fruit, nectar and insects and are particularly partial to the flowerheads of mango trees and figs.

The female makes an open, cup-shaped nest in a tree, using fine plant material. She incubates the 2 or 3 eggs and does most of the work of feeding the young, although the male does help.

White-vented Euphonia *Euphonia minuta*

RANGE Mexico, Central and N. South America to Amazonian Brazil

HABITAT Rain forest, secondary growth, scrub, clearings

SIZE 3½ in (9 cm)

The white-vented euphonia lives in pairs or small groups and forages high in the trees, feeding primarily on mistletoe berries but also on insects and spiders. The birds may have to travel considerable distances to find the berries. The hard seeds of the mistletoe are excreted in due course, usually up in the trees, where they stick to the branches and germinate. All the euphonia species feed on mistletoe berries, and they are the birds most responsible for the spread of this parasitic plant. The male bird is a colorful mixture of yellow, white, black and gray-blue while the female is green, gray and yellowish. Both have short bills and tails.

Like the chlorophonias, the white-vented euphonia builds a rounded nest with a side entrance. The nest is made of moss or dry plant material and is placed in a cleft in bark or rock or in a hole in a tree trunk. The female incubates her 2 to 5 eggs for 14 to 18 days. Both parents feed the young.

Silver-beaked Tanager *Ramphocelus carbo*

RANGE N. South America east of Andes, south to Bolivia, Paraguay, Brazil

HABITAT Woodland, secondary growth, cultivated land

SIZE 7 in (18 cm)

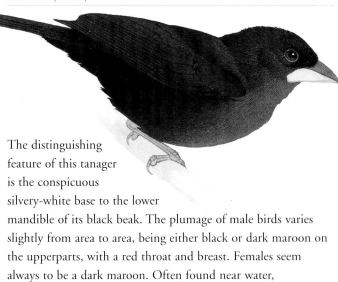

The distinguishing feature of this tanager is the conspicuous silvery-white base to the lower mandible of its black beak. The plumage of male birds varies slightly from area to area, being either black or dark maroon on the upperparts, with a red throat and breast. Females seem always to be a dark maroon. Often found near water, silverbeaked tanagers tend to live on or near the edge of wooded areas, rather than inside them. Alone or in small groups they forage actively for insects and fruit from the lowest branches to the middle story of trees.

The female bird builds a large nest in a bush or thicket. Her mate brings food to her while she incubates the 2 eggs for about 12 days. The young birds are able to leave the nest about 11 to 13 days after hatching.

Paradise Tanager *Tangara chilensis*

RANGE N. South America east of the Andes, south to Bolivia and Amazonian Brazil

HABITAT Rain forest

SIZE 5½ in (14 cm)

An extremely beautiful bird, the paradise tanager has gleaming, multicolored plumage. Males and females of the species look alike. In groups that often include other species, paradise tanagers forage for berries, spiders and insects in the middle and upper layers of the forest.

The breeding habits of this species are probably similar to those of other tanagers.

Purple Honeycreeper *Cyanerpes caeruleus*

RANGE Trinidad; N. South America to Bolivia, Paraguay, Brazil

HABITAT Rain forest, forest edge, mangroves, plantations

SIZE 4 in (10 cm)

Groups of purple honeycreepers frequent flowering trees in many different types of wooded areas. Fruit, especially bananas, and insects are important foods, but these birds also perch by flowers and suck nectar from them with their long, curved bills. Male and female differ in plumage; the male is largely bluish-purple and black, with yellow legs, while the female is rich green, with buff and blue patches on the head and breast.

The female builds a cup-shaped nest in the fork of a tree or bush and lays 2 eggs, which she incubates for 12 to 14 days. The young leave the nest about 14 days after hatching.

Giant Conebill *Oreomanes fraseri* **LR:nt**

RANGE South America: Andes in S. Colombia to Bolivia

HABITAT Forested and scrub slopes

SIZE 6¾–7¼ in (17–18.5 cm)

Although not really a giant, this conebill is distinctly larger than other conebills. It has fairly sober, mainly gray and chestnut plumage and a straight, sharp bill about ½ in (1.25 cm) long. Little is known about this bird, which inhabits the Polylepsis woods at high altitudes in the Andes – between 10,000 and 13,000 ft (3,000 and 4,000 m). These woods are cold and impoverished, with only the *Polylepsis* trees and little other vegetation except for mosses and ferns. The giant conebill explores the trunks and branches of the trees for insects, its plumage providing good camouflage against the bark of the trees. It is usually found in chattering groups, sometimes along with mixed flocks of flycatchers and finches.

FINCHES, BUNTINGS AND TANAGERS CONTINUED

Swallow-tanager
Tersina viridis
RANGE E. Panama to Bolivia, Paraguay, N.E. Argentina, S.E. Brazil
HABITAT Open forest, clearings, parks
SIZE 5½ in (14 cm)

The swallow-tanager is a gregarious bird out of the breeding season and moves in pairs or small groups. It forages at all levels, from the ground to the highest branches of trees, eating fruit and catching insects on the wing. Both sexes are eye-catching birds, the male has mainly turquoise and black plumage, and the female bright green, with a brownish face and throat and touches of yellow on flanks and belly.

The male establishes and defends the breeding territory, and the female makes a cup-shaped nest at the end of a burrow, which she digs in a bank, or in a hole in a wall. She lays 3 eggs, which she incubates for 14 to 17 days. In some parts of their range, swallow-tanagers breed in highland regions.

Plush-capped Finch *Catamblyrhynchus diadema*
RANGE Andes, from Venezuela to N.W. Argentina
HABITAT Cloud forest, forest edge, clearings
SIZE 5½ in (14 cm)

This bird has a golden-yellow crest of short, erect feathers. Male and female have similar plumage. Little is known of this species, which occurs in inaccessible mountain forest, but it appears to live alone or in pairs, foraging in low vegetation and on the ground for its insect food.

Rose-breasted Grosbeak *Pheucticus ludovicianus*
RANGE S. Canada, central and E. USA, south to N. Georgia; winters from Mexico to N. South America
HABITAT Woodland, borders of swamps and streams, cultivated land
SIZE 8 in (20.5 cm)

The male rose-breasted grosbeak is easily identified by his black and white plumage and his red breast patch; the female has streaked brown and white plumage. This grosbeak forages in trees, for seeds, buds, blossoms and insects. It is a popular bird with farmers because it eats the harmful potato beetles and their larvae.

The nest is made on a low branch, usually by the female. The 3 or 4 eggs are incubated by both parents for 12 or 13 days.

Buff-throated Saltator *Saltator maximus*
RANGE Mexico; Central and South America: Panama to Brazil
HABITAT Forest edge, tangled secondary growth, plantations
SIZE 8 in (20.5 cm)

A long-tailed, thick-billed bird, the buff-throated saltator is identified by the black-bordered buff patch on its throat. Male and female look alike. They forage in pairs or small flocks in the treetops, feeding on

berries and fruit such as the fruiting catkins of *Cecropia* trees.

The female builds a bulky nest in a tree or bush close to the ground. The male stays near her, singing and feeding her from time to time. She incubates the 2 eggs for 13 or 14 days, and both parents feed the young. There may be two or more broods.

Painted Bunting *Passerina ciris*
RANGE S. USA, Mexico; winters from Gulf states to Central America
HABITAT Woodland edge, thickets beside streams, gardens, roads
SIZE 5–5½ in (13–14 cm)

An extremely colorful bird, the male painted bunting would look quite at home in a tropical forest; the female is bright yellowish-green. Painted buntings feed on a variety of grass seeds, and also on spiders and insects such as grass hoppers, caterpillars and flies. The male is strongly territorial and will battle fiercely with intruders.

The cup-shaped nest, made of grasses, stalks and leaves, is built in a bush, low tree or vine a meter or so above ground. The female incubates her 3 or 4 eggs for 11 or 12 days.

Dickcissel
Spiza americana
RANGE USA: Great Lakes, south through Midwest to Gulf states; winters from Mexico to N. South America
HABITAT Grassland, grain and alfalfa fields
SIZE 6–7 in (15–18 cm)

The common name of this little bird is derived from its constantly repeated call, which sounds like "dick-dick cissel". The male is characterized by his heavy bill, yellow breast and black bib and chestnut wing patches. The female is sparrowlike, with streaky plumage, but has a yellowish breast and small chestnut wing patches. Dickcissels feed mainly on the ground on weed seeds, grain, spiders and insects such as crickets and grasshoppers.

The male establishes the nesting territory by calling from a conspicuous perch. The cup-shaped nest, made of weed stems, grasses and leaves, is built on the ground, often in the shelter of alfalfa or grain crops, or in a tree or bush. The female usually lays 4 eggs, which she incubates for 12 or 13 days. There are generally two broods a year.

Northern Cardinal *Cardinalis cardinalis*
RANGE Canada: S. Ontario; E. USA: Great Lakes and New England, south to Gulf Coast, S. Texas and Arizona; Mexico, Guatemala
HABITAT Woodland edge, thickets, parks, gardens
SIZE 7¼–9 in (20–23 cm)

The male cardinal is an unmistakable, brilliant red bird, while the female is buffy-brown, with a reddish tinge on wings and crest and a red bill. Cardinals are strongly territorial and aggressive birds and have a rich and varied repertoire of songs; both sexes are heard singing at all times of year. They feed on the ground and in trees on seeds and berries and, in the breeding season, also take insects.

The female builds the nest on a branch of a small tree or bush, usually among tangled foliage and vines. She incubates the 3 or 4 eggs for 12 or 13 days. Two or more broods may follow.

FINCHES, BUNTINGS AND TANAGERS CONTINUED

Bananaquit *Coereba flaveola*

RANGE Mexico, Central and South America to N. Argentina; West Indies

HABITAT Forest, mangroves, gardens, parks, plantations

SIZE 3¾ in (9.5 cm)

An extremely adaptable, widespread bird, the bananaquit is equally at home in dense rain forest or dry coastal areas, but must have some cover. It lives alone or in pairs and never forms flocks. Bananaquits feed mainly on insects and fruit, but also on nectar, probing blossoms with their curved bills or piercing large blooms at the base to obtain the nectar.

A globular nest is built, usually suspended from a branch or vine. The female incubates the 2 or 3 eggs for 12 or 13 days, and both parents feed the nestlings with nectar or insects. There are at least two broods a year.

Black-and-White Warbler *Mniotilta varia*

RANGE Breeds S. Canada, USA, east of Rockies; winters S. USA to N.W. South America

HABITAT Deciduous and mixed forest, parks, gardens

SIZE 4½–5½ in (11.5–14 cm)

Both male and female of this species are boldly striped with black and white, but the male has a black throat while the female's is white. Insects are their main food, and these warblers creep over branches and tree trunks, searching for caterpillars, ants, flies and beetles and also spiders.

The cup-shaped nest is made on the ground at the foot of a tree or by a rock and the female incubates the clutch of 4 or 5 eggs for between 10 and 12 days. The young are tended by both parents until they leave the nest 8 to 12 days after hatching.

Golden-winged Warbler *Vermivora chrysoptera*

RANGE Breeds N.E. USA; winters south to Central America and Venezuela

HABITAT Woodland, thickets

SIZE 4¼–5½ in (11–14 cm)

Identified by their bright yellow wing patches and crowns, male and female golden-winged warblers look similar, but the female has a lighter throat and eye patch. They forage at all levels of trees and bushes, searching the foliage for insects and spiders.

The nest is made on the ground or just above it in vegetation, and the female incubates the 4 or 5 eggs sometimes 6 or 7, for about 10 days. Both parents feed the young, which leave the nest about 10 days after hatching. This warbler often interbreeds with the blue-winged warbler, *V. pinus*, where their ranges overlap.

Northern Parula *Parula americana*

RANGE Breeds S.E. Canada, eastern USA; winters S. Florida, west Indies, Mexico to Nicaragua

HABITAT Coniferous forest, swamps, mixed woodland in winter

SIZE 4¼ in (11 cm)

A sedate little warbler, the northern parula forages for insects, especially caterpillars, in the trees, creeping over the branches and hopping perch; it also feeds on spiders. Male and female look similar, but the female is slightly duller.

The nest is usually built in hanging tree lichen or Spanish moss. The female incubates the 4 or 5 eggs for 12 to 14 days. Both parents tend the young.

Yellow Warbler
Dendroica petechia

RANGE Alaska, much of
Canada, USA, Mexico, Central and South America to Peru; West Indies

HABITAT Damp thickets, swamps

SIZE 4¼–5 in (11–13 cm)

An extremely widespread species, the yellow warbler varies considerably over its range, but the male breeding plumage is, typically bright yellow with chestnut or orange streaks. Males are duller outside the breeding season, and females are generally more greenish. Yellow warblers forage in trees and shrubs for insects, mainly caterpillars but also beetles, moths and spiders.

The female builds a cup-shaped nest in a tree or bush and incubates the 4 or 5 eggs for about 11 days.

Ovenbird *Seiurus aurocapillus*

RANGE Breeds central and E. Canada and USA to N. Gulf
states; winters Gulf of Mexico to N. South America

HABITAT Forest

SIZE 5½–6 in (14–15 cm)

The ovenbird has a brownish-orange crown, edged with black, and its white eye rings. It finds most of its food on the forest floor. It eats insects, spiders, slugs, snails and other small creatures; it also eats seeds and berries.

The female builds a domed, oven-shaped nest on the ground. She incubates her 4 or 5 eggs for 11 to 14 days.

Mourning Warbler *Oporornis philadelphia*

RANGE Breeds central and E. Canada, N.E. USA;
winters from Nicaragua to Ecuador and Venezuela

HABITAT Thickets, wet woodland

SIZE 5–5¼ in (12.5–14.5 cm)

Male and female mourning warblers both have gray hoods, and the male has a black patch on the throat. This species forages among low vegetation for insects and spiders.

The bulky nest is made on the ground or in a low bush, and the female incubates the 3 to 5 eggs for 12 to 13 days.

Painted Redstart *Myioborus pictus*

RANGE S.W. USA, Mexico to Nicaragua

HABITAT Woodland, mountain canyons

SIZE 5–5¾ in (12.5–14.5 cm)

Both sexes of painted redstarts have distinctive bright red breasts and white bellies. They eat insects, most of which are caught in the air.

The nest is made in a small hollow in the ground near a boulder or clump of grass. The female incubates the 3 or 4 eggs for 13 or 14 days.

Golden-crowned Warbler *Basileuterus culicivorus*

RANGE Mexico, through Central and South America
to N. Argentina; Trinidad

HABITAT Rain forest, plantations, scrub

SIZE 5 in (12.5 cm)

This warbler has a yellow or rufous-orange patch on the crown, bordered with black. Alone or in pairs, it forages in the lower levels of dense vegetation and rarely flies into the open. Insects are its main food – caught among the foliage or on the wing.

The female builds a domed nest on the ground and incubates her clutch of 3 eggs for 14 to 17 days.

FINCHES, BUNTINGS AND TANAGERS CONTINUED

Yellow-rumped Cacique *Cacicus cela*

RANGE Panama, south to N. Bolivia, E. Brazil; Trinidad

HABITAT Rain forest, secondary growth, open country with scattered trees

SIZE 9–11 in (23–28 cm)

The yellow-rumped cacique is gregarious. Much of its food, such as fruit and insects, is found in the trees but it may also catch flying termites.

The female cacique weaves a long, pouchlike nest, from grass and plant fibers, which is suspended from a branch, close to other nests of the colony. The 2 eggs are incubated for about 12 days.

Chestnut-headed/Wagler's Oropendola

Psarocolius wagleri

RANGE S. Mexico, through Central America to N.W. Ecuador

HABITAT Forest, clearings

SIZE 11–14 in (28–35.5 cm)

Wagler's oropendola has dark plumage, with a chestnut head and yellow tail feathers. The male is larger than the female and has a crest of hairlike feathers. It hops and flutters in the middle and upper layers, in search of fruit, seeds and insects.

Colonies of 50 to 100 pairs make their nests in the same tree or clump of trees. Females weave long, pouchlike nests, which hang from outer branches.

Common Grackle *Quiscalus quiscula*

RANGE S. Canada, USA, east of Rockies

HABITAT Open woodland, fields, parks, gardens, orchards

SIZE 11–13¼ in (28–34 cm)

The common grackle is glossy black, with a sheen of purple or other colors, depending on the race. Females are smaller than males. Common grackles gather in large noisy flocks and roost in groups. They forage in trees and bushes for nuts, fruit and the eggs and the young of small birds. On the ground, they probe for worms and chase insects, mice and lizards, and will wade into water to catch aquatic creatures such as frogs and crayfish.

A bulky nest of twigs, stalks and grass is made in a bush or tree or on a building. The birds usually nest in colonies. The female incubates the 5 or 6 eggs for 13 or 14 days, and both parents tend the young. Most populations winter just south of their breeding range, but some are resident.

Northern Oriole

Icterus galbula

RANGE S. Canada, much of USA except Gulf Coast and Florida, N. Mexico; winters from S. Mexico to Colombia

HABITAT Woodland, parks, gardens

SIZE 7–8¼ in (18–21 cm)

There are two forms of this species – the Baltimore oriole (left), found in the east, and Bullock's oriole, found in the west. The western race is similar, but the male has an orange head and white wing patch. Northern orioles eat insects, fruit and berries.

The female weaves a deep pouchlike nest from plant fiber hung from a forked twig. She lays 3 to 6 eggs.

Bobolink

Dolichonyx oryzivorus

RANGE S. Canada;
USA, south to Pennsylvania,
Colorado, California;
winters in South America

HABITAT Prairies, cultivated land

SIZE 6–7¼ in (15–20 cm)

In breeding plumage the male bobolink is
largely black, with a white rump, a white streak
on the back and a yellow nape. In winter, however, he looks
like a larger version of the female, with yellow-brown plumage.
Insects are the main food source of the bobolink in summer,
but in winter, as it migrates south, it feeds on grain crops – in
former times particularly on rice.

The bobolink performs the longest migration of any
member of its family, travelling at least 5,000 miles (8,000 km)
on its trek from Argentina to northern USA and Canada. Once
they arrive at the breeding grounds, males court females with
display flights and bubbling songs. Each male may have many
mates. The female builds a nest on the ground and lays a clutch
of 5 or 6 eggs, which she incubates for 13 days.

Brown-headed Cowbird *Molothrus ater*

RANGE S. Canada, USA; winters south of breeding range, from Maryland
to Texas and California; Mexico

HABITAT Woodland, farmland, fields, open country

SIZE 6–7¼ in (15–20 cm)

As the common name suggests, the male of this species is
distinguished by his shiny brown head; the female is uniformly
gray. They are gregarious birds, forming large flocks in winter
and gathering in small groups of up to 6 in the breeding season.
They feed largely on plant food, such as grain, seeds, berries and
fruit, and on some insects, spiders and snails.

These cowbirds are brood parasites: the female lays her eggs
in the nests of other birds. She lays up to 12 eggs a season, each
in a different nest. The eggs each need to be incubated for 11 or
12 days. This cowbird has been known to use over 185 different
species as hosts. Most of the host species have smaller eggs than
the cowbird. The young cowbirds hatch more quickly and are
bigger than the hosts' young, which usually perish.

Eastern Meadowlark *Sturnella magna*

RANGE S.E. Canada; USA: New England to Minnesota,
south to Florida, Texas and New Mexico; Mexico,
Central and South America to Brazil

HABITAT Open country: prairies, fields, grassland

SIZE 8¼–11 in (21.5–28 cm)

The eastern meadowlark bears a close resemblance to the yellow-
throated longclaw, *Macronyx croceus*, of the Wagtail and Pipit
family. The two are not related but they have adapted to a
similar way of life in a similar habitat.

The eastern meadowlark often perches in a conspicuous spot,
such as wires and posts, but it finds much of its food on the
ground. It eats insects, such as grasshoppers, ants, beetles and
caterpillars, as well as grain and weed seeds. It will also consume
the remains of other birds which have been killed by traffic.

After wintering just south of their breeding range, eastern
meadowlarks return to it in the spring, the male birds arriving
before females in order to establish their territories. Each male
may have more than one mate. The grass nest is made in a dip
in open ground and is often dome-shaped. The female usually
lays a clutch of 5 eggs, which she incubates for 13 or 14 days.
Both parents feed the young.

GLOSSARY

Abdomen
The part of an animal's body that lies between the **thorax** and pelvis in vertebrates. In mammals, the abdomen is separated from the thorax by the diaphragm.

Adaptation
Part of the process of evolutionary change that animals undergo to occupy a **niche**. Changes can concern the structure, physiology, development or behavior of animals, and are driven by **natural selection**.

Adult
A fully developed and mature individual, capable of breeding.

Air sac
Non-respiratory air bags connected to the lungs of a bird.

Albino
An animal lacking coloring, or pigment, and therefore having pale or white skin or fur, and pink eyes. This characteristic is passed down in the **genes**.

Alimentary canal
The passage that extends from the mouth to the anus, for the digestion and absorption of food and elimination of waste matter.

Algae
Primitive marine and aquatic plants that lack a system of roots, stems, and leaves.

Amphibian
Cold-blooded animals belonging to the class Amphibia, such as frogs, which live on land but breed in water.

Anadromous
Fish, such as salmon and certain species of herring, which migrate from the sea to freshwater to spawn.

Anal fin
Fin that lies along the underside of the body, behind the anus in fishes. The anal fin works in conjunction with other fins for swimming and turning.

Alpine
Of the Alps in Europe; or any mountainous region having an altitude of over 4,500 ft (1,500m)

Anatomy
The study of the internal structure of plants and animals. Also the physical structure of an animal or plant, or any of its parts.

Antarctic
Pertaining to the south polar region.

Aquatic
Living mainly or wholly in water.

Arboreal
Living mainly in or among trees.

Archipelago
A large group of islands.

Arctic
Pertaining to the north polar region.

Asexual reproduction
Reproductive process that is not **sexual**; the parent organism splits into two or more organisms, or produces buds.

Avian
Pertaining to birds.

Baleen
Horny slats that hang vertically from the roof of a whale's mouth, with fringed inner edges for filtering food.

Barbel
A fleshy, thin, antenna-like protuberance found around the mouth of many species of fish

Basking
A form of temperature regulation whereby some animals, especially reptiles, expose themselves to sun to raise their body temperature.

Bill
The beak of a bird or the jaws of a fish.

Bioluminescence
The production of light by some organisms, such as the hatchetfish, by biochemical means.

Biome
A community of plants and animals occupying a large geographical area. For example, **rain forest**, **desert**, or **tundra**.

Bipedal
Walking on two legs. Some primates may travel bipedally for short distances; only humans exhibit habitual bipedalism.

Bipolar
Occurring in both polar regions.

Bird
A class of animals called Aves, consisting of feathered, warm-blooded **tetrapods** with forelimbs adapted for flying. Examples include eagles, ostriches, and parrots.

Bisexual
Pertaining to animals and plants that have both male and female reproductive organs. Also known as **hermaphrodite**.

Blubber
A layer of fatty insulating tissue found directly beneath the outer layer of skin (**epidermis**) in marine mammals.

Brackish
Water that is a mixture of seawater and freshwater. May be found in river estuaries where seawater enters the river mouth.

Brood
The eggs or offspring of a single female from one mating; any group of young animals being cared for by an adult.

Browser
A **herbivore** that feeds on the leaves and shoots of shrubs and trees, as opposed to grasses.

Buccal cavity
The cheek or mouth cavity leading to the pharanx, and (in vertebrates) the esophagus.

Calf
A young cow or bull, buffalo, seal or whale.

Camouflage
When an animal conceals itself by adopting the color and texture of its surroundings, either physically or by concealing itself in a suitable place.

Canine teeth
In **carnivorous** mammals, the two long and pointed teeth in the upper and lower jaws, behind the **incisors** that are used for seizing and holding prey. In Pinnipedia, a suborder that includes sea lions and walruses, they can take the form of tusks.

Canopy
In forests, an almost continuous layer of foliage at the level of the tree tops, produced by the intermingling of vegetation. The crowns of some trees may project above the canopy layer and are known as emergents.

Carapace
A skeletal shield of bone or chitin (tough fibrous material) covering the bodies of reptiles such as tortoises or terrapins.

Carcass
The dead or rotting flesh of an animal, which is a source of food for scavengers.

Carnassial teeth
An opposing pair of teeth adapted especially to shear with a scissor-like, cutting edge.

Carnivore
A flesh-eating animal (but not necessarily a member of the order Carnivora).

Cartilage
Strong elastic connective tissue between bones; also called gristle.

Cementum
Hard material coating the roots of teeth in mammals. In some **species** it is laid down in layers annually, and the number of layers can be used to help determine an animal's age.

Cell
The basic structural unit of all living organisms.

Chromosome
An assembly of **genes** (units of **DNA**), which determine hereditary characteristics.

Cladogram
A diagram used to show how groups of organisms have evolved from a common ancestor.

Class
A **taxonomic** rank superior to **order**, but subordinate to **phylum**.

Clutch
The number of eggs laid, and simultaneously incubated, by a female.

Cock
A male bird, crab, lobster or salmon.

Cold-blooded
An animal with no internal temperature mechanism, such as a **reptile** or an

amphibian, whose body temperature is determined by external temperatures.

Colony
A **population** of animals living and breeding together in one place.

Communal
Cooperative behavior between animals, such as can be found in the nest building of some birds.

Coniferous forest
Forest comprising largely evergreen conifers, such as pines, spruces, and firs. Usually found in northern latitudes.

Conservation
Preservation of the environment and natural resources.

Continental shelf
An area of relatively shallow water adjacent to a continental land mass and rarely deeper than 600 ft (200m).

Coral reef
An organic marine reef composed of solid coral and coral sand.

Courtship
Communication between individual animals of opposite sexes of a species to facilitate breeding.

Crepuscular
Mainly active during the twilight hours around dawn and dusk.

Crest
A prominent tuft of feathers on the heads of some species of bird.

Cue
A signal produced by an animal to elicit a response in another individual, for example, in **courtship**.

Deciduous forest
Temperate and tropical forest with moderate rainfall and marked seasons. Trees normally shed their leaves during cold or dry periods.

Dentition
The arrangement of the animal's teeth, which varies according to the species.

Desert
An area with low average rainfall, with sparse scrub, or grassland vegetation, or no vegetation at all.

Detritus
Dead organic or inorganic material.

Digit
A finger or a toe.

Dispersal
Movement of animals away from their home range as they reach maturity. Distinct from dispersion, where animals or food sites are distributed or scattered.

Display
Conspicuous behaviour to convey specific information to others, usually to other members of a species. May be visual or vocal, and used as a threat to **predators** or in **courtship**.

Distal
Farthest point away from center of the body, for example, the tip of an animal's tail.

DNA
Deoxyribonucleic acid, a long molecule resembling a chain made up of four kinds of link, the sequence of which codes hereditary information. **Genes** are units of DNA. The DNA molecule consists of two strands joined in a spiral, an arrangement known as a double helix.

Dormancy
A period of inactivity. For example, many bears are dormant for a period during winter. This is not true **hibernation** as the animal's pulse rate and body temperature do not drop significantly.

Dorsal
The upper surface or plane of an animal's body.

Dorsal fin
In fishes, the **fin** that lies along the spine on the upper side of the body. The dorsal fin works in conjunction with the other fins in swimming, turning and balancing.

Eardrum
A thin membrane in the middle ear which vibrates in response to airborne sounds.

Echolocation
A process used by Cetaceans (whales, dolphins), bats and some species of birds to detect distant or invisible objects (in darkness), by means of sound waves that are reflected back to the emitter from the object.

Eclipse plumage
Dull plumage of birds, which is superseded by more striking plumage in the breeding season.

Ecology
The study of plants and animals in relation to their natural environmental setting.

Ecosystem
A part of the environment in which both living and non-living elements exist and interact.

Eft
A lizard or newt.

Egg tooth
A specially modified tooth that a new-hatched reptile or bird uses to break free of the egg on hatching.

Elongate
Relatively long. For example, canine teeth are elongate compared to adjacent teeth.

Embryo
The developing egg until it hatches. Or the early stages of a developing mammal. Once the mammalian embryo begins to resemble an adult animal, it is known as a **fetus**.

Emigration
The departure of an animal, or animals, from its group or from its place of birth, often on reaching maturity. Also known as **dispersal**.

Enamel
A hard substance that forms the outer layer of a vertebrate tooth.

Environment
External surroundings; the physical, biological, and chemical influences that act on an individual organism.

Enzyme
An organic substance produced by living cells that catalyses biochemical changes.

Epidermis
The outermost layer of cells comprising the outer layer of skin of a mammal, or the outer tissue of stems or leaves in plants.

Equator
A theoretical line around the Earth's surface midway between the north and south poles. Equatorial regions are those areas located at, or lying close to, the equator.

Estrus
When female mammals are receptive to mating and are attracted to males. Also when ovulation occurs and mature eggs are released from the ovaries.

Estuary
The mouth of a river where the tide enters, the resulting body of water is a mixture of **freshwater** and seawater.

Eutherian
Pertaining to mammals whose **embryos** receive nourishment from the placenta.

Evolution
The act or process of gradual change where the characteristics of a **species** or **population** alter over many generations.

Excretion
The elimination of waste products from the body.

Extant
Living, still in existence, and therefore not **extinct**.

Extinct
According to available evidence, no longer in existence, having died out.

Family
A **taxonomic** rank superior to **genus**, but subordinate to **order**.

Fang
In carnivorous mammals, a **canine** tooth. In snakes, a modified tooth carrying poison.

Fauna
All of the animal life of a region, geological period, or special environment.

Feces
The remains of indigestible food excreted from an animal's bowels.

Feral
A wild or undomesticated animal, descended from domestic animals.

Fertilization
The process of union of two sex cells (**gametes**) to form a new animal. In mammals, reptiles, and birds, fertilization takes place within the female's body, whereas in most species of fish and amphibians, fertilization takes place externally.

Fetus
An **embryo** of a mammal in the later stages of development, when it shows the features of the fully developed animal.

Filter feeders
Animals, such as certain whale species, that obtain their food from straining or filtering water to sift out small organic particles.

Fin
A flat, projecting organ, used by fishes and other aquatic animals, such as whales and seals, to swim, turn, and balance in the water.

Fish
Streamlined **vertebrates** adapted to life in the water. Examples include hagfish, sharks, salmon, and coelacanth.

Fledgling
A young bird that has recently learned to fly.

Flora
The plant life of a particular region, geological period or special environment.

Fluke
In Cetaceans (whales, dolphins) and Dugongs, the flat, horizontal tail fins.

Forage
To search for food.

Fossil
The remains of dead organisms, or their imprint, which have been preserved in rocks. Fossils therefore reveal the history of life on earth in the fossil record. Palaeontology is the study of fossils and the fossil record.

Freshwater
Water that is not saline, as found in a river or lake.

Fusiform
Streamlined. Sometimes referred to as "torpedo-shaped." Cetaceans (whales, dolphins) are said to have fusiform-shaped bodies, aiding propulsion in water.

Gamete
A sex cell. When sexual **fertilization** takes place, the male sex cell or **sperm** fuses with the female sex cell or **ovum**.

Gelatinous
A substance having a jelly-like consistency.

Generalist
An animal that does not rely on specialized strategies for feeding or surviving, as distinct from a **specialist** animal that does.

Gene
A unit of **DNA** carrying hereditary information that is passed on from generation to generation. An assembly of genes make up a **chromosome**.

Genital
Pertaining to the genitalia, the reproductive organs.

Genus
A t**axonomic** rank superior to **species**, but subordinate to **family**.

Gestation
The period from conception to birth in mammals. Elephants have the longest gestation period of any animal, that is, 22 months.

Gills
Organs found in fish and other animals that are completely or mainly aquatic to obtain oxygen from the surrounding water. Consists of membranes through which exchange of oxygen and carbon dioxide takes place.

Grazers
Herbivorous animals that feed on grasses (if land-based) or other plant material, such as **algae** or plankton (if **aquatic**).

Gregarious
Sociable animals that often live in large groups, such as many species of **Old World** and **New World** monkey.

Guano
Phosphate deposits resulting from the accumulation of bird excrement or droppings.

Gut
Forming part of the **alimentary canal**, the gut is a hollow tube for the digestion and absorption of food, and for the elimination of waste material.

Habitat
The place or **environment** in which an animal or plant lives. Usually described in terms of the predominant vegetation of the area, and by its physical features and characteristics.

Harem group
A group of animals consisting of one dominant mature male and two or more breeding females. A common social arrangement among mammals.

Hen
A female bird.

Herbaceous
Pertaining to herbs; resembling leaves.

Herbivore
An animal that feeds mainly on plants, or parts of plants, for its source of energy.

Hermaphrodite
An animal which has both male and female sex organs, or which functions as both male and female at the same time. Some hermaphrodites alter their sex at different stages of their lives.

Herpetology
The scientific study of **reptiles** and **amphibians**.

Hibernation
A period of sleep-like inactivity for some mammals, reptiles, and amphibians, usually during winter. The animal reduces its normal physiological processes in order to minimize energy requirements.

Hierarchy
The pattern or structure of divisions within a social group or **population**, whereby some animals come to dominate others. Dominant individuals have control over the resources available in terms of access to food and mates.

Higher primate
The more advanced primates – monkeys, apes, and man – are also known as anthropoids.

Homing
The capability of an animal, or group of animals, to return to its original location following **migration**.

Hoof
The horny sheath that encases **digits** and bears the weight of certain **ungulate** mammals.

Hormone
A chemical substance produced by glands that regulates and controls many bodily functions, such as growth, digestion, and sexual development.

Host
The organism which a **parasite** organism lives on and receives food or shelter from.

Hybrid
The offspring resulting from crossbreeding two different species. Hybrids are often sterile;

the best known example is a mule, the result of crossbreeding a horse and a donkey.

Hyoid arch
One of the bony arches that supports the gills in primitive vertebrates.

Implantation
The process in which the early **embryo** becomes attached to the wall of the uterus in mammals, resulting in the development of the complex network of blood vessels linking the **embryo** to the mother's **placenta**.

Incisors
Chisel-shaped teeth in **carnivores**, used for cutting rather than tearing or grinding. In certain animals, such as rodents, the incisor teeth continue to grow throughout life as they are worn down by use.

Incubation
The period between the laying of eggs and their hatching. During incubation the eggs are kept warm by a parent.

Insectivore
An animal whose primary source of food is arthropods – insects and spiders. Not necessarily of the mammal order Insectivora.

Introduced
Species which are brought by man, either accidentally or deliberately, from regions where they occur naturally to other regions where they previously were not represented.

Intertidal zone
Intermediate area of shore that is exposed between high and low water marks.

Juvenile
The growth stage of development spanning the period between an infant and a full-grown **adult**.

Juvenile plumage
The plumage of a young bird, when it departs from the nest. Later replaced by **adult plumage**.

Keratin
A tough fibrous protein that produces an impervious outer layer in the **epidermis** of mammals, birds, amphibians, and reptiles. Thicker layers of keratin form the major part of hair, scales, feathers, nails, claws, and horns.

Kingdom
The second highest **taxonomic** category in the hierarchy of classification, one of which is Animalia – the animals.

Krill
Crustaceans that are an abundant source of food for marine mammals, particularly baleen whales.

Lactation
Discharge of milk from the mammary glands in mammals, occurring after the birth of young. Lactation is controlled by **hormones**.

Larynx
The upper part of the wind pipe which contains the vocal chords, used to produce vocal sounds.

Larva/Larvae
A pre-adult stage in species where the young of an animal has a completely different appearance and way of life from the adult. Amphibians and some fish have a larval stage.

Lek
A traditional "display ground," used year after year, where animals of one sex display themselves to members of the opposite sex in order to attract potential mates.

Lateral
On or toward the right or left side of the body.

Life cycle
The sequence of different stages in an animal's life. In **vertebrates**, the production of sex cells (**gametes**) is followed by fertilization and the development of an **embryo**, followed by birth or hatching, growth to adulthood, and repetition of the cycle.

Litter
A number of young produced by an animal at one time.

Longevity
A record or estimate of an animal's life span. May refer to the maximum recorded longevity or to the average life expectancy at birth.

Lower primate
A primitive primate known as a Prosimian.

Lung
An internal chamber, nearly always air-filled, used for the exchange of respiratory gases between the **environment** and the animal's body. The structure varies from a simple, unfolded chamber in some amphibians to the complex systems of tubes in mammals and birds.

Mammal
Vertebrate animals that are warm-blooded, breathe air using **lungs**, and give birth to live young. Mammals live in the air, land, and water. Examples include bats, monkeys, and dolphins.

Mammillae
Nipples or teats belonging to female mammals through which milk is passed to the young from the mother.

Mammary glands
The milk-producing organs in female mammals.

Mandible
The lower bone of the jaw, or the lower part of a bird's bill.

Mangrove forest
Tropical forests containing salt-tolerant trees and shrubs, located on the shores of **estuaries** and river deltas.

Marine
Living in the sea.

Marsupial
Unlike **eutherian** mammals, marsupial mammals such as kangaroos, wombats, and bandicoots have a very short gestation period, after which the immature young finish their development inside a pouch on the mother's belly.

Mating
Pairing of individuals for reproductive purposes.

Maturation
The attainment of sexual maturity, that is reaching reproductive age.

Membrane
Thin tissue covering or connecting organs and other bodily structures.

Metabolic rate
The speed at which chemical changes in the body occur.

Metabolism
The chemical changes in living cells by which energy is supplied for vital processes and other activities, for example, the production of protein from amino acids, and the extraction of energy from foods.

Metamorphosis
A transformation in the shape and structure (**morphology**) of an animal. For example, metamorphosis occurs when a tadpole is transformed into an adult frog.

Microplankton
Plankton so small they are not easily visible to the naked eye.

Migration
The seasonal movement of a population from one area to another – often over large distances – for the purpose of feeding or breeding.

Mimicry
A species development of a superficial similarity to another species or to natural objects in its environment, often for protective purposes.

Molar teeth
In mammals, cheek teeth used for crushing and chewing food. The biting surface is made up of a series of ridges and the teeth have several roots.

Monogamous
Having only one mate per breeding season.

Morphology
A branch of biology that deals with the structure and shape of animals and plants.

Moult
The shedding of fur, feathers, or skin. Reptiles shed their outer dead layers of skin when they grow; moulting in mammals and birds occurs seasonally.

Musk gland
A gland used for secreting musk, a strong smelling odor produced by animals such as badgers and musk deer. Such secretions usually occur during the breeding season.

Nasal plugs
Found in toothed whales, these are muscular flaps at the base of the nasal passage used to close the airway when diving. May be used to produce sounds.

Natal range
Home **range** into which an individual animal is born.

Natural Selection
The key evolutionary process whereby animals with the most appropriate **adaptations** are more successful at reproducing than others.

Nerve cell
Specialized cells which transmit information in the form of electrical signals. All types of animal behavior, from a blink of the eye to complicated body movements, are controlled by the action of the nerve cells.

New World
A term used to describe the western hemisphere, the Americas, and the animals from those regions, as distinct from the **Old World**.

Niche
Role of a **species** within its **community**, defined in terms of its lifestyle, that is, food, competitors, predators, and other resource requirements.

Nocturnal
Mainly active during the night.

Nomadic
Moving from place to place, not settled or resident in any particular area.

Nomenclature
A system used for naming and classifying animals and plants using **scientific names**.

Old World
A term used to describe the eastern hemisphere, Europe, Africa, Asia and Australasia and the animals from those regions, as distinct from the **New World**.

Olfactory
The sense of smell which relies on the receptors inside the nasal cavity.

Omnivore
An animal which feeds on both plant and animal material. The digestive system is specially adapted to cope with both sources of food.

Operculum
Any type of hard cover or flap used for protection of tissue, such as the flaps that protect fishes' **gills**.

Opportunistic
A type of feeding behavior. Many species of **carnivore** are opportunistic feeders, taking advantage of circumstances to exploit varied food resources.

Opposable
A finger or toe which can be used in conjunction with other **digits.**

Order
A **taxonomic** division superior to a **family**, but subordinate to a **class**.

Ornithology
The scientific study of birds.

Ovum
An egg or female sex cell (**gamete**). Develops into a new individual of the same **species** on **fertilization** by the male sex cell or **sperm.**

Oviduct
The tube between the ovaries and the uterus used to carry eggs. **Fertilization** and early development occur in the oviduct of mammals and birds.

Oviparous
Egg-laying animals. The young hatch outside the body of the female.

Ovoviviparous
An animal that produces eggs, but retains them inside the body until the release of the live young.

Pair-bond
Prolonged association between a mating pair of animals for breeding purposes. In some species, the association may last until the death of one partner.

Palaeontology
One of the earth sciences, a branch of geology which deals with the scientific study of **fossils** and the fossil record.

Palmate
Palm-shaped.

Pampas
Extensive grassland plain found in South America.

Parasite
A relationship between two organisms, whereby one, the parasite, obtains its food from the other, the **host.**

Passerine
In birds, where one toe is directed backward and the others are directed forward.

Patagium
A membrane found in bats and flying squirrels, situated along the sides of the body between the fore and hind limbs, that helps them glide through the air.

Pectoral fin
A pair of fins in fishes, situated immediately behind the head on either side of the body, which work in conjunction with other fins for swimming, turning, and balancing.

Pelvic fin
A pair of fins in fishes, situated in the pelvic region (on the underside of the body), which work in conjunction with the other fins for swimming, turning, and balancing.

Photophores
If fish, an organ which can produce **bioluminescent** light.

Phylogenetic
Pertaining to the **evolutionary** relationships within and between groups of animals.

Phylum
A **taxonomic** rank superior to a **class**, but subordinate to a **kingdom**.

Physiology
The scientific study of processes and metabolic functions of living organisms.

Pigment
The natural coloring of living tissue.

Placenta
The organ that develops inside the uterus, allowing the exchange of oxygen, food, and waste to and from the **fetus** in **eutherian** mammals during **gestation**. The placenta is discharged after birth.

Plankton
Tiny water-borne organisms, eaten by whales and some fishes.

Plastron
The lower section of the shell of tortoises and turtles, connected to the **carapace** by a bony bridge.

Plumage
The feather covering of birds.

Pod
Name for a family group of Cetaceans (whales and dolphins), which may remain together for life.

Polar
Pertaining to the north or south polar regions of the earth.

Polygamous
Mating of one male with several females or one female with several males.

Polygynous
Mating of one male with several females during the breeding season.

Polyandrous
Mating of one female with several males.

Population
A group of animals of the same **species** that live separately from other similar groups.

Pouch
Female **marsupial** mammals have a pouch on their abdomen in which the young complete their development, following a short **gestation** period.

Prairie
The grassland steppe of North America, treeless and flat.

Predator
Any animal which hunts for live prey to feed on. Predation is the killing of one **species** by another for food.

Prehensile
Capable of grasping or seizing, as in monkeys' or lizards' tails and the trunks of elephants.

Premolar teeth
The cheek teeth of mammals, in front of the **molars** and behind the **canine teeth**, which are normally preceded by milk teeth and are used for chewing and crushing food.

Primary forest
A mature forest that has lain undisturbed for a long period.

Primate
A member of the order of animals that includes lemurs, monkeys, apes, and humans. Primates have larger brains than other animals and their **digits** are adapted for grasping and holding.

Proboscis
A protruding organ used for sensing and food-gathering, such as an elephant's trunk.

Progeny
Offspring.

Protein
A long chain molecule made of amino acids, essential to all living organisms.

Protrusible
Capable of protruding, jutting out, as in the tongue of a lizard or other reptile.

Quadrumanous
An animal that uses both hands and feet for grasping or holding.

Quadruped
An animal that walks on four legs.

Rain forest
Tropical or subtropical forest that receives high levels of year-round rainfall and supports rich and diverse **flora** and **fauna**.

Race
A subgroup of a **species** in the hierarchy of classification of living things.

Range
Area in which an individual animal or a social group usually lives. The range may not be exclusive to the animal or group, and may overlap with the range of other animals or groups of animals. It typically contains regular areas for feeding and resting/sleeping.

Receptive
A female mammal that is ready to mate.

Regeneration
Having the capability to regrow an organ or limb after accidental loss.

Reingestion
The extraction of the maximum amount of energy from food by digesting it more than once. The animal brings up food from the stomach for further chewing.

Reproduction
The process by which living organisms produce other organisms similar to themselves by **sexual** or **asexual** means.

Reptile
Vertebrate animals that are **cold-blooded**, breathe air using lungs, and lay eggs. They need an external heat source to maintain their body temperature and are therefore found in the hotter regions of the Earth.
Examples include lizards, snakes, and turtles.

Respiration
The system of breathing that involves the exchange of oxygen and carbon dioxide between an organism and its **environment**.

Retractile
Capable of being pulled back into the animal's body, for example, claws.

RNA
Ribonucleic acid, a long molecule that is used in several ways to carry out a cell's genetic instructions. RNA is chemically similar to **DNA**.

Rostrum
The upper jaw in Cetaceans or the forward projection of the snout in fish.

Rufous
Reddish-brown in color.

Ruminant
An animal, such as a camel or cow, with a complex stomach designed for chewing the cud, or regurgitating its food in order to chew it again.

Saddle
Distinctive markings on the back of whales and dolphins.

Salivary gland
A gland for the secretion of saliva that aids the digestive function.

Savanna
Grassland areas of the tropics and subtropics with few scattered trees and receiving seasonal rainfall. A transition zone from forest to open grassland.

Scales
Modified skin in the form of overlapping plates that serve as the outer protective covering in reptiles and fish.

Scavenger
An animal that feeds mainly on dead animal **carcasses**.

Scientific name
The precise Latin name of a **species** of animal, as distinct from its common name.

Scent mark
A place where chemical secretions from **scent glands** are left. Scent marks act as a form of communication between animals, often for breeding or territorial purposes.

Scent gland
Organs that secrete chemical "messages" to other animals.

School
A large number of fishes or Cetaceans (whales, dolphins) swimming together.

Scrub
A pattern of vegetation characterized by shrubs and low trees.

Sedentary
Animals that habitually remain in one place, or occupy a small range and do not migrate.

Sexual dimorphism
Differences between males and females of the same **species** in terms of size, color, and so on.

Sexual reproduction
The process by which living organisms produce new organisms similar to themselves by sexual means.

Siblings
Brothers and sisters, that is, animals who share one or both parents.

Simian
A monkey or ape, or having their characteristics; used colloquially to mean any of the **higher primates**.

Shoal
A large number of fishes swimming together.

Skeleton
The internal structure in an animal that provides support for the body and protects internal organs. In higher vertebrates, the skeleton consists of a system of bones.

Solitary
Animals which habitually live on their own, as distinct from social animals which live in family groups.

Sonar
Part of the facility of **echolocation** used by bats and some marine mammals to help them navigate.

Spatulate
Shaped like a spatula, that is, broad and rounded in shape.

Spawn
In **aquatic** animals, the act of producing and laying eggs.

Specialist
An animal that uses specialized strategies or techniques for feeding or surviving, as opposed to a **generalist**.

Species
A species is the basic **taxonomic** rank comprising a set of individuals having common attributes which can interbreed to produce fertile offspring. Related species are grouped together in a **genus**.

Sperm
The male sex cell (**gamete**), also known as spermatazoon (plural spermatazoa).

Spermatophores
A case enclosing the **sperm** in certain amphibians.

Sphagnum
Moss found in boggy areas in temperate regions, forming peat as it decays.

Steppe
Large areas of open grassland, known as **prairie** in North America; steppe lands receive low rainfall and may experience wide temperature variation.

Subfamily
A division of a **family**.

Suborder
A division of an **order**.

Subadult
Developmental stage between a **juvenile** and an **adult** animal.

Subspecies
A division of a **species**.

Swim bladder
A fish's gas-filled bladder that helps maintain buoyancy. Certain fish use them for breathing.

Taxonomy
The study of the classification of plants and animals. Animals that share common features are grouped together. The categories are: **species, genus, family, order, class, phylum, kingdom**; these can be divided further into subspecies, subfamily and so on.

Temperate
A climate that does not experience either hot or cold extremes.

Testis
The organ in which **sperm** are made in most mammals.

Tetrapod
Any **vertebrate** with four limbs.

Terrestrial
Living on the land.

Territory
An area defended from intruders by an individual or group of animals.

Thorax
In mammals, the chest or middle part of the body between the head and the **abdomen**.

Thermoregulation
The regulation and maintenance of body temperature in mammals.

Toxin
Any poisonous substance of animal or plant origin.

Trachea
The windpipe in air-breathing **vertebrates**, used to carry air from the throat to the bronchi.

Transluscent
Partially, but not completely transparent.

Tropical zone
Located between 15 and 23.5 degrees in the southern and northern hemispheres.

Tundra
A region of sparse vegetation and extremely low temperatures, where only lichens and mosses are able to grow.

Ultrasonic
Very high-frequency sound produced by some marine mammals, possibly as a form of communication.

Ungulates
Hoofed herbivorous mammals. Examples include horses, deer, cows, goats, and pigs.

Venom
A **toxic** secretion produced by some animals, used to kill their prey.

Vertebrate
Any animal with a backbone – mammals, birds, reptiles, amphibians, and fish. More than 40,000 species of vertebrates exist.

Vestigal
An organ which is no longer useful and is consequently diminished in size.

Viviparous
Giving birth to live young, as opposed to laying eggs.

Vocalization
The production of songs, calls and other vocal sounds by animals.

Warm-blooded
Animals that regulate body temperature independent of external temperature. Examples include mammals and birds.

Yolk sac
A sac containing the yolk of the egg, which contains food for the use of the **embryo**.

CLASSIFICATION

CLASS MAMMALIA: MAMMALS
Subclass Prototheria: Egg-laying Mammals

Order Monotremata: Monotremes
Family Tachyglossidae: Echidnas
Family Ornithorhynchidae: Platypus

Subclass Theria: Live-bearing Mammals
Infraclass Metatheria: Marsupials

Order Didelphimorpha
Family Didelphidae: Opossums

Order Paucituberculata
Family Caenolestidae: Shrew Opossums

Order Microbiotheria
Family Microbiotheriidae: Colocolo

Order Dasyuromorpha
Family Myrmecobiidae: Numbat
Family Dasyuridae: Marsupial Carnivores and Insectivores

Order Peramelemorpha
Family Peramelidae: Bandicoots and Bilbies
Family Peroryctidae: New Guinean Bandicoots

Order Notoryctemorpha
Family Notoryctidae: Marsupial Moles

Order Diprotodonta
Family Phascolarctidae: Koala
Family Vombatidae: Wombats
Family Phalangeridae: Phalangers
Family Potoroidae: Rat Kangaroos
Family Macropodidae: Kangaroos, Wallabies
Family Burramyidae: Pygmy Possums
Family Pseudocheiridae: Ring-tailed and Greater Gliding Possums
Family Petauridae: Striped and Lesser Gliding Possums
Family Tarsipedidae: Honey Possums
Family Acrobatidae: Pygmy Gliding Possum, Feather-tailed Possum

Infraclass Eutheria: Placental Mammals

Order Xenarthra: Edentates
Family Myrmecophagidae: Anteaters
Family Bradypodidae: Three-toed Sloths
Family Megalonychidae: Two-toed Sloths
Family Dasypodidae: Armadillos

Order Pholidota
Family Manidae: Pangolins

Order Lagomorpha
Family Ochotonidae: Pikas
Family Leporidae: Rabbits

Order Rodentia
Family Sciuridae: Squirrels
Family Geomyidae: Pocket Gophers
Family Heteromyidae: Pocket mice
Family Aplodontidae: Mountain Beaver
Family Castoridae: Beavers
Family Anomaluridae: Scaly-Tailed Squirrels
Family Pedetidae: Spring Hare
Family Muridae:
    Subfamily Sigmodontinae: New World Rats and Mice
    Subfamily Cricetinae: Hamsters
    Subfamily Calomyscinae: Mouse-like Hamster
    Subfamily Mystromyscinae: White-tailed Rat
    Subfamily Spalacinae: Blind Mole-rats
    Subfamily Myospalacinae: Eastern Asiatic Mole-rats
    Subfamily Rhizomyinae: Mole- and Bamboo Rats
    Subfamily Lophiomyinae: Crested Rats
    Subfamily Platacanthomyinae: Spiny Dormice
    Subfamily Nesomyinae: Madagascan Rats
    Subfamily Otomyinae: African Swamp Rats
    Subfamily Arvicolinae: Voles and Lemmings
    Subfamily Gerbillinae: Gerbils
    Subfamily Petromyscinae: Rock Mice, Swamp Mouse
    Subfamily Dendromurinae: African Climbing Mice
    Subfamily: Cricetomyinae: African Pouched Rats
    Subfamily Murinae: Old World Rats and Mice
Family Dipodidae: Jerboas and Jumping Mice
Family Myoxidae: Dormice
Family Ctenodactylidae: Gundis
Family Hystricidae: Old World Porcupines
Family Erethizontidae: New World Porcupines
Family Caviidae: Guinea Pigs
Family Hydrochaeridae: Capybara
Family Dinomyidae: Pacarana
Family Dasyproctidae: Agoutis
Family Agoutidae: Pacas
Family Chinchillidae: Chinchillas and Viscachas
Family Capromyidae: Hutias
Family Myocastoridae: Coypu
Family Octodontidae: Octodonts
Family Ctenomyidae: Tuco-tucos
Family Abrocomidae: Chinchilla-rats
Family Echimyidae: Spiny Rats
Family Thryonomyidae: Cane Rats
Family Petromuridae: Dassie Rat
Family Bathyergidae: African Mole-Rats

Order Macroscelidea
Family Macroscelididae: Elephant Shrews

Order Insectivora: Insectivores
Family Solenodontidae: Solenodons
Family Tenrecidae: Tenrecs
Family Chysochloridae: Golden Moles
Family Erinaceidae: Hedgehogs, Moonrats
Family Soricidae: Shrews
Family Talpidae: Moles, Desmans

Order Scandentia
Family Tupaiidae: Tree Shrews

Order Primates: Primates
Family Cheirogaleidae: Mouse Lemurs, Dwarf Lemurs
Family Lemuridae: Lemurs
Family Megaladapidae: Sportive Lemurs
Family Indridae: Indri, Sifakas, Avahi
Family Daubentoniidae: Aye-aye
Family Loridae: Lorises, Pottos
Family Galagonidae: Galagos
Family Tarsiidae: Tarsiers
Family Callitrichidae: Marmosets and Tamarins
Family Cebidae: New World Monkeys
Family Cercopithecidae: Old World Monkeys
Family Hylobatidae: Gibbons
Family Hominidae: Apes and Humans

Order Dermoptera
Family Cynocephalidae: Flying Lemurs or Colugos

Order Chiroptera: Bats
Family Pteropodidae: Fruit Bats
Family Rhinopomatidae: Mouse-tailed Bats
Family Emballonuridae: Sheath-tailed Bats
Family Craseonycteridae: Hog-nosed Bat
Family Nycteridae: Slit-faced Bats
Family Megadermatidae: False Vampire Bats
Family Rhinolophidae: Horseshoe Bats
Family Noctilionidae: Fisherman Bats
Family Mormoopidae: Moustached Bats
Family Molossidae: Free-tailed Bats
Family Phyllostomidae: New World Leaf-nosed Bats
Family Vespertilionidae: Evening Bats
Family Natalidae: Funnel-eared Bats
Family Furipteridae: Smoky Bats
Family Thyropteridae: Disc-winged Bats
Family Myzopodidae: Old World Sucker-footed Bat
Family Mystacinidae: New Zealand Short-tailed Bats

Order Carnivora: Carnivores
Family Canidae: Dogs, Foxes
Family Ursidae: Bears, Pandas
Family Procyonidae: Raccoons
Family Mustelidae: Mustelids
Family Viverridae: Civets
Family Herpestidae: Mongooses
Family Hyaenidae: Hyenas
Family Felidae: Cats

Family Otariidae: Sea Lions, Fur Seals
Family Odobenidae: Walrus
Family Phocidae: True Seals

Order Tubulidentata
Family Orycteropodidae: Aardvark

Order Artiodactyla: Even-toed Ungulates
Family Suidae: Pigs
Family Tayassuidae: Peccaries
Family Hippopotamidae: Hippopotamuses
Family Camelidae: Camels
Family Tragulidae: Mouse Deer
Family Moschidae: Musk Deer
Family Cervidae: Deer
Family Giraffidae: Giraffes
Family Antilocapridae: Pronghorn
Family Bovidae: Bovids

Order Cetacea: Whales
Family Platanistidae: River Dolphins
Family Phocoenidae: Porpoises
Family Delphinidae: Dolphins
Family Monodontidae: Narwhal, White Whale
Family Physeteridae: Sperm Whales
Family Ziphiidae: Beaked Whales
Family Eschrichtiidae: Grey Whale
Family Balaenopteridae: Rorquals
Family Balaenidae: Right Whales

Order Perissodactyla: Odd-toed Ungulates
Family Equidae: Horses
Family Tapiridae: Tapirs
Family Rhinocerotidae: Rhinoceroses

Order Hyracoidea
Family Hyracoidea: Hyraxes

Order Proboscidea
Family Elephantidae: Elephants

Order Sirenia: Sea Cows
Family Dugongidae: Dugong
Family Trichechidae: Manatees

CLASS AVES: BIRDS
Order Struthioniformes: Ratites
Family Struthionidae: Ostrich
Family Rheidae: Rheas
Family Casuariidae: Cassowaries, Emu
Family Apterygidae: Kiwis

Order Tinamiformes: Tinamous
Family Tinamidae: Tinamous

Order Craciformes: Curassows, Guans, Megapodes
Family Cracidae: Curassows, Guans, Chachalacas

Family Megapodiidae: Megapodes

Order Galliformes: Gamebirds
Family Phasianidae: Quails, partridge, francolins, pheasants, grouse, turkey
Family Numididae: Guineafowl
Family Odontophoridae: New World Quail

Order Anseriformes: Waterfowl
Family Anhimidae: Screamers
Family Anseranatidae: Magpie goose
Family Dendrocygnidae: Whistling ducks
Family Anatidae: Geese, swans, ducks

Order Turniciformes: Buttonquail
Family Turnicidae: Buttonquail

Order Piciformes: Barbets and woodpeckers
Family Indicatoridae: Honeyguides
Family Picidae: Woodpeckers
Family Megalaimidae: Asian barbets
Family Lybiidae: African barbets
Family Ramphastidae: New World barbets and toucans

Order Galbuliformes: Jacamars and Puffbirds
Family Galbulidae: Jacamars
Family Bucconidae: Puffbirds

Order Bucerotiformes: Hornbills
Family Bucerotidae: Hornbills
Family Bucorvidae: Ground-hornbills

Order Upupiformes: Hoopoes
Family Upupidae: Hoopoe
Family Phoeniculidae: Wood-hoopoes
Family Rhinopomastidae: Scimitar-bills

Order Trogoniformes: Trogons
Family Trogonidae: Trogons

Order Coraciiformes: Kingfishers, Rollers, Bee-eaters
Family Coraciidae: Rollers
Family Brachypteraciidae: Ground-rollers
Family Leptosomidae: Cuckoo-roller
Family Momotidae: Motmots
Family Todidae: Todies
Family Alcedinidae: Alcedinid kingfishers
Family Dacelonidae: Dacelonid kingfishers
Family Cerylidae: Cerylid kingfishers
Family Meropidae: Bee-eaters

Order Coliiformes: Mousebirds
Family Coliidae: Mousebirds

Order Cuculiformes: Cuckoos
Family Cuculidae: Old World cuckoos
Family Centropodidae: Coucals

Family Coccyzidae: American cuckoos
Family Opisthocomidae: Hoatzin
Family Crotophagidae: Anis and guira cuckoos
Family Neomorphidae: Roadrunners and ground-cuckoos

Order Psittaciformes: Parrots
Family Psittacidae: Parrots

Order Apodiformes: Swifts
Family Apodidae: Swifts
Family Hemiprocnidae: Crested-swifts

Order Trochiliformes: Hummingbirds
Family Trochilidae: Hummingbirds

Order Musophagiformes: Turacos
Family Musophagidae: Turacos

Order Strigiformes: Owls and Nightjars
Family Tytonidae: Barn owls
Family Strigidae: True owls
Family Aegothelidae: Owlet nightjars
Family Podargidae: Australian frogmouths
Family Batrachostomidae: Asiatic frogmouths
Family Steatornithidae: Oilbird
Family Nyctibiidae: Potoos
Family Eurostopodidae: Eared-nightjars
Family Caprimulgidae: Nightjars

Order Columbiformes: Pigeons
Family Columbidae: Pigeons

Order Gruiformes: Cranes and Rails
Family Eurypygidae: Sunbittern
Family Otididae: Bustards
Family Gruidae: Cranes
Family Heliornithidae: Limpkins and sungrebes
Family Psophiidae: Trumpeters
Family Cariamidae: Seriemas
Family Rhyncochetidae: Kagu
Family Rallidae: Rails
Family Mesitornithidae: Mesites

Order Ciconiiformes: Waterbirds and Birds of Prey
Family Pteroclididae: Sandgrouse
Family Thinocoridae: Seedsnipes
Family Pedionomidae: Plains wanderer
Family Scolopacidae: Woodcock, snipe, sandpipers
Family Rostratulidae: Painted snipe
Family Jacanidae: Jacanas
Family Chionididae: Sheathbills
Family Burhinidae: Stone curlews
Family Charadriidae: Oystercatchers, avocets, plovers
    Subfamily Recurvirostrinae: Oystercatchers, avocets, stilts, ibisbill
    Subfamily Charadriinae: Plovers, lapwings
Family Glareolidae: Coursers, pratincoles, crab plover

Family Laridae: Skuas, skimmers, gulls, terns, auks
    Subfamily Larinae: Skuas, skimmers, gulls, terns
    Subfamily Alcinae: Auks
Family Accipitridae: Osprey, birds of prey (eagles, kites, hawks, buzzards, harriers, Old World vultures)
Family Sagittariidae: Secretarybird
Family Falconidae: Falcons
Family Podicipedidae: Grebes
Family Phaethontidae: Tropicbirds
Family Sulidae: Gannets, boobies
Family Anhingidae: Anhingas
Family Phalacrocoracidae: Cormorants
Family Ardeidae: Herons, egrets, bitterns
Family Scopidae: Hammerkop
Family Phoenicopteridae: Flamingos
Family Threskiornithidae: Ibises, spoonbills
Family Pelecanidae: Pelicans, shoebills
Family Ciconiidae: New World vultures, storks
    Subfamily Cathartinae: New World Vultures
    Subfamily Ciconiinae: Storks
Family Fregatidae: Frigatebirds
Family Spheniscidae: Penguins
Family Gaviidae: Divers or loons
Family Procellariidae: Shearwaters, petrels, albatrosses, storm petrels
    Subfamily Procellariinae: Petrels, shearwaters, diving petrels
    Subfamily Diomedeinae: Albatrosses
    Subfamily Hydrobatinae: Storm petrels

Order Passeriformes: Songbirds
Suborder Tyranni: Primitive passerines
Family Acanthisittidae: New Zealand wrens
Family Pittidae: Pittas
Family Eurylaimidae: Broadbills
Family Philepittidae: Asities
Family Sapayoidae: Sapayoa
Family Tyrannidae: Tyrant flycatcher, cotinga, and manakin family
    Subfamily Pipromorphinae: MionectIne flycatchers
    Subfamily Tyranninae: Tyrant flycatchers
    Subfamily Tityrinae: Tityras, becards
    Subfamily Cotinginae: Cotingas, plantcutters, sharpbill
    Subfamily Piprinae: Manakins
Family Thamnophilidae: Antbirds
Family Furnariidae: Ovenbirds, woodcreepers
    Subfamily Furnariinae: Ovenbirds
    Subfamily Dendrocolaptinae: Woodcreepers
Family Formicariidae: Ground antbirds
Family Conopophagidae: Gnateaters
Family Rhinocryptidae: Tapaculos
Family Climacteridae: Australian treecreepers
Suborder Passeri: Advanced passerines
Family Menuridae: Lyrebirds, scrub-birds
Family Ptilonorhynchidae: Bowerbirds
Family Maluridae: Fairywrens, emuwrens, grasswrens
Family Meliphagidae: Honey-eaters
Family Pardalotidae: Pardalotes, bristlebirds, scrubwrens, thornbills
Family Eopsaltriidae: Australian robins
Family Irenidae: Leafbirds, fairy-bluebirds
Family Orthonychidae: Logrunners
Family Pomatostomidae: Australasian babblers
Family Laniidae: Shrikes
Family Vireonidae: Vireos
Family Corvidae: Crow family
    Subfamily Cinclosomatinae: Quail thrushes, whipbirds
    Subfamily Corcoracinae: Australian chough, apostlebird
    Subfamily Pachycephalinae: Sittellas, mohouas, shrike tits, whistlers
    Subfamily Corvinae: Crows, magpies, birds-of paradise, currawongs, wood-swallows, orioles, cuckoo-shrikes
    Subfamily Dicrurinae: Fantails, drongos, monarchs
    Subfamily Aegithiniae: Ioras
    Subfamily Malacotinae: Bush-shrikes, helmet-shrikes, vangas
Family Callaetidae: New Zealand wattlebirds
Family Picathartidae: Rock-jumpers, rockfowl
Family Bombycillidae: Palmchat, silky-flycatchers, waxwings
Family Cinclidae: Dippers
Family Muscicapidae: Thrushes, Old World flycatchers, chats
    Subfamily Turdinae: Thrushes
    Subfamily Muscicapinae: Old World flycatchers, chats
Family Sturnidae: Starlings, mockingbirds
Family Sittidae: Nuthatches, wallcreeper
Family Certhiidae: Wrens, treecreepers, gnatcatchers
    Subfamily Troglodytinae: Wrens
    Subfamily Certhiinae: Treecreepers
    Subfamily Polioptilinae: Gnatcatchers
Family Paridae: Penduline-tits, titmice
    Subfamily Remizinae: Penduline tit
    Subfamily Parinae: Titmice
Family Aegithalidae: Long-tailed tits
Family Hirundinidae: River martins, swallows, martins
Family Regulidae: Kinglets
Family Pycnonotidae: Bulbuls
Family Hypocoliidae: Hypocolius
Family Cisticolidae: African warblers
Family Zosteropidae: White-eyes
Family Sylviidae: Warblers
    Subfamily Acrocephalinae: Leaf-warblers
    Subfamily Megalurinae: Grass-warblers
    Subfamily Garrulacinae: Laughingthrushes
    Subfamily Sylviinae: Babblers, parrotbills, typical warblers
Family Alaudidae: Larks
Family Nectariniidae: Sugarbirds, flowerpeckers, sunbirds
Family Melanocharitidae: Berrypeckers, longbills
Family Paramythiidae: Paramythias
Family Passeridae
    Subfamily Passerinae: Sparrows
    Subfamily Motacillinae: Wagtails, pipits
    Subfamily Prunellinae: Dunnocks
    Subfamily Ploceinae: Weavers
    Subfamily Estrildinae: Grass finches, parasitic whydahs
Family Fringillidae
    Subfamily Peucedraminae: Olive warbler

Subfamily Fringillinae: Chaffinches, cardueline finches, Hawaiian honeycreepers
Subfamily Emberizinae: Buntings, wood warblers, tanagers, cardinals, icterids

CLASS REPTILIA: REPTILES
Order Chelonia: Turtles and Tortoises
Family Emydidae: Emydid Turtles
Family Testudinae: Tortoises
Family Trionychidae: Softshell Turtles
Family Carettochylidae: Plateless River Turtle
Family Dermatemydidae: Central American River Turtle
Family Kinosternidae: American Mud and Musk Turtles
Family Cheloniidae: Marine Turtles
Family Dermochelyidae: Leatherback Turtle
Family Chelydridae: Snapping Turtles
Family Pelomedusidae: Greaved Turtles
Family Chelidae: Matamatas

Order Sphenodontia
Family Sphenodontidae: Tuataras

Order Squamata: Lizards and Snakes

Lizards
Family Iguanidae: Iguanas
Family Agamidae: Agamid Lizards
Family Chamaeleonidae: Chameleons
Family Gekkonidae: Geckos
Family Pygopodidae: Scaly-footed Lizards
Family Dibamidae: Old World Burrowing Lizards
Family Gymnophthalmidae: Microteiid Lizards
Family Teiidae: Teiid Lizards
Family Lacertidae: Lacertid Lizards
Family Xantusiidae: Night Lizards
Family Scincidae: Skinks
Family Cordylidae: Girdled and Plated Lizards
Family Xenosauridae: Crocodile Lizards
Family Anguidae: Slow Worms and Alligator Lizards
Family Varanidae: Monitors
Family Helodermatidae: Gila Monsters

Amphisbaenians (Worm Lizards)
Family Bipedidae: Bipeds
Family Trogonophiidae: Trogonophiids
Family Amphisbaenidae: Amphisbaenids

Snakes
Family Leptotyphlopidae: Thread Snakes
Family Typhlopidae: Blind Snakes
Family Anomolepididae: Dawn Blind Snakes
Family Uropeltidae
Family Aniliidae: Pipe Snakes
Family Xenopeltidae: Sunbeam Snake
Family Loxocemidae: Loxocemid Snake
Family Boidae: Boas and Pythons
Family Boyleriidae: Round Island Snakes

Family Tropidophiidae: Neotropical Ground Boas
Family Acrochordidae: Wart Snakes
Family Atractaspidae: Burrowing Asps
Family Colubridae: Colubrid Snakes
Family Elapidae: Cobras and Sea Snakes
Family Viperidae: Vipers and Pit Vipers

Order Crocodilia: Crocodiles, Alligators and Gavial
Family Crocodylidae: Crocodiles
Family Alligatoridae: Alligators
Family Gavialidae: Gavial

CLASS AMPHIBIA: AMPHIBIANS
Order Anura: Frogs and Toads
Family Ascaphidae: Tailed Frogs
Family Leiopelmatidae: New Zealand Frogs
Family Discoglossidae: Discoglossid Frogs
Family Pipidae: Pipid Frogs
Family Rhinophrynidae: Mexican Burrowing Frog
Family Pelodytidae: Parsley Frogs
Family Pelobatidae: Spadefoot Toads
Family Centrolenidae: Glass Frogs
Family Heleophrynidae: Ghost Frogs
Family Bufonidae: Bufonid Toads
Family Brachycephalidae: Gold Frogs
Family Hylidae: Treefrogs
Family Pseudidae: Pseudid Frogs
Family Rhinodermatidae: Mouth-brooding Frogs
Family Leptodactylidae: Leptodactylid Frogs
Family Myobatrachidae: Myobatrachid Frogs
Family Sooglossidae: Sooglossid Frogs
Family Dendrobatidae: Poison-dart Frogs
Family Hyperoliidae: Reed Frogs
Family Microhylidae: Narrow-mouthed Frogs
Family Ranidae: True Frogs
Family Rhacophoridae: Rhacophorid Treefrogs

Order Caudata: Salamanders and Newts
Family Sirenidae: Sirens
Family Amphiumidae: Congo Eels
Family Plethodontidae: Lungless Salamanders
Family Rhyacotritonidae: Rhyacotritonid Salamanders
Family Proteidae: Olms and Mudpuppies
Family Salamandridae: Newts and Salamanders
Family Ambyostomatidae: Mole Salamanders
Family Dicamptodontidae: Dicamptodontid Salamanders
Family Cryptobranchidae: Giant Salamanders
Family Hynobiidae: Asiatic Land Salamanders

Order Gymnophonia: Caecilians
Family Rhinatrematidae: Rhinatrematid Caecilians
Family Ichthyophidae: Ichthyophid Caecilians
Family Uraeotyphlidae: Uraeotyphlid Caecilians
Family Scolecomorphidae: Scolecomorphid Caecilians
Family Caeciliaidae: Caeciliaid Caecilians
Family Typhlonectidae: Typhlonectid Caecilians

FISH
Class Myxini
Order Myxiniformes: Hagfishes

Class Cephalaspidomorphi
Order Petromyzontiformes: Lampreys

Class Chondrichthyes: Cartilaginous Fish
Order Heterodontiformes: Bullhead, Horn Sharks
Order Lamniformes: Sand Tigers, Goblin Sharks, Megamouth
  Sharks
Order Carchariniformes: Cat Sharks, Hound Sharks, Requiem
  Sharks
Order Orectolobiformes: Wobbegons, Nurse Sharks, Whale
  Sharks
Order Squatiniformes: Angel Sharks
Order Hexanchiformes: Frilled Sharks, Cow Sharks
Order Squaliformes: Bramble Sharks, Sleeper Sharks, Dogfish
  Sharks
Order Pristiphoriformes: Saw Sharks
Order Rajiformes: Rays, Skates, Sawfishes
Order Chimaeriformes: Chimaeras

Class Osteichthyes: Bony Fish
Subclass Actinopterygii: Ray-finned Fishes
Order Polypteriformes: Bichirs
Order Acipenseriformes: Sturgeons, Paddlefishes
Order Lepisosteiformes: Gars
Order Amiiformes: Bowfin
Order Osteoglossiformes: Bonytongues, Butterflyfish, Mooneyes
Order Elopiformes: Tarpons, Tenpounders
Order Albuliformes: Bonefishes, Halosaurs, Spiny Eels
Order Anguilliformes: Freshwater Eels, Moray Eels, Conger Eels
Order Saccopharyngiformes: Bobtail Snipe Eels, Swallowers,
  Gulpers
Order Clupeiformes: Herrings, Anchovies
Order Gonorynchiformes: Milkfish, Beaked Sandfishes, Snake
  Mudhead
Order Cypriniformes: Carps, Minnows, Loaches
Order Characiformes: Characins, Trahiras, Headstanders
Order Siluriformes: Catfishes
Order Gymnotiformes: Knifefishes, Electric Eel
Order Esociformes: Pikes, Mudminnows
Order Osmeriformes: Smelts, Slickheads, Noodlefishes
Order Salmoniformes: Salmon, Trout, Chars
Order Stomiiformes: Bristlemouths, Marine Hatchetfishes,
  Lightfishes
Order Atelopodiiformes: Jellynose Fishes
Order Aulopiformes: Telescope fishes, Greeneyes, Barracudinas
Order Myctophiformes: Lanternfishes
Order Percopsiformes: Trout-perches, Cavefishes
Order Ophidiiformes: Carapids, Cuskeels, Brotulas
Order Gadiformes: Cods, Hakes
Order Batrachoidiformes: Toadfishes
Order Lophiiformes: Anglerfishes
Order Beloniformes: Flying fishes, Needlefishes, Halfbeaks
Order Cyprinodontiformes: Killifishes, Rivulines, Splitfins,

Pupfishes
Order Atheriniformes: Rainbow Fishes, Blueeyes, Silversides
Order Lampridiformes: Crestfishes, Oarfishes, Ribbonfishes
Order Stephanoberyciformes: Whalefishes, Gibberfishes
Order Beryciformes: Beardfishes, Lanterneyes, Squirrelfishes
Order Zeiformes: Dories, Oreos
Order Gasterosteiformes: Sticklebacks, Sand Eels, Tubesnouts
Order Synbranchiformes: Swamp Eels, Spiny Eels
Order Dactylopteriformes: Flying Gurnards
Order Scorpaeniformes: Scorpionfishes, Velvetfishes, Sculpins
Order Perciformes: Perchlike Fishes
  Suborder Percoidei: Percoid Fishes
  Suborder Elassomatoidei: Pygmy Sunfishes
  Suborder Labroidei: Cichlids, Damselfishes, Wrasses,
  Parrotfish
  Suborder Zoarcoidei: Eelpouts, Wrymouths, Gunnels,
  Wolffishes
  Suborder Notothenioidei: Icefishes
  Suborder Trachinoidei: Sand Lances, Weeverfishes, Stargazers
  Suborder Blennioidei: Blennies
  Suborder Icosteodei: Ragfish
  Suborder Kurtoidei: Nurseryfishes
  Suborder Acanthuroidei: Spadefishes, Scats, Rabbitfishes,
  Surgeonfishes
  Suborder Mugiloidei: Mullets
  Suborder Scombrolabracoidei: Scombrolabracoid Fishes
  Suborder Scombroidei: Barracudas, Mackerel, Tunas, Marlin
  Suborder Stromateoidei: Medusafishes, Squaretails,
  Butterfishes
  Suborder Anabantoidei: Gouramis
  Suborder Channoidei: Snakeheads
Order Pleuronectiformes: Flounders, Soles
Order Tetraodontiformes: Puffers, Triggerfishes, Porcupinefishes

Subclass Sarcopterygii: Lobe-finned Fishes
Order Ceratodontiformes: Australian Lungfishes
Order Lepidosireniformes: African and South American
  Lungfishes
Order Coelacanthiformes: Coelacanth

INDEX

Q

R

ACKNOWLEDGEMENTS

The Publishers received invaluable help during the preparation of the Animal Encyclopedia from: Heather Angel, who lent us reference slides, Angus Bellairs, who gave advice, Dr H. G. Cogger, who lent us reference slides; Rosanne Hooper and Zilda Tandy who assisted with research, Dr Pat Morris of Royal Holloway College, London and Dr Robert Stebbings of the Institute of Terrestrial Ecology, Huntingdonshire, who both helped with reference on the Mammal section, Ed Wade, who helped with reference on the Fish section, the staff of the Herpetology Department of the British Museum (Natural History), London, particularly Colin McCarthy and Barry Clarke, who allowed us access to specimens and reference, the staff of the Ornithology Department of the British Museum (Natural History) outstation at Tring, particularly Peter Colston, who gave assistance with the specimen collection, the staff of the Science Reference Library, London, the IUCN Conservation Monitoring Centre, Cambridge, England, for data on threatened species, and the Zoological Society of London, which allowed us to reproduce information from its *International Zoo Yearbook*.

We acknowledge the contribution of Professor Carl Gans in his book *Reptiles of the World* (Bantam 1975).